GETTING RESPECT

GETTING RESPECT

Responding to Stigma and Discrimination in the United States, Brazil, and Israel

Michèle Lamont, Graziella Moraes Silva,
Jessica S. Welburn, Joshua Guetzkow,
Nissim Mizrachi, Hanna Herzog,
and Elisa Reis

PRINCETON UNIVERSITY PRESS
Princeton and Oxford

Published by Princeton University Press, 41 William Street,
Princeton, New Jersey 08540
In the United Kingdom: Princeton University Press, 6 Oxford
Street, Woodstock, Oxfordshire OX20 1TR

press.princeton.edu

Jacket art: Bharti Kher, *A Love letter*, 2009.
Bindis on painted board. 188 × 249 × 7 cm. / 74 × 98 × 2 ¾ in.
Courtesy of the artist and Hauser & Wirth.
© Bharti Kher

ISBN 978-0-691-16707-7

Library of Congress Control Number: 2016935762

British Library Cataloging-in-Publication Data is available

This book has been composed in
Sabon Next LT Pro & Univers LT Std

Printed on acid-free paper ∞

Printed in the United States of America

1 3 5 7 9 10 8 6 4 2

CONTENTS

LIST OF TABLES

PREFACE AND ACKNOWLEDGMENTS

This is a conjointly written book—not an edited volume. It is the result of a rewarding and demanding collective adventure. It required collaboration across three continents separated by several time zones over a number of years. Regular discussion of all the usual aspects of data collection, analysis, and writing was essential to ensure consistency in approach and methods and to develop in dialogue the comparative analysis that anchors our contribution. For this purpose, the seven authors (joined periodically by other collaborators) held regular Skype meetings, at times weekly, at other times monthly. We also met face-to-face at least once a year for a few days in Rio de Janeiro; Tel Aviv; or Cambridge, Massachusetts; or at conferences and workshops elsewhere. We debated, argued, disagreed, and mostly learned from one another. We believe that our book demonstrates the value of collaboration—when complementary perspectives shed light on realities that could not be illumined adequately by a single mind.

The pace of our work accommodated our other writing commitments as well as the demands of our respective professional trajectories, which ranged from completing dissertations and finding academic positions or postdoctoral fellowships to coming up for tenure and chairing a department or a research center. The major milestones of human life (from having babies to becoming a grandparent) also intervened. We became significant others amidst the chaos, challenges, and multiple demands we faced.

The idea for the project germinated in 2005 in a paper written by Michèle Lamont and Christopher Bail on group boundaries in Brazil, Israel, Northern Ireland, and Québec, with the cases of France and the United States in the background (Lamont and Bail 2005). The idea was to compare equalization strategies in countries where group boundaries are strongly policed (Israel and Northern Ireland) and where they are more permeable (Brazil and Québec). This led to a workshop titled "Ethnoracism and the

Transformation of Collective Identity," held in February 2005 with the support of the Weatherhead Center for International Studies at Harvard University. This event brought together potential collaborators as well as other experts.[1] After the meeting, several of us agreed on the value of comparing the cases of Brazil, Israel, and the United States, guided by a combination of theoretical and practical reasons (described in the Introduction).

The following year was dedicated to defining the project further and seeking funding to cover several years of collaboration. The research in the New York metropolitan area was supported by a grant from the National Science Foundation ("African-Americans Respond to Racism and Discrimination;" grant 0701542). The US-Brazil comparison was made possible by a grant from the Weatherhead Center for International Affairs ("Bridging Boundaries: Destigmatization Strategies of African-Americans and Black Brazilians"). In Israel, research was supported by a grant from the United States–Israel Binational Science Foundation ("Destigmatization Strategies among Ethnic Groups in Israel") and from the Van Leer Jerusalem Institute ("Crossing Boundaries: Processes of Destigmatization among Palestinans and Mizrahi Jews in Israel"). A Weatherhead Initiative grant from the Weatherhead Center for International Studies ("A Comparative Study of Responses to Discrimination by Members of Stigmatized Groups") supported most of our meetings and other costs associated with the collaboration. Finally, each team benefited from additional sources of funding. The Israeli team received funds from the Department of Sociology and Anthropology at Tel Aviv University, and the Brazil team received funds from National Council for Scientific and Technological Development (CNPq), the Rio de Janeiro State Agency for Research Support (FAPERJ), and the Coordination for the Improvement of Higher Education Personnel (CAPES).

The bulk of the data collection was conducted in 2007 and 2008, with slight variations across sites. Coding started in 2009 and continued intermittently until 2012, with additional work on specific issues being conducted as we wrote. The bulk of the writing was completed in 2012–2015.

The core of the US team was composed of Michèle Lamont, Crystal Fleming, and Jessica S. Welburn. Crystal remained part of the team until we started drafting the book in the fall of 2012. She then chose to move on to write her own book on slavery in French collective memory. Her input on a number of conceptual issues and in the creation of the interview schedule and the coding key was crucial and is gratefully acknowledged.

Most of the US interviews were conducted in northern New Jersey by Crystal and Jessica, together with Cassi Pitman (with a few interviews conducted by Michael Jeffries). The coding team, supervised in turn by Crystal Fleming, Jessica S. Welburn, and Anthony Jacks, also included Monica Bell, Moa Bursell, Jeffrey Denis, Nicole Hirsch, and Cassi Pittman. Sabrina Pendergrass, Matthew Clair, and Monica Bell helped with the review of the literature, while Steven Brown, Nathan Fosse, and Charlotte Lloyd provided technical assistance with the quantitative data analysis. Christy Ley assisted with the preparation of the final manuscript. Several Harvard undergraduates were involved in various phases of the project: Melissa Bellin, David Clifton, Nafisa Eltahir, Veronique Irwin, Christina Nguyen, and Natalie Smith. Travis Clough, Joe Cook, Kristen Halbert, Kathleen Hoover, Heather Latham, and Hunter Taylor offered excellent staff and administrative support at various times.

While most of the American graduate research assistants involved were not part of the core writing team, they had access to the data, and several published their first publications based on it. Their papers came out in two special issues of journals that were connected to the project: "Responses to Discrimination and Racism by Members of Stigmatized Groups: Brazil, Canada, France, Israel, South Africa, Sweden, and the United States," *Ethnic and Racial Studies* (February 2012), co-edited by Michèle Lamont and Nissim Mizrachi, and "Varieties of Responses to Stigmatization: Macro, Meso, and Micro Dimensions," *Du Bois Review* 9:41–200 (2012) co-edited by Michèle Lamont, Jessica S. Welburn, and Crystal M. Fleming.

The core of the Brazilian team was Graziella Moraes Silva and Elisa Reis, who published several papers based on the data from the project. Interviews were conducted by Suzana Mattos, Jonas Henrique de Oliveira, Carla Ramos, Marcio André Santos, Graziella Moraes Silva, Guilherme Nogueira de Souza, and Simone Souza. Most interviewers also participated in coding, but other researchers from the Network for the Study of Inequality (NIED) also contributed in later stages of the project and relied on the interviews to write their own papers, namely, Luciana Souza Leão, who published with Graziella Moraes Silva a paper on the identity of pardos in Brazil ("O Paradoxo da Mistura: Identidades, desigualdades e percepção de discriminação entre brasileiros pardos," *Revista Brasileira de Ciências Sociais* 27.80 (2012)), and Patricia Guimarães, who relied on the project to write her first publication ("Distância social e produção de estigmas nas relações raciais brasileiras," *Revista Habitus* 11.2 (2013)). Several social science undergraduates at the Federal University of Rio were involved in various phases of the project: Ruan Coelho, Gustavo Fernandes, Barbara Grillo, Daniel Lourenço, Marta Mello, Jéssica Nonato, and Diego Povoas. We also thank Lia Rocha and Luciana Souza Leão for their collaboration in a second round of coding.

The core of the Israeli team was composed of Joshua Guetzkow, Hanna Herzog, and Nissim Mizrachi. A graduate student, Idit Fast, was responsible for the coding. Sophia Abexis, Ibtesam Amoury, Motti Gigi, Avi Golzman, Yossi Harpaz, Dima Kanan, Adane Zawdu, and Assia Zinevich conducted the interviews and transcribed them. Joshua Guetzkow and Idit Fast published part of the findings in the *American Behavioral Scientist* 60:2 (2016), "How Symbolic Boundaries Shape the Experience of Social Exclusion: A Case Comparison of Arab Palestinian Citizens and Ethiopian Jews in Israel."

Over the years we had the opportunity to discuss our work with colleagues and to tap different networks of experts for the various aspects of our research. For the project as a whole, we benefited from the input of scholars associated with the Successful Societies Program of the Canadian Institute for Advanced Research. We single out particularly the input of Gérard Bouchard, Peter Gourevitch, Peter A. Hall, Clyde Hertzman, Danielle Juteau, Will Kymlicka, Ron Levi, Bill Sewell, and Ann Swidler, as well as James Dunn, Leanne Son Hing, and Dan Keating, who advised us on measures of the impact of perceived discrimination on well-being (as did David Williams and Nancy Krieger (Harvard University) at the start of the project). Michèle Lamont is particularly grateful for the support of the Canadian Institute for Advanced Research, which enabled her work on this project and supported academic leaves in 2010 and 2014.

The American team in particular benefited from discussion and feedback from several colleagues as our research was unfolding. We thank especially Christopher Bail, Erik Bleich, Lawrence Bobo, Bart Bonikowski, Matthew Desmond, Frank Dobbin, Nicolas Duvoux, Peter Hall, Christopher Jencks, Riva Kastoryano, Devah Pager, James Sidanius, William Julius Wilson, and Andreas Wimmer. Conversations with Elijah Anderson, Joe Feagin, Peggy Levitt, Jane Mansbridge, Edward Telles, and Howard Winant were useful at the onset of the project. Other colleagues engaged with our argument while we presented our results at various conferences and department colloquia. We acknowledge the opportunities and hope they will recognize the many ways in which these conversations shaped our analysis.

For the Brazil case study, Stanley Bailey and Edward Telles gave us important feedback during the early phases of the research. Samara Mancebo, Mani Tebet, and Verônica Toste, post-doctoral students at Network for the Study of Inequality (NIED), also contributed during later stages with important feedback and suggestions for analysis.

In Israel, the project benefited from presentations of some of the study's results to various audiences. These included talks given in departmental seminars of the Department of Sociology and Anthropology at Tel Aviv University and the Department of Sociology at Hebrew University by Michèle Lamont. We thank Jose Bruner for his comments regarding our presentation of Israel's ethnic demography, as well as Tel Aviv University graduate students for their comments on the data presented in several university forums.

The group as a whole also benefited particularly from meetings hosted at Sciences Po by Patrick Le Galès, Nonna Mayer, Marco Oberti, and Tommasso Vitale in the spring of 2011. We thank the colleagues who commented on our work at these occasions: Bruno Cousin, Nicolas Dodier, Nicolas Duvoux, Cyril Lemieux, Daniel Sabbagh, Patrick Simon, Laurent Thévenot, and others. A meeting hosted by Elisa Reis and Frances Hagapian in Rio de Janeiro was also especially fruitful. A meeting held in August 2014 with graduate students from the Department of Sociology at Harvard

University, where the entire manuscript was discussed, was singularly significant. Participants included Asad Asad, Monica Bell, Matthew Clair, Caitlin Daniel, Kim Pernell, and Eva Rosen, in addition to visiting scholar Thomas Koenig and Anna Sun. Others who commented on sections of the book manuscript or the book in its entirety include Stanley Bailey, Christopher Bail, Bart Bonikowski, Matthew Desmond, Frank Dobbin, Nicolas Duvoux, Crystal Fleming, Nathan Fosse, David Harding, Leanne Son Hing, Alexandra Kalev, Devah Pager, Mario Luis Small, William Julius Wilson, and Andreas Wimmer.

Others who deserve thanks include Carolyn Bond and Cyd Westmoreland, who helped make our writing style more consistent, our marvelous editor Meagan Levinson at Princeton University Press, and our respective families who provided love, support, and encouragement during the years when this project was unfolding.

It should be noted that several coauthors are members of stigmatized groups (as African American, Jewish, Mizrahi, and Québécois), and that their own experiences (from a range of contexts) shaped their understanding and analysis of the phenomena at hand. Conversely, not belonging to such a group influenced the work of the other coauthors. Our collective conversation around our respective and different perspectives was an essential and unavoidable component of the dialogical research process over the years. As this project comes to an end, we believe our cojointly written book was greatly enriched by such dialogues, and we acknowledge their centrality to our collective endeavor.

The book was written primarily for social scientists, but we also intend for it to be read by members of stigmatized groups who are not researchers, as well as by other individuals who have an interest in the everyday experiences of those confronting stigma and discrimination. At a time when many feel powerless in the face of growing racial tensions and interethnic conflicts, our hope is that *Getting Respect* may help communities and individuals find ways forward and alternatives to hopeless handwringing. From our book, readers will learn that experiences of exclusion are the result of a range of factors, some of which can be changed and engineered (for instance, through the diffusion of more solidaristic images of the polity). Policymakers, cultural intermediaries, experts, and ordinary citizens all have a role to play in reducing stigmatization and discrimination, and social suffering more generally. This is an urgent task, as social inclusion remains a crucial dimension by which one can assess collective well-being and the relative success of our societies.

We conclude by expressing our deepest thanks to the men and women who are at the center of this book, and who gave us their time and generously answered our questions. We can only hope that our words do justice to the often painful complexity of their experiences.

ABOUT THE AUTHORS

MICHÈLE LAMONT is a professor of sociology and African and African American studies, the Robert I. Goldman Professor of European Studies, and Director of the Weatherhead Center for International Affairs at Harvard University. She is also codirector of the Successful Societies Program of the Canadian Institute for Advanced Research. She serves as the 108th President of the American Sociological Association in 2016–2017.

GRAZIELLA MORAES SILVA is assistant professor at the Graduate Institute of International and Development Studies in Geneva, Switzerland. She is also affiliated with the Graduate Program in Sociology and Anthropology (PPGSA) and the Interdisciplinary Network for the Study of Inequality (Núcleo Interdisciplinar de Estudos sobre Desigualdade—NIED), both at the Federal University of Rio de Janeiro (UFRJ), Brazil. She served on the research team of the Project on Ethnicity and Race in Latin America (PERLA).

JESSICA S. WELBURN is assistant professor of sociology and African American Studies at the University of Iowa. Her research interests include race and ethnicity, cultural sociology, and urban inequality. She is currently working on a book exploring how African Americans in Detroit, Michigan, navigate the city's limited public infrastructure.

JOSHUA GUETZKOW is assistant professor in the Department of Sociology and Anthropology and the Institute of Criminology at the Hebrew University of Jerusalem. His research bridges cultural sociology, social stratification, the sociology of punishment, and the study of policy making.

NISSIM MIZRACHI is Chair of the Department of Sociology and Anthropology, Tel Aviv University. He earned his PhD in sociology from the University of Michigan, Ann Arbor, as a Fulbright Scholar and was a Postdoctoral

Research Fellow at Harvard University. He is a recipient of the 2008 Clifford Geertz Prize for the Best Article in the Sociology of Culture, awarded by the American Sociological Association.

HANNA HERZOG is professor emerita of sociology at Tel Aviv University. She is codirector of WIPS— the Center for Advancement of Women in the Public Sphere at Van Leer Jerusalem Institute. She specializes in political sociology, ethnic relations, and sociology of gender. Her books include *Gendering Politics—Women in Israel*, *Sex Gender Politics—Women in Israel* (written with others), and *Gendering Religion and Politics: Untangling Modernities* (edited with Ann Braude).

ELISA REIS is professor of political sociology at the Federal University of Rio de Janeiro and Chair of the Interdisciplinary Research Network on Social Inequality (NIED). An expert in political sociology and perceptions of inequality, she currently serves as Vice-President for Science of the International Social Science Council (ISSC).

GETTING RESPECT

INTRODUCTION

This book examines how ordinary people understand stigma and discrimination, and how they respond to such experiences. We conducted more than 400 in-depth interviews with middle- and working-class men and women—African Americans in New York suburbs, Black Brazilians in and around Rio de Janeiro, and Arab Palestinian citizens of Israel and two Jewish ethnic groups in and around Tel Aviv. When asked about incidents where they were treated unfairly, these individuals described interactions where they felt underestimated, overscrutinized, misunderstood, feared, overlooked, shunned, or discriminated against. They discussed their responses, including how they confronted stigmatizers, aimed to avoid confirming racial stereotypes, used humor, and chose to ignore the incident—often motivated by a desire to get respect. They also discussed what affected their courses of action. Three examples, one from each country, illustrate some of these experiences and what they have in common.

First, take the case of Joe, a middle-class African American man who found himself alone with several white men in an elevator at work. He remembers the interaction as follows:

> One made a joke about blacks and monkeys. I said, "Man, listen, I ain't into jokes." . . . His demeanor changed, my demeanor changed. All of the positive energy that was in there was being sucked out because of the racial part. . . . [I told myself] get out of it because if I stay in it, I'm going to be in that circle and [won't be able to] get out. . . . The stress level rose. My tolerance was getting thin, my blood pressure peaking and my temper rising. By the grace of God, thank you Jesus, as I stepped off the elevator, there was a black minister walking past. I said, "Can I speak to you for a minute because I just encountered something that I got to talk about because I'm this far [from exploding]. . . ." I had been at the job for a week. This is all I need to get me fired. . . . [Now]

I'm trying to get through the affair [to decide] if I should go to the city [to complain].

In the second case, Ana, a Black Brazilian journalist, is traveling for work. After attending a fancy party, she gets to her hotel late at night and gives the receptionist her room number to get her key. Instead of handing it to her, he calls the room. When no one answers, he winks and says, "Sorry, he is not answering." Ana replies that it is the key to *her* room she is asking for. The hotel clerk blushes and gives her the key. When asked to reflect on what happened, she says:

> He thought I was a prostitute and was there to visit a client. A well-dressed *negra*, in the hotel, at 1:00 a.m., he could not register. When he realized [his mistake], he immediately gave me the key. He was embarrassed. I was embarrassed. Usually I am prepared to react, to complain. But in this situation, nothing was said. It was a game of impressions—the half smile he gave me when my "client" was not answering and his embarrassment once he realized his mistake. But he never apologized because he did not "do" anything wrong. I could not call him out because he could say I was crazy. So he did not say anything. It was just a misunderstanding. That really hurt me! It made me cry! There was nothing I could do because there was nothing explicit—no offense, he did not refuse to give me the key, there was nothing.

Once in her room, she calls home, hoping to be comforted by her husband, who happens to be white. Instead of reassuring her, he tells her that she is overreacting, which adds to her aggravation and feeling that she is isolated and misunderstood.

In the third case, Abir, a single Israeli Palestinian woman, faces harassment at a border crossing between Israel and the West Bank during a routine weekend outing. She pounds the table to express her anger as she describes the incident:

> Not long ago, I was [traveling] with my girlfriends. All of us, including myself, are Israeli citizens and we had our standard identity cards with us. We spent time in Bethlehem, and on our way home we went through a security checkpoint. There a soldier came up to us. He was a lot younger than me, about 18, so what does he know about life? He asked for our identity cards went away to check them. . . . He kept us waiting for half an hour. He came back and told us to pull over to the side. And then he began a series of humiliations as he "played" with us. He came up to the car and pretended to give us our identity cards through the window. But when I raised my hand to take them,

he pulled his hand away. Offering them a second time, he did not let them go. . . . I started to get irritated, but because I was afraid I didn't say anything. . . . All of this was just because we are Arabs. This is just humiliation and provocation.

These three cases illustrate how the same course of action—outwardly *not* responding—is the result of very different contextual dynamics. In the first case, it is without hesitation that Joe interprets "the monkey joke" as a case of racism, but he does not respond because he wants to avoid a violent escalation and needs to keep his job. He controls his anger and finds comfort thanks to a chance encounter with an African American pastor who "can relate." In the second case, Ana, the Black Brazilian journalist, does not respond to being stereotyped as a black prostitute because she believes she cannot prove harm and fears denial and being ridiculed. In the third case, Abir, the Israeli Palestinian woman, cannot respond to mistreatment since doing so could result in arrest or further harassment.

We argue that responses are enabled by the broader context in which these individuals find themselves. Joe initially feels he should confront the man in the elevator. Confrontation is the most frequent response to racist incidents reported by our American interviewees; we will argue that this is the result of African Americans' shared understanding of the legacy of the Civil Rights Movement and familiarity with a legal context that strongly discourages racial slurs. However, confrontation is not the only response possible. Joe ultimately retreats; he fears losing his job (not surprisingly, given the high unemployment rate that prevailed in 2007–2008, when we conducted our interviews). When factoring pragmatic considerations, he is reluctant to engage given prevalent stereotypes of black men as violent and dangerous. The silence of Ana, the Black Brazilian journalist, is likewise shaped by the context, one in which, compared to the United States, there is less shared understanding about the appropriateness of calling out people who engage in what may be racist actions. As for the Arab Palestinian, Abir, she also avoids confrontation. She does not hope for redress given a national context where Arab Palestinians are often viewed as "the enemy within." Instead, she simply wants to be on her way. But she does not miss the opportunity to vent her anger and denounce the abuse when interviewed.

OUR APPROACH, CHALLENGES, AND QUESTIONS

Our approach in this book is to explore the experiences of and responses to stigmatization and discrimination across contexts. We further analyze how national configurations of cultural repertoires and group boundaries enable and constrain different experiences of and responses to stigmatization and discrimination. We focus on three countries and some of their most excluded groups: African Americans;[1] Black Brazilians;[2] and in Israel, Arab Palestinian citizens,[3] Ethiopian Jews, and Mizrahim* (Jews of North African and Middle Eastern descent). While much of the literature on racial attitudes most often focuses on the perpetrator's prejudice (conceptualized as a biased view of the out-group), we shift the attention to the experience of the stigmatized and on his/her subjectivity.[4] We offer a counterpoint to the fascination with the pathology, criminality, and social problems of the stigmatized, which is particularly salient in the internationally influential US literature on race.

As described in Chapter 1, we examine microphenomena (the phenomenology of experiences) through a macrocomparative approach (focused on history and case commonalities and differences), while focusing on how mesophenomena (e.g., cultural repertoires, groupness, and institutions) interpolate the two.[5] Our five groups live in different sociopolitical contexts and face social boundaries that are permeable to varying degrees. These groups experience different levels of residential or job market segregation or access to marital partners from outside their own ethnoracial group. Their places in the histories of their countries vary, as does their access to cultural repertoires (e.g., the American Dream, Brazilian racial democracy, Zionism, but also human rights), with which they make sense of their situations and make claims for equality and respect. Moreover, they differ in the extent to which their members perceive themselves as belonging to a group (this is part of what we call "groupness"). These dimensions, we argue, help us make sense of how these groups experience and respond to stigmatization and discrimination. Thus, we go beyond the analysis of individual cases to consider how macropolitical structures and meso-level explanations help account for micro-level experiences.

Why study these groups in particular? Originally, we wanted to compare ethnoracial groups marginalized within their respective countries by their degree of social exclusion in both the symbolic and the social boundaries they face.[6] Our focus was the United States, Brazil, and Israel, as our goal was to compare cases where boundaries ranged from fluid (Black Brazilians) to rigid (Arab Palestinians), with a case somewhere in between (African Americans): we wanted to assess whether those who face more heavily policed boundaries have more elaborate ways of dealing with those experiences.[7] As our understanding of the cases and the puzzles at hand deepened,

---

* In Hebrew, the suffix "–im" denotes a plural noun. We have chosen to preserve the Hebrew term, and so throughout the text we refer to this group as "Mizrahim" rather than "Mizrahis." We use the term "Mizrahi" as a modifier, for example, when we refer to "Mizrahi responses."

the rationale for including each group changed. We came to examine the role of groupness in shaping people's experiences and responses, as well as the influence of cultural repertoires, based on the historical locations of groups in their respective polities, and various characteristics of their societies. Consequently, we included Mizrahi Jews, who are stigmatized ethnically in relation to Ashkenazim (European Jews) but whose ethnic self-identity is not very salient, with the goal of comparing them with another group whose groupness is partial and contested (at least relative to African Americans): Black Brazilians. We also brought into the comparison Ethiopian Jews living in Israel, who are stigmatized as phenotypically black (among other markers). The inclusion of these groups in our study informs the differences in the experiences of three phenotypically black groups living in different national contexts. It also serves to put the comparison between United States and Brazil (both former slave societies) in a broader perspective, through a comparison with Israel, a society where one ethnic group (Arab Palestinians) is both symbolically and institutionally excluded from full national membership. Finally, the intranational Israeli comparison enables us to consider "difference in difference," that is, how experiences and responses differ among groups that are exposed to varying levels and types of exclusion based on phenotype, ethnicity, and national belonging.[8] While comparative studies on race and ethnicity are generally Europe-centered (see Bail 2008 for a review), we made the gamble that bringing together this quintet of cases would be a theoretically generative strategy and a fruitful empirical puzzle. We also made the decision to not include a comparison of various ethnic groups in the United States and Brazil, but to privilege instead a comparison of the middle class and the working class across countries. This decision was motivated by growing economic inequality and the relative neglect of comparative class analysis within and across countries. We hypothesized that the varying life conditions and degree of material security across these two class groups would enable different types of responses.

Incidents: Assault on Worth and Discrimination

Racism as it is experienced has been written about by a great many classical and contemporary authors,[9] as well as analyzed in its multifarious manifestations in the United States and elsewhere, creating a vast literature that has generated a large number of definitions across the disciplines.[10] What distinguishes our inquiry is our effort to trace inductively, systematically, and in a detailed fashion (using software-assisted content analysis) (1) the relative salience of various experiences and class patterns across groups and selected national contexts and (2) the different ways experiences are interpreted. In discussing each group under study, we describe the typologies of incidents and responses, their meanings, as well as their frequency. Our contribution also stands out by offering an analysis of what enables and constrains these experiences by reference to groupness, repertoires, and historical contexts. Few studies of responses to racism offer a sustained explanatory framework.

We examined how our interviewees responded when asked: "Have you ever been treated unfairly?" "Can you described what happened and where?" "Do you think you have been discriminated against at work?" "Can you remember encounters with racism outside of work?" and "Do you remember cases where you interacted with whites and felt misunderstood?"[11] We explored how they described their own responses to actual incidents they experienced and how they think people should respond (what we call "ideal" or "normative" responses). We inductively analyzed what they said by conducting detailed coding of narratives of incidents and responses in their contexts. We categorized narratives based on similarities and differences, and we developed meta-codes that enabled us to theoretically make sense of what interviewees said they were experiencing.

Are these accounts worthy of our attention? We think so. While some dismiss narratives as "merely" representations of subjective experience, we share a sociological perspective that takes what social actors say seriously (as sui generis social facts) instead of aiming to show how they are blind to their own reality (see Boltanski's 2008 critique of Bourdieusian sociology). In our view, establishing that an assault-on-worth incident has occurred requires establishing the participant's belief in such an incident, as instantiated in his or her narrative. Narratives guide action (Somers 1994) and enable and constrain it (Polletta et al. 2011).[12] They influence micro-interactions, even when they are contested.[13]

Discrimination was highly salient in the interviews. Our use of the term "discrimination" refers to incidents in which our interviewees believe they were deprived or prevented from getting access to opportunities and resources (e.g., credit, jobs, housing, access to public places) due to their race, ethnicity, or nationality. It also includes instances of racial profiling, being excluded from public places, and the like.

Even more frequent were mentions of incidents of stigmatization. Under this category, we include a wide range of subjective experiences, namely, incidents in which respondents experienced disrespect and their dignity, honor, relative status, or sense of self was challenged. This occurs when one is insulted, receives poor services, is the victim of jokes, is subjected to double standards, is excluded from informal networks (e.g., is not invited to parties), is the victim of physical assault, or is threatened physically. It also includes instances where one is stereotyped as poor, uneducated, or dangerous, or where one is misunderstood or underestimated. These instances can be described as targeting an individual qua individual or as targeting the individual's group.

Discrimination (being deprived of resources) generally goes hand in hand with feeling stigmatized (being assigned low status)—although the reverse is not necessarily true. As Link and Phelan (2013) point out, steps leading to discrimination are often overlooked or difficult to prove, but they often involve stigmatization, intolerance, exclusion, fear, and mistrust on the part of the "perpetrator."[14] According to Pescosolido and Martin (2015), discrimination may also entail social distancing, traditional prejudice, exclusionary sentiments, negative affect, perception of dangerousness, and more. However, as described by our respondents, stigmatization is frequently experienced without discrimination. Thus, we use the term "assault on worth" to refer explicitly to stigmatization that is not perceived as leading to or is not associated with discrimination. But we also use the terms "stigmatization" and "assault on worth" interchangeably at times. We refer to stigmatization and discrimination as forms of *ethnoracial* exclusion (for short), because we are concerned with groups that are excluded based on phenotype, ethnicity, nationality, or some other ascribed characteristics.[15]

Note that with stigmatization, we are concerned not only with micro-aggressions and the experience of being stereotyped but also with the experience of being ignored and overlooked (which are not cases of aggression per se but of non attention).[16] We also view the notion of "assault on worth" as more encompassing than the kindred notion "implicit association" (Greenwald, McGhee, and Schwartz 1998), which is concerned with sorting and classifying but not with narratives as a means for meaning-making. We focus on assault-on-worth experiences that are at times hard to identify as incidents and are difficult to measure, because much of their manifestation is intrapsychic, the result of neglect, and they often generate (and are generated by) non-responses. Yet, as we will see, such experiences are often what people actually talk about when they are invited to reflect on their quotidian experiences with ethnoracial exclusion. These are consistent with the experience of "laissez-faire racism" (Bobo and Smith 1998), which points to experiences of neglect more than to overt aggression or blatant racism. Such experiences, we will argue, are an essential, yet too often undertheorized and unnoticed, component of a phenomenology of experiences of ethnoracial exclusion.

As a specific example of the distinction between stigmatization and standard discrimination, consider the following case from our interviews: an African American teacher is not greeted by her coworkers when she enters the teachers' room in the morning, while her white male colleague who walks in with her is. She cannot readily sue her peers for not greeting her, yet such an experience, especially when repeated, affects her well-being. It adds to the "wear and tear" that accompanies perceived racism, factoring into the large racial disparities in health found in the United States (Williams, Neighbors, and Jackson 2003; Williams and Sternthal 2010; Krieger 2014). Stigmatization is of particular importance in the symbolic ordering of ethnoracial inequality, just as symbolic violence is essential to class domination (Desmond and Emirbayer 2009).

Across our three societies, incidents of stigmatization are more frequently mentioned compared to those of discrimination. Their prominence is one of the most significant findings of our study. Indeed, the literature has primarily focused on discrimination, especially on instances where being deprived of resources (in housing, employment, education, healthcare, banking, etc.) meet legal standards of proof. This is hardly surprising, given that meritocracy and the myth of the American Dream are predicated on equal opportunity and access to resources. But to focus too exclusively on these forms of unfair treatment misses important aspects of the experience of living with a stigmatized identity. Tackling this challenge has become particularly important in the current context, where self-worth, respect, and dignity have gained centrality in social debates as multicultural societies become more concerned with recognition as an essential dimension of equity and social justice (Fraser 2000; Hodson 2001; Honneth 2012; Misztal 2013). In multicultural societies, such concerns are often associated with educated liberals (see Mizrachi 2014 on "liberal isomorphism"), but they are shared by many who are concerned with asserting self-worth. Against this background, it is important to examine how stigmatization manifests itself and to document its relative salience in relation to discrimination. We aim not to downplay the importance of discrimination but to situate it within the full range of incidents that individuals experience.

The greater salience of stigmatization for our interviewees was unexpected, particularly given what appears to be a greater attention given to discrimination in the US literature on race,[17] in line with US laws and social policies that are concerned with protecting access to opportunities for minorities (affirmative action, antidiscrimination laws, Moving to Opportunity, etc.). This is in strong contrast with most European antiracist law, which puts more emphasis on the control of blatant racism and hate speech than on protection against discrimination.[18] As shown by Bleich (2011), American social policy does comparatively little to limit stigmatization (often in the name of the defense of the First Amendment), as policymakers and the American public are mostly concerned with equality of opportunities. Bleich mentions that less attention is paid to how condoning stigmatizing symbolic acts (e.g., public cross burning by the Klu Klux Klan) signals implicit support for assigning low status to specific groups (in this case, denying African Americans equal respect and cultural citizenship). Such indignities contribute to processes of inequality and should be given full consideration. This is a lacuna we hope to correct.

We are also concerned here with how victims interpret and respond to incidents they identify as stigmatizing or discriminatory. There is often unequal power between stigmatizer and stigmatized such that the definition of reality produced by the former minimizes that of the latter. The perspective of the stigmatizer cannot be a necessary or sufficient condition for demonstrating that stigmatization has occurred; instances of assault on worth are to be inferred via the subjective experience of the stigmatized as conveyed by narratives. Intersubjective data would be needed to document how widely diffused stigmatization's effects are and whether a negative label "sticks" in such a way that one indeed gets stigmatized in ongoing interactions. Establishing this would require determining the extent to which meaning is shared within networks. This is an object of inquiry beyond the scope of our study. By documenting patterns in narratives of the stigmatized across our three sites, we hope to gain significant knowledge of how stigmatization is experienced across places.

Responses to Incidents: Actual and Ideal

In addition to examining experiences of assaults on worth and discrimination, we also explore how people respond to such incidents, because responses to acts of ethnoracial exclusion are fundamental to social and cultural processes that contribute to the transformation of group boundaries and the reinforcement of inequality.[19] This is true both in terms of how people actually respond to spontaneous incidents and in terms of what they perceive as the ideal responses for dealing with racism—what they feel people should do. Our analysis thus focuses both on how people report reacting (or not) to being stigmatized or discriminated against and on the individual and collective strategies that our respondents perceive as fruitful, which include their views on race-targeted policies and lessons for children about racism (among other topics).

Responses matter, because the stress (or "wear and tear") generated during responses may compound inequality and disadvantages. Types of responses may affect health differently, depending on the social context. In such contexts as the workplace, for example, confrontational responses may impact health negatively, in part because of the necessity of maintaining an occupation for mental well-being.[20] Normative responses raise important questions concerning how social change can be produced moving ahead, through individual and collective strategies aimed at social transformation.

We innovate in relation to the available literature by paying close attention to how individuals think about the consequences of responding and coding how respondents consider the emotional, material, or legal costs of various types of responses. As suggested in Hirschman's (1970) classic *Exit, Voice, and Loyalty*, which models three basic types of responses, there are many reasonable ways to respond to a challenge.[21] Our inductive analysis reveals five categories of responses: confronting (including taking legal recourse), management of the self, not responding, a focus on hard work and demonstrating competence, and self-isolation/autonomy.

Interviewees most frequently confront the stigmatizer, especially in the United States. While the high frequency of this meta-category of response could be explained as a desirability effect, descriptions of how confrontation occurs are so varied as to confirm its de facto centrality.[22] Yet, it is as prevalent as no response and management of the self in Brazil: there, interviewees are more hesitant to describe an incident as demonstrating racism and prefer a polite exchange to "educate racists."[23] And they spend considerable energy managing relationships so as to deflate conflict. Compared to African Americans, Arab Palestinians also confronted somewhat less frequently, often opt to stay silent due to cynicism over the perceived intractability of their situation.

Management of the self, the second most common type of response, entails individual calculations (in terms of emotion, energy, reputation, and resources) concerning the personal cost of responding.[24] In Goffmanian terminology, it involves managing the "front stage" presentation of the self in a way one considers satisfactory. This may mean making the effort not to be perceived as a "loud black woman" or to confirm other stereotypes frequently applied to one's group. It may also mean wanting to preserve energy or avoiding getting caught in a vicious cycle of anger, which depletes resilience. With this category, we capture the fact that respondents spend substantial energy considering what response is best to offer in an incident. While some scholars have analyzed the salience of such a response in various contexts (Lacy 2007; Wingfield 2010; Patterson and Fosse 2015), its relative significance vis-à-vis other types of responses to stigmatization and discrimination has not been systematically assessed to date, even within a single context.

A third common response type (as frequent as management of self) is simply not responding. Like management of the self, this is a category where the response is not obvious to an onlooker. While the literature rarely theorizes the meaning of non-response, we pay careful attention to how people account for their not responding. While "management of the self" responses result from deliberation about the personal costs of responding, there are cases where respondents do not give consideration to the consequences of not responding, because they are surprised or inattentive. In other cases, they don't respond due to habit or other circumstances. Or else they say that they chose to not respond because they believed it was pointless or that the stigmatizers should be ignored or forgiven, or because ignoring is perceived as a way to insult the stigmatizer.

Other salient responses are to demonstrate a strong work ethic and competence in professional and educational (especially formal educational) contexts, or to engage in isolation or autonomy, a strategy of making the group more self-sufficient and less dependent on the socially dominant group. We will see that these are less common forms of response across sites.

However, self-improvement, which can be achieved through work or education, is in most cases particularly salient among ideal strategies that respondents offer as ways to deal with ethnoracial exclusion. We consider whether in these cases the beneficiary is the individual or the collective. This is important in a neoliberal context, where the social conditions that may have encouraged collective mobilization in earlier decades are receding, given the current emphasis on the privatization of risk and individualism (Bobo 1991; Hall and Lamont 2013).[25] Considering ideal responses raises many questions for the future of social movements and of individual and collective strategies.

Class, Gender, and Age Cohorts

The selection of interviewees in all three sites was originally inspired by a desire to consider whether the resources at the disposal of middle- and working-class individuals affect patterns of responses to incidents. To take the case of African Americans, Drake and Cayton (1945) have argued that the black middle class has historically been more conscious of discrimination than its working-class counterpart and has been more eager to confront (see the "race man/race woman" theory; Drake and Cayton 1945: 394). Du Bois (1899) has written to great effect on the same question. Thus, we pondered whether individuals with more resources are more likely to confront racism across the three societies under consideration. Here we also drew on the broader literature on American middle- and working-class culture, which has documented middle-class norms of conflict avoidance (Morrill 1995; Jackall 2010) and this group's attachment to professional identity (Brint and Proctor 2011), which could prompt its members to downplay racist incidents and avoid confrontation. Alternatively, would experiencing racism be so similar across classes as to deflate class difference in responses?[26] Having a small number of respondents in each of our Israeli groups, we could not draw conclusions about class in this national context.

Even if our main focus was class similarities and differences in the US and Brazil, we also considered gender differences. As with class differences, patterns of gender differences in interviewees' responses are much less than originally expected and revolve around specifically gendered areas of discrimination, such as racial profiling. Their responses also resonate with gendered narratives of behavior, for instance, violence and confronting. In the United States, interviews suggest that African American men perceive themselves slightly more frequently to be stigmatized and discriminated against, and in particular to be more often feared and underestimated, and men mention more incidents than do women. In Brazil, gender differences in the number of excluding experiences and types of responses were quite limited, even if we found more mentions of experiencing sexualized stereotypes by women and more mentions of being stereotyped as violent among men.

In the US case we also considered the relevance of age cohort differences. The differences, though small, are worth noting. In the United States, those born before the Civil Rights Movement are more likely to refer to the law and legal recourse in their responses. Because Brazil interviewees are somewhat younger, cohort differences are not relevant. In Israel there were fewer respondents for each group, which also prevents discussion of cohorts (and gender). However, the secondary literature suggests that the younger generation of Arab Palestinians is more ready to confront stigmatizers and to be involved in political activities than previous generations (Rabinowitz and Abu-Baker 2005). Similarly, Sansone (1997) has argued that younger Black Brazilians are more affirming of their black identity than the older generation. But it is unclear from his findings whether the younger generation would be more likely to respond to an incident of exclusion with confrontation.

Before delving into the details of our objectives, we turn to the making of the study to further specify how our comparison fosters a novel perspective. In Chapter 1, we describe our explanatory strategy as well as some of our contributions. This discussion is more theoretical and can be skipped by those not interested in the scholarly conversation in which we locate our work.

HOW WE DID OUR STUDY

Our Cases

Our study honors the tradition of comparing race relations in the United States and Brazil, which are often regarded as reversed mirror images of one another when it comes to racial relations.[27] Our third point of comparison, the Israeli case, serves to denaturalize widely shared and deep-seated notions about the centrality of the racial divide that characterizes US and Brazilian societies. It also permits a broad reframing of the question of exclusion, as social scientists typically treat Israel as an exception that would require distinct analytical lenses to understand. Approaching the three countries through similar lenses, we hope to unsettle widely held assumptions and offer new analytical leverage in our understanding of all three national cases.

Originally, we thought of incorporating only Arab Palestinians into the study, as this population represents the most deeply and explicitly excluded group in the Israeli landscape, and as such it is the most comparable to African Americans and Black Brazilians. However, as spelled out earlier, as the investigation proceeded, we came to appreciate the heuristic value of considering the interplay among different sources of stigma, so we included two additional, differently marked, Israeli groups, Ethiopian and Mizrahi Jews.[28] Initially, we treated these as "shadow cases," thinking that it was simply too overwhelming for the reader to go into the same depth and detail for the Ethiopian and Mizrahi Jews as for the Arab Palestinians. In practice, however, it became difficult to maintain this shadow status throughout. Thus, in the introductory section of the Israeli chapter (Chapter 4), they receive equal weight, more or less. But in later sections they are treated as foils to compare to the Arab Palestinian case, and we highlight mainly how they are different from that group. In places where it makes sense to compare them to the groups in the United States and Brazil, we do that. In a sense, we have given them more space when discussing the explanatory factors, and less space and emphasis when it comes to the explanandum (experiences and responses).

Mizrahi Jews are Israeli citizens who immigrated from Arab or Muslim countries or whose parents or grandparents did. Like Brazilians, they experience an ambiguous status in their society because of the historical denial of the existence of discrimination against their group. While not strongly marked in part due to their relatively large size (Mizrahim and Black Brazilians represent, respectively, 27 percent and 51 percent of the population of their countries),[29] both groups are relegated to an inferior position in their country's status and economic systems.

Ethiopian Jews represent only 2 percent of the population, and they are strongly marked phenotypically, as the size of Israel's black population is very small (it also includes some African migrant workers) and the Israeli population is not multiracial, although there is significant ethnic heterogeneity. While religion is the basis of their national inclusion, their phenotype and recent migration from Africa are often viewed as markers of inferior status. The fact that they share their phenotypical marking with Black Brazilians and African Americans enables us to consider the impact of skin color in ethnoracial inequalities across three national contexts (Banton 2012; Telles and PERLA team 2014).

In short, the fact that our analysis concerns not only three countries, but also, in one national case, three groups, enriches our analysis. It allows us to explore not only how middle- and working-class men and women experience and react to stigma and discrimination, but also how different types of boundaries (ethnic, national, phenotypical, and religious) operate in relation to one another in one national context. We can also consider how, even within the confines of a single nation, one principle of exclusion (e.g., being stereotyped as poor) operates differently across groups.

Although our analysis is largely organized around cross-national comparisons, we are mindful of the dangers of methodological nationalism (Wimmer and Glick Schiller 2002), and we also pay attention to similarities and exchanges across settings, particularly in the mobilization of transnational narratives for making claims pertaining to such issues as racism, social justice, human rights, and reparation. We locate our three national contexts within the global landscape in several ways. First, we consider how transnational movements have informed the way individuals look at difference, equality, and inequality, and how their responses are shaped by transnational cultural repertoires, whether those of human rights (Jenson and Levi 2013; see Mizrachi 2014 for the concept of liberal isomorphism) or others. Second, we pay attention to cross-national influences, such as how the United States has been an important point of reference for current debates on recognition (e.g., Mizrachi and Herzog 2012; Roth 2012) and the black diaspora (see Bourdieu and Wacquant 2001b for a critique). Third, we maintain a comparative emphasis on differences in how national laws, customs, and practices evolve. Countries and nation-states remain important structuring actors and objects of analysis, even in the context of increased globalization and interdependency.

A reminder of the importance of national contexts is the fact that our interviews captured these three countries at different phases in their respective social and economic trajectories. During the phase of data collection (2007–2008), the United States was in a recession, and Brazil and Israel were experiencing economic growth. While in the United States and Israel inequality has been growing in the past decades, the reverse has been the case in the Brazil (even if inequality is still substantially larger in this country compared to the other two).[30] Consequently, the gap between the middle and working classes (or between the working class and the unemployed) may be getting larger (in the United States and Israel) or smaller (in the case of Brazil).

Finally, the three societies vary in their ethnoracial diversity. The United States faces a rapid expansion of its immigrant population, especially Latinos, and is quickly becoming a minority-majority society. In Israel, the 1990s were a period of accelerated immigration from Russia, and the 2000s, from Africa (both Jewish Ethiopians and non-Jewish migrant workers). In Brazil, while the 1980s were a period of emigration to the United States and Europe, the 1990s saw increased immigration from other Latin American countries.[31] These changes have influenced the overall ethnoracial hierarchy in each country in the past couple of decades. For example, some authors have referred to the Latin Americanization of the color line in the United States, which is moving from the "one-drop rule"[32] to a color spectrum.[33] In Brazil, there has been growing recognition of racial differences (Costa 2001), partly attributed to the increasing mobility of Brazilian immigrants to and from the United States (Joseph 2013). In Israel, this period has witnessed a decline of the dominant Ashkenazi groups and the emergence of subgroups that challenge the dominant national identity (Kimmerling 2001). These different contexts surely impact perceptions about opportunities and constraints for social change among our interviewees.

Our Participants and Methods

Our study is based on in-depth interviews conducted between 2007 and 2008[34] in or around a prominent multiethnic metropolis in each of the three countries under consideration: New York, Rio de Janeiro, and Tel Aviv. Our aim is not to generalize from our three metropolitan contexts to the countries themselves. In each national case, there are important regional differences in the character of race/group relations.[35] Instead, the logic of our analysis is one of theoretical sampling in which each group is considered a case study in and of itself (Small 2009). When possible, we mobilize national data to consider whether and how our interviewees' views resemble those of the broader population. But overall, our goal is to contribute by improving the analysis of cultural processes of ethnoracial exclusion than to describe national trends for which data are not always available.

Our approach incorporates a cultural and cognitive approach to consider how groupness is organized around race, ethnicity, phenotype, nationality, or religion. We understand ethnicity and race as cognition, with a focus on how groups classify and differentiate themselves from one another.[36] We capture this boundary work through narratives produced in interview situations. We take these to be significant expressions of intersubjectively shared classification systems or collective representations as they manifest and are captured at one point in time. While a focus on boundary work as it manifests in interactions and is captured through ethnography would be useful (e.g., Sherman 2005), ethnography is insufficient for tapping broadly shared classification systems across different participants (Lamont and Swidler 2014). An ideal approach would combine observation and interviews, which is not feasible in the context of this already sprawling study.

An additional limitation of our interview-based approach is that it taps only the perspective of the subordinates and ignores that of the dominant group they are exposed to—except as captured through the descriptions by the subordinates. However, the dominants are also present in the background to the extent that they share some of the contexts experienced by the stigmatized (e.g., through cultural repertoires). We hope that our contribution will inspire other scholars to examine the worldview of the dominant in a complementary fashion (e.g., DiTomasso 2013).

In-depth interviews were conducted among 150 residents in New York suburbs, 160 in the Rio de Janeiro metropolitan area, and 137 in and around

Tel Aviv. While slightly different protocols were followed to recruit respondents across sites (Appendix 1 provides details on the methodology), our sample composition was overall similar across sites (unless otherwise noted) to maximize their comparability. In each case, we aimed to interview a roughly equal number of men and women, and of middle- and working-class individuals (adjusting the boundaries of the class groups to the distinctive class structure of each country). Although the American and Brazilian research procedures largely parallel one another, in Israel these procedures were less parallel, in part because three groups were studied, with smaller numbers for each group.

In interviews, we pay attention to how respondents describe stigmatizing and discriminatory incidents, although we cannot say with certainty that the incidents actually occurred in the way they were perceived. Indeed, respondents' certainty about viewing an incident as an example of racism, is likely to vary with the character of the specific event, the typical relationship between the stigmatized and the dominant groups, the time lag between the interview and the incident, and broader expectations based on past modes of interaction between groups. To illustrate, in some instances, the respondents reported feeling hesitant to label an event or individual as "racist" for fear of not having proof, as recounted at the beginning of this chapter in the case of the Brazilian woman Ana. We regard such hesitations as data, not evidence that our respondents do not experience racism.

When analyzing the interviews, we used content-analysis software to categorize inductively the most salient aspects of identification and the types of subjective experiences of such incidents that our interviewees described. This inductive approach reveals many dimensions of the life-world of our respondents that we had not suspected beforehand that are quite variable when looked at comparatively. Because researchers do not inhabit the world of respondents, it would be easy to overlook or exaggerate differences without the benefit of specific inductively derived information about similarities and differences. Thus, this approach makes possible a much more detailed empirical portrait of our groups' experiences and responses to ethnoracial exclusion.

This analysis also reveals differences in raw or absolute numbers of experiences and responses across sites. These differences depend on how likely interviewees were to interpret experiences through the lens of ethnoracial exclusion, which is one of the main focuses of our analysis. They are also influenced by how extensively interviewees were probed during the interviews at each site, despite the extensive efforts we made to increase consistency in our interviewing procedures and in the training of interviewers. Nevertheless, we believe comparing the relative frequency of incident types for each group of respondents (as opposed to across groups) is an informative and significant contribution.

So far, we have described the book as offering:

1. A phenomenological analysis of experiences and responses of eth-noracial exclusion that explains micro-phenomena by the meso- (cultural repertoires, groupness) and the macro- (societal character-istics, history, etc.) levels;
2. A fine-grained analysis that brings to light the relative frequency of types of experiences of stigmatization and discrimination and responses to those incidents;
3. The salience of stigmatization in relation to discrimination in inci-dents mentioned by our interviewees;
4. Different patterns of responses across cases, such as the greater promi-nence of confrontation in the United States; and
5. Surprising results through our inquiry into class, gender, and cohort differences in the United States and Brazil.

Now we turn to our multidimensional explanation. Here we will see three other contributions: (1) a multidimensional explanation that focuses on groupness and the cultural tools available to make sense of reality; (2) a multidimensional operationalization of groupness that takes into consider-ation both self-identification and group boundaries; and (3) an analysis of the varied types of groupness across our five cases.

. . . .

Before proceeding to the next chapter, we visit the story of another respon-dent to signal that, with all the detailed analysis deployed in this study, above all, we are concerned with the challenging experiences that taint the daily lives of individuals belonging to stigmatized groups. We quote from an African American artist who recalls his experience while attending an almost all-white elite high school as a teenager. He describes how he dealt with the fact that he was made to feel invisible by his white schoolmates and his uncertainty about the ambiguity of these racial incidents. His de-scription alludes to themes reminiscent of Ralph Ellison's classic *Invisible Man* (1952). He describes how his friends helped him by corroborating his interpretation of reality and bolstering his self-confidence:

When I first started getting hit with that invisibility trick . . . oh man, I was like, "Did I say it wrong?" But fortunately I didn't spend a lot of time on that because I had my buddies and we would always be hang-ing out. . . . On Saturday we would be going to play baseball and I'd say, "You know what happened to me?" They [would] say, "That hap-pened to you—oh man, let me tell you what happened to me!" . . . Even though for the rest of that week I felt like "Was it me? Was it something

I said?" by the time I got to the weekend, just because of the fact that I had a positive group of people around me, I had a way of talking about it, and I couldn't talk about it like the way I am talking about it now. I mean, we understood it from the perspective of somebody who was like 16. Oh it's "the man," you know, "The man does that stuff." . . . You might not really understand the true dynamics of it or how you really want to deal with it, but at least it got me out of feeling inferior. . . . I had a sounding board that would reflect back to me: "No, it's not you, man."

This passage illustrates the importance of intersubjectivity as a resource for defining and confirming definitions of reality (Sauder 2006), and, conversely, the dangers of self-isolation. The uncertainty surrounding the appropriate interpretation of an event is part of the event, just as being able to establish legally the fact that discrimination has happened is itself part of the event. Assaults on worth are frequently more open to varying interpretation than are discrimination events, because they do not involve specific effects that can be demonstrated, such as being deprived of education, a job, housing, or other resources. Subjectively experienced and defined, the harm is no less real for those who believe they are being underestimated, ignored, or stereotyped. The need to better understand such painful human experiences is what motivates our study. While these experiences are all too familiar to members of stigmatized groups, it is particularly crucial that we engage fellow human beings across color and class lines in an effort to work together toward the transformation of racial and class hierarchies.

CHAPTER 1

ACCOUNTING FOR DIFFERENCES

HOW TO EXPLAIN

In this chapter, we develop a multidimensional framework to help account for experiences and responses to ethnoracial exclusion. Our analytical strategy is meant to be suggestive of how patterns are set in place rather than to provide a parsimonious causal analysis of patterns sensu stricto.[1] At the most abstract level, our approach resembles that used by historical institutionalists interested in configurational explanations,[2] by sociologists of immigration, and by social movement scholars who pursue discursive opportunity structure explanations. The latter group has analyzed emotions and the availability of religious and human rights frameworks and their impact on mobilization (e.g., Williams 2004; Bröer and Duyvendak 2009), while scholars of immigration have argued that discursive opportunity structures influence the claims-making of minorities (e.g., Koopmans and Statham 2000).[3] Similarly, we zoom in on a few dimensions to account for the patterns of experiences, responses, and groupness that we identify in the evidence we have collected.

THREE DIMENSIONS OF NATIONAL CONTEXT

Our explanatory framework analytically distinguishes between three dimensions to make sense of how they influence experiences and responses (see also Falleti and Lynch 2009). More specifically, we focus on the dimensions listed in Table 1.1 that pertain to (1) history and the socioeconomic and institutional context (which we capture by the notion of background factors); (2) the strength and mode of groupness (i.e., the extent to which individuals conceive of themselves as part of a group, which itself includes several dimensions, e.g., self-identification and group boundaries); and (3) available

TABLE 1.1. DIMENSIONS ENABLING AND CONSTRAINING NARRATIVES
OF EXPERIENCES AND RESPONSES

Historical, socioeconomic, and institutional elements	Cultural repertoires	Groupness
• Size of group and its relative demographic weight • Ethnoracial demographic diversity of the region and society • History of group relations and inequality • Changes in levels and national patterns of inequality • Economic context (e.g., economic recession and expansion) • Concentration of ethnoracial minorities across classes and recent transformation of class structure • Spatial and institutional segregation (including incarceration) • Institutional and legal reforms (including those dealing with race, ethnicity, and nationality) • Political transformation (progressive, liberal, and conservative eras)	• National myths and ideologies (e.g., American Dream, Zionism, racial democracy) and models of incorporation in the polity (e.g., melting pot, multiculturalism) • Transnational antiracist repertoires (e.g., human rights, social justice, black diaspora) • Empowering ideologies (e.g., black nationalism) • Available repertoires of group disadvantages and shared experiences; ready-made scripts about exclusion and universalism • Hierarchy of class cultures (e.g., dominance of middle-class culture, stigmatization of the poor) • Class- and gender-specific cultural repertoires (e.g., masculinity, self-actualization) • General cultural repertoires (e.g., meritocracy, therapeutic culture, identity politics) • Neoliberal repertoires (e.g., competition, privatization of risk, self-reliance)	• Self-definition and self-labeling • Meaning of identity and perceived cultural distinctiveness of group • Salience of racial, class, and national identification in the group • Reported network composition and homophily • Symbolic boundaries toward dominant group and its perceived advantages • Census categories and policies making group identity salient • Homophily in cohabitation/marriage and friendship • Perceived spatial segregation

cultural repertoires (themselves the product of history). In the three country chapters (Chapters 2–4), we detail how these various elements are more or less salient as broad contextual factors, how they are connected, and how they may help explain aspects of the puzzle. We also spell out the configuration of groupness for each of the five groups being studied. Although this approach could be criticized for having too many explanatory dimensions for too few cases—what Stanley Lieberson (1992) termed the "small N, big conclusion" problem—again, our goal is not to offer a parsimonious explanation but to improve our understanding of why and how patterns contrast across groups, in line with the classical Weberian tradition in comparative sociology. Each of the three dimensions we focus on has several components that define in important ways the context in which the lives or our five groups evolve. We argue that these components need to be considered when trying to account for individuals' experiences of and responses to ethnoracial exclusion.

Historical, Socioeconomic, and Institutional Elements. Among the main background elements shaping experiences and responses, one has to consider the history of the country, particularly as it pertains to ethnoracial relationships. Other relevant factors (see Table 1.1, column 1) include the level of inequality in the country and whether it and the economy are growing or contracting; the size of the group under consideration and its salience; the ethnoracial diversity of the country's population; the concentration of the stigmatized group in low-income categories; the extent to which the middle class is diversified racially; the extent of spatial and institutional segregation each group experiences; and the historical transformation of politics, which brings about conservative and progressive changes, as well as neo-liberal moments (e.g., Phillips-Fein 2009 and Waterhouse 2013 for the United States). Finally, we also include the institutional and legal structures and reforms of the society, particularly those that bear on race, ethnicity, and nationality. The explanatory dimensions under this heading are the mainstay of background explanations for contemporary forms of American racism (e.g., in the analysis of laissez-faire racism by Bobo and Smith 1998). They are also the main focus of most macro-historical comparisons of race relations (e.g., Marx 1998; Winant 2001).

Cultural Repertoires. Individuals do not develop narratives in isolation; instead they construct narratives from historically constituted, culturally available narrative templates, public narratives, or meta-narratives and in conversation with other narratives (Somers 1994; Ewick and Silbey 2003). Although many terms are used to describe these sources of meaning (scripts or frames, among others) and there are nuances in what each of them highlights (Lamont and Small 2008), we favor the term "repertoires," defined as a set of tools available to individuals to make sense of the reality they experience.[4] Table 1.1, column 2 lists the explanatory elements that pertain to such cultural repertoires. Some repertoires may be more readily available in one national context than in another.[5] The cultural repertoires considered include national myths of incorporation in the polity (e.g., the American Dream, Zionism, and racial democracy). There are also models of incorporation (Portes and Borocz 1989) or philosophies of integration

(Favell 1998) that speak to the principles by which the polity holds together (e.g., multiculturalism, diversity, and Republicanism). Cultural myths of belonging as defined by collective memory are often related to these two broad categories. Other significant repertoires include transnational anti-racist repertoires ranging from human rights to social justice and the Black Pride promoted by members of the black diaspora during the Civil Rights Movement. Such repertoires may be widely available to group members as cultural resources as they are looking for scripts to make sense of experiences of exclusion and group stereotypes. Also relevant are class-related cultural repertoires (e.g., the self-actualization so crucial in the middle classes), as well as broader cultural repertoires, such as those pertaining to therapeutic culture and individualism. Repertoires pertaining to the relative standing of various classes (the cultural hegemony of the upper middle class) also matter. References to neoliberal repertoires are most prominent in our analysis of the United States and are least prominent in Brazil: in some contexts, neoliberal narratives have resulted in an increased emphasis on the privatization of risk, competitiveness, and hard work and have intensified demands on stigmatized groups to be more self-reliant (Moraes Silva 2012; Hall and Lamont 2013; Sharone 2014). After the Civil Rights Act, blacks have the de jure right to confront, and self-reliance places de facto the burden of overcoming racism on their individual shoulders. This has important effects on the decline of collective responses among African Americans, one of the main themes developed in Chapter 2 on the United States (see also Harris 2014).

Of course, other authors consider the impact of repertoires on identity. For instance, Dawson (2009) focuses on media exposure, Essed (1991) is concerned with public narratives, and Lipsitz (2011) factors in national myths of belonging, while racial formation and systemic racism approaches also consider the impact of frames.[6]

Our approach takes into consideration a broader range of cultural repertoires than most. We look toward not only repertoires that feed into racialization but also those tied to specific class cultures and positions, national ideologies and myths, and economic transformation. We also consider how such repertoires interact with one another to enable subjective experiences and responses.[7]

Groupness. The third column of Table 1.1 isolates groupness as a distinct explanatory dimension. For our purpose, groupness is a function of self-identification and perceptions of out-groups (symbolic boundaries). But it is conditioned by background conditions that include network composition and homophily (spatial and social boundaries), as well as the size and visibility of the group and the multiracial character of the national context (which are discussed as part of the background against which the group stands, with more or less contrast; Zerubavel 1991; Alba 2005). Because groupness is a less familiar concept than that of repertoire, we discuss it in some detail below and explain how we went about operationalizing this notion already present in the contemporary literature (Brubaker 2009). The configuration of groupness for each of our five cases is revisited in greater detail in the second section of each country chapter.[8]

Brubaker and Cooper (2000: 20, 7) define groupness as "the sense of belonging to a distinctive, bounded, solidarity group" and a "fundamental and consequential sameness among members of a group or category" (see also Brubaker 2009).[9] In our case, we focus on groupness as experienced by our interviewees. While previous accounts have tended to treat groupness as a one-dimensional category that varies from weak to strong (Bailey 2009a), we operationalize it as multidimensional, so as to capture both the symbolic bases according to which groupness is defined and its potentially contradictory character when relevant (i.e., the fact that groupness can be considered weak on certain dimensions and strong on others).

For the groups we consider, we draw a detailed picture of their degree of groupness. Contrary to dualistic images of group identity that oppose in-group and out-group, this picture combines:

1. The *self-identification* of our interviewees, as captured by questions concerning self-definition and self-labeling, the perceived cultural distinctiveness of the group, and the use of distinctive referents when defining the meanings of racial, ethnic, religious, or national identity (cultural symbols such as Kwanza, African-American history, expressions of pride and honor, etc.);[10] and

2. The strength of *group boundaries*, as revealed by perceived closeness to in-group members, including friendship, dating, and marriage, and by boundary work toward out-groups (toward whites in particular in the United States and Brazil), including concerning white privilege.[11]

We also consider perceived background conditions that could be identified (spatial separation, network structures, etc.).[12] We put particular weight on the availability and institutionalization of public narratives in shaping the experience of and responses to stigmatization and discrimination. This dimension of groupness has often been overlooked by dominant approaches to racial inequality and racism, which are typically overwhelmingly descriptive and when explanatory, mostly focus on macro-level explanations of racism in the US context (as argued by Emirbayer and Desmond 2015).

Also relevant to groupness are the demographic weight of the group and the diversity of the environment in which it is located. That Black Brazilians make up roughly 50 percent of the Brazilian population—including those who identify as browns (*pardos*) and as blacks (*pretos*)—and evolve in a highly multiracial landscape certainly influence how prominent they are as a group. Similarly, it matters that Ethiopian Jews began immigrating relatively recently and make up only 2 percent of Israel's population in a relatively homogeneous racial context and that Mizrahi Jews constitute a narrow majority of the Jewish population of Israel. The extent to which any group stands out against a background of greater or lesser ethnoracial demographic diversity matters not only for the definition ("brightness") of the boundaries and thus groupness, but also as a dimension of the context in which that group operates. Nor does the size of a group mechanistically translate into weak or strong groupness. One also needs to take into consideration historically constituted racial classification systems, how diversity and other policies influence group formation, political strategies of political parties and minority social movements, and much more (e.g., Loveman 2014; Paschel 2016).

The three country chapters (Chapters 2–4) show variations in the groupness of the five groups under consideration. As shown in Table 1.2, these variations can be broken into two dimensions: self-identification and group boundaries. Table 1.2 provides details on the characterization of groupness for each dimension. It shows that our approach to groupness is multidimensional: it considers both internal (self-identification) and external (toward outgroups) boundaries, which can be characterized as strongly policed, blurred, fuzzy, ambiguous, and the like.

African Americans, Ethiopian Jews, and Palestinian Arabs are at the high end of the spectrum on the strength of groupness, whereas Black Brazilians and Mizrahim are at the low end. While again, we acknowledge that referring to the strength of groupness may flatten out what is after all a multidimensional reality, in Table 1.2 we use strength as a heuristic device to aid comparison across cases. We consider the very different configurations of identification (including national and class identifications) in which these groups find themselves. Patterns of groupness figure prominently in the arguments deployed in each of our country chapters. The construction of this explanatory dimension is also an empirical contribution of the study, as this dimension could not be captured without the mediation of clear conceptualization and operationalization. Thus, the empirical analyses of groupness figure prominently in each country chapter and are revisited in the Conclusion to the book.

In the United States, the *strong racial groupness* of African-Americans manifests as a combination of strong group identification; strong social boundaries based on perceived high spatial segregation; strong racial homophily (despite our interviewees' valuing friendship with people of diverse backgrounds); and high awareness of racial stigmatization and discrimination, which are perceived as existing independently of class stigma. There are also few differences in self-identification or experiences of stigmatization/discrimination across classes, as if being black overrides class-specific experiences.

TABLE 1.2. CHARACTERIZATION OF GROUPNESS FOR THE FIVE ETHNORACIAL GROUPS STUDIED

| | UNITED STATES | BRAZIL | ISRAEL | | |
	African Americans	Pretos and pardos	Palestinian citizens	Ethiopians	Mizrahim
Characterization	Strong but contradictory	Blurred	Strong	Dissonant	Weak
Primary bases of groupness	Race	Race	Nationality	Race/Immigrant status	Ethnicity
SELF-IDENTIFICATION					
Self-definition and self-labeling as group member	Strong	Strong	Strong	Medium	Weak
Perceived cultural distinctiveness/meaning of identity	Strong	Weak	Strong	Strong	Mixed
National identification	Mixed	Strong	Weak	Strong	Strong
GROUP BOUNDARIES					
Reported social boundaries					
Perceived spatial segregation	High	Low	High	High	Low
Homophily	High	Low	High	High	Low
Symbolic boundaries					
Symbolic boundaries toward dominant out-groups	Strong but contradictory	Porous	Strong	Weak	Weak
Available repertoires of group disadvantages and shared experiences	Strong (racism, slavery)	Mixed (racism, slavery, and class)	Strong (colonialism)	Strong (versus Ashkenazim)	Weak

Respondents also identify slightly more with their racial group than with the nation. Their strong racial groupness coexists with a *pro-universalist orientation*: they proclaimed universalism or openness to out-group members despite their awareness of discrimination. This is why we described their groupness as *strong but contradictory*.

In Brazil, our interviewees display *blurred racial groupness*, with *racial identification*, as they largely identify as black but do not view themselves as sharing a culture distinct from the majority culture. They make up 51 percent of the Brazilian population according to the 2010 census, and their expressive culture largely defines the majority culture. Also, they identify racially as black and nationally as Brazilian (i.e., they combine both national and racial identification). They experience less perceived spatial segregation than African Americans do, based mostly on class rather than race. They also experience low salience of racial preference in personal relationships and a conflation of race and class in experiences of stigmatization and discrimination. But they are aware of being racially stigmatized (especially among those who have strong racial identification—although we do not make a causal claim here). Here our analysis resembles Sansone (1997), who describes Black Brazilians as having "blackness without ethnicity." However, while Sansone focuses on cultural distinctiveness captured by the notion of ethnicity (equating the latter with having a shared culture), our approach is to examine the nuances of the boundedness of groups.

In Israel, ethno-national identity based on religious identification is at the center of Israeli life and organizes the formation of the polity, which shapes how different types of stigma are framed and experienced. The three Israeli groups experience groupness in highly differentiated ways. The first two groups are categorized by the majority group as "other," one because of its local political history (Palestinians) and the other because of skin color and ties to Africa (Ethiopians). The third group (Mizrahim) largely perceives itself as unmarked, yet its members face social boundaries (mostly class-based spatial segregation and discrimination in education and the workplace) and Orientalist stereotypes (i.e., a patronizing attitude toward non-Western cultures; Said 1978). We describe Mizrahi Jews as demonstrating *weak ethnic groupness*, which we contrast with the *strong national groupness* of Arab Palestinians and the *dissonant racial groupness* of Ethiopian Jews. These three groups connect in diverse ways to the Zionist national polity (with Arab Palestinians symbolically and institutionally excluded from the polity despite full citizenship, while Ethiopian and Mizrahi Jews feel fully identified with the nation-state of Israel despite varying degrees of ethnoracial exclusion).

Wimmer (2008, 2013) represents a parallel and kindred effort to our own, particularly in that we also regard groupness as an issue to be ascertained empirically.[13] As elaborated in elsewhere (Lamont 2000; see also Brubaker et al. 2006), we share an inductive approach to self-identification that does not start with the assumption that ethnoracial identity is most salient for members of the group under consideration (even if our sampling strategy used specific externally defined categorizations—ethnoracial self-identification, education, and occupation—as a basis for inclusion in the population to be studied; see also Brubaker 2009).[14] While we are agnostic about the salience of self-identification across groups and contexts and consider this an empirical issue, we also acknowledge that there is no "view from nowhere" and that so-called unmarked or universal categories are dominant categories turned into *doxa* (Bourdieu 1977: 164).[15] Thus, our aim is to tackle the challenge of maintaining an open-ended perspective on groupness without obliterating the politics of categorization.

While a few authors have explored a taxonomy of how actors change ethnic boundaries through expansion, contraction, transvaluation, boundary crossing and repositioning, and blurring (Alba 2009; Zolberg and Woon 1999; Wimmer 2013), our goal is to produce a phenomenology of group boundaries by relying on the in-depth narratives of stigmatized groups. Whether they do it by confronting or not, our respondents structure the types of boundary changes discussed by these authors. We are interested less in the general configuration and reconfiguring of boundaries than in the processual experiences that produce them.[16]

There are other important differences between our position and major contributions to the relevant literature: Instead of emphasizing the cognitive and the motivational, including the self-enhancing and self-protecting dynamics that social psychologists often privilege (Major 1993), we consider feelings of similarities and differences described by the social actor.[17] Identities are factored in, but we also locate these in a network of self-reported relationships in time and space shaped by such factors as spatial segregation, homophily, and classification systems.[18] In the African American case, for instance, this approach leads us to reconstruct a multidimensional, and in some ways contradictory, portrait of ethnoracial groupness, which we describe as strong by some criteria (identification, in-group preference, out-group boundaries) but paradoxically mixed by other criteria (friendships with whites, normative commitment to a culture of diversity or to a desire to weaken group boundaries).[19] Again, Table 1.2 captures the different dimensions of groupness for each of the cases under consideration.

CONNECTING FINDINGS AND EXPLANATION

A close examination of our cases suggested a complex and textured explanation that takes into consideration a range of dimensions enabling various types of experiences. We need to explain how two groups with a high degree of groupness but different relationships with the polity—African Americans and Arab Palestinians—experience exclusion differently and respond to it differently. How can we explain that African Americans provided more narratives of experiences of stigmatization and discrimination and offered a wider range of responses than did Arab Palestinians? We suggest that it is in part because the latter largely do not define themselves as full members of the polity and have low expectations about equal treatment. Comparably, two groups with low groupness (or boundedness)—Black Brazilians and Mizrahi Jews—are located differently in their respective countries' polities and interpret their experiences of exclusion in contrasting ways: Mizrahi Jews systematically downplayed personal experiences of stigmatization, while Black Brazilians perceived high levels of stigmatization, especially based on status and social class stereotypes. In both comparisons, there is no linear relationship between the degree of groupness or boundedness and the frequency of incidents or types of responses to incidents mentioned in interviews. Instead, responses to incidents appear to be shaped by the distinctively structured contexts in which these groups find themselves, so it is necessary to refer to these contexts to make sense of the reported experiences and responses.

Tables 1.3 and 1.4 summarize a few of the patterns of experiences of ethnoracial exclusion and responses to those experiences along with the causal argument for each of our five groups. These dense tables will also be discussed in detail as each country chapter unfolds, with the full list of experiences and responses provided in tables in Appendix 2. Because the total frequency of types of experiences and responses varied across sites, when Tables 1.3 and 1.4 compare the frequency of different types (low, medium, or high), this refers to their relative frequency within that site. For now, it suffices to mention that, as shown on Table 1.3, being insulted or disrespected is the primary form in which assault on worth is experienced across all sites (ranging from very high to medium for all groups). African American interviewees most often mention being misunderstood compared to other groups. In contrast to African Americans, Black Brazilians more often interpret incidents of assault on worth as being about negative stereotypes relating to being poor, having low status, or being uneducated. This suggests that racial stigmatization is experienced somewhat separately from class stigmatization for blacks in the United States, an area where they diverge from their Brazilian counterparts. Being stereotyped as threatening is more frequent for African American and Black Brazilian men, as well as Arab Palestinians. The incidence of being denied opportunities ranges from high to medium for all groups. Similarly, when it comes to responses, we find that confrontation is the most frequent response everywhere, but it is as predominant as management of the self and no response among Black Brazilians (unlike for the other groups); that African Americans, Ethiopians, and Mizrahim most frequently offer self-improvement as an ideal response; that

TABLE 1.3. RELATIVE NUMBER OF MENTIONS OF TYPES OF INCIDENTS AND RESPONSES FOR THE FIVE ETHNORACIAL GROUPS STUDIED

	UNITED STATES	BRAZIL	ISRAEL		
TYPE OF INCIDENT	Blacks	Pretos and pardos	Palestinian citizens	Ethiopians	Mizrahim
Assault on worth	Very high	High	Very High	High	Medium
Insulted/disrespected	High	Medium	High	Medium high	Medium
Misunderstood	Medium high	Low	Never	Low	Never
Stereotyped as low status/low class/uneducated	Medium	Medium high	Low	Medium	Medium low
Stereotyped as threatening	Medium for men	Medium for men	Medium	Low	Low
Discrimination	High	Medium high	High	Medium	Low
Denied opportunities	Medium high	Medium	High	Medium high	Medium high
Profiling (men only)	Medium	Medium	High	Medium low	Low
RESPONSE TO INCIDENTS					
Confront	Very high	Medium high	High	Very high	Very high
Management of self	Medium high	Medium high	Medium	Medium	Medium
Not responding	Medium	Medium high	Medium high	Low	Medium
Competence/work	Low	Low	Low	Medium	Low
Isolation/autonomy	Low	Low	Low	Low	Low
IDEAL RESPONSE					
Self-improvement	High	Medium low	Low	High	High
Collective mobilization/solidarity	Medium	Low	Medium	Medium	Low
Redistributive policies	Low	Very high	Low	Medium	Medium
Affirmative action policies	Very high	Medium	Low	Low	Low

Note: The number of mentions refers to the relative frequency of the various types of incidents and responses, which was calibrated for each site and category based on the frequencies reported in Appendix 2. For the United States and Brazil, the scale is: 1–20% = low; 21–45% = medium; 46–60% = medium high; 61–80% = high; and 81%+ = very high. For Israel, slightly different scales were used due to different sample sizes. These are available upon request.

TABLE 1.4. PARTIAL SUMMARY OF EXPLANATORY DIMENSIONS

HISTORICAL, SOCIOECONOMIC, AND INSTITUTIONAL ELEMENTS	UNITED STATES	BRAZIL	ISRAEL		
	Blacks	Pretos and pardos	Arab Palestinians	Ethiopians	Mizrahi
Size of group demographic (%)	Minority (14)	Slight majority (51)	Minority (20)	Very small (2)	Slight majority of Jewish population (52)
Concentration in lower income group	Mixed	High	High	High	Mixed
Social and spatial segregation	High	Mixed	Almost total	High	Mixed
Institutional discrimination (army, schools, work)	Mixed	Mixed	High	Mixed	Low
GROUPNESS					
Self-identification	Strong	Mixed	Strong	Mixed	Low
Boundaries toward dominant out-groups	Strong but contradictory	Porous	Rigid	Medium	Porous
CULTURAL REPERTOIRES					
National myth and ideology	Melting pot	Racial democracy	*Nakba* (catastrophe)	Zionism (In-gathering of exiles)	Zionism (In-gathering of exiles)
Model of incorporation	Civil Rights/multiracialism	Transnational blackness	Rights of citizenship	Jewish melting pot	Jewish melting pot
Neoliberal repertoires	High	Low	Low	Mixed	High
Universalist repertoires (religion, human rights, pro-diversity)	High	High	High	Mixed	Mixed

non-response is one of the most frequent reactions for Black Brazilians and Arab Palestinians; and that, among ideal responses, Black Brazilians most value the use of universal redistributive policies. Finally, Mizrahim most rarely offer collective responses. While such responses are also rare for Black Brazilians, their support for the black movement has grown in recent years.

Some of our explanations for these patterns are presented in Table 1.4. We argue that a combination of elements interact with cultural repertoires and groupness to enable various types of excluding experiences and responses to those experiences across contexts. Instead of providing a list of explanatory factors for each of our cases, we will consider how various explanatory dimensions are articulated differently in each instance.

ADDITIONAL CONTRIBUTIONS

We characterize our contributions in relation to several approaches in the literature. One of them is social psychology. Social psychologists typically predefine what we call incidents. To take one example, in their influential experimental research, Steele and Aronson (1995: 797) analyze stereotype threat, defined as "being at risk of confirming, as self-characteristic, a negative stereotype about one's group." These authors activated the racial identity of blacks to establish whether it would depress their performance on intelligence tests, but they neglected to consider in depth other types of responses, such as confrontation. We complement this work by exploring how individuals interpret their experiences.

By adopting an inductive approach, we open possibilities for a finer analysis of a broad range of experiences and responses to stigmatization, and of how those responses are enabled by various dimensions of their contexts. Thus, while psychologists working on stigma typically consider identities and boundaries as cognitive phenomena located in peoples' heads (with a focus on in-group favoritism and out-group dynamics (e.g., Major 1993) and adopt a top-down approach with a priori constructs and deductive hypotheses, we focus on narratives about lived experience.[20] Also, while political scientists typically focus on institutions and material factors (Marx 1998) or on identity politics as an area for political struggle (Walzer 1997), we redirect inquiry by adopting a bottom-up approach to boundary formation that locates groups in their local and historical contexts and considers which aspects (including identity politics) are actually relevant for actors.

At the same time, we do not deny that different individuals may react to similar incidents in different ways. While psychologists may focus on such personality traits or states as grit or self-efficacy to explain these differences (see Duckworth et al. 2007; Reich, Zautra, and Hall 2012), we focus on various types of social and symbolic resources and how societies may enable some responses rather than others. Thus, our emphasis is on the empowerment of social resilience by cultural repertoires and institutions across national contexts, instead of on individualized resilience embodied in personality traits (Hall and Lamont 2013; see also Komarraju, Karau, and Schmeck 2009).

Our approach is also a complement to studies of cultural change resulting from social movements and political ideology. Instead of privileging the impact of those involved in identity politics and activists whose numbers are often exaggerated and who receive disproportionate attention from sociologists,[21] we focus on the often-neglected experiences of ordinary men and women and on the way that responses to ethnoracial exclusion may contribute to change.[22] We also advocate an open-ended approach that captures the full range of responses possible instead of romanticizing one particular type, such as resistance, which is the focus of much attention (Lamont and Mizrachi 2012). In the context of a rapid transformation of racial consciousness in Brazil (Sansone 2003) and of identity politics among Mizrahi activists in Israel (Hever, Shenhav, and Motzafi-Haller 2002), we want to renew the conversation about racial formations (Omi and Winant 1994) and how to influence them. We also want to consider and answer whether it makes sense to ask if one of the three societies under consideration in our research offers a better path forward from the perspective of the victims of ethnoracial exclusion. In the Conclusion, we argue that the contexts in which these groups' lives are structured are so different that to ask which group is worse or better off is almost nonsensical.

Unsurprisingly, this book also dialogues with the comparative literature on race and ethnicity. This literature most often adopts a macro-historical comparative perspective and focuses on historical legacies variously defined (e.g., Fredrickson 1988; Marx 1998; Winant 2001). We take legacies into consideration as a source of social-structural constraints (e.g., patterns of socioeconomic inequalities, neighborhood segregation, and state institutions) and as cultural sources of scripts for interpreting racist and other incidents. This comparative literature has been criticized for not considering the mechanisms through which historical legacies are reproduced or transformed (Cooper 1996). By focusing on the quotidian experiences of ordinary people (i.e., nonactivists), we aim to enrich our understanding of how such legacies play out in contemporary narratives—for example, in the ready availability of legal tools to address hate crimes and discrimination in the United States (Bleich 2011) and in the role played by the state in distributing resources and arbitrating among groups in Brazil and Israel (Santos 1979), which influence responses to racism in each national context.

Our multimethod comparative and interview-based case study is structured around three country chapters concerning the United States (Chapter 2), Brazil (Chapter 3), and Israel (Chapter 4) that build on one another. For each country we proceed as follows. First, we describe the historical, institutional, and structural contexts in which the ethnoracial group (or groups, in the case of Israel) live, as well as the metropolitan areas where we conducted interviews. Second, we describe how their members understand their relationship to their ethnoracial group (i.e., their groupness). Third, we identify the ways in which each group experiences ethnoracial exclusion. Fourth, we turn to their responses, through both specific experiences and through what they consider ideal responses. We account for these patterns as the analysis unfolds. The conclusion of each country chapter brings together patterns of experiences and responses and analyzes how these result from different forces and constraints that operate for each group. The book's Conclusion steps back to capture comparisons across the three countries and five groups. It also synthesizes some of our main arguments and proposes an agenda for future research.

CHAPTER 2

THE UNITED STATES

The first of our three country chapters sets the course for the book by exploring (1) background conditions and the place of African Americans in US society and in the New York metropolitan area, where our interviewees reside; (2) how African Americans experience strong groupness, which influences how they perceive and react to racism; (3) how they experience specific incidents of stigmatization and discrimination; (4) how they say they responded to specific incidents and what they view as the best responses from a normative perspective; and (5) how the patterns of experiences and responses can be accounted for. These sections do not proceed in a linear order, with *explanans* (what explains) following *explanadum* (what is to be explained). Instead, we intermix both. We first provide background information, which will help place our interviewees in their context. Several of the factors described here will be salient in the configurational explanation developed throughout the chapter. This is also true of factors discussed in the second section on groupness. We anticipate similarities and differences between our five groups that will be described fully in the Chapters 3 and 4 on Brazil and Israel, respectively, so that the argument of the book unfolds cumulatively as we move through country chapters to produce a complex and nuanced portrait of how contexts enable the experiences of ordinary people who are victims of ethnoracial exclusion.

SECTION 2.1: BACKGROUND FACTORS: HISTORICAL AND SOCIOECONOMIC CONTEXT

A HISTORICAL LEGACY OF RACIAL DOMINATION

Since its founding, the United States has grounded its identity in the promise of freedom, equality, and meritocratic individualism (Weber 1905; de Tocqueville 2004; Bouchard 2013). However, as Myrdal (1944: 80) famously argued, anti-black violence, racism, and discrimination have always clashed with these founding myths.

From the time the first ship carrying African slaves arrived in Virginia in 1619, the United States has struggled to come to terms with the continued oppression of African Americans. It is estimated that more than 1 million Africans were brought to the United States as slaves. In his detailed history of plantation slavery, Stampp (1956: 7) argued that "prior to the Civil War Southern slavery was America's most profound and vexatious social problem." From the brutality of the journey from Africa to the United States to the deplorable conditions of Southern plantations, slaves were forced to navigate racial boundaries in a country that did not see blacks as humans deserving of the rights of American citizenship.

When slavery ended after the American Civil War, many African Americans saw only marginal improvements in their situation. Promises of a sustained reconstruction effort went unfulfilled (Du Bois 1935). The majority of African Americans lived in the South, where they often became trapped in exploitative sharecropping arrangements with white farmers. African Americans in the South also faced Jim Crow segregation laws (solidified in the 1890s) that enforced racial segregation in all public areas of life. Jim Crow laws not only prevented African Americans from interacting with whites but also ensured that the former had limited access to resources, such as housing and schools. Blacks were denied employment in many industries and as a result had limited means to support themselves. In addition, they were deprived of the right to vote and faced constant threats of violence if they made efforts to challenge racial boundaries (Blair 2005; Grossman 2005). Circumstances were somewhat more favorable in the northern United States, where blacks did not face brutal Jim Crow laws. Indeed, limited job opportunities and omnipresent legal segregation caused many African Americans to migrate north during the first and second waves of the Great Migration (1910–1930 and 1940–1970, respectively).[1] Although African Americans did not face the same rigid racial boundaries in the North that they did in the South, they still faced significant racism and discrimination in housing, employment, and educational opportunities (Du Bois 1899).

The continued racial oppression of African Americans led to the mid-twentieth-century Civil Rights Movement, which brought legal victories. Most importantly, in the 1954 *Brown v. Board of Education* case, the US Supreme Court ruled that the separate-but-equal doctrine that had enabled legalized racial segregation was unconstitutional. Other victories included the Civil Rights Act of 1964, the Voting Rights Act of 1965, and the Civil Rights Act of 1968. The change in racial dynamics brought about during the Civil Rights Era shaped African Americans' responses to racism by legitimizing their right to speak up, confront, and sue.

Civil rights legislation ended state-sanctioned racial segregation and improved opportunities for African Americans. As a result, more African Americans were able to move into the middle class (Pattillo-McCoy 1999; Lacy 2007). The percentage of African Americans living below the poverty line decreased from 39.3 percent to 27.6 percent between 1967 and 2011, and overall incomes increased (DeNavas-Walt, Proctor, and Smith 2013). In 1967 the median income for African Americans was $25,464; in 2011 it was $32,229 (in 2011 dollars) (DeNavas-Walt, Proctor, and Smith 2013). In addition, college degree attainment rates rose dramatically. In 1965 just 4.7 percent of African Americans had attended college compared to 22.7 percent in 2012 (US Bureau of the Census 2012). Opportunities for employment in white-collar jobs (particularly government jobs) also increased. In 1983 approximately 40 percent of African American workers were employed in lower- and upper-middle-class white collar occupations, including clerical, sales, teaching, finance, medical, and legal jobs. The proportion of African Americans employed in these types of jobs grew to more than 50 percent by 2010 (Landry and Marsh 2011).

PERSISTENT STRUCTURAL INEQUALITY AND RACIAL SEGREGATION

Despite gains made in the post-Civil Rights Era, African Americans continue to face a number of socioeconomic obstacles. While more African Americans secured white-collar jobs, these jobs are likely to be in sales and clerical occupations (Pattillo-McCoy 1999; Landry and Marsh 2011). This shapes economic circumstances. In 2012, the median household income for African Americans was $33,321 compared to $57,009 for whites (DeNavas-Walt, Proctor, and Smith 2013). While middle-class African Americans fare better than economically disadvantaged African Americans, they still earn less money than middle-class whites and face more obstacles to finding well-paying, stable jobs than middle-class whites: In 2014 the median weekly income for blacks with a bachelor's degree was $895 in contrast to $1,132 for their white counterparts (US Bureau of Labor Statistics 2015).

African Americans also have considerably less wealth than whites. When we take into account savings, stocks, bonds, and property values and subtract the sum of debt, the economic gap between African Americans and whites is considerable (Oliver and Shapiro 2006; Kochhar, Fry, and Taylor 2011). In 2009, the median net worth of white households was $113,149, compared to $5,677 for African American households (Kochhar, Fry, and Taylor 2011). The gap has grown since the 2008 recession. Kochhar, Fry, and Taylor (2011) find that while white households lost an average of 16 percent of their wealth between 2005 and 2009, African American households lost an average of 53 percent of their wealth during the same period.

African Americans are also more likely to be among the urban poor than are whites. Wilson (1987) shows that in the postindustrial era, African Americans have become increasingly isolated in declining cities, as many jobs have been moved to the suburbs, to the South, and abroad. Unemployment rates for African Americans are approximately double the rates for whites—2014 seasonally adjusted labor force participation rates indicate that an estimated 10.7 percent of blacks were unemployed compared to an estimated 5.3 percent of whites (US Bureau of Labor Statistics 2014). In 2013, the poverty rate for African Americans was 27.2 percent, compared to 9.6 percent for whites (DeNavas-Walt and Proctor 2014).

In addition, African Americans face high rates of racial residential segregation, which places them in neighborhoods that have fewer resources than white neighborhoods enjoy. These neighborhoods may have higher crime rates and other elements of social disarray (Wilson and Taub 2007). Based on an analysis of tract-level data from the 2010 Census, Logan and Stults (2011) show that the average white person residing in metropolitan America lives in a neighborhood that is 75 percent white. In comparison, a typical African American lives in a neighborhood that is 35 percent white (a situation not much different from 1940) and as much as 45 percent black. Although middle-class African Americans have been able to move out of some of the most disadvantaged inner city neighborhoods, they are more likely than middle-class whites to live in segregated neighborhoods in declining suburbs or on the outskirts of large cities.

In *American Apartheid*, Massey and Denton (1993) suggest that patterns of spatial segregation translate into patterns of social distance that reinforce class differentiation—with ethnoracial groups living largely parallel and separate lives. Social boundaries between groups are produced and reinforced by symbolic boundaries (Lamont 1992; Alba 2009; Brubaker 2012) and by cognitive distance (Massey 2007; Ridgeway 2013). Charles (2000) argues that the racial attitudes of both whites and minority groups play an important role in perpetuating these patterns of residential segregation. For example, using data from the 2000 General Social Survey, Bobo et al. (2012) explore the neighborhood racial composition preferences of African

Americans and whites. They find that, on average, whites prefer a neighborhood that is more than half white and less than a third African American. For their part, on average, African Americans prefer a neighborhood that is a third African American and less than half white. Both groups prefer to live near in-group members, but African Americans prefer to live in more racially mixed neighborhoods than do whites.

Research has also shown that housing discrimination is persistent. For example, according to a study by the Department of Housing and Urban Development, when searching for homes to rent or to buy, African Americans are told about and shown fewer housing units by real estate agents than are whites (US Department of Housing and Urban Development 2013). On average, African Americans searching for rental homes are told about 11.4 percent fewer units and are shown 4.2 percent fewer units than are whites. This gap is larger for African Americans who are looking to buy a home. On average, they are told about 17 percent fewer homes and are shown 17.7 percent fewer homes than are whites (US Department of Housing and Urban Development 2013).

African Americans also face disproportionately high incarceration rates (Alexander 2012). Using data from the Pew Public Safety and Mobility Project, Western and Pettit (2010) find that African American men born between 1975 and 1979 have a 26.8 percent chance of being incarcerated, in contrast to 5.4 percent for white men born during the same period. Incarceration can have a negative impact on various socioeconomic factors, including family stability, future earnings, and health outcomes (see also Schnittker, Massoglia, and Uggen 2011; Alexander 2012).

In the post-Civil Rights Era, social and symbolic boundaries between African Americans and whites remain relatively strong, as shown by analyses of patterns of racial homophily. Using data from the National Longitudinal Survey of Adolescent Health to explore the racial composition of the friend groups of white, African American, Asian, and Hispanic students in grades 7–12, Quillian and Campbell (2003) found that friendships between African Americans and all other groups are the least likely to occur. Interracial marriage rates for African Americans are also low. In 2010, approximately 17 percent of newly married blacks were married interracially, compared to approximately 9 percent of newly married whites (Taylor et al. 2012). Seventy-two percent of blacks are in favor of interracial marriage, compared to 61 percent of whites (Taylor et al. 2012). But levels of homophily are declining (Passel, Wang, and Taylor 2010).

The American workplace remains largely segregated: while public employment and the armed forces are highly integrated, other realms of employment are less so. Stainback and Tomaskovic-Devey (2012) argue that some industries, such as transportation, construction, and securities and commodities, have actually become more racially segregated since the 1970s. Hamilton,

Austin, and Darity (2011) show that 87 percent of US occupations can be classified as racially segregated. Using 2005–2007 American Community Survey data, they find that black men are proportionally represented in only 13 percent of occupations. Moreover, black men are underrepresented to a greater extent in more highly paid occupations: the percentage of black men employed in an occupation decreases by 7 percent for every $10,000 increase in annual salary. School racial segregation largely goes the way of residential segregation, with segregated neighborhoods feeding into a school system that remains largely segregated (Tyson 2011). An estimated 76.5 percent of African American children attend schools that are more than 50 percent minority students, compared to just 15.9 percent of whites (Krogstad and Fry 2014).

Understanding factors that contribute to the disadvantages of African Americans in the so-called post-Civil Rights Era has been a central task for scholars of race and ethnicity. One such factor is whites' attitudes toward race. Social scientists have documented a shift in whites' attitudes that contribute to persistent racial disparities. At the very end of the twentieth century, Bobo and Smith (1998: 186) argued that most whites subscribe to "laissez-faire racism," which "involves persistent negative stereotyping of African Americans, a tendency to blame blacks themselves for the black-white gap in socioeconomic standing and resistance to meaningful policy efforts to ameliorate America's racist social conditions and institutions." A little more than a decade later, Bonilla-Silva (2010) argued that whites subscribe to colorblind racism; that is, they do not believe that blacks are innately inferior to whites. Instead, they believe that formal barriers for African Americans were eliminated with the abolishment of Jim Crow, that African Americans are primarily responsible for their own fate, and that the remaining disparities between African Americans and whites are due to African Americans' failing to work hard enough to get ahead.

Scholars have also studied the impact of the 2008 elections, which resulted in the election of the first African American president. (We conducted the bulk of our interviews in 2007 and during the 2008 presidential campaign, so our data do not reflect Barack Obama's election as president.) For instance, Welburn and Pittman (2012) found that among 35 African Americans they interviewed who grew up in the middle class and live in New Jersey, many believe that Obama's election serves as evidence that hardworking African Americans have a chance to get ahead despite persistent racial inequality. Poll data also suggest that African Americans have become more optimistic about racial equality since Obama's election (Pew Research Center and NPR 2010). However, some scholars caution that Obama's election does not necessarily signal a postracial era (Bobo and Dawson 2009; Brooks 2009; Bonilla-Silva 2010; Tesler and Sears 2010). Tesler and Sears (2010: 5) argue that despite Obama's efforts to promote unity and avoid detailed discussions of race on the campaign trail, "Obama's campaign for the presidency in 2008 . . . was anything but post-racial." Instead, the racial hopes and fears evoked by his potential to become the country's first black president sharply divided racial conservatives from racial liberals. Racist incidents, and continuous conflict with political foes that journalists, scholars, and political commentators have described as racially motivated have plagued the Obama presidency (see Bobo and Dawson 2009; Cobb 2014). This should be kept in mind as we interpret our interviewees' perspectives against the background of this presidency.

It is also important to consider the position of African Americans in the current context of growing economic inequality. After World War II, economic inequality decreased significantly in the United States, allowing increased intergenerational mobility among the general population (Beller and Hout 2006). However, since the early 1970s, and especially since the mid-1980s, income has become increasingly concentrated at the top (Piketty and Saez 2003). In the United States, the standard measure of inequality, the Gini coefficient, was 0.38 in 2012 (after taxes and transfers), up from 0.36 in 2000. This is higher than in most other Western countries (OECD 2012). Levels of inequality in the United States are on par with Israel (also with a 0.38 Gini coefficient in 2012) and significantly lower than in Brazil, whose Gini coefficient is 0.52 (World Bank 2012). Economic mobility is particularly challenging for African Americans: only 23 percent of African Americans who grow up in the middle fifth of the socioeconomic spectrum exceed their parents' income, compared to 56 percent for their white counterparts (Taylor et al. 2012). While their circumstances have improved in the post-Civil Rights Era, persistent racial discrimination coupled with growing levels of overall inequality have weakened their group's relative position.

At the same time, inequality among blacks has increased considerably over the past decades. According to Hochschild and Weaver (2015), African Americans "show the most intragroup income inequality in 2013" (with a Gini coefficient of 0.492 compared to 0.472 for Asian Americans, 0.465 for non-Hispanic whites, and 0.453 for Hispanics). These changes are consistent with Wilson's (2012: 22) thesis in *The Declining Significance of Race*: "As the black middle class rides the wave of political and social changes, benefiting from the growth of employment opportunities in the growing corporate and government sectors of the economy, the black underclass falls behind the larger society in every conceivable respect."[2]

Many of the socioeconomic conditions described above influence how African Americans interviewees experience and respond to racism. Particularly salient are the legacies and collective memory of slavery and Jim Crow segregation and the various forms of racial inequality fostered by these. Inequality in wealth, income, education, and occupational status come first and foremost. Also relevant are the high degree of spatial segregation and racial homophily, and the high level of incarceration for blacks. Equally significant are the African American collective project of upward mobility, which feeds an engagement with the American Dream, and the growing differentiation of the American class structure, concomitant with the growth of the black middle class. The overrepresentation of African Americans among low-income Americans is another important factor, one that feeds many of the stereotypes about blacks that our respondents struggle with and respond to. For our respondents, these conditions were aggravated by the timing of our interviews—in 2007, at the beginning of an economic recession that put pressure especially on working- and middle-class African Americans. These conditions are captured in Table 1.1 in Chapter 1. We analyze how interviewees make sense of racial progress and continued inequality as we explain narratives of experiences and responses we collected.

THE RESEARCH SITE: THE NEW YORK METROPOLITAN AREA

Our respondents reside in the New York Metropolitan Statistical Area (NYMSA). This area is 59.2 percent white, 22.9 percent Latino, 17.8 percent African American, and 9.9 percent Asian (US Bureau of the Census 2010). The NYMSA has the largest African American and the second largest Latino populations of any metropolitan area in the United States. While the NYMSA remains one of the most diverse areas in the country, the racial and ethnic composition of the population has been shifting, with an influx of Hispanic residents and an outmigration of African Americans.[3] The Hispanic population grew by 21 percent between 2000 and 2010, while the African American population decreased by 2 percent (Frey 2011). Thus, black/white polarization in this area should be considered within a broader ecology of interracial relationships. Blacks do not stand out as the only minority—far from it. However, their relation to racism deserves particular attention in part because their historical position in the country, and the region has many implications for how they and others experience race relations today.[4] Their demographic weight is less than a fifth of the population—far smaller than that of their counterparts in Brazil, who make up half of the population (if those who identify as pretos/dark blacks and pardos/browns according to the census categories are considered together). They are located in a more multiracial environment than Ethiopians in Israel, who represent only 2 percent of the population, yet may stand out more. Such factors of visibility influence how they and other groups experience ethnoracial exclusion.

Our interviewees live in towns in northern New Jersey, including Orange, Plainfield, and Montclair. Northern New Jersey was chosen as a research site for two reasons. First, it is a typical American context. McLafferty and

Preston (1992: 410) argue that northern New Jersey, "with its more dis-persed employment opportunities, lower densities, and higher rates of auto ownership, may be more typical of US metropolitan areas." Second, north-ern New Jersey has a large native-born African American population, due to the area's popularity during the first and second waves of the Great Migra-tion of blacks from the South.

The families of many of our respondents moved to this area from the South during that mid-twentieth century migration. They migrated because northern cities provided the promise of greater racial equality and more chances for upward mobility than the South did. However, African Ameri-cans continued to face persistent racism and discrimination in the North. As the number of African Americans in the North grew, racial tensions in-creased, unrest ensued, and whites began leaving cities for suburbs. In New Jersey, racial tensions culminated in the 1967 race riots, which lasted six days. Smaller uprisings—all lasting several days—occurred in other New Jersey towns and cities, including Irvington, Plainfield, and Montclair. These riots contributed to white flight and increased levels of racial residential segregation, which have had a lasting impact on the life circumstances of our respondents.

Levels of racial residential segregation are quite significant, and some pre-dominantly African American cities, such as Newark and Irvington, con-tinue to struggle with disproportionately high poverty and unemployment rates and criminal activity. Although many of our professional respondents live in typical middle-class suburbs dotted with lush lawns, others reside in more mixed areas where strip malls, public housing projects, and middle-class homes sit next to one another, reflecting a less homogeneous popula-tion (see also Pattillo-McCoy 1999; Pattillo 2005).

New Jersey's current economic situation has improved from its low point in the 1970s, when traditional American industries were leaving the region to reestablish themselves in the South or abroad. In fact, NYMSA has fared slightly better than the United States as a whole. In 2012, the poverty rate was 14.8 percent compared to 15.9 percent for the entire United States, and the median income was $63,982 compared to $55,030 for the country (US Bureau of the Census 2012). The unemployment rate, however, has hovered at or slightly above the national average—in May 2014 it was approximately 6.7 percent compared to 6.1 percent for the country as a whole (US Bureau of Labor Statistics 2014).[5] Young, Varner, and Massey (2008) examined Amer-ican Community Survey data from 2000–2006 and found that in this period, New Jersey continued to experience growth. They argue that the relatively high cost of living, however, did contribute to outmigration among the state's low-income population.

New Jersey benefits economically from its proximity to New York City and the commuters who make their way into the city every day. Some of our respondents are commuters, but most live and work in northern New Jersey, in such towns as Newark, Patterson, Irvington, Plainfield, and West Orange. When we conducted our interviews in 2007 and 2008, the recession was hitting hard. Many were facing significant economic difficulties, such as home foreclosure and loss of employment. Working-class and lower-income residents did continue to receive some state support during this period. Nevertheless, the economic crisis shaped our respondents' experiences of and responses to racism.

It is within this context that our US respondents understand American race relations. Northern New Jersey has provided important opportunities for upward mobility for African Americans, particularly historically for those who fled the more segregated southern United States. However, a history of racial tension and deindustrialization has created a tenuous environment for African Americans in the area.

SECTION 2.2: ETHNORACIAL GROUPNESS

As spelled out in the Introduction, in this study we draw a detailed and at times contradictory picture of groupness that combines (1) the *self-identification* of our interviewees, as captured by questions concerning self-definition and self-labeling, and the perceived cultural distinctiveness and meanings associated with their group (including in relation to class and nation); and (2) *group boundaries* as revealed by perceived closeness to in-group members (including marriage and friendships), and boundary work toward out-groups (toward whites in particular). Although not dimensions of groupness, we also consider background factors that influence it: the demographic composition of the population and social and spatial boundaries (as they are perceived) as well as the repertoires of universalist inclusion and group disadvantages that are made available to group members.

In this section we draw a complex portrait of African American ethnoracial groupness—complex because we find it is strong by some criteria (identification, in-group preferences, anti-white boundaries, awareness of white privilege), yet weak by other criteria (low salience of race in response to the question "what kind of person are you?," friendships with whites, and a normative commitment to a culture of diversity or to a desire to weaken group boundaries). In other words, we portray African Americans as presenting strong but contradictory groupness in a universalist context where openness to out-group members is the norm. In the other country chapters, we contrast this particular type of groupness with those found in the other four groups under consideration. We will see that the groups vary in terms of not only what ties individuals together (phenotype, ethnicity, religion) but also the strength and characteristics of group boundaries.

SELF-IDENTIFICATION

Writings on African American racial identification have tended to emphasize its stability over its fluidity. For instance, Morning (2011) makes the case for the lasting influence of essentialism in racial thinking (due in part to the lasting impact of institutional racial categorizations in medicine and science), while Dawson (2011) offers evidence that African Americans remain strongly bounded as a group (see also Roth 2012; Hochschild et al. 2012). However, in a well-received longitudinal study of black men and women between 1979 and 2002, Saperstein and Penner (2012) found that individual racial identification changes over time in response to changes in social position: successful and high-status people tend to redefine themselves as white (or not black) and unsuccessful or low-status people as black (or not white), suggesting that racial identification is a result of stratification processes. For us to weigh in on this debate would require different type of evidence than we have here. However, our data suggest that African Americans take their racial identity to be highly salient to their lives and to the distribution of resources in US society. Thus, they form by some measure a tightly bounded group—even if they favor weak boundaries toward out-groups and support universalism.

We can learn a lot about ethnoracial identification by considering how individuals respond to the most open-ended question possible: "What kind of person are you?" As was the case in Brazil and Israel, nearly all African Americans we talked with answered this question by describing themselves in moral terms ("caring," "disciplined," or "honest") or by referring to their temperament ("easy going," "friendly," etc.). This is in line with psychological and sociological studies showing that Americans tend to define themselves in terms of moral attributes (Lamont 1992; Markus 2010: 364; see Lamont and Thévenot 2000 on self-definition and morality). Only 11 interviewees (out of 150) responded to this question by making reference to their racial identity. This is in tension with the literature on African American identity, which emphasizes the centrality of racial identity for individuals of this group (Krysan 2012). Yet it is possible that our respondents regarded their racial self-identification as a given, and thus did not mention it, because they were being interviewed by a co-ethnic,[6] and because we mentioned their racial identity as a criterion of selection in our letter inviting them to be part of the project.[7] But these aspects of our research protocol could also have made racial identity more salient. A detailed look at our data suggests a complex picture of ethnoracial self-identification: strong racial identification is revealed by the respondents' preferences when self-labeling—preferences that range from habitual and highly routinized to highly purposive and contextual.

Black and/or African American Self-Labeling

Consistent with sociological and social psychological research on ethnic identity (Portes and Rumbaut 2001; Phinney and Ong 2007), our African American interviewees say they use a variety of in-group labels, depending on the social setting or type of interaction.[8] They also distinguish between the labels they believe out-group and in-group members should use to designate their group and are particularly sensitive about labels outsiders use. This variety of labels, as well as the complexity and nuances of their thinking on the topic, suggests that ethnoracial identity is salient and central to most respondents. In our analysis of interviewees' responses, we attend to both dimensions—the centrality of ethnoracial identity and the diversity of meaning.[9]

The main question we used to examine these topics asked interviewees which ethnoracial label they typically use to describe themselves and why they use that particular label. There was some variation in how the question was framed, with some interviewers asking respondents whether they prefer to be called "black" or "African American," while others asked respondents about their preference for self-labeling categories they had used spontaneously in earlier parts of the interview. Four interviewees out of five indicated a preference for the category "black" and almost a third expressed a preference for "African American."[10] Several—a third of middle-class and a handful of working-class respondents—declared using these terms interchangeably (which explains why these percentages add up to more than 100 percent). Consistent with this flexible attitude, a fifth volunteered that they are indifferent to which label is applied to them.[11]

While the majority of Black Brazilians responded to questions about self-labeling by describing themselves as *Negros* (a political category) or multiracial, and few mentioned skin color (light, "high yellow," dark) the latter was also rarely mention by African Americans—perhaps a legacy of the one-drop rule (Davis 1991; Omi and Winant 1994). It should be noted that while only one of our interviewees self-defines as multiracial, another study finds this is currently the case for 7.4 percent of African Americans and 2.9 percent of Americans (Jones and Bullock 2012).[12]

Our interviewees' responses to the question of self-labeling suggest that racial self-identification is self-evident for all but a few of them. The three who reject the use of ethnoracial categories when self-describing offer various reasons. One rejects the predominant ethnoracial labels because he views himself as "mixed" or interracial. Another explains his position by referring to his commitment to universalism: he does not pay attention to color—only to the fact that "we are all human beings." These respondents stand out as exceptional, revealing the extent to which ethnoracial self-labeling is the rule among the individuals we spoke to.

Respondents vary in terms of the degree of purposefulness with which they privilege one racial self-labeling category over another, reflecting variations in how they think about their racial identification. A minority of our respondents describes self-labeling preferences as reflecting existential issues: they choose one label over another because they believe it is "who they are." Some of these respondents talk about the term "black" as connected to political consciousness and group pride and note that the meaning of the term "black" changed during specific historical moments (described as "the '60s," "the Black Power Movement," or simply "James Brown" in reference to a historical moment defined by the release of the singer's popular hit "Say It Loud—I'm Black and I'm Proud"). However, many tie preferences to habit or do not provide a reason for using one label over another. For instance, a cook explained that he uses the term "African American" "just . . . [to] fill out applications and stuff, you know." Only a few simply account for their preference in reference to their skin tone (also rarely mentioned in Brazil).

Against this diversity of labels and meanings invested in a range of terms, the presence of black/African American identification in our respondents' lives is strong (in line with Krysan 2012). But how does this racial identification relate to national identity? Our interviews suggest that, contrary to what we found in Brazil, national identification is weaker than racial identification in the case of African Americans.

Racial and National Identity

Racial identification can be tempered by national identification. When asked to explain the meaning they attach to being African American, several interviewees affirmed their identification with being American and stressed pride in their country, using the language of American exceptionalism (Lipset 1997). Few of these respondents appear to see a contradiction between national and racial self-identification. Some based both national pride and African American pride on black racial progress as well as on pride in values held sacred, such as the freedom of speech guaranteed by the First Amendment. For instance, one teacher said she explains to her young students that the United States is "a land of opportunity. I can go back at least as far as my father's uncle, who fought in World War I in Europe, okay? So I'm very patriotic. . . . And here I can criticize the government and those running it, and this too [is] okay. . . . This is still the best country of the world for anybody." Another respondent, an attorney, referred to his many ancestors who have died fighting for the country and concluded, "I have just as much right as anyone to say I am an American. Africans, my folks, have earned that for us. It's just that I am connected to here."[13]

However, many of these same respondents also perceive American society as flawed and unfair. They point to the history of racism and to what has yet to be overcome, as does an administrator who notes that inner city kids have no hope: "kids with looks in their eyes, they're vacant, there's nothing there." A youth worker connects the country's racist past and what has been accomplished to the fortitude of his people when he says, "Being an African American, it's pride to me, when I think of all the hardships that they had to endure and still forged ahead and still opened doors for the next generation."[14]

Most of our respondents, however, value their American identity while also expressing skepticism about American ideals. These findings are consistent with previous research (Phinney and Onwughalu 1996; for a counterexample, see MacLeod 1987). On average, national identity (measured in various ways) is weaker for blacks than for whites. This remains the case when education and class are controlled for (Sidanius et al. 1997; Huddy and Khatib 2007). This point is important, as we will see it strongly contrasted with the Brazilian case, where race and national identity are less in tension with one another, and Brazilian national identity is more salient than racial identity and is taken for granted by Black Brazilians (Moreas Silva 2013). This is in part because racial mixture is quintessential to the Brazilian founding myth, just as immigration is to the American founding myth. It also stands in contrast to the case of Arab Palestinians, whose Israeli nationality is very much at odds with their group identity.

Meanings of Racial Identity

To get a clearer sense of the extent to which interviewees were concerned with their racial identity, we considered their responses to a question about what being African American or black meant to them. We coded whether they included the following in their responses:[15] expressions of racial pride or honor; spontaneous references to racial identification; or references to distinctive cultural practices and traditions (e.g., Kwanza), to racial responsibility or African American history, to racially salient institutions (e.g., Historical Black Colleges and Universities), to group-based identification (e.g., "our people"), and to group struggle or overcoming obstacles. We also considered whether interviewees downplayed racial identity: by self-identifying as "a person" rather than as a racial group member, by rejecting the importance of race or ethnicity, by referring to a "postracial identity" (as "American" or "a human being"), or by describing race as incidental. Of the 93 respondents who responded to our question about the meaning of being

African American, two-thirds (67) attributed importance to racial identity at least once, while almost a quarter (26) downplayed it. We take these results to be evidence of the high salience of racial referents for the majority of respondents.

The meanings most frequently associated with being black concerned the shared history and experience of slavery (mentioned by 39 percent of the respondents who answered this question), followed by a feeling of black pride (31 percent), resilience (25 percent), shared culture (19 percent), color of skin (12 percent), and discrimination (11 percent), with other categories, such as shared genetic or physical characteristics and aesthetics, being mentioned by very few respondents. In general, the meanings these interviewees associate with their racial identity contrast sharply with racist stereotypes associated with African Americans, such as laziness, poverty, low intelligence, family dysfunction, and educational underperformance (Bobo 2011; see also Kluegel 1990; Steele and Aronson 1995; Schuman et al. 1997; Bonilla-Silva 2010).

Collective memory contributes to consolidating a sense of groupness and to providing points of reference that individuals can use to make sense of their current experiences. For African Americans, this collective memory is grounded in and empowered by the shared history of slavery, segregation, discrimination, and experiences of inequality. For instance, one interviewee explained that "my wife's father had a garage in South Carolina. The Ku Klux Klan burned it down. That's why they moved up here, to get away from it. A lot of older people, they don't even like to talk about it. . . . We just had to deal with it." The availability of ready-made repertoires of group disadvantage for interpreting events reduces the hesitancy and anxiety often associated with labeling an incident "racist."[16] Interviews are peppered with references to the American racial history of oppression and exploitation, including 302 mentions of landmark historical events. This adds up to roughly two mentions of history per respondent on average, which we consider a relatively high level of awareness of shared history. Thirty percent of these mentions concerned slavery,[17] 16 percent concerned the 2008 elections, 15 percent mentioned the Civil Rights Movement, and 11 percent mentioned the race riots.[18] We will argue later that this shared background encourages our interviewees to "name it" when they witness or experience racism. This is in contrast to the situation that prevails in Brazil, where shared historical background is tempered by other factors.

Social scientists have argued that the perception of shared significant experience and linked fate strengthens racial identity. This applies to African Americans. Indeed, Bobo and Simmons (2009: 58) argue that "in a 2009 National Survey of Blacks, more than a third said that 'what generally happens to black people in this country' would have 'a lot' to do with what would happen in their own lives." In 1984, 31 percent had responded similarly, suggesting a relatively stable sense of linked fate. Based on the 2009 survey, another third (33.6 percent), said that it would have some connection to their own lives, with a third seeing no connection. A related measure, the "perceived racialization index" (based on "shared fate, economic inequality, and racial equality"), indicates that one in four blacks has a consistently highly racialized view of these dimensions of society (Bobo 2012: 60).[19] Older respondents scored higher on this perceived racialization index than the youngest cohort (34 and 18 percent, respectively). Perceived racialization was the highest among those who have completed college (38 percent). This leaves little doubt that the shared experience of perceived discrimination contributes considerably to the sense of groupness among African Americans. Concomitantly, we will see that the black middle class is also more invested in collective responses to racism than the black working class.

The relatively low awareness of class stigmatization among the African Americans we talked to also adds to the strength of their racial identification. Only a third of them refer to class stigmatization during the interview. More generally, class was not very salient when we asked respondents to self-identify, with only 7 respondents mentioning class in response to our open-ended question, "What kind of person are you?" And, only 17 respondents referred more or less directly to their subjective class position as middle or working class by describing themselves with terms such as "normal," "regular," "average," or "humble."

However, this low salience of class may be surprising, as the economic inequality among African Americans has increased in recent decades. Non-blacks have always downplayed the internal class diversity of this group, often blind to the existence of a black middle class at the same time as they stereotypes blacks as poor (Gilens 1996). At times, the class differentiation has also often been downplayed by blacks themselves, who have tended to emphasize their linked fate through a shared experience of spatial segregation and discrimination. The growing literature on the black middle class (see the work of Bart Landry, Mary Pattillo, Karyn Lacy, Adia Wingfield, Patricia Banks, and others) has done a lot to correct the illusion of internal homogeneity of a "black community."

However, that African American ethnoracial groupness is taken for granted by our interviewees is hardly surprising in the face of the one-drop rule, which is de facto still operative in how many Americans perceive racial identity. The latter helps explain why most Americans grossly overestimate the percentage of the US population that is black, with the average American believing that blacks constitute 33 percent of the American population according to a 2001 Gallup poll.[20]

To recap, the strong racial identification of Black American interviewees is evidenced by their responses to questions about self-labeling, which reveal a plurality of labels while suggesting that racial self-identification is a given. This is also confirmed by our data and the secondary literature on the relationship between national and racial identity (which gives slight prevalence to the latter) and on the use of racial referents in definitions of what it means for most interviewees to be African Americans. Their sense of collective identity points to an emphasis on a shared vibrant expressive culture, history, pride, and resilience—positive (and often pleasurable) aspects of a shared identity that often go unnoticed in the sociology literature on African Americans.[21] The interviews also indicate familiarity with a shared history that feeds collective identity. Finally, only a third refer to class stigmatization during the interview. Thus, the aspects of racial identification we have examined up to this point lean in the direction of strong groupness among African American respondents. This, we shall see, contrasts with the cases of Mizrahi Jews (who have a weaker identity), and with Ethiopian Jews and Arab Palestinians, who have strong ethnoracial identification that combines very differently with national identity. For their part, Black Brazilians can be described as having a blurred sense of groupness, with porous group boundaries but relatively consistent identification (as *Negros*). This is often a source of pride, as we discuss in Chapter 3.

GROUP BOUNDARIES

Here we consider broader social dynamics that feed a sense of groupness, such as whether interviewees favor in-group relationships and whether they draw strong symbolic boundaries in opposition to out-groups, whites in particular. We also consider background factors, such as patterns of spatial segregation, and whether symbolic boundaries and spatial boundaries work hand-in-hand to produce groupness and inequality.[22]

Experiences of Spatial Segregation and Integration

In Section 2.1, we described national patterns of racial segregation. Now we turn to spatial segregation as it is experienced and described by respondents in their neighborhood, at work, at school, and elsewhere. We approximated the extent of the spatial integration and segregation that our respondents experience from what they told us in the interview in response to open-ended questions probing them about their schooling (K–12, college, and postgraduate), past and current neighborhoods of residence, past and current workplaces, and social interactions (in the context of friendships, community organizations, and religious organizations). We found that, like the majority of African Americans, many of our interviewees say they live largely segregated lives, which is likely to reinforce their sense of groupness and racial identification. This is not surprising, given that we located our respondents from census tracts with at least 20 percent African American residents. For those who live in predominantly white environments, being a "token" in the workplace is associated with heightened visibility, negative stereotypes, and social isolation (Wingfield 2010: 252). Both types of experiences are likely to make racial identity more salient and to increase groupness (Purdie-Vaughns et al. 2008).

Our respondents' most segregated environments (those they described as majority black) are their current and past neighborhoods, followed by their religious organizations, friendship networks, K–12 schools, and community organizations. Indeed, almost three times as many live in majority-black neighborhoods compared to multiracial neighborhoods (85 compared to 32), with only 4 living in predominantly white neighborhoods.[23] Forty percent of respondents belong to majority-black religious organizations, and 5 percent belong to multiracial religious organizations.

The environments perceived as least segregated by respondents are their workplaces, colleges, and postgraduate degree institutions. They reported the most integration in their current workplaces (with 33 mentions of working in a majority-black workplace, compared to 34 in a majority-white workplace and 53 in a multiracial workplace).[24] This is in a context where black-white desegregation in the American private sector workplaces nearly flatlined from 1980 through at least 2005 (Stainback and Tomaskovic-Devey 2012) or even increased between 1990 and 2000 by some accounts (Hellerstein, Neumark, and McInerney 2008), with blacks working in workforces that were 23.7 percent black in 1990 and 28.7 percent black in 2000.[25]

The past and current neighborhoods of middle- and working-class respondents are equally segregated, but the former live in slightly less segregated environments than the latter. Further, the middle class experienced more integration through their college years—an experience that working-class respondents do not have.[26] Also noteworthy is the slightly greater segregation of working-class workplaces compared to middle-class workplaces.[27] This is in line with patterns of class differences in workplace segregation in the United States (Alonso-Villar, Del Rio, and Gradin 2012).

Boundaries and Friendship

Our interviewees' perceptions of similarities and differences, likes and dislikes, and inferiority and superiority between groups inform us about the symbolic boundaries they draw in relation to other groups. We explored these boundaries by asking questions about respondents' close friends, such as, "Do you have close friends of racial backgrounds other than yours?" We similarly asked respondents about their wider circles: "Does race have an impact on how you choose your friends?" In response to the second question, 30 percent of interviewees responded that race is important in choosing close friends. As we will see, this is an astonishingly high figure compared with the responses of Black Brazilians, the vast majority of whom perceive this question as nonsensical.

Among US interviewees, 69 percent responded that race is irrelevant in selecting friends (with roughly equal percentages among middle- and working-class respondents), and 68 percent say that they have at least one close non-black friend. This suggests a pattern of relatively weak out-group boundaries, which is confirmed by the interviewees' reports of interracial friendship and dating. It is also in line with the "color-blind," "diversity," and "social justice" frames discussed by Bonilla-Silva (2010), Feagin (2006), and Warikoo and de Novais (2014)—frames that these scholars regard as manifestations of current American normative expectations about openness to differences. American national identity is premised on democratic ideals, including the notions of universalism, equality, and openness to differences, whereas particularism is considered incompatible with our social contract (Lipset 1979; Anderson 2010). Yet interview data also suggest that blacks are considerably more negative toward whites than toward any other ethnic group and that their most intimate relationships are with other African Americans.

Closer, In-Group Circles. Most interviewees say their closest bonds are with other African Americans "because of what we have gone through together." Though some respondents explain that most of their friends are African Americans because they mostly live with blacks, many describe the feelings of cultural intimacy or familiarity that they share with blacks, mostly from having similar experiences.[28] For instance, they describe shared tastes or habits. As one insurance salesman says: "I just feel more at ease with our own ... because that's what I was brought up around even though we were brought up around Caucasians but I never went out to seek their companionship." This shared experience is at times contrasted with negative experiences with whites. This is the case for a councilwoman who explains that her closest friends are blacks because she does not trust whites—even while acknowledging that one should not judge "a whole class or race of people." Her position is not unusual. Referring to a classic article used in antiracist training that describes white privilege as "an invisible weightless knap-sack of special provisions, maps, passports, codebooks, visas, clothes, tools, and blank checks" (McIntosh 2007: 188), this woman explains: "It's not an indictment on a whole class or race of people, but.... When they are put to the test, they start to take out that knapsack and feel like they're on that whole superiority thing. You know, that's the real test of friendship: be friends with someone and you two get in a jam when you're under pressure, and see how they hold up."

This observation is consistent with previous research on African Americans and interracial friendship. Race and ethnicity play a particularly salient role in shaping friendship networks (McPherson, Smith-Lovin, and Cook 2001; Mouw and Entwisle 2006). This is typically attributed to factors such as spatial distance from out-group members and shared experiences with in-group members (Massey et al. 2003; Quillian and Campbell 2003; Fischer 2011).

This preference for blacks is also present in more intimate relationships, as evidenced by responses to questions probing past experience with inter-racial dating, which remains a rare phenomenon among African Americans, once again in stark contrast to the case of Black Brazilians. Only a dozen African American interviewees responded that they have dated inter-racially, and twice as many had not (but note that only one-third of our sample addressed this question). And 22 said they were either indifferent toward or supportive of it, with no distinct class patterns. These responses about interracial relationships resonate with national trends documented by survey data, with a majority of all Americans favoring interracial marriages (see Taylor et al. 2012).

Wider, Out-Group Circles. Because 87 out of 120 individuals who answered the question about the impact of race on the selection of people they associate with work in majority-white or multiracial environments, it is not surprising that 85 percent of the total say that they have many non-black acquaintances.[29] Moreover, many include whites when they are asked to describe their circles. And when asked how they select their friends, many say they "treat people as people" and provide the normatively correct responses: they declare that they don't pay attention to race when deciding with whom to associate. As a parole officer puts it, "I don't see him as my white friend, I just see him as my friend. You see what I am saying?" This possibly reflects their hopes concerning how others will approach them. As a minister said, "I'm not looking for anything from anyone except respect, as I would give them. That's something that all of us should want."

The experiences described as solidifying friendships are universal ones, like being "able to laugh, able to laugh at yourself, able to look past some of the hardships and still laugh," as a counselor said. Others explain that race does not affect their selection of friends, because there are many in-group members, too, from whom they feel great distance. For instance, a correction officer explains: "To me, it's more the quality of the person and their own views rather than their race, because there are people from my race that I don't like."

The non-black friends referenced are most often whites from the workplace and school. Other sites/activities where non-black friends are found are in sport and leisure activities (e.g., traveling, running marathons, playing basketball, or playing golf), at church, or in volunteering (including for political campaigns). These relationships lead to casual socializing. As one interviewee puts it, "We talk, eat, go to amusements parks. . . . Go get some ice cream at Friendly's ... I look at life as 'people are people.'" The only context in which our middle-class respondents are more segregated than their working-class counterparts is in their volunteering and religious activities.

Given the racially mixed work environment of all but 33 respondents, many describe interracial friendship as a necessity, as opposed to a preference or taste, as if integrated sociability was not optional but essential to daily life and particularly to social mobility. Indeed, describing a recent experience, one interviewee reflects thus on the role of sociability in business relations: "I could see myself being uncomfortable in some situations, like on the golf course perhaps where there is still that good old boy network.... A lot of business is conducted on the golf course.... I have invited [coworkers,] and there are some people that still consider me part of their network because they will call me for information and if there is a job opportunity they might feel I would fit, they will call me."

There is reason to believe that friendship networks may be becoming more diverse for all groups, including African Americans. Recent survey data from the Pew Research Center shows that younger Americans are more likely to have friends who are out-group members. These surveys also revealed greater openness to diversity (Pew Research Center and NPR 2010). This is in line with the increase of prodiversity institutional culture, in elite colleges and beyond (Warikoo and de Novais 2014; Berrey 2015), and converge with our finding that our respondents either embrace or perceive weakening group boundaries. Although many African Americans are critical of the notion that the United States is now in a postracial era when it comes to racial justice (e.g., Bobo 2011), there is support among Americans for a weakening of racial boundaries. The stability of this trend remains to be determined and may be challenged by highly publicized incidents of police violence against African Americans.[30]

Universalism, Essentialism, and the Constructions of Racial Similarities and Differences

In the post–Civil Rights Era United States, where universalism is routinely reaffirmed as the grounding principle on which the polity's unity stands, it is not surprising that many of the African Americans we spoke to uphold egalitarian or universalist views when it comes to discussing similarities and differences between groups—whether they do so in practice or not. When probed on such questions, the majority of middle- and working-class respondents said they believe that racial groups are either equal (43 percent) or partly equal (14 percent). Only 14 percent of respondents believe that groups are not equal. Some of these responses refer to positions that are normative ("we are equal as human beings"), prescriptive ("we should be treated as equal"), or descriptive ("we are not treated as equal"). The evidence given for equality is wide ranging yet often pertains to common life experiences. For example, one landscaper says, referring to blacks and non-blacks, "We are all equal because we all do the same thing." And as a police-man puts it, "The more we talk, the more we find out we are the same. His manager messed up, my manager messed up."

Given that a significant number of respondents took a resolutely univer-salist or a relativist position and refused to make clear distinctions between racial groups, it is important to note that a minority drew strong boundaries against whites, suggesting a fairly complex constellation of views among African Americans about in-group/out-group dynamics. This discrepancy leads us to describe African Americans as presenting a unique combina-tion of strong groupness, paradoxically coupled with openness to diversity and weak group boundaries. This tension cannot be captured by alternative models of collective identity and groupness (Sellers et al. 1998; Bailey 2009).

Those who are strongly committed to a universalist view of human be-ings downplay differences between ethnoracial groups as surface-level dis-tinctions or emphasize the universal character of human nature, human weaknesses, wants and needs, or life experiences (see also Lamont 2000: chapter 2; Shelby 2014). This is the case for a cafeteria worker who, when asked about similarities and differences between whites and blacks, says, "The white people that I know work jobs, two jobs, trying to make ends meet, like me." Some adopt a principled universalist position based on basic beliefs. For instance, referring to her religious beliefs, an interior designer states: "God made everybody out of the same substance. . . . We're here to get along. That's the ultimate goal here. Love thy neighborhood and all that other stuff."

This anti-essentialist perspective is also expressed by an entertainer when he says about racial groups, "I think there are downsides to everybody, I mean, not only white people. I mean, all of us have good and bad, and ups and downs, white people, too!" When asked to compare whites and blacks, a fashion buyer says, "I think that's an individual thing, you know, because I can't group them all together and say, 'All white people are like this, or like that.'" This respondent also notes that the media present groups as mono-lithic. He advocates for the introduction of more complexity to the depictions of groups in contemporary America. A graphic designer concurs, pointing to the need for more nuanced depictions of African Americans.

In contrast, when questioned about differences between whites and blacks, other respondents describe what they believe to be natural or incon-testable essential differences between the two groups (see also Morning 2011: chapter 2). These include differences in "our handshake; theirs are limp," "sense of rhythm," tastes in food ("we like hot sauce, they like mayon-naise"), in hair or skin ("whites get sunburns "), in habits ("we seem to be louder"), in attitudes toward money ("whites seem to be better at saving"), and in attachment to family tradition (expressed through the greater popularity of family reunions among African Americans for instance). A dental technician summarizes the differences comprehensively, "It's the way we talk, the way we walk, the way we make love, the way we raise our children, the way we deal with each other." Several interviewees also note having observed different approaches to childrearing, with more communication and encouragement, less authoritarianism, and more public display of affection by white parents, while others critique whites for not demanding respect from their children. Still others, referring to the crisis of African American families, note that white parents are more likely to send their kids to college and less likely to leave one another. Yet others say the only difference between groups is "skin color," implying that no real differences exist between groups. We will see that this position is predominant in Brazil.

Anti-white Moral Boundaries and White Privilege

While interview questions were open ended and most did not mention specific out-groups, our respondents mentioned whites more often than other non-black groups in their answers.[31] We coded all spontaneous references to ethno-religious or racial groups, and whites were the most frequently mentioned (39 percent of total mentions), followed by Latinos (26 percent), Asians (13 percent), non-US blacks (10 percent), and Jews (9 percent). Whites are also the group that receives the most negative mentions—and by a large margin (114 out of 274 mentions). These range from casual negative comments to more significant and damning statements of moral boundaries. For all the other groups considered, the number of negative mentions is much smaller than for whites (the largest number being 20 negative comments about Latinos). This suggests the existence of relatively strong anti-white boundaries, which are in tension with the universalist positions toward racial differences, described above, that undergird the weak boundaries toward whites voiced by many respondents. This also suggests that the tensions between whites and blacks remain particularly deep and deserve special attention, counter to the view expressed by some social scientists that black-white relationships should not be as central to scholarship moving forward.

Morality is salient in the boundary work of our respondents toward whites. (As we have seen, it was also salient when we asked respondents to define themselves.) This is in line with Lamont's (2000) finding that African American working-class men value a caring self, which they contrast with a more disciplined and domineering self among whites. An insurance salesman draws similar moral boundaries as he ties differences between whites and blacks to the American history of discrimination: "It's not a downside about the things that they bring to the country; it's the downside of the things that they do to other people not like themselves. That's been their history for so long, whether it's because they were scared, because they didn't know any better. They don't know about others because they choose not to or they don't want to." Similarly, comparing whites and blacks, a recreation specialist says: "We're more of a forgiving race of people than white folks are. I think white people are just born vicious. There are some vicious black people too, but it's like the nature of a white man is they'll do anything for success." Along the same lines, a history teacher said about whites: "I think they're barbaric. I really think they're ruthless people. A lot of them are people with evil intent, a lot of them are uneducated, and they're nasty. Loud, they're loud, they're really loud." His comment, by implication, alludes to what he perceives to be the moral strengths of blacks.

Anti-white boundaries are bolstered by our interviewees' awareness of contemporary racial inequality and historical racial domination and exploitation in the United States. It is also fed by awareness of the sense of entitlement that they believe many white Americans seem to have—a topic that prompted particularly vivid us/them contrasts and contributes to a strong sense of groupness. As one interviewee, a court clerk, puts it clearly, "It just seems as if with them they think they better. Everything, you know, has got to be their way. They know more than we know. They just think they superior when it comes to us." This sense of entitlement and superiority manifests in many circumstances—for instance, through their impatience when they have to wait for service in a public space, according to a parole officer. Similarly, a recreation specialist voices widely held views when he says of whites: "They act as though they are God's gift to the Earth. It was implanted in them that you are the hierarchy: 'Black folk are beneath you and anyone else.' My parents didn't say 'Individuals are beneath you.' They said, 'Respect everyone and you can achieve anything you choose to do.'"

Respondents' descriptions of white privilege are reminiscent of Blumer's (1958) theory of race prejudice as a sense of group position, which refers both to racial hierarchies and to whites' desire to maintain the current pecking order and to defend white privilege. Respondents are acutely aware of this racial hierarchy. As a teacher puts it, "White folks got the get-out-of-jail card. They got the superiority card, and black folks got the inferiority card. . . . We always the last hired, first fired, so we already know the deal. We know that sooner or later we going to be separated from the payroll when we come on the job." And for some, white privilege lies in the fact that whites don't have to think about dealing with racism on a daily basis. "They don't get up in the morning with the thought that 'I'm not going to be waited on because I'm black.' I get up knowing I am going to face this. They get up with not a clue. So that's a big difference right there."

Views about group disadvantage and the sense of privilege found among whites appear so broadly shared among our respondents as to constitute widely available scripts or frames that contribute to a strong sense of group-ness: they empower a collective construction of identity easily agreed on among group members, as it is repeated intersubjectively often enough to become taken for granted and institutionalized (Berger and Luckmann 1967).

DiTomasso (2013) describes the experience of white Americans as grounded in the transmission of white privilege. While her white middle-class and working-class respondents are critical of blacks' benefiting from affirmative action, they are blind to the myriad ways they help their own relatives and friends gain access to jobs and other resources. Here, we find that blacks are well aware of the advantages of whiteness. In this sense one could argue that the two groups operate in parallel universes, with defini-tions of reality that are largely incommensurate. This situation is enabled by the spatial racial segregation discussed above. As we will see in Chap-ter 3, this is largely absent in Brazil, revealing the uniqueness of the US case. This also demonstrates the importance of adopting a multidimensional view of boundaries that takes into consideration not only self-identification but also symbolic, social, and spatial boundaries (intersubjective boundaries located in networks and space).

CONCLUSION

This section paints a paradoxical portrait of the groupness of African Amer-icans that is quite different from approaches that focus exclusively on racial identity and offer familiar theories that focus on dichotomies of black and white and in-group and out-group. We presented evidence of strong racial identification: that self-identification as black/African American is frequent; that interviewees attribute many (often positive) meanings to their racial identity and make references to a shared history; that African Americans subordinate national identity to racial identity; that our respondents made fewer references to class identity than to racial identity. We argued that strong racial identification is fed by a common history of slavery and segre-gation, and by shared experiences of racial inequality.

But this is only half of the story. Against a background of low spatial boundaries in work settings and high neighborhood segregation, we have sketched a picture of groupness that combines strong racial identification with openness to diversity in personal relationships (more so in friend-ships than in intimate relationships) and with relatively frequent anti-white boundaries. These apparent contradictions are fed by the cultural and struc-tural context in which our interviewees live. More specifically, openness to universalism is in line with American ideals of equality, while strong anti-white boundaries resonate with the quotidian experience of racial inequality and white privilege, the latter drawing on readily available scripts about group disadvantage and the historical plight of African Americans.

SECTION 2.3: EXPERIENCES OF STIGMATIZATION AND DISCRIMINATION IN THE UNITED STATES

As captured in Section 2.1, through its history of slavery, white supremacy has been a defining feature of American society from its inception. It has shaped the contexts in which the lives of African Americans unfold (from Jim Crow to contemporary spatial segregation and racial economic inequality). In this section we argue that these contexts, along with African Americans' strong sense of groupness and available cultural repertoires, enable and constrain how our African American interviewees experience ethnoracial exclusion.

We first examine how our interviewees responded when asked a series of questions about their experiences of stigmatization and discrimination: "Have you ever been treated unfairly?" "Do you think you have been discriminated against at work?" "Are there contexts at work where you feel you have been disrespected?" "Can you remember encounters with racism outside of work?" and "Do you remember cases where you interacted with whites and felt misunderstood?"[32] We inductively analyzed their responses by coding narratives of incidents and comparing them with the responses of other groups considered in this book, as well as across gender, class, and age cohort (specifically, respondents who came of age during the Civil Rights Movement, immediately in its aftermath, and in the 1980s).

We found that African American respondents mention more incidents of stigmatization and discrimination than the other interviewed groups considered in this book. What we defined as stigmatization or assault on worth is more frequently mentioned than discrimination. These most frequently mentioned assault-on-worth incidents are often quite blatant, yet they coexist with more subtle experiences of stigmatization. Discrimination manifests most frequently as denied opportunity and racial profiling.

We also found that the number of respondents who believe they are stereotyped as poor, low status, or uneducated is surprisingly low—only one in four. Contrary to our expectations, given the growing inequality among blacks, narratives about stigmatizing and discriminatory incidents are largely similar for the African American middle class and working class, except that middle-class blacks are twice as likely to say they have been underestimated or stereotyped as poor, low status, or uneducated. Also, working-class blacks report more often than middle-class blacks that they experience double standards, which we tie to their low autonomy at work. Gender differences are smaller than expected. However, we found that when probed, men mentioned more incidents of being treated unfairly than women did. Finally, differences in incidents across generations are also fewer than expected. Two such differences are that while members of the oldest cohort said having been denied opportunities more often, members of the youngest cohort believe having experienced racial profiling more often.

The incidents mentioned in response to our questioning about unfair treatment occurred at diverse phases of the life cycle and in a plethora of contexts, including friendships, work, and family relationships. These incidents are generally described vividly, with emotion, as interviewees recall injustices that have scarred them:

- A young woman is dismayed that, contrary to custom, the year she graduated, her high school yearbook did not include pictures of sports award winners, all African Americans.
- A web director recalls that while she was not allowed to go to the high school prom because her parents still owed tuition to her private school, a white girl who was in the same situation was not penalized in this way.
- A patient-care employee notes that the worksite where white employees are in the majority has a daycare center, while the worksite where most workers are non-whites does not.
- A female editor discovers that a job she applied to was downgraded after management decided to hire her.
- A lumberyard worker gets more jail time than his codefendant, who is white, even though they committed the same crime.

When asked "Have you ever been treated unfairly?" and "Do you think you have been discriminated against at work?" the African American interviewees described a total of 687 incidents.[33] This is more than what we found in Brazil and Israel (with 522 incidents mentioned by Black Brazilians, 347 by Arab Palestinians, 75 by Mizrahim, and 157 by Ethiopians for a total of 574 in Israel). This suggests a high salience of narratives about racism in the daily lives of African Americans, which we see as stemming from various factors, such as their strong groupness, the ready availability of repertoires about group disadvantage, and others to be described below.

· ·

For all sites, the mentioned incidents were categorized into two broad groupings—stigmatization and discrimination—whose boundaries were derived inductively after extensive discussion among researchers across sites. As previously noted, we define stigmatization as assaults on worth, whereas discrimination refers to experiences of denied access to opportunities or resources. For the African American interviewees, the first category represents 81 percent of all incidents mentioned ($N = 555$—note that this is not the same as the number of interviewees who mention a category of incidents). The second category represents 32 percent ($N = 220$)—see Table A2.1 in Appendix 2 for a comprehensive list of the types of incidents.[34] Eighty incidents were coded as both assault on worth and discrimination.[35]

Stigmatization or assaults on worth include incidents in which respondents experienced disrespect and their dignity, honor, relative status, or sense of self was challenged. Our detailed coding of the interviews revealed that this occurs when one is insulted, receives poor services, is the victim of jokes, is subject to double standards, is excluded from informal networks, is threatened physically, or is a victim of physical assault. It also occurs when one is stereotyped as poor, uneducated, or dangerous, or is misunderstood or underestimated. Again, here we are concerned not only with the experience of being stereotyped but also with the experiences of being overlooked, misunderstood, ignored, feared, and underestimated. While some of these are experienced as micro-aggressions, others do not manifest themselves as aggression but as non-events (they are invisible) and thus are harder to respond to.

Discrimination broadly refers to incidents in which respondents were denied opportunities or resources due to their race or ethnicity. It also includes being excluded from access to services or public spaces. Typically, experiences of discrimination also entail stigmatization, even if our respondents are generally not explicit about the stigmatizing dimension in the interview.

We find that incidents dubbed "assault on worth" are more pervasive than those that concern discrimination across all groups. Keeping in mind unavoidable variations in interviewing skills and experience among interviewers and that the number of respondents vary in each case (which calls for caution in comparing percentages), it is interesting to note that 96 percent of the US interviewees mentioned at least one such incident, compared to 72 percent for discrimination incidents. In Brazil, 79 percent of the interviewees mentioned experiencing assault-on-worth incidents, compared to 60 percent who mentioned experiencing discrimination. In Israel, 84 percent of Arab Palestinians mention at least one assault-on-worth incident, and 58 percent mention an instance of discrimination. For Ethiopians, these figures are 78 percent and 48 percent, respectively. They are 57 percent and 36 percent, respectively, for Mizrahi.

The salience of assault-on-worth incidents is an important finding across all three sites. It has particular significance for the US site, since the bulk of the American literature on racism concerns discrimination, with a strong focus on documenting hidden discrimination around a specific measurable outcome—typically wage, employment, health services, banking, housing, or occupational status (e.g., Quillian 2006: 302; Krieger 2014). This focus is not surprising, given that the 1964 Civil Right Act restricted freedom to discriminate in favor of equality of opportunity and equality of outcome, emphasizing services (Title II) and employment (Title VII). Partly as a result of pressures from civil libertarians, some Supreme Court decisions in the 1960s and 1970s have expanded freedom of racist expression in the United States (Bleich 2011: 6)—with freedom of speech and freedom to protest generally trumping restriction of racist speech, except in the work environment, where employment law has been evoked to restrict freedom of speech (Bleich 2011: 78–79).

American law does not punish racist attitudes and display (e.g., display-ing the swastika), but it does punish discriminating or acting on racist opinion, which results in discrimination or hate crimes.[36] Compared to many European countries, American law is more oriented toward equal-ity of opportunity and access to material resources than it is toward the protection of dignity and recognition. For instance, when it comes to racial discrimination and sexual harassment law, the goal of rectifying assault to protect dignity is not as much of a concern as the production of and access to resources (Saguy 2003; Berrey 2015). This speaks volumes about the on-tological assumptions about fairness and justice that ground the American symbolic community, solder it together, and generate solidarity (see Ban-ting and Kymlicka forthcoming).

Consistent with this observation, in the United States, discrimination in-cidents can typically be subject to legal procedures and legal sanction.[37] In contrast, this is often not the case for stigmatization or assault-on-worth incidents, as these generally do not concern the types of experiences one can sue for, that is, interactions where individuals believe that they are not re-garded or treated as worthy or equal (except for incidents in the workplace).

STIGMATIZATION OR ASSAULT ON WORTH

Social scientists have been writing about the transition from blatant racism to more subtle forms of racism for a few decades. Because blatant racism has been on the decline over the past decades (Pearson, Dovidio, and Gaert-ner 2009), they have proposed various terms and theories to capture these new forms of racism: "symbolic racism" (Tarman and Sears 2005), "cultural racism" (Anthias 1995), "modern racism" (McConahay 1986), "laissez-faire racism" (Bobo and Smith 1998), and "color-blind racism" (Bonilla-Silva 2010)—to mention only some of the most popular approaches (see Quil-lian 2006 for criticism of this literature).

We find that many of the types of incident our respondents mentioned most often when questioned about past incidents where they were treated unfairly cannot be described as subtle. Indeed, 67 percent of them mentioned being explicitly insulted or disrespected. It is followed by more subtle experiences, such as being misunderstood (note, however, that we explicitly probed interviewees about this type of experience). The other assault incidents mentioned are distributed across a range of experiences, with receiving poor services and facing double standards each mentioned by a third of the respondents. These are the types of experiences that are often considered micro-aggressions in the literature on racism.

African Americans have an extensive repertoire to describe racist experiences and denounce racist encounters, even if denouncing racism may be perceived by non-blacks as making excuses for problems that blacks face. Indeed, only six African American interviewees did not mention any incidents. In the African American context, denying ever being a victim of racism may be interpreted as an attempt to mark social distance toward the in-group, to put oneself above others, or to acquiesce to racial stereotypes (as in "I don't get excluded because I know how to act"). African Americans' strong groupness helps explain why adopting distancing self-narratives is unpopular—indeed, anathema for some. We will see different dynamics in Brazil and in Israel—among Black Brazilians an awareness that poor whites are also discriminated against, and among Arab Palestinians a relative hopelessness about the future.

Blatant Racism: Being Insulted or Disrespected and Physical Assault

Their first encounter with racism is deeply etched in memory for many respondents. These incidents often involve being insulted or disrespected. This is where experiences with stigmatization most resemble traditional forms of blatant or overt racism. Take the case of a recreation specialist who remembers an experience from his youth in which his mother was threatened:

> Me and my mom are in the kitchen, and we hear this yelling out the back of my building. We look and there is a cop, white cop, beating up on this black guy. . . . And there's a couple of cops watching. . . . So my mother is like, "Hey, stop beating up on that guy!" And the cop screamed out obscenities: "Shut up you bi-, you black b and mind your mf-ing business before I come up there and arrest your ass." And I'm sitting there with this, with this guy talking to my mom and calling her a black bitch. That was my first encounter, to see that it was like, a mean white guy, not the white guy that you see on TV. This is not Elvis or *The Brady Bunch*. That ain't nothing like that!

Again, more than two-thirds (67 percent) of our respondents mentioned being insulted or disrespected.[38] This compares with a quarter of Black Brazilians and less than half of the Arab Palestinians, who live in a country where intergroup violence is reputed to be pervasive. For African Americans, these experiences range from being told one is dirty because one is dark; being called "a black piece of shit" (UPS driver); being called a "nigger" or "boy;" facing a neighborhood petition asking their family to move out from the neighborhood; being told that someone cannot work with you, because you are black (graphic designer); having an employer not wanting to put a check in one's hand for fear of touching you (housing manager); being spit on; being told that you are inferior (minister); being told to go back to Africa (circuit assigner); and so forth. When asked to describe such instances, an entrepreneur replies: "There were so many you just tune them out." These insults often play on widespread racial stereotypes that many Americans believe are a thing of the past. For instance, a policeman tells the following anecdote:

> I worked [at Lockheed Electronics] for 14 years. I was only the second black guy in management. I was a production control coordinator. We had dinners for the management group. This one particular dinner . . . , this guy, Frank Fish, I'll never forget. [He said,] "You know, Gene, there's watermelon on the [menu]." [I thought:] Oh no! You didn't take me there! No you didn't! I said, "Excuse me? I'll take care of you." Monday morning, I was in Monty Conway's office, he's the president of Lockheed. "Let me explain something to you, Mr. Conway." "Hey, Gene, sit down." "No, I don't want to sit down. We were at this meeting the other day, your buddy, your manager Frank Fish talking about some watermelon! I don't eat watermelon. He's got to go." He looked, he said, "What do you mean?" "He's got to go, or we're going to have some problems up in here." . . . Two days later he came to me crying to apologize. [Monty] fired him.

This same policeman remembers being told by a coworker with whom he worked side by side for a number of years "I hate black people to the core."[39] This left a critical imprint on his sense of belonging and identification with his workplace.

Particularly striking in this so-called postracial era is the number of interviewees who say they have been told "nigger jokes" or been called "nigger."[40] This racial slur is often used as a putdown when the sense of group positioning of whites is threatened (Blumer 1958), as when the racial hierarchy is challenged and needs to be reasserted (e.g., by yelling racist insults after a predominantly black baseball team won a game against a predominantly white team). A similar effect is achieved through the use of visual racist symbols. A New Jersey contractor remembered that on his first day at William Patterson College in central New Jersey, there was "a dummy being lynched from the top of a water cooling tower."

Symbolic acts of racial dominance, whether verbal or visual, aim to affirm the traditional racial order and are part of the experience of everyday racism for many of our interviewees. Such acts may be rare, but together with more subtle forms of racist experiences, they contribute to the creation of a hostile environment. So does being exposed to racist jokes, which is mentioned by 13 percent of our respondents. It may be that incidents interpreted as an insult by African Americans (e.g., a reference to watermelon) would be interpreted as a joke by Black Brazilians.

Also indicative of the lasting presence of blatant racism was the occurrence of incidents of physical assaults, being reported by one respondent in five (18 percent). This figure is not unexpected, given the abundant media coverage of recent incidents of racial violence. Such events serve as a powerful reminder that African Americans continue to face violence and threats to their personal safety (from in-group and out-group members) at a higher rate than non-Hispanic whites and Hispanics.[41] Somewhat surprisingly, incidents that involved racial profiling were mentioned by respondents less frequently than expected (they represent only 11 percent of all incidents mentioned), although 38 percent of all respondents had experienced them.

Less than one in ten interviewees recall being threatened with violence or being a victim of vandalism. One gripping example of such an incident is that of a utility worker, John, who remembers that a noose was found in the locker area at work. The evidence vanished before the culprit could be found. John regarded this as evidence that his supervisors were willing to cover over the event and support his racist coworkers. Another interviewee faced verbal and physical abuse from his boss, and when he complained, he was told by the union to transfer. Such experiences leave individuals feeling unsupported, vulnerable, helpless, and often emotionally depleted.

More Subtle Racism: Being Misunderstood

While blatant racism undoubtedly remains the most salient form of racism experienced by the African Americans we interviewed, also crucial are more subtle forms of racism, including the experience of being misunderstood. This finding demonstrates the subtle complexity and multidimensionality of the forms of racism that African Americans experience, in contrast to accounts that emphasize a linear shift from blatant to subtle forms of racism accompanying the end of segregation and the move toward integration.

In Section 2.1, we saw that, according to an analysis of tract-level data from the 2010 census, the average white person residing in metropolitan America lives in a neighborhood that is 75 percent white, while a typical African American lives in a neighborhood that is 35 percent white and up to 45 percent black (Logan and Stults 2011: 2). This means that large numbers of whites and blacks live lives that do not intersect with others of different ethnoracial groups, which may feed cultural distance (Massey and Denton 1993). This is also true for our interviewees, as they were selected from neighborhoods that were at least 20 percent African American. Thus, it is not surprising that in response to our questioning about past experiences of being misunderstood, half of our respondents (77) describe having had such experiences.

When asked if there are times when he feels misunderstood because of his race, John, a 48-year-old employee, says that he does:

> all the time. I can't even say nothing in a meeting without being misunderstood. Every time I say something, it's misunderstood. . . . They don't share your philosophies. They don't understand my tastes. . . . They just don't understand anything about me. They look at me like I got two heads or something. You know where you try to make a point, it's really a valid point, but they just don't seem to get it. . . . Also, I'm constantly getting many black issues. . . . Or you get the black comments like, "Hey, I look pretty good. I'm dressed like a black guy tonight, aren't I?" . . . Any racial biases get tested or directed to you when you're the only one in the workplace.

John's response echoes Kanter's (1977b) description of the experience of tokenism. The scarcity of corroboration of one's interpretation of reality is one of the most painful aspects of racism. It can lead to isolation and self-doubt. This kind of experience has prompted some African Americans to turn to entrepreneurship and self-employment (Light and Rosenstein 1995). This is the case for John: "I just got tired of playing the politics, got tired of the phoniness that's in the workplace."[42]

Like him, many African Americans experience a clash between how they view situations compared to non-African Americans. This can be precipitated by the cultural distance between in-group and out-group members, by their divergent experiences of past interactions, by racial tensions, and by high levels of distrust. Such experiences often leave blacks feeling emotionally isolated, deflated, and powerless. They also demonstrate the importance of intersubjective confirmation of interpretations of reality when trying to make sense of moments of exclusion or stigmatization. Strong groupness helps individuals identify an incident as racist, even if they have little contact with in-group members. So does access to ready-made scripts about the historical experience of white supremacy, white privilege, and how African Americans repeatedly face racism in their daily life.

We will see later that some interviewees believe that ignorance or lack of exposure ("they know nothing about us") leads non-blacks to misunderstand or misinterpret the behavior of blacks. In comparison, in Brazil, only eighteen interviewees believe they are misunderstood by whites when explicitly probed on this same question. This is one of the most striking differences in the interactions between whites and blacks in the two countries, and it is enabled in part by the vastly different levels of spatial segregation, miscegenation, and other forms of intergroup contacts in the two countries, as well as by policies and others factors to be discussed in Chapter 3. The contrast is even greater in Israel, where this type of experience is simply not mentioned—note that interviewers did not probe Israeli interviewees about it.

Poor Service and Double Standards

Those who write on the contemporary experience of African Americans as consumers continue to document the ways in which consumption remains a site for discrimination broadly defined, notably in the form of receiving poor service (e.g., Pittman 2011; for a summary, see Molnár and Lamont 2002). Thus, it is not surprising that a third of our interviewees (32 percent) described incidents having to do with receiving poor service—whether at restaurants, while shopping, or while dealing with repairmen, which may be connected to a perception that they are not able to afford goods or services.[43] These incidents range from subtle to blatant.

Al, an insurance salesman, describes the poor service provided by an appliance repair person at his mother's house. After spending less than 5 minutes looking at a broken washing machine, this worker declared that a belt needed to be replaced, while in fact the problem was more serious. Al pursued the case to ensure that the careless worker would cover the costs of full repairs. Al was livid, in part because he believes his own self-presentation signals respectability and his ability to consume and thus entitles him to proper service:

> My money is green like everyone else's. . . . I dress pretty comfortable, and a lot of people always comment they think I have a lot of money. I don't consider myself [as having] a lot of money, but I carry myself in a way that you would think I did. I'm always clean. My clothes are always neatly pressed, things of that nature.

Al notes that when he goes to stores and does not get "automatic attention . . . I as a person really get offended by this." Al specifically recalls an instance when, although he had in no way indicated that he could not pay cash for an appliance, he was offered a layaway plan by a sales clerk. Recalling the incident, Al commented that "I think that's one of the hardest things for me to deal with, stuff like that outside of the workplace."

As is the case for poor service, double standards are a means of maintaining historical racial hierarchies and of protecting the racial privilege of the dominant group. Pager and Shepherd (2008) discuss double standards as unequal treatment and discrimination, but such an experience can also be interpreted as assault on worth: it signals distrust in an individual's ability to do his or her job competently, indifference toward treating this person fairly, or even a desire to humiliate and cut down to size the other party. A third of our interviewees (31 percent) mentioned such incidents when asked about past experiences of being treated unfairly. In one telling example, his superior told a teacher that he could not receive a raise because he received a bad teaching evaluation and, in his superior's words, was "already making a significant amount of money." The teacher added, "So, my family's not as important as his family, my family doesn't need as much as [his] family needs." Such interactions also symbolically reassert the ethnoracial pecking order of the workplace and legitimate the superior position for the dominant group (Blumer 1958). Those in the dominant group who have few resources, for whom small distinctions acquire precious symbolic power, can heavily invest in such pecking orders.[44] This explains their proliferation in multi-ethnic workplaces.[45]

DISCRIMINATION

National surveys provide ample evidence of the centrality of perceptions of discrimination in the lives of African Americans. Using data from the General Social Survey, Bobo (2011) finds that African Americans (59 percent) are twice as likely as whites (30 percent) to believe that discrimination contributes to the persistence of the socioeconomic gap between blacks and whites (see also Hunt 2007; Bobo and Charles 2009).[46] In the 2006 Washington Post/Kaiser Family Foundation African American Men survey, when queried about which of a list of topics is "a big problem, a small problem, or no problem for black men today," 68 percent of the black men and 69 percent of the black women in the sample chose racial discrimination as a big problem, compared to 41 percent for the white men in the sample and 53 percent of the white women in the sample.[47]

Complementing the work of other scholars,[48] we look at how our US interviewees understand discrimination, focusing on the categories of experiences that emerged as the most salient from our inductive analysis: racial profiling and denial of opportunity. Seventy-two percent of our respondents mentioned discrimination incidents when questioned; of these, half (47 percent) mentioned being denied opportunities, and more than a third (38 percent) mentioned being a victim of racial profiling.

While these incidents all entail a loss of resources (our criteria for distinguishing between assault on self and discrimination), some also entail an attack on worth, as illustrated in the following three examples. A policeman who believed he outperformed a white coworker but was not recommended for promotion by his supervisor recalls that when the promotions were announced during a precinct meeting, "They didn't call my name. My supervisor was listening to the speaker. So [when] they said 'Petty Officer Bates,' he was like, 'Yes!' and walked out the room. He was pushing for [Bates] to make rank. So I felt I was unfairly treated.... That got to me." This policeman is denied an opportunity, but he is also hurt, because he believes his superior underestimated him. Along similar lines, a bank clerk who had been repeatedly posted to branches in dangerous areas of the city that were not well served by public transportation notes: "When I got promoted, most of [my coworkers] tried to say I got promoted because of affirmative action. Forget the fact that I was getting to all these branches without a car. Forget the fact that I was working all these crazy hours without a car. Working 65 hours, getting paid 40!!" He is upset both because he feels his poor work conditions translated into a lower hourly pay (a form of discrimination) and because reactions to the news of his promotion did not acknowledge his contribution. Another respondent was repeatedly asked by her manager to stay longer at work than the other workers: "She dismissed them and not me.... I don't hang onto that kind of stuff. I just recognize it and keep moving on." Alluding to past practices of whites asking blacks to use the back entrance, she pragmatically states that this poor treatment is a means to reassert a racial pecking order: "Believe me, I've been told about the back doors, and I come in and out the back door. [I know] what they think my place is supposed to be."

A number of our respondents also described in detail their personal experiences with law enforcement, and more specifically, with racial profiling. A drycleaner who was pulled over for making a U-turn said the incident happened "'cause I have a black face, that's the way I figure. Why is he gonna flash me, approach me in that manner, and this other car is still sitting there?"

Racial profiling is particularly prevalent in shopping malls, which explains the emphasis put on wearing brand-name clothing to go shopping so as to deflect racist stereotypes. But even this strategy is not always effective. John, who used to work at Saks, gives a telling example:

My wife comes in a $2,000 Armani suit. That's what I sell. She has an orange leather coat, orange Gucci bag. She comes, speaks to me, goes downstairs and shops, and as she's shopping, [a security guard] is hiding and following her around the store. I go downstairs to meet her, and I see two security guards, and I say, "Hey guys, what's going on? That's my wife. Why are you following her around the store?" That same day, a white gentleman came into the store with a suit on, a trench coat, laid 25 Armani ties at 150 bucks a piece across his arm, looked at them all at one time, cuffed his arm [to hide the ties] and walked right out the store, and they didn't even see him. But you're following my wife around, and this guy's stealing ties upstairs, and you don't see him because he doesn't fit the description of who you think a criminal is.

This unequal treatment when "shopping while black" serves as a painful reminder of the racial hierarchy that prevails in public spaces (Lamont and

Molnár 2001). Even wearing expensive goods is not enough to signal cultural membership in an emotionally invested consumers republic (Cohen 2003).

Yet, we cannot establish a pattern between types of incidents and types of contexts in our data, although there are a few exceptions: assaults-on-worth incidents are most frequent in school contexts, public places and retail/commerce establishments, and personal relationships (roughly one out of ten cases in each), while discrimination is most frequent in encounters with the police (one out of five) and in retail/commerce establishments (one out of ten).[49] We did find that middle-class respondents are twice as likely to mention incidents in public spaces as working-class interviewees,[50] and they are slightly more likely to mention incidents in retail or professional services, school, interactions with the police, and family relationships, but the numbers are small and therefore difficult to interpret. That the middle class is more concerned with incidents in public space speaks to the challenges of signaling class status in anonymous contexts.[51]

CLASS, AGE, AND GENDER DIFFERENCES

We now turn to intraracial group differences in experiences of stigmatization and discrimination. In particular, we analyzed variations in African Americans' experiences by class, age, and gender. Overall, we identified fewer differences within each of these three categories than were expected, suggesting that racial categorization primarily influenced our respondents' experiences of stigmatization and discrimination. We begin with differences across class before focusing on age and gender.

Experiencing Racial or Class Stigma? The Role of Class Boundaries

When asked whether they believe that all groups are treated fairly in the United States, 86 percent of our middle-class respondents and 83 percent of those from the working class replied in the negative. And when queried about the bases of inequality, all African American interviewees are far more likely to discuss racial discrimination than class discrimination. For instance, a city councilwoman mentioned that people are not treated fairly "through discrimination, through racism, through the way that different systems are set up." In response to the same question, a court administrator explained, "[Unfair treatment] goes back to race. That goes back to color." Fifty-four percent of interviewees referred to the unfair treatment of African Americans explicitly. After African Americans, the second group most frequently mentioned as being treated unfairly was "minorities" (racial or other), mentioned by 37 of the respondents. When queried about unfair treatment in an open-ended question, only 29 percent of respondents brought up unfair treatment due to class."[52]

Their views about the role of class in ethnoracial exclusion are multi-layered and at times paradoxical. For example, some interviewees are concerned with being excluded on class basis—their own class identity being misrecognized is the most frequently voiced concern—but few express concerns about the stigmatization of the poor, even if they are highly aware that the poor are stigmatized. However, overall racial exclusion remains most salient for respondents, in keeping with Omi and Winant's (1986) theory that race is a master category. We first explore cases of misrecognition of the respondents' own class identity before turning to their views on the stigmatization of another social class, the poor.

Middle-class respondents are almost twice as likely to mention being stereotyped a low status, uneducated, or poor as working-class respondents (30 percent versus 18 percent). As we saw above, many want to be viewed as middle-class Americans who are able to consume. There was the case of Al—the smartly dressed insurance salesman who takes pains to signal by his dress and manners that he "has a lot of money." Like John, the Saks Armani salesman whose wife dressed in an orange leather coat, Al strongly dislikes being perceived by sales clerks and security agents as unable to consume luxury goods and services. Similarly, Jimmy, a parole officer, fumes when he is asked to provide additional identification when purchasing an expensive watch to add to his personal watch collection: "When I put my credit card up there, people ask me for ID with the credit card. And I say to them, 'That's enough ID right there!'" When asked why he believes he faces this request for additional identification, Jimmy says "probably the way I was dressed. My race, and the way I was dressed, and their perception." He believes he is being stereotyped based not only on phenotype but also on perceived socioeconomic status, as signaled by what he wears.

Jimmy, Al, John, and others are appalled that non-blacks are unable to read their middle-class status and that the intraracial differences that are so significant to them are invisible or inadmissible to others outside their racial group. This concern with being recognized as middle-class is not surprising in a context of growing inequality among blacks. Not being recognized as middle-class, or being stereotyped as poor, is a double injury to their sense of self as African American and middle class). It is experienced as an unacceptable violation, perhaps because it attacks not only who they believe they are but also the sacred premises of the American Dream and its correlate, possessive individualism, which promise that success opens all doors and is the key to cultural belonging in the United States.[53]

Martin Gilens (1999) has shown that many white Americans conflate being African American with being poor. Indeed, "despite the fact that African Americans constitute only 36 percent of welfare recipients and only

27 percent of all poor Americans, whites' attitudes toward poverty and welfare are dominated by their beliefs about blacks" (Gilens 1999: 5). When Americans are asked, "What percentage of all the poor people in this country would you say are black?" the median response is 50 percent (Gilens 1999: 68). Against this background, it is striking that only one respondent in four mentioned incidents where they were being stereotyped as low status, poor, or uneducated (compared to half of the respondents in Brazil). Equally surprising is the fact that only 5 percent of all incidents mentioned concerned being stereotyped this way.

In some cases, the desire to not have one's middle-class status go unrecognized is reinforced by views that having a college degree should guarantee respect and that higher status justifies better treatment. Such beliefs can be in tension with the universalist support for equality that regards all human beings, including low-income blacks, as deserving cultural membership.

This position is illustrated in the following three examples. A teacher (and part-time singer) recalls performing at an alumni reception at a prestigious law school. On her way to the event, she gets in an elevator with a white alum who addresses her as "girl." She feels that this expression betrays an inappropriate degree of familiarity or stereotypical views of blacks as low status. She observes, "I could be a doctor or PhD or whatever," implying that high professional status should entitle one to being addressed respectfully, independent of phenotype.

Judy, a councilwoman, reported that when she enrolled her daughter in a youth basketball league, her daughter was offered financial assistance, despite being from a middle-class family, because the team coach assumed all African Americans living in their area were economically disadvantaged. Judy found out that only the African American players on the team were receiving scholarships after conferring with parents of white players. She discussed the issue with the coach, who explained, "Well, I just thought the girls being from [Jonesville] and all, they could use a little extra help." Judy believes that the coach was hiding his racial prejudices by referring to residence in a low-income neighborhood instead of race to justify his action—and that he stereotyped all blacks, including herself, as low income. She finds this unacceptable.

A social worker explains that she has trouble maintaining professional boundaries between herself and her clients. As part of her job, she visits disabled adults in their homes and helps them develop the skills necessary for independent living. At times, one of her white clients believe she is there to clean their homes, "I am not here to do it for him. I am here to teach him how to do it for himself, and it's a big difference 'cause I'm not the maid and I'm not the housekeeper, you know?" For middle-class respondents, this misrecognition may be troubling because of their general concerns about hard work and social mobility.

The fact that these middle-class respondents found misrecognition of their class status so appalling is also explained not only by growing inequality among African Americans but also by the prominence of consumption for American cultural citizenship, and the prestige and influence of middle- and upper middle-class lifestyles and culture in this country.[54] Some respondents believe in the American Dream and expect full participation in the American polity. That these expectations are not met is not surprising in the context of contemporary American race relations, particularly following a recession that has considerably weakened the economic position of most African Americans (Bonnet and Théry 2014).

A strongly shared belief in meritocracy in US culture is another element that feeds concern about misrecognition of class identity. Verba and Orren (1985: 180) showed that most elite Americans feel there should be a substantial income gap between occupations, as "the ideology of individual achievement remains potent." Meritocracy leads Americans to view inequality as legitimate, which reinforces the belief that those who succeed deserve the rewards of success (McCall 2013). The International Social Survey Program confirmed this tolerance for inequality in the United States. In 2009, nationally representative samples were asked whether they agree or disagree that differences in income are too large. While only 29.4 percent of the US sample responded affirmatively, 53.5 percent of the Israeli sample said yes. Brazil was not included in the 2009 survey, but in the 2001 survey, Brazilians were asked whether income differences were too high in their country. Eighty-six percent agreed completely and 10 percent agreed partly (Scalon 2004). These different attitudes toward inequality certainly influence how racial inequality is understood in each country. If class differences are largely viewed as a legitimate principle for distributive justice, Americans may be far more accepting of class inequality (and stigmatization) than they are of racial discrimination (McCall 2013). This is suggested by the fact that as a group, African Americans are less stigmatized than the poor (Clair, Daniel, and Lamont 2015).

Paradoxically, the notion of poverty discrimination may be a misnomer in the American context, where policies deal more readily with racial discrimination than with class discrimination—in fact, many means-tested redistributive social policies contribute mightily to the stigmatization of the poor. Under the influence of market competition, which gained greater legitimacy in the neoliberal era, even workers have come to blame themselves for their inability to complete college, their job instability, and their lower status (on the self-blaming American working class, see Sharone 2014; Silva 2013; also see Cherlin 2014). Concomitantly, a growing number of African Americans have come to embrace individualist explanations of racial inequality (which blame individual failings) over structural explanations (which emphasize systemic discrimination) (see Hunt 2007). But this attitude is less prevalent among them than among whites: comparing African Americans, whites, and Latinos, Bullock (2008: 57) writes, "Among all three groups, structural attributions for poverty were favored over individualistic causes, but again African Americans and Latinos expressed stronger support for structural explanations than whites." Further reflecting a belief in meritocracy, Americans across racial categories favor individualistic explanations over structural explanations for others' obtaining wealth (Hunt 2004). Here again, though, African Americans and Latinos were more likely than whites to believe that structural factors were also important (Hunt 2004).

It should be remembered that the language of class-based discrimination has lost considerable influence since the Reagan era, with the spread of neoliberalism and social conservatism (Rodgers 2011). While populism and anti-elitism remain an influential cultural trend in American culture (exemplified by the impact of the Tea Party), the American embrace of success makes class boundaries toward the lower half more punitive than they are in Brazil. Cultural repertoires associated with the neoliberal era, which has contributed to legitimizing class boundaries based on competitiveness, earning, and social status (Hall and Lamont 2013), are likely to enable stronger class boundaries among blacks (in favor of high-status people) and to influence which experiences of racism become more salient for middle-class blacks. Yet, using the American National Election Survey, Hochschild and Weaver (2015: 1253) show that "College-educated blacks evinced less support for government services in general and for spending on the poor in 2012 than did college-educated blacks in the 1980s, while poorly educated blacks did not shift. . . . In all three arenas (government services, spending on the poor, and spending on crime control), class differences that were minimal or nonexistent among blacks in the 1980s became statistically and substantively significant by 2012." However, they also find that in "support for government aid to blacks or minorities, blacks evinced no class differences in either the 1980s or 2012" and that support for the notion that the fate of blacks is linked remains as strong in the black middle class in 2012 it was in 2008. There again, shared racial identity appears to trump class differences, in line with the strong groupness argument developed above.

Neoliberalism is far less influential as an ideology and set of policies in Brazil than in the United States (Diniz 2007; Bresser-Pereira 2009; Bresser-Pereira and Theuer 2012). At the same time, Black Brazilian interviewees are more likely to hesitate in labeling an incident (or person or situation) as racist or not. Brazilians appear to be more concerned with class generally and with the class hierarchy especially, which is perceived as particularly steep in Brazil, as compared to the United States—although the countries' Gini coefficients of inequality have been converging (Lara 2013). That African

Americans are less hesitant to label an incident as racist is enabled not only by the strength of their groupness, the salience of collective memory about the racist history of American society, and wide availability of ready-made scripts concerning what defines and how to recognize a racist act, situation, or person—it is also explained by the low salience of the notion of class discrimination.

Surprisingly Few Differences across Classes

Overall, middle-class respondents report a slightly larger number of stigmatizing incidents than do working-class respondents: out of 687 incidents, 365 are reported by middle-class respondents, compared to 322 by working-class respondents (with comparable proportions for assault on worth and for discrimination). At the same time, class differences for each type of incident mentioned are fewer than expected. Middle-class interviewees are twice as likely to mention being underestimated as the working-class respondents (30 percent versus 16 percent). They are also slightly more likely to mention receiving poor service (35 percent versus 29 percent) and being ignored (18 percent versus 9 percent, but the numbers are small). And we saw that they are almost twice as likely to mention being stereotyped as low status, poor, and uneducated (30 percent versus 18 percent). For Brazil, the figures are 58 percent for the middle class and 30 percent for the working class. We will see that this is one of the main differences in how groups experience ethnoracial exclusion in Brazil and the United States. These class differences hold whether we compare the working class with the middle class defined broadly (as including semi-professionals) or narrowly (as including only college-educated professionals and managers). In all cases, the class difference points toward middle-class people having more expectations of being respected than working-class people have.

The only type of incident that our working-class respondents report more frequently than middle-class respondents is the use of double standards (34 percent versus 27 percent for the middle class.) Although the difference is very small (only six respondents), it is worth pondering, as it sheds light on how work conditions may shape the types of racist incidents each group faces. If working-class respondents complain that their boss keeps a closer eye on them than on their white coworkers—for instance, by making sure that they punch in on time—it is in part because they have less job autonomy and discretionary power at work than do middle-class professionals (Hodson 2001).

Several working-class respondents observe that their attire and appearance are also the object of more policing—connected to boundary work against what may be regarded as racial differences in habitus or bodily displays (hexis) (Bourdieu 1977). In one case, a boss insists that a female restaurant worker removes her braids, although she wears a net over them. She regards this level of scrutiny as illegitimate interference in her private life. This experience is directly tied to her work conditions and to the forms of control present in her workplace, which are absent in middle-class workplaces. In another case, when a black worker comes back from lunch late, he gets written up, but his white coworkers who returned at the same time do not. In addition, he is docked an hour of pay, although he was late by only 15 minutes.

Nevertheless, the overall high level of similarity in incidents across classes strikes us. We had expected class differences to be greater, given not only the increasing inequality among blacks but also the class differences in degree of professional autonomy, discretion, work conditions, and so on.[55] The surprisingly few differences across classes imply that, independent of social class, there is great uniformity in the experience of "living while black" in the United States. Middle-class blacks enjoy relatively fewer class privileges than do middle-class whites (DiTomasso 2013). Despite that notion that money whitens, and despite recent research showing that African Americans in middle-class occupations are perceived as more white (or less black) (Saperstein and Penner 2012), when it comes to everyday experiences of racism, class differences are fewer than expected.[56]

The way the shared experience of racism flattens out expected differences across classes may be a function not only of the frequency of experiences but also of the strength of groupness, the wide availability of scripts concerning group disadvantage, and the pervasive character of white privilege, as discussed in Section 2.2. Both the frequency of experiences and these other factors influence the certitude with which African Americans can point to an event as having to do with race but not with class. This speaks to the pervasiveness of stigmatization and discrimination of African Americans in the United States, even 40 years after the victories of the Civil Rights Movement and at a time when a large number of college-educated blacks are joining the ranks of the middle class (Landry and Marsh 2011).

Our findings are to be interpreted against the background of a growing body of interview-based literature on how middle-class African Americans experience racism. Most notably, Feagin and Sikes (1994) examine discriminatory action across various social domains and argue that middle-class status does not provide a refuge from racism and discrimination. Pattillo-McCoy (1999) demonstrates how intertwined the lives of the black middle class are with those of the poor who live in their neighborhood and how they manage class boundaries, even within a single family. Lacy (2007) studies the experiences of upper-middle-class African Americans and argues that they have a varied cultural toolkit to manage their position as middle-class minorities, which is composed of various identities: public, status-based, race-based, class-based, and suburban (see also Banks 2009). Although aspects of our results are consistent with this research,[57] we open up new lines of inquiry by using inductive coding to demonstrate similarities in the experiences of African Americans from different class backgrounds. Further, complementing this literature on the black middle class, a few rare studies, such as Annette Lareau's influential book *Unequal Childhood*, compare blacks across classes.[58]

We still lack sufficient comparative studies of the experience of racism across classes. Moreover, the literature has not been particularly attuned to the distinctive attributes and resources of the upper middle and middle classes, which can potentially operate as buffers against racism—attributes such as expertise, professional autonomy, or the discretionary power that knowledge can offer (Brint and Proctor 2011). Further, this literature typically has not fully considered this group's cultural orientation toward self-actualization and conflict avoidance (Morrill 1995). A broader view of the contexts of class cultures is necessary to make sense of the push and pull factors that shape the experiences of the black middle and working classes and how they respond to racism. These various repertoires are intertwined with the ideal of meritocracy and national myths of mobility and the American Dream and have to be considered together if we are to fully understand their impact. Class cultures, political, ideological, and groupness factors work together to fashion the quotidian experiences of individuals—helping us to move beyond a simple "us versus them" perspective to consider the various factors that enable and contrast various of experiences.

Gender Differences and Gender Discrimination

That experiences of ethnoracial exclusion are gendered is well established (Choo and Ferree 2010). In our study we documented how people interpret their experiences and the kinds of incidents men and women most often encounter. We find significant differences in the experiences described by the men and women we interviewed, which indicates the gendered character of stigmatization and discrimination. These patterns are shaped by, and resonate with, the predominant constructions of black men and women in the media and elsewhere: a general antagonism and lack of sympathy toward black men, with exaggerated views of their criminality and violence (Opportunity Agenda 2011), and the stereotypes of Jezebel, the welfare queen, and the angry black woman (Collins 1990; Moody 2012; see also Entman and Rojecki 2000).

For instance, national level data suggest that black men are pulled over while driving more frequently than black women are. In the 2006 Survey of Black Men,[59] when asked, "Have you ever been unfairly stopped by police because of your racial background?" 48 percent of the black men surveyed answered affirmatively, compared to only 13 percent of the black women (out of 1,835 black respondents). Given the high level of incarceration for black men, it is not surprising that several interviewees mention racial profiling and similar experiences, at the same time as they voiced their fear of cops (white cops in particular) and their desire to avoid all contact with them. They associate the police with arbitrariness in the exercise of power and with a degree of lawlessness that strongly clashes with mainstream views about the police force. Thus, teaching black children (young men in particular) how to deal with cops is a salient theme in the lessons that respondents give kids about racism, as discussed in Section 2.4.

The men reported 378 incidents in which they were treated unfairly compared to 309 for women, and the men are more likely to describe themselves as being misunderstood (65 percent of men versus 40 percent of women). In addition, twice as many male respondents believe they are viewed as threatening (22 percent versus 10 percent for women). This is not surprising, given prevailing stereotypes of African American men as both violent and threatening (Entman and Rojecki 2000; Collins 2005). Further, among our respondents, twice as many men have been victims of physical assault (24 percent versus 12 percent for women), and more men describe incidents where they believe they were insulted and disrespected (74 percent versus 62 percent). While the differences are small, they all go in the same direction. However, roughly the same number of men say that they are stereotyped as low status, low income, and uneducated as women (24 percent versus 26 percent). We will see that the gender difference is larger in Brazil, with women being more often stereotyped as low status (e.g., domestic workers).

These reports from interviewees should be considered against the background of relative distrust toward black men in the American context. The 2006 Survey of Black Men reveals that when asked how often respondents have experienced people acting as if they were afraid because of their race, 21 percent of the black men surveyed answered "somewhat often," and 13 percent answered "very often." This is compared to 8 percent and 1 percent, respectively, for white men, and 13 percent and 6 percent for black women.[60] Thus, it is not surprising to learn that, among our interviewees, men are more likely than women to mention having experienced racial profiling (9 percent more likely) and having been stereotyped as threatening (also 9 percent more likely). Here again, although these differences are not large, they are consistent with stereotypes of black men as dangerous and violent (Collins 2005). Interviewees are acutely aware of this perception, as noted by a parole officer:

> I'm six-seven, 295 pounds. You understand? Certain situations where I walk in different places, people think that I might want to rob them

or I might want to take something from them. . . . And I'm supposed to take certain things, and I shouldn't hurt. I shouldn't have feelings. You should be able to say certain things to me, and I should be able to brush it off my shoulders because of my size.

Another male respondent explains:

I [have] a beard. People don't like that. A lot of people have a hard time dealing with this figure, this persona here. It's something that's threatening to them, and I am no more threatening than anybody else as long as you are not trying to hurt people or my family.

When respondents are queried about unfair treatment, gender is brought up the least frequently (by 9 percent of the respondents, with no significant class differences) compared to race (91 percent of respondents) and class (29 percent). These differences are compatible and probably enabled by the strong groupness of African Americans, with racial discrimination overpowering other experiences of unfair treatment. The contrast between the figures for gender, race, and class may be at odds with some of the literature on intersectionality, which frames stigmas as additive (i.e., effects are the sum of multiple stigmatized identities) or combinatory (i.e., effects vary by individuals' unique gender, race, class, or other identity combinations). However, both of these views primarily emphasize the effects of the individuals' characteristics instead of examining how experiences for certain groups with different histories of ethnoracial relations vary with context.[61]

In a few cases, respondents stressed that gender and racial discrimination are often intermixed. When asked whether she believes everyone is treated fairly in the United States, a fashion buyer quickly responds, "Hell no!" She goes on to explain that "I'm African American and I'm a woman. It has been a little rough in the workforce, competing with the guys. And nothing is harder, I've found, in my life than to be a smart black woman. You have to go and compete with the white male, or you have to go and compete with the white female." Congruent with some intersectionality literature (McCall 2005), which says that disadvantages can be cumulative, a woman insurance adjuster stresses that there is a "black tax" that is harder for women who face a glass ceiling, implying that African Americans have to simultaneously navigate multiple stigmatized identities as they negotiate both race and gender exclusion.[62]

Age Cohorts

We categorized interviewees into three cohorts: those who came of age during the Civil Rights Movement, immediately after it, and in the 1980s.[63] The goal was to consider groups that have been exposed to different types of historical conditions and that live where legal protection against racism was more or less accessible. We found that the changes in race relationships over the past few decades (skillfully analyzed by Bobo 2012) indeed have influenced the types of incidents respondents from each age cohort mention, but not nearly as much as we had expected. Surprisingly, the three cohorts mention very similar types of assaults on worth and in similar proportions. However, a few differences across cohorts exist. While members of the oldest group are more likely than the youngest group to say that they have been denied opportunities (29 percent versus 18 percent), the youngest group more often mentions incidents of racial profiling (25 percent versus 13 percent), which resonates with widely spread stereotypes about aggressive behavior among African American youth (see also Patterson and Fosse 2015).

Besides this qualitative difference, we find that incidents of discrimination are slightly more numerous in the oldest group (81 percent mention such incidents, compared to 71 percent of the middle group and 65 percent of the youngest group). This is not surprising, given that the oldest group has lived longer, and some in that cohort experienced Jim Crow (directly or indirectly) in the South.

The experience of discrimination varies across cohorts, reflecting the legal and cultural changes that have taken place through the decades since the 1960s. A network technician in the oldest cohort speaks of how segregation and discrimination shaped his trajectory:

> When you have a conversation with someone . . . somebody that is not of the black race, it's like you have to explain to them [that] you come from poverty . . . I used to tell [my coworkers] my parents didn't have as much fortune as yours. . . . They had a lot of things behind them pushing them down, because when I came before the 70s, you know, everybody was against blacks. . . . When my generation came along, we were a little bit better than that. They let us have jobs a little bit better. . . . I took the test for Verizon. For some reason, they didn't qualify me to take the network technician test straight out of college. . . . Even though the company that I work for, you know, is diverse, the hiring staff didn't think that, you know, us as black people deserve those jobs. . . . I did take the test again eight years later, and I passed it.

Several older respondents spoke of how their responses to racism evolved through the decades. One teacher recalled how he dealt with his former school principal, whose father was a grand wizard of the Ku Klux Klan. He told a higher-up in the school that he could not work under this principal, "They wanted to know why, and I told all the reasons why, and I didn't hold my tongue. And you know that I live in the era where I can do that and at least I feel like I can." The post–Civil Rights historical context shaped how experiences came to be understood by members of the oldest cohort, just as the contemporary context, with growing rates of incarceration for young black men, shapes the youngest cohort's perceptions.

CONCLUSION

The main finding of this section is the preponderance of narratives of experiences of stigmatization (which we identify as assault on worth) over experiences of discrimination reported by the African American interviewees. This is in tension with the US literature on race, which treats discrimination as the primary issue. American law and social policy have made stigmatization invisible by addressing discrimination primarily and at times, exclusively. A second significant finding is that African Americans' everyday experiences of racism are largely blatant in character, although they coexist with more subtle experiences (e.g., being misunderstood). This challenges standard accounts, which emphasize a linear transition from blatant to subtle racism as American society becomes more socially progressive.

We saw that respondents mention racial discrimination more often than class and gender discrimination in interviews. This is surprising, given the growing inequality among African Americans. We explained this finding by the strength of groupness of African Americans, itself the product of a historical legacy of racial domination that may also feed directly into awareness of racial discrimination.

We also discussed the concern about class misrecognition by middle-class blacks. We connected this concern to the salience of meritocracy and the myth of the American Dream, which feed the belief that cultural membership is achieved with middle-class status (although not all respondents embrace the American Dream). There is an inner tension between middle-class blacks' feelings of linked fate with all African Americans and their anxiety about misrecognition of their class position. This is perhaps fed by the growing stigmatization of the poor, as measured by the decline in governmental programs dedicated to them, by growing inequality, and by the hegemony of middle- and upper-middle-class culture in American society in conflict with aspects of groupness.

Otherwise, we found generally only small differences in how the middle- and working-class respondents experience racism: the middle-class interviewees more often express feeling misunderstood and ignored than the working class. This is consistent with the strong groupness of African Americans—suggesting that linked fate in the form of a common legacy of racial domination overpowers class differences. The differences in the experiences of the three age cohorts also turned out to be smaller than we had expected. Finally, gender differences in experiences of unfair treatment resonate with familiar stereotypes associated with African American men and women.

We have suggested that growing inequality, spatial segregation, a strong sense of groupness, and several intertwined cultural repertoires (pertaining to neoliberalism, such national myths as, the American Dream, meritocracy, and middle class culture) as well as access to ready-made cultural scripts concerning racism and group disadvantage, inform how African American interviewees experience stigmatization and discrimination. In the next section, we will see how they respond to their plight.

SECTION 2.4: RESPONSES TO STIGMATIZATION AND DISCRIMINATION

Much has been written on African American responses to racism as expressed through political parties and mobilizations, marches and riots, religious manifestations and music, and arts and literature. Yet, the actions and reactions of ordinary people have not often received appropriate consideration. Just as one cannot understand how gender inequality was transformed over the past decades without taking into consideration the quotidian behavior of women bucking social norms and unequal treatment, one cannot make sense of major changes in how African Americans live and practice various forms of diversity, including racial diversity, without taking a close look at the everyday responses to ethnoracial exclusion.[64]

This section reconstructs inductively the range of responses to incidents reported by African American interviewees and discussed in Section 2.3. These responses were provided when we queried interviewees about instances where they were treated unfairly and how they reacted. They fall into the five meta-categories described in the Introduction: confronting the stigmatizer; management of the self; not responding; demonstrating strong work, educational, and professional competence; and isolating oneself (plus "miscellaneous," which we do not discuss).[65] (For details, see Table A2.2 in Appendix 2.)

We also consider normative or ideal responses, which we elicited by asking the interviewees three sets of questions:

- "What do you teach your kids about how to deal with racism?"
- "What is the best way to deal with racism?"
- "What do you think are the best tools that African Americans have at their disposal to improve their situation?"[66]

The latter captures their views on group tools for dealing with racism, which we distinguish from responses concerning the best way or best approach for dealing with racism. To elicit respondents' views on normative and ideal responses, we asked questions about both collective and individual responses to racism. We understand their responses as revealing taken-for-granted conceptions about the norm (what blacks should do) and possibilities conceived in the abstract (what they can do), unconstrained by the pragmatic considerations that figured prominently in their descriptions of responses to actual incidents.[67]

While some of the responses to incidents that our US interviewees shared have been discussed in current literatures on coping with stigmas and racism, others have not.[68] The added value of our analysis is to provide a comprehensive and fine-grained description of such responses,[69] along with their relative salience, and to explain them in context. Also unique is that we compare narratives concerning actual responses with views on normative responses. This section highlights how groupness and available cultural repertoires enable both actual and ideal responses, which resonate with shared myths about the character of American society, such as how cultural membership is acquired and how to be successful.

We found that when describing their responses to actual incidents, African American interviewees most often confront the stigmatizer—mostly by speaking out followed by using legal tools. (See Tables A2.1 and A2.2 in Appendix 2 for a distribution of types of incidents and types of responses for all incidents and all US interviewees by class). Their high degree of groupness and readily available scripts about the racist character of American society, as well as feeling empowered by the legal gains made by the Civil Rights Movement (among others), make confronting a legitimate response. Confrontation also comes easily, because blacks may be less hesitant to label an incident as race-related (in contrast to Black Brazilians).

The second most frequent group of responses for our US respondents is what we call "management of the self," the act of considering the pragmatic implications of responding one way or the other and acting accordingly. Because management of the self is an internal process, the resulting external action may sometimes also be one of the other coded responses, such as confrontation. In these cases, the responses were double-coded as "management of the self" and the corresponding external response. We argue that high unemployment, ready-made scripts about discrimination, and a climate of economic uncertainty encourage a pragmatic attitude of factoring in the cost associated with different types of responses. The third most frequent responses are "non-response," where interviewees state that they spontaneously did not respond due to surprise, inattention, or because not responding was the only option. While both management of the self and non-response may look like non-events from the perspective of an observer, they differ in that management of the self implies weighing alternatives, while non-response does not.

Neither of the two remaining categories of responses—working hard/demonstrating competence, and self-determination/self-isolation—is very salient among the US interviewees' responses to actual incidents, but the first looms large when it comes to normative responses. Indeed, hard work/demonstrating competence is particularly prominent when interviewees are queried about the tools that their group has at its disposal for dealing with exclusion. Most of the responses to this question center on self-improvement, where individual strategies (through social mobility, the pursuit of education, and moral reform) are almost three times as salient as collective strategies (e.g., in-group solidarity and becoming involved in community organizations and social movements). This is consistent with a general retrenchment (until recently) from collective responses that were pervasive during the Civil Rights Era, which is enabled by neoliberalism, an ideology associated with individualism, the promotion of market competitiveness, and the privatization of risk. We also find that very few respondents spontaneously mention race-based policies (e.g., affirmative action) when queried about the tools that African Americans have at their disposal as a group to fight racism. This is perhaps because such policies are taken for granted by our respondents or because they believe that they do not represent a solution to racial inequality, given public opinion about reverse discrimination. We note that the respondents' explanations of racism emphasize unchangeable factors (stupidity, human nature) and discuss the diversity of normative lessons that respondents teach their kids about how to deal with racism. We conclude with underscoring that normative responses resonate with belief in the American Dream.

Throughout this section, we weave in a comparison of responses across class, gender, and age group. In all categories but "confronting," middle-class and working-class respondents are almost equally constrained with respect to how they react, contrary to our predictions. As was the case with their experiences of stigmatization and discrimination discussed in Section 2.3, racialized experiences seem to overpower class differences. This may be because even middle-class individuals experience considerable constraints due to lasting discrimination, as well as less wealth and high unemployment compared to the white middle class. Class differences increase only slightly when we consider normative responses: more middle-class respondents favor collective responses to ethnoracial exclusion and promote the moral reform of African Americans, while slightly more working-class respondents favor the self-improvement of blacks. Thus, the working class may be more inclined to favor responses that are more in line with neoliberalism. This may be a function of their lack of resources—making a virtue of necessity, as Bourdieu (1972: 260) would put it—or an indication of their having less freedom than the middle class from means of institutional control and normalization.[70]

As we saw in Section 2.3, men mention more incidents of racial profiling, being stereotyped as threatening, and being misunderstood than do women. They also provide slightly more responses of all types than women—specifically, confrontation (mentioned by 86 percent of men versus 77 percent of women), management of the self (59 percent versus 38 percent), and not responding (50 percent versus 41 percent). Although confronting may resonate with a widespread construction of masculinity, management of the self and not responding may be ways to avoid violent escalations and feeding racial stereotypes of black men as prone to violence. Differences in responses across age cohorts are even smaller, although the three age cohorts experience slightly different types of racist incidents, and those in the oldest cohort report experiencing the most discrimination.

Beyond these structural dimensions, we initially expected that whether and how respondents react to incidents may have a lot to do with where incidents occurred. As a youth advocate pointed out concerning his experience of not being served promptly in a restaurant after also having heard an insulting remark, "I came here to eat. I didn't come here to pick into your politics or whatnot. And if you had said it ten feet further [away] I wouldn't have heard it at all." Responding or not may have to do with how hungry you are, the mood you are in, what happened earlier in the day, and whether people in the restaurant know you. Thus, we spent considerable energy assessing systematic variations in responses across types of contexts by coding each incident, where it occurred, and how the interviewee responded. Our hunch was that one cannot respond the same way in a public setting and at work. As a UPS driver said about dealing with racism, institutional support matters:

> At work . . . you can document, you got his boss you can go to. You've got a shop steward, you've got a union involved, you can document certain things, how he treats you as opposed to how he treats other people. . . . But on the streets, . . . you don't want to do something where you could wind up doing some time. . . . Think about your next move, right then and there. Don't be so quick to jump.

But to our surprise, a close look at our evidence suggests there is no clear-cut relationship between context and response.[71] Specifically, we find no systematic pattern of variation in responses based on whether the incident occurs in a public or a private space, whether it involves people with whom one interacts regularly or in an anonymous relationship, or whether the context is institutional or not.[72] A range of responses accompanies both meta-types of incidents—stigmatization and discrimination—with no significant differences.[73]

ACTUAL RESPONSES TO INCIDENTS

Confronting

Confrontation is the most frequent response to stigmatization and discrimination among African Americans. This response is enabled by the civil rights gains of the 1960s, which declared discrimination illegal; the widely available repertoires of group disadvantage; and the experiences of blatant and subtle racism described in Section 2.3. We find that four out of five respondents (81 percent) say they respond to specific incidents through confrontation. This represents 52 percent of all the 529 responses to incidents mentioned by our respondents. Confrontation is also the most frequent response among all four of the other groups studied. However, only roughly half of the Black Brazilians, Ethiopians, and Mizrahi mention this response, while it is the case for fewer than half of Arab Palestinians (38 percent). These figures are indicative of the belief that members of each group have in their ability to create change, the clarity they have about the racial or nonracial nature of incidents, and their views on the risk associated with various responses. The differences across groups are not stark, rather they are differences in emphasis and the salience of strategies.

Inductive analysis revealed four types of responses that are related to confrontation: speaking out, using formal mechanisms or the law, engaging in physical threat or intimidation, and screaming and insulting. Of these responses, the most popular among all five groups studied is "speaking out." In the United States, this response was used by 67 percent of respondents. Three-quarters of the middle-class respondents said they confronted verbally or by speaking out, compared to more than half of the working-class respondents (76 percent compared to 57 percent). In an example, Meagan, a teacher, describes how she deals with white people who cut in front of her when she is at the Pathmark (a supermarket):

> They do that all the time here. Just they're trying to be superior. . . . So I say, "You know better than this. You're not telling me, you know, [that] you're not doing that because I'm black. You're actually doing that because you're white. Because my being black has nothing to do with you." And you know, of course it comes as a shock to them. . . . [The lady who cut in front of me] never said a word. They don't want a confrontation! . . . And if you confront them, they're not going to

give you a word back, because you are not there! You understand? So I think she won't be doing that to too many black women. One woman, I actually put my foot out and tripped her.

Meagan's response is set against a history of previous and equally frustrating interactions. She feels empowered to confront the offender, so she presumes that she is in the right and that her interpretation of the situation is correct. Her confidence is enabled by ready-made scripts about racist interactions between blacks and whites, which are sustained by an awareness of racial exclusion, inequality, and history, and which confirm that she is witnessing racist behavior. A legal culture, backed by the Civil Rights Acts, convinces her that it is legitimate to stand up for oneself when facing racial slights. Her strong sense of groupness (which makes her race salient and convinces her that being cut in line has to do with racism) also feeds her confidence to respond in this way. The anonymity of the context may further enable this response. In Brazil, confronting is often done in a more low-key way, with an orientation toward educating non-blacks; but in the United States, responses are far more varied and cover the spectrum, with "scream and insult" representing a small number of responses (7 percent).

We coded what the US respondents said they were trying to accomplish by confronting and found that the response is multipurpose: in 19 percent of the incidents, respondents mentioned that they were motivated by a need to vent anger; in 15 percent they aimed to prevent further incidents; in 12 percent they aimed to seek reparations; in 12 percent they wanted to expose racism; in 10 percent they aimed to educate; and in 10 percent they aimed to demand an explanation. As such, confronting can be viewed as an antiracist response that serves long-term purposes (e.g., redefining the racial hierarchy and educating whites) as well as short-term needs (i.e., emotional release for victims or preventing other incidents).

Many respondents discuss at length the conditions that empower an effective confrontation—conditions that may include management of self. For example, in describing her response to her coworkers' jealousy of her working from home because she just had a baby, an insurance adjuster states:

> My response is usually to go somewhere and calm down because my first instinct is to curse somebody out [laughs]. But I have to go, breathe, take it easy, bring it back, calm down. And then I usually don't go to them directly. I usually go talk it out with somebody else first and say, "Look, hear me out, what do you think? Am I wrong?" And then when they say, "No," it's like, "Okay, now let me bring you and tell you how I feel, and then I take it that way."[74]

One astute interviewee reasons that it is important to confront, as some non-blacks will try to "turn it on you" and pretend that you are the racist—drawing on a repertoire of reverse racism that has gained prominence since the reversal of affirmative action in higher education by the Supreme Court in 1996. This response is in dialogue with familiar scripts about possible reactions that also inform the management of the self-response. The interviewee describes at length the importance of confronting micro-aggressions with a detailed explanation to the perpetrator, so that he or she can come to understand why his behavior is problematic.

One-third of the interviewees (35 percent) responded in ways that involved formal legal mechanisms (through unions, human resources departments, or courts). This response was used less frequently in Brazil, and it was almost totally absent in Israel, which illustrates the lack of faith members of these groups have in obtaining justice. In the United States, the Civil Rights Acts of 1964 and 1968 legislate equality based on the founding principles of the American Constitution, which has played a huge role in constructing African Americans as a group officially recognized as discriminated against de jure—unlike Mizrahi Jews in Israel (Bitton 2008). Human resources departments played a crucial role in making affirmative action a reality, and employees of large organizations are empowered to draw on these legal tools in antidiscrimination cases (Dobbin 2009). In addition, the United States has a culture of litigation that permeates all aspects of social life, with many more lawyers per capita than most advanced industrial societies (Ramseyer and Rasmusen 2010).

Lodging formal complaints through unions is an option for working-class interviewees, bolstered by the antidiscrimination rules imposed by the Equal Employment Commission created in 1965. Johnny, a man who works for UPS, describes how his Hispanic manager allowed the Hispanic workers to leave work early while requiring that black workers stay longer to retape boxes. He explains emphatically how his understanding of the union's role allowed him to deal with the situation:

> So when I [am about] to leave, [my boss] says, "No, you have to re-tape all this stuff." And I looked at him, I said, "Well, how come all your Spanish-speaking friends got to leave, and you did their re-tapes, but now because there's three black guys here left, you are not trying to—." I said, "As a matter of fact, I want my union rep over here now. I handle things in a different way. I'm not going to get loud or irate with you. I want your supervisor, I want the union rep over here because they're discriminating." ... The union rep came, and I said, "What do you see?" He said, "Three black guys taping up boxes." I said, "What else don't you see?" He said, "All the Hispanic guys are gone, and everybody else is gone." I said, "Yeah, why is that? Why did he not help us re-tape our packages? They left a whole hour before we did." He said, "All these things are going on?" I said, "You see it right here." So [my boss] got it

written up. See, because I'm one of the people that I know the system, so don't play with me. You know, the worst thing in the world is a man with knowledge. Once that man attains that knowledge, you can't do anything to him because you can't take it from him either.

Middle-class respondents also had experiences using the law or formal mechanisms. In one telling example, the son of a law administrator was suspended from a predominantly white private school because, together with other black athletes, he had attacked a white student who had started a fight. The others who were involved were also suspended and charged with assault. The son's record was cleared, because the law administrator had a prominent Newark firm write the school a legal letter. Feeling both guilty for having received privileged treatment and victimized by in-group members who were less fortunate, the administrator explained:

> Now, yes, [it was] unfair treatment [that the other teens were not absolved]. I get a letter saying he's reinstated, there's no absenteeism on his records, blah, blah, blah! It was the result of the fact that [the principal] got a letter from a prominent law firm saying "Your ass is going to get sued." Nothing else! You can see how this still bothers me. My son and I get ostracized because I had his case taken care of.... Other [black kids] that were involved got school suspensions, got some penalties at proms, suspension from teams, and had to make other appearances in court.... This is the way of the world.

Because their work life is more often regulated by union conventions and human resources departments, responding to incidents through formal complaints and legal tools is slightly more prevalent among working-class interviewees (37 percent versus 32 percent of middle-class interviewees); however, middle-class people are more likely to have the financial and emotional resources to take a legal route. As we saw in Section 2.3, the American approach to ensuring equality of opportunity in the workplace has focused on the control of discrimination instead of penalizing hate speech. US laws are extremely protective of freedom of speech (even Nazi and openly racist propaganda).[75] In Brazil, we will see that legal tools are also available, but are used more rarely and not as efficiently (see Chapter 3). In Israel it was only in 2008 that the Equality of Opportunity Commission established mechanisms for dealing with discrimination in the workforce, and the law is only sporadically enforced (Ben-Israel and Foubert 2004).

Other less popular forms of confrontation are making physical threats and intimidating stigmatizers. These may be unavoidable in a context of continuous tensions, but such responses are widely condemned, and many respondents express concern about the aggravated intergroup tensions that result. The same can be said about responding through screaming and insulting (an even less frequent response). In the American context, in which a universalist orientation is normative, confronting is best accomplished by staying calm.

Confronting is also salient as an idealized response to racism. When we asked interviewees, "What is the best approach for dealing with racism?" a large number (64 percent) favored responses involving confronting. Again, the recent history of the Civil Rights Movement and of legal gains reaffirms their view that it is legitimate for African Americans to stand up and denounce bigotry and social injustice. Only a small number (13 percent) believe the best approach to deal with racism is what we coded as "conflict deflating" approaches—that is, accepting, ignoring, forgiving, or walking. The other respondents (33 percent) spoke of mixed strategies, consisting of both picking battles and tolerating—responses that correspond broadly to our "management of the self" category.

When it comes to confrontation as a response to actual incidents or as an ideal response, class differences are noticeable. Among middle-class respondents, 86 percent used confrontation in response to actual incidents, compared to 71 percent of the working-class respondents. The numbers for confronting as an ideal response are similar, with 79 percent of the middle class using this approach, compared to 65 percent of workers. These figures are consistent with our expectations: we predicted that middle-class interviewees would react more aggressively to racism and choose confrontation more often than would working-class respondents. Our prediction was based on literature showing that middle-class people have more resources, better market positions, a greater sense of entitlement (Skeggs 2004: 173–74), higher political participation (Bartels 2009), and a tradition of collective mobilization for the promotion of their class and racial group (Brown 2013). However, the literature also points to reasons we could expect the middle class to be less confrontational and to engage in more individualistic responses— what Lacy (2004) calls "strategic assimilation." Specifically, our middle-class respondents experience slightly more integrated environments at work and at school than do the working-class respondents, and middle-class blacks, compared with working-class blacks, in general face implicit as opposed to blatant racism, which may be more difficult to confront (Hochschild 1996: 216.) This is compounded by the fact that conflict avoidance is more often the norm in bureaucratic middle-class work environments (Morrill 1995), where the risks of confrontation impacting one's career may be higher (Jackall 2010) compared to working-class environments, where a strong culture of resistance (Willis 1977) and culture of masculinity may encourage confrontation (Nixon 2009). Moreover, a desire to avoid confirming stereotypes about "angry blacks" and blacks "making excuses" by decrying racism may also discourage confrontation and encourage resorting to individual strategies of mobility. It is possible that these different pulls and pushes produce more confrontation in the middle class relative to the working class, but contradictory forces temper what may otherwise be even more confrontation in the middle class.

With regard to the use of confrontation among the three age cohorts, we expected that older groups (those who came of age before or slightly after the Civil Rights Movement) would be more assimilationist in orientation and that younger respondents might adopt an oppositional stance, promoted by hip hop culture, and express more concern for "getting respect" and for giving voice to their racial and cultural authenticity than for being accepted by whites (Kitwana 2002; Carter 2005; Patterson and Fosse 2015). Alternatively, younger African Americans could be less confrontational and draw weaker boundaries in relation to members of other ethnoracial groups, because they have had more exposure to a discourse of universalism, diversity, multiculturalism, and openness (Warikoo and de Novais 2014) and because this group is more sensitized to multiculturalism and the celebration of diversity (Alba and Nee 2005; Hochschild, Weaver, and Burch 2012).

But there is more: the Black Power Movement, and the Civil Rights Movement generally, were extraordinarily successful at mobilizing African Americans to assert their rights and to affirm and celebrate their cultural distinctiveness and collective identity in the 1950s and 1960s. They also transformed the meaning of blackness for both whites and blacks, effectively contesting once-dominant stereotypes about the innate inferiority of African Americans and making blatant racism normatively unacceptable in American society. We believed that this changing backdrop and associated generational experiences would influence the responses to racism, making older respondents more likely to choose confrontation, because their generation participated in the social movements leading to social change.

What we found is that there are great similarities in responses across age groups, with small differences in emphasis: the older group is more likely to confront, but by a very small margin (nine out of ten compared to three out of four for the younger group). The older group engages in management of the self in similar frequency and does not respond slightly more often than the younger group (half of the older group versus a third of the younger group). Otherwise, few differences stand out. While the sample numbers are very small and thus difficult to interpret, they do show consistency in the patterns of differences, which is compatible with the fact that older respondents say they experience discrimination more often than younger ones do.

This is consistent with the fact that the Civil Rights Movement and the desegregation era left a profound impression on those growing up during that time. For instance, an insurance adjuster reported that when she was a child, her family moved into a predominantly white neighborhood in northern New Jersey. The neighbors would taunt her family by yelling,

"N[igger] go home! N[igger] go back!" The family never felt comfortable in their new home and did not socialize with their neighbors. Similarly, a social worker remembers facing a confrontation in the school parking lot when all the white students came to school with bricks in their car trunks. "It was our version of the Ku Klux Klan because they were so prepared. Even the guys that played football with blacks, they had all the rocks and stuff in their car. It was so strange. I ran, and I went to hide in the school." The school principal suspended half of the black kids and only about ten of the white kids, although both groups engaged in violence. Such experiences of blatant racism have left their mark on older respondents and how they understand and deal with racism.

Management of the Self and Not Responding

The second most frequent type of response by African Americans (26 percent of all responses, offered by half of the respondents) is what we have dubbed "management of the self," which involves considering various scenarios prior to responding. The third most popular response is not responding (22 percent of all responses to incidents, adopted by 45 percent of the interviewees). Considering these two types of responses together, it is striking that 48 percent of all responses to incidents could be seen by an outsider as non-events.

With management of the self, the individual spends substantial time considering pragmatic constraints, including the material, professional, and emotional costs (and benefits) of various types of responses. US respondents report reflecting on the best response with the goal of, for instance, presenting themselves in a positive light,[76] saving their energy, or avoiding confirmation of stereotypes about blacks (e.g., the angry black woman). This response is also popular in Brazil, where management of the self was mentioned by 55 percent of all respondents. Interestingly, it is quite rare across the three Israeli groups, among whom non-responses are more frequent.

Our inductive analysis led us to identify five subcategories of management of the self responses: acting against stereotypes, preservation of self or energy, humor, managing anger (picking one's battles), and strategic silence (see Table A2.2 in Appendix 2). For instance, in responding to the fact that white clients frequently mistake his white employees as "the boss," a financial expert wants to avoid being seen as "paranoid," thus confirming a widely held stereotype about African Americans. Rather than confronting, he favors fostering his reputation as a competent professional, because, as he puts it, "numbers are numbers," and he purposefully "hides behind" numbers, his area of expertise. Still he adds, "When they meet me in person, it's like [they think], 'Was it you I was trusting?'" This respondent combines a display of competence and management of the self to avoid being perceived as the "angry black" (coded as "acting against stereotypes"). Another chooses to not respond, so as to avoid being emotionally drained or "caught in a spiral" and risking being permanently angry (which we coded as "self-preservation" and "manage anger/pick battles"). Still others (only 6 percent) may choose to respond through humor (for a detailed analysis of our interviews concerning this question, see Hirsch 2014) or to not respond so as not to reveal their inner feelings (what we call "strategic silence"). The active consideration of various ways of responding is not without consequence, as the deliberating and worrying may contribute to the toxic stress that results in racial disparities in health (Shonkoff et al. 2012).

Of all these types of management-of-the-self responses, management for self-preservation is the most common, being mentioned by 30 percent of the interviewees. For instance, a social worker who talks about white people trying to cut in front of her as she waits in line in stores (a frequently mentioned issue) says she is tired of fighting and draws on religious repertoires. Her response contrasts strongly with the response described earlier of another woman to the same type of incident:

> A: I try not to look at that [as racism] . . . I see family members and friends cussing someone out, saying, "Oh that, just cause she white." I don't tend to think like that at all. However, there have been times where I'm saying, "I'm next . . . I am standing here." [I have an] aunt that would say [to me], "You just don't want to recognize it for what it is." [She] says [that] I'm naïve, and maybe I am, but I just don't want to fight all the time. You have to pick your battles.
> Q: Why do you not want to focus on race all the time?
> A: Because [I feel] tired. . . . I mean, there could be a thousand other reasons as to why the incident occurred. . . . That again could be my faith and what I'm taught spiritually. As a spiritual person you always want to see the good and say, "No, Lord, I know this ain't what it is." . . . I'm a woman of peace.

Another respondent, a teacher, explains that he suffered discrimination at work where he "became marginalized." In response to being advised to be a team player and less confrontational, he tried to conform to racialized expectations to keep his job:

> Honestly, you know, I'm bo-jangling and tap dancing. I'm doing a lot more smiling. You want to be liked so that you'll debunk the stereotype that you inevitably have of you being hostile . . . because you find yourself not having the economic roots to sort of just be in a position to say, "You know what? I don't need this, and I can be free to say what I want." So, you bo-jingle it out of there, and you say, "Okay, well, I'll keep that in mind."

This quote illustrates how this man, while responding, is in dialogue with widely held stereotypes about blacks at the same time as he considers constraints on how he can respond. Along similar lines, a former nurse explains her attitude toward an Indian patient who believed that Indians are better than blacks: "I said to myself, 'Just sit quietly and listen and learn, because he is full of himself, and he's ignorant enough to actually voice these opinions. So learn from it.' . . . In my younger days, I might have cussed him out and gotten mad and all that stuff. But as I was saying, I want the job a little longer."

Several respondents mention the importance of managing their anger and picking their battles (26 percent), the second most popular form of management of the self. For instance, an educator describes his reaction to an insulting interaction: "I try to be cool and collected. I try to think about all my upbringing and stuff." Similarly, a minister describes his reactions as anger management motivated by a desire not to confirm stereotypes: "I don't react in a negative way. I win them over with kindness. . . . Just let them know I'm not what you think, and I'm sorry that you feel that way because if you understood history you wouldn't think that way. . . . Pick up a book and read. Understand my history as well as I understand yours." A female coordinator reflects on her transition toward anger management from a more confrontational response to whites:

When I went through the militant period, I didn't trust white people at all. Maybe [it lasted] a year or two. I would go to black events, I hung out with black people. . . . With my black friends we would vent about things they had experienced, racial experiences, so you weren't by yourself. . . . Eventually I changed because it wasn't going anywhere. And I felt like I was being eaten up with hate and I was standing still. I could just continue to hate or I could maybe do something to change it, you know. And so I just decided to become more people-friendly and to see if maybe I could try to work to create a fair environment.

While the responses that we coded as management of the self are ones where interviewees reported reflection, planning, and deliberation with regard to their responses, we coded as "non-response" instances where they said they simply did not respond. To explain their non-responses, they reported a range of circumstances, such as "I was startled," "My mind was on other things," "I really did not care," "I kind of expected it; it does not surprise me," "I just moved on," or "It's their problem, not mine." One interviewee recalls that when he was a teenager, one of his teachers was telling ethnic jokes and he let it slide, "I didn't really say anything because, being that young, you view it as that stuff being funny, as him being a comedian, stuff like that. So, you really kind of look at it and say, 'Well he really can't be a racist or a bigot because he talks about everybody.'"

In the US case, 45 percent of the respondents engaged in non-responses at least once, compared to 53 percent of the Black Brazilians and only respectively 24, 21, and 5 percent, respectively, of Arab Palestinians, Mizrahi, and Ethiopians. (Note, however, that the numbers for Israel are small.) In the United States, non-responses represent 22 percent of all responses.

We included in this category three types of non-response: ignoring an incident; avoiding a stigmatizing situation or people; and not responding due to circumstantial reasons, shock, or passivity. Nearly all non-responses in the United States pertain to not responding due to shock, passivity, or circumstances. More than a third (37 percent) of our interviewees reported this kind of response. A case in point is a graphic designer who was stopped by the police:

> Basically, I show them my ID, give them all my information, they go check it out, and then they come back, give me the stuff and says, "Have a nice day," and I'm like—. It just is one of those things where they take their chances figuring that they're gonna find something, and when they don't, they don't feel like they've lost any sleep. So I'm not gonna lose any sleep over it.

We find minimal class differences with regard to management of the self. Again, this is not what we expected. Based on social science literature, which has pointed to the great salience of emotional work in service jobs (Hochschild 1983; Leidner 1993) and in the largely middle-class-based therapeutic culture of self-actualization more generally (Illouz 2008), we expected a higher frequency of management of the self among the middle class, with its culture of moral pragmatism, and lower frequency in the working class, where management of the self is somewhat antithetical to a working-class habitus centered on sincerity and authenticity (Bourdieu 1984; Lamont 2000; Nixon 2009).

We only found class differences in management of the self after we refined our class categories to compare a narrowed middle class (only professionals and managers with a college degree—results not included in Table A2.2) to all other respondents. With this refinement, we found that slightly more working-class than middle-class respondents (narrowly defined) engage in management of the self (52 percent versus 41 percent). Differences are starkest when it comes to statements we coded as "managing the self for preservation" (only 8 professionals and managers, compared to 37 workers). This finding may be accounted for by the lower job autonomy that workers experience in the workplace, and the fact that workers live in environments where physical violence may be more frequent, and guarded responses are therefore more necessary.

Among all categories of responses, the biggest gender difference is in management of the self, where 59 percent of men mention it compared with 38 percent of women. This resonates with broadly available gendered scripts construing black males as prone to aggressiveness and physical violence (Jackson and Wingfield 2013). Men may feel they must engage in management of the self if they want to eschew perilous situations that can lead to violence or to more racial tension. An insurance salesman remembers one such interaction with a former boss:

> A: Some of the supervisors that I deal with, they have a problem with a "black man with a beard." Some study has shown from sales that a lot of people have a hard time dealing with this figure, this persona here.
> Q: What kind of signals did they send you that they might be uncomfortable?
> A: The dismissive nature in how they do business, that's the main thing, especially with the one. Her name is Angela. . . . It's just that holier-than-thou, dismissive attitude, that condescending tone that they take. . . . I give you that respect, I'm demanding it in return, and she is just very standoffish. . . . [What I do then is] kill them with kindness. You go that little bit extra, but you have to do it in a strong, confident manner because if you show a sign of weakness, yeah, they are going to keep on doing it. . . . It's that you have to exude that confidence even in the roughest situation

The challenge of not being viewed as threatening and yet showing confidence to avoid being dominated is acute for black men. So are the dangers of racial profiling and potential incarceration, which are less salient for black women. A graphic designer explains that his responses to racism are always constrained by possible consequences, "because you gotta think of where you are. All you need is for them to call the police and get in trouble. Me, I am like the person that always tells people, 'Don't ever add fuel to the fire,' you know." For this respondent and many others, the high incarceration rate for African American men looms large as they consider appropriate responses. We will see that this affects the lessons they give their children about how to deal with racism.

IDEAL AND OTHER ACTUAL RESPONSES

Competence/Hard Work, Self-Improvement, Education, Religion, and Moral Reform: The Neoliberal Responses

We now turn to responses that are connected to the focus on self-improvement and individualism encouraged by neoliberalism. While some of these responses (e.g., demonstrating hard work) are related to actual incidents, others concern ideal responses as tapped through queries about group tools and best approaches for responding to racism. This is particularly the case for responses regarding self-improvement, education, religion, and moral reform.

In our interviews, only one respondent in five (or 19 percent) described actual incidents to which they responded by demonstrating their work ethic or by trying to establish their equality through competence. This is a surprisingly low proportion when one considers the salience of hard work and effort in the myth of the American Dream (Hochschild 1996). While these interviewees' responses to actual incidents are constrained by necessity, this is not the case with their reflections on ideal responses. Indeed, demonstrating competence and willingness to work hard make up a significant portion of the interviewees' ideal responses to racism, where interviewees may be implicitly dialoguing with dominant cultural repertoires about how to gain cultural membership and with stereotypes about the lack of self-reliance among African Americans.

One example of such a work/competence-focused response comes from a teacher who, while in graduate school, felt that her professors asked more from black students than from others. Her response was to "just work harder. If a professor gives an assignment and they say read a book, I'll go beyond. They say, give 100 percent. I give 110 percent, 120 percent." However, other respondents are more skeptical of this strategy and explain that they are not encouraging their children to follow a similar path. A legal administrator compared what his mother taught him about how to respond to racism with how he approaches this issue with his own children:

> My mother told me . . . "Don't worry about it, you'll be successful if you outwork everybody." Did I instill that in my kids? Probably not! I taught my kids, "Fuck 'em! You're as good as anybody else." [laughter] I didn't say it like that to them, but essentially [I tell them], "You're as good as anybody else, you're equal to anybody else. Do what you have to do, but be mindful that you're going to have to compete against everybody. And, you don't step on people, okay? I mean you'll find out in this world that you have to have some sense of what's right and wrong."

The focus on work ethic and education as means for mobility follows from individualist explanations of the lower achievements of blacks that have gained popularity in recent years, in part under the influence of neoliberalism. Indeed, Hunt (2007) has shown the declining importance of discrimination in explanations among blacks of racial inequality between 1997 and 2004. This change parallels a turn toward individual effort and work ethic when explaining the reasons for differences in socioeconomic status.

In the same vein, if blacks are blamed for their plights (teen pregnancy, violence, and crime) by whites, and to a lesser extent by blacks themselves,[77] then the idealized solution is to be found in moral reform, with a renewed focus on self-improvement, education, and upward mobility. Indeed, when queried about normative responses, and specifically about group tools that blacks have at their disposal to improve their situation, the majority of respondents (73 percent) offer responses that are centered on self-improvement. As is the case for most Americans experiencing long-term unemployment studied by Sharone (2014), many of our interviewees appear to embrace self-reliance and self-blaming when faced with unemployment (see also Silva 2013). Similarly, Welburn and Pittman (2012) find that the majority of middle-class African Americans they interviewed believe that mobility results from individual efforts, although they also believe structural factors limit their mobility. This paradoxical response, which Hunt (1996) has described as "dual consciousness," is again confirmed by our results.

This insistence on self-improvement is implicit in dialogue with the dominant stereotypes of blacks that are widely held by whites. According to Krysan (2012: 241), who draws on General Social Survey data, between 1990 and 2002 "the percentage of whites rating blacks as lazier than whites declined from 65 to 44 percent . . . [as did] the [lower] intelligence stereotypes (from 56 percent to 32 percent). Moreover, in 2002, the reason most often offered by whites for racial inequality was 'blacks' lack of motivation and will power to work their way out of poverty.'" But our interviewees' responses are also shaped by how they view the obstacles that African Americans face. Drawing on responses to the same question, Hirsch and Jack (2012) found that both our middle- and working-class interviewees believe that racism remains the most significant problem facing African Americans. Middle-class respondents believe that lack of racial solidarity and economic problems, respectively, are the second and third most significant problems facing African Americans. In contrast, working-class respondents believe that fragility of the African American family is the second most significant problem, and that racial solidarity comes in third place. Being not so distant from lower-class blacks (Pattillo-McCoy 1999), members of this group may be more concerned with the moral issues often associated with the fragility of the black family, such as father absenteeism, teen pregnancy, and low levels of child supervision (Edin and Kefalas 2005; McLanahan and Garfinkel 2012). At the same time, as Hirsch and Jack (2012) comment, concerns for fragile families and economic problems point to the importance of self-reliance among blacks.

Neoliberal transformations have increased the emphasis on individualism and the privatization of risk in institutionalized conceptions of worth and in the redistribution of resources (Hall and Lamont 2013; Block and Somers 2014; see also Pew Forum on Religion & Public Life 2008), intensifying demands that blacks be more self-reliant. Regardless of whether

African Americans embrace this injunction, they are in dialogue with it as they reflect on how to respond to racism, just as they are in dialogue with widely held stereotypes about the fragility of the .black family and moral issues.

Based on Lamont and Fleming (2005), we expected middle-class interviewees to respond to racism by referring to self-improvement and by affirming their membership in American society at large through conformity to the standards of consumption and liberal individualism, even at the risk of promoting norms of membership that exclude poor African Americans (i.e., implicitly or explicitly defining those who cannot consume as outsiders). This would mean seeking opportunity and education as the bases of social membership. Middle- and working-class people value both education and seeking opportunity roughly equally in the context of recession (as in 2007–2008, when our interviews were conducted), when insecurity is high. In addition, given that, compared to the black upper-middle class, black working-class and lower-middle-class people have less social and spatial distance from the poor (Pattillo-McCoy 1999), we could expect working-class individuals to want to distance themselves from the poor and aim to show that widely held stereotypes of African American men as violent or criminal (Quillian and Pager 2001) do not apply to them. This may lead to a particularly strong investment in self-improvement among the black working class and lower-middle class. Indeed, we find a slight difference: 78 percent of our working class respondents zeroed in on self-improvement as a group tool against racism, compared to 69 percent for the middle class.

Individual versus Collective Self-Improvement; The Case of Self-Segregation. Having outlined various neoliberal responses above, we now delve into particular self-improvement responses. Considering again ideal responses, we find that interviewees are generally more concerned with individual, as opposed to collective, self-improvement. However, the two are often understood as deeply intertwined, which adds a distinctive wrinkle to the question of the impact of the privatization of risk and individualism in response to neoliberalism. Among the US interviewees' responses centered on self-improvement (offered by three-fourths of the interviewees, or 73 percent), self-improvement is to be demonstrated through seeking education (in 60 percent of the responses), seeking opportunities (20 percent), seeking work (11 percent), and gaining financial acuity (4 percent).

We closely analyzed patterns of responses to identify (1) whether education, opportunity, work, and financial acuity have to do with the improvement of oneself, society as a whole, or African Americans in particular; and (2) whether respondents were more concerned with gaining human capital (market-related skills) and cultural capital or with improving their knowledge of their group's culture and history. We wanted to ascertain the relationship between the pursuit of education, culture, and knowledge on the one hand, and individual and collective mobility and self-pride on the other hand. These questions are important, given the centrality of individualism under neoliberalism and also the rich legacy of black mobilization in favor of social justice and collective empowerment.

In a little more than half of the cases (59 out of 111 mentions), references to education concerned improvement of the self, primarily through gaining human capital (28 mentions) or cultural capital (22 mentions). In only three cases were interviewees concerned with improving society in general, while in 36 cases they were concerned with improving the situation of African Americans (with 18 of these instances referring to improving knowledge about collective identity and history). Thirty-four mentions of "seeking opportunities" concerned the improvement of an individual's prospects, while 16 out of 18 mentions of "work" viewed it as a tool for self-improvement. Therefore, although there were mentions of self-improvement that concerned the situation of blacks as a group (46 out of 169), the focus was more often improvement of the individual (102 out of 169). These findings about the relative scarcity of a collectivist orientation are of relevance to contemporary discussions about black solidarity and the role of the black elite in social change (e.g., Shelby 2007), and they deserve further analysis.

Given the low salience of collective approaches, it is not surprising that less than one in five interviewees (14 percent) respond to incidents via maximizing his/her autonomy from whites, including through self-segregation or boycotting white institutions. This is a small number, given the important traditions of black nationalism, separatism, Afrocentrism, and self-determination in African American thought, as articulated by some of the most prominent African American intellectuals, from Booker T. Washington to Marcus Garvey and Malcolm X (on black nationalism as a major strand of black political ideologies, see Dawson 2001). The strong focus on individual self-improvement and the relative scarcity of isolation and autonomy as a response to racism are fed by a similar decline of black nationalism and separatism in favor of individualist approaches that are at the heart of the American Dream and of neoliberalism more generally.

Of course, it is quite possible that black nationalist respondents were not inclined to participate in our study and are thus underrepresented among our interviewees. Such respondents would draw the starkest distinctions between blacks and non-blacks and emphasize the power relationship between whites and blacks, as does this operations manager, who recalls his mother's view of whites: "My mother would always make statements like 'You have to deal with them, you don't have to live with them.'... She would say, 'You have to go out in the world, and they control a lot of things. But at the end of the day, you come home and you are with yourself.'"

This man's mother pointed to the necessity of interaction with whites, because whites make up a large portion of the population. However, this situation can be antithetical to friendship or mutuality. A historical relationship of domination, exploitation, and racism is the background for such a response. It is enabled by repeated experiences of being isolated and discriminated against when with whites, and, in some cases, of being supported, validated, and more comfortable with blacks. An army employee who explains why she moved to a predominantly black university after attending an integrated college where she was the only black student in the nursing program expresses this perspective. She describes how at the integrated college, her teachers were:

> not giving me the attention I needed, and I just felt like this is not for me. When I had assignments, nobody was there to talk with me [or] to lead me into what I am supposed to do. So I said, "You know, I will go through this for a year, but I am not staying. I am going to go to an all-black university." . . . That's where I went, and I was happy because I was around black folks, and they would talk to you. . . . Being in a black university where I was with people like me, you know, I felt more comfortable and everything.

As the high number of ideal responses focused on individual self-improvement indicates, to choose to be "with your own" after facing discrimination is not the only possible course of action. In the twenty-first century, black solidarity is challenged by growing individualism, at a time when neoliberal values encourage a privatization of risk, greater distancing between the middle class and the poor, and growing competition among blacks.

"It All Begins with Education." The pursuit of education looms large as a response to ethnoracial exclusion, as many interviewees echo the view of one respondent who commented, "It all begins with education." As many as 60 percent of our interviewees mention education as a group tool for responding to racism. This is not surprising, as the sociological literature has offered ample evidence of the high level of investment in education by African Americans—in particular, of African American students (together with Asian students) consistently report more positive attitudes about school than do white students (Ainsworth-Darnell and Downey 1998; on the importance of education to black professional women, see also Higginbotham and Weber 1992). Our US respondents voiced a variety of reasons for why they value education: the pursuit of personal growth and development, increased mobility (often stemming from formal education), gaining informal knowledge or broadening African American understanding of how society works, or gaining self-knowledge (i.e., familiarizing blacks with their heritage, history, and identity).

The quest for formal education is particularly salient in our interviews and is given many meanings, with a focus on intrinsic or extrinsic rewards.

Some value it as leading to individual development. A female entrepreneur explains that "reading is fundamental, education is fundamental so that you have more to expound on. . . . It's kind of like a father teaching a son how to use a hammer or something like that." Others value access to information per se. This is the case for a court administrator who, in response to our question about best group tools to improve the African Americans' situation, points to the value of all aspects of learning, including going to school, going to the library regularly, using the internet, and having a computer at home. Similarly, a fashion buyer stresses self-education:

> I was one that was pretty much self-taught. I'd go through the *Reader's Digest*, and I'd learn a new word every week. There were certain things I'd seek out. If I had a question about why black and why white, why are you prejudiced, I would ask, you know. . . . A lot of people are afraid to take that step or to ask questions or even to leave their neighborhood because they don't know what's on the other side of the river.

Thus, education is about gaining information, which is at the time connected to the broader goal of self-development. In the words of a school counselor, the goal is to gain "resources of information to broaden your mind, yourself for personal growth, anyway." Yet for others, education is approached more instrumentally and is, above all, a resource for gaining employment. It is directly tied to jobs and opportunities for which knowledge is a tool or a means of access. This is the view of an auditor who says about African Americans: "[They should have] the opportunity to get an education and to be gainfully employed, and to have their children have more access to social and economic, how should I say it, potential. You know, to be what they want to be the best that they can."

Most of the mentions of education as a best approach to address racism stress improving the situation of the individual rather than that of the community. A detailed analysis of these references to education ($N = 42$) reveals that respondents are concerned with both formal education (schooling) and informal education (combating ignorance among both white racists and blacks) and that these mentions concerned informal or formal education for blacks (18 mentions), for whites and blacks (13 mentions), and for whites only (11 mentions). It is remarkable that no other non-black groups (such as Latinos or Asians) are mentioned. This reflects the history of racial relations but not the current ethnoracial landscape of the New York metropolitan area, where immigrants make up almost half the population (Kasinitz et al. 2008).

Another group of respondents is primarily concerned with blacks' self-knowledge, which is a crucial condition for fostering recognition, strong collective identification, and mobilization. A prison instructor said that, for him, getting an education means "not even just running to the universities.

I'm talking about a self-education. Run to the library, learn your history, you know?" He values knowledge as a tool for strengthening group identity through gaining familiarity with the history of black Americans. Along the same lines, a law administrator connects self-knowledge with the pursuit of success. Bringing together knowledge of the history of African Americans and the tools for upward mobility, he says of young African Americans: "If they understand 'from whence we came,' as the saying goes, they'd understand 'where we have to go.' There would be . . . a better sense of history, there would be a greater urgency as a whole."

Some interviewees also discuss the importance of educating non-blacks about black culture, that is, making racists and non-blacks more aware of black culture or of the life conditions of blacks, as many consider whites in particular as cut off from the broader reality and diversity of American society. This is hardly surprising, given the high degree of spatial segregation discussed in Section 2.1 and the frequency with which respondents say they are misunderstood by whites. Fourteen percent of responses to the question concerning the best way to deal with racism fall under this category (which we labeled "informal education" as an approach for dealing with racism). More working than middle-class respondents advocate this strategy (21 percent compared to 8 percent), which is likely related to their frequent exposure to bigotry—while symbolic racism is more prevalent in middle-class milieus (Kinder and Sears 1981). Other class differences are much smaller, even insignificant.

Greater identification with one's group has been associated with higher educational success among children of low-income minority groups (Oyserman, Bybee, and Terry 2006) and is a significant factor in building collective resilience (Hall and Lamont 2013). Greater awareness of a collective identity provides intersubjective validation and supports a form of recognition that sustains collective well-being (Honneth 1995; Sandelson 2014). Many respondents point to the decline of such knowledge among African Americans and deplore its detrimental effects. Commenting on the messages circulating in the broader environment in which he grew up, a social worker notes:

> When I was coming up, they talked about slavery, they talked about Sojourner Truth, and they talked about the Underground Railroad. So you had things to identify with that brought you from there to here. The young people today, they don't know about that, so they really have nothing to identify with. And I think that's a part of the problem.

In line with the literature (e.g., Chandler and Lalonde 1998 on aboriginals in Canada), this social worker points to the importance of self-knowledge for building pride and collective resilience. He also stresses the need for more moral reform (particularly in the family) and for leadership for young people: "If you're in your home, your parents, they have to lead you, they have to guide you.... They're not being guided, so they have no direction. So that's why the jailhouses are full." Similarly, many other respondents connect education to moral reform. When asked about group tools to improve African Americans' situation, one respondent answers: "If the families stick together, they are going to tell the kids, 'Okay, you got to go to school! You got to learn to take care of yourself! You can't be on welfare! Okay, you got to stand on your own feet!'"

The topic of moral reform requires closer examination. When asked about best tools for improving the situation for blacks, a small group of respondents expressed concern with strengthening the black family and strengthening values (one out of five, or 19 percent). There is a perceived crisis of moral values in the black community, as described dramatically by an investor:

> Some leader needs to come up with commandments and say, "Listen, black people, listen, this is where we go on from right now, you need to be blah-blah-blah-blah. We are going to agree to not kill each other! We are going to agree to get educated! We are going to agree to love our family. We are going to agree to stay without those drugs, and we are going to agree to own more stuff!"... You got to have a chart of agreements, values, and standards that we live by, and if you do that, guess what, our kids ... will grow up adhering to that. Right now there is no guidance, there is no guidelines.... The churches have failed miserably because a lot of blacks can't relate to Christianity, they can't relate to Baptism and Methodism.

Child-rearing is often singled out as an area in need of improvement. An insurance adjuster, for instance, notes that black and Latino parents don't show up for parent-teacher conferences. Remembering a recent experience, she says, "Me and my husband were the only parents in the class that showed up, out of the 20-something kids.... Parents need to be more involved.... By the time they come to 16, it's not 'Well, where is he?' [He's] where you sent him—to the streets!" This woman implicitly dialogues with the culture-of-poverty arguments that blame the plights of African Americans (drugs, low marital rates, high out-of-wedlock birth rates, high incarceration rates, high unemployment, etc.) on a dysfunctional culture (for a critique, see Harding, Lamont, and Small 2010). Implied in her words is the view that blacks should take responsibility for the problems they face and engage in moral reform.

The Surprisingly Low Salience of Religion and Spirituality. Only 16 of our respondents (12 percent) pointed to religion and spirituality as tools for improving the situation of blacks. Why there were so few is puzzling and may be tied to the relatively low religious involvement of our respondents compared to most African Americans. Only 84 (out of 150) say they are involved in a faith-based community organization (with 59 self-described as Christian, 18 as Muslim, and 7 as "other"). Moreover, when asked, "what is the most important aspect of your life?" only 26 interviewees spoke of a church or organized religion, and only 26 mentioned spirituality, faith, or their relationship with God or a higher power. This level of religious involvement is considerably lower than that found in the African American population as a whole. Indeed, according to the US Religious Landscape Survey, conducted in 2007, 87 percent of African Americans describe themselves as belonging to some religious group (Pew Forum on Religion & Public Life 2008: 40). These percentages are slightly smaller in the Northeast, where our research site is located, than in the South (86 percent versus 91 percent; Pew Forum on Religion & Public Life 2008). Fifty-two percent of the Northeast black population surveyed said they belong to a historically black church against 64 percent for black Southerners (with a national average of 59 percent).

Among the 16 who spoke of religion and spirituality as group tools, a few interviewees single out the strength they get from faith or prayer, which they connect with the cultural identity and history of African Americans. A minister (who is also a part-time salesman) not surprisingly responds to our question about group tools by pointing to spirituality. He says blacks should respond "spiritually. We always go back to, to our roots. God is the only reason that we have come this far, because we didn't have anything else to lean on." Similarly, a social worker describes the group tools to combat racism with one word: "Jesus!" She explains that if improvement is to come, "it's gonna have to be through their faith. They have to start there and start believing in they can change." Another minister explains how religion can serve as a collective resource, using the "crab-in-the-barrel" metaphor (which refers to the collective holding back an individual who attempts to leave and get ahead of the collective) as a counterexample:

> I found that those that have strong spiritual ties, no matter what they believe in, tend to gyrate and play off of the strengths, and upon doing so, were able to get further and do better.... But here with the African American people, once that was our strength, but it seems as though it's become a weakness because we're like crabs in the pail. I will say that our strongest asset should be our ties to God.

A respondent who works as an army contractor points to the importance of religious institutions as a group tool when he says, "Church should be there, should be number one—the pastor, the leaders of the church, the youth leaders. You got to have a strong youth leader in the church to help to connect the community of young folks." Taking a slightly different tack, a development expert explains: "If there's one institution that a lot of people may go and support, it is the church. They have to play a bigger role."

Thus, religious institutions as well as spirituality are viewed as having an important role to play in supporting collective resilience. Studies have demonstrated the positive role of religion in relation to health (e.g., Williams and Sternthal 2007) and in constructing moral boundaries around the in-group, thus ensuring a sense of responsibility and collective worth (Higginbotham 1994; see also Lamont 2000). Moreover, religion and spirituality are often constructed as essential sources of strength (e.g., in giving up smoking, where it has been shown that African Americans put more faith in God than in taking medication; Shields, Najafzadeh, and Schachter 2013).

Decline of Collective Mobilization

When questioned about the best tools African Americans have to improve their situation, a subgroup of respondents (27 percent, $N = 37$) mentioned collective tools having to do with in-group solidarity and networks of support as well as collective mobilization. Indeed, they value helping other in-group members (26 out of 37 respondents mention this). An even larger number of respondents value belonging to such organizations as the NAACP (with 41 respondents mentioned belonging to such organizations when probed in a separate question). Finally, they emphasize the importance of providing role models (mentioned by ten individuals), who at times are also seen as leaders of moral reform.

An editor who advocates developing more role models stresses the importance of narratives for resilience. She says she values the stories that are exchanged in the media and elsewhere about the achievement of African Americans: "Reading other peoples' stories definitely serves as inspiration and just seeing that somebody else has done it before you." When asked what can bring African Americans together, she says: "Definitely celebrating the people in the community who are doing things that need to be celebrated. Seeing examples of people doing well [helps]. . . . And it's just, like, a race toward mediocrity. People don't strive for excellence. . . . It wasn't always like that, so I'm told." Similarly, a male educator reminisces about a time when role models were more readily available:

> We have self-esteem problems in our community. In order to rectify this, I try to be somebody that not only children can look up to and relate to, but somebody that can help them nurture what talents and gifts they have. . . . When I was coming up, you could see people in the community that were role models, like Dr. John [who] lived around the corner. . . . And then we had things like "father and son dinners" in

school, and that we couldn't even do now. The gym teacher Mr. Milter, he was the father of two guys like myself.... Now, he was a role model to me, and he was my first black male teacher.

A dozen respondents mention, as valuable group tools, using and developing social networks for support or as sources of information essential to success. Echoing the literature on the impact of social networks on well-being (Berkman and Glass 2000), these respondents understand the very existence of black communities as collective resources for success. When asked about group tools, an employee of a job center says, "We have each other, for one. We usually have good support systems, be they work, church, family, friends." A train conductor answers by saying, "We have to work with each other and uplift each other, and that's the only way we can do it. We have to pool our knowledge, our resources.... It takes a village to raise a child." Along the same lines, pointing to the importance of community organizations, a developer says: "Church needs to play a bigger role in bringing back the family. We've got to look at more of our men organizations.... Anything from 100 Black Men, to Big Brothers/Big Sisters, and those other types [of] little community-based organizations. We've got to use those social networks to begin to address some of our ills."

Several respondents mention collective resources (such as money) as important for developing African American communities. A carpenter stresses the importance of self-determination (led by the black elite) when he explains that in the United States, "billions of dollars circulate through our fingers. If we start channeling [it], we could empower ourselves. Our own institutions could have a global impact, you know.... It's not going to be as a people, it's going to be as the intellectual community—come together and structure a plan for the people. This is where we'll get our empowerment, you know."

That only a quarter of our respondents mention collective resources as a type of group tool is evidence of the decline of the collective approaches to social change that were behind the success of the Civil Rights Movement (Payne 1995; McAdam 1988; Polletta 2002). Some respondents are nostalgic about a time when African Americans were more oriented toward helping one another. A female minister remembers how things were "back then":

If I'm a teacher for a living, I go to the after-school program to make sure that Sally can read above grade level. If I make a lot of money, I will pick three kids to make sure, [that you get] whatever you need, because you've demonstrated the drive and all. When I was in school, I used to get these little envelopes from one of my aunts, once a month. She scrubbed floors for a living and ironed white people's clothes. "Five dollars, that's for you, baby." That five dollars said, "I believe in you! I got your back." And we don't do that with our kids enough.

The decline in collective orientation goes hand in hand with the focus on individual self-improvement as a response to our question about group tools. This decline seriously challenges the work of such scholars as Dawson (2011), who celebrate racial solidarity as a privileged tool for social change for African Americans. Ordinary African Americans, who are typically not invested in social movements, may not embrace this perspective as fully as members of the intellectual elite; indeed, we know that only 11 percent of the non-college-educated African Americans had attended a protest or signed a petition between 1978 and 2008 (see Caren, Ghoshal, and Ribas 2011).[78] Thus, our interviews include very few mentions of collective projects of social change and political mobilization beyond the desire for community uplift. This may be in part because respondents feel that mobilization is pointless, or, alternatively, they believe that many of the legal and institutional barriers for mobility have already been lifted (even if they are regularly threatened by Supreme Court decisions). Or it is quite possible that reforming African American youth and addressing the drug or incarceration issues are viewed as more urgent goals and more efficient ways to intervene directly in the moral fabric of the community than supporting a broader agenda to transform American racial hierarchies. In this reformist orientation of eschewing the call of identity politics for more short-term and narrow objectives, African American respondents resemble their Brazilian and Israeli counterparts. Paradoxically, however, members of this group can also mobilize and take the streets in response to racist incidents, such as those in Ferguson and Staten Island during the summer of 2014.

The largest class difference with regard to group tools concerns the importance of in-group solidarity and collective mobilization, which are 13 percentage points higher in the middle class (broadly defined) than in the working class (34 percent versus 21 percent) among respondents who mentioned them. The only group tool mentioned more often by the working class than the middle class is self-improvement (78 percent compared with 69 percent). This is in line with recent research showing that the language of self-improvement is particularly salient among the unemployed when discussing how to improve their situation (Silva 2013; Sharone 2014). This is also a basis for moral boundary work toward those of lower socioeconomic status (Lamont 2000; Duvoux 2014). Gender and age cohort differences regarding types of group tools valued are minimal.

Race-Targeted Policies

Another striking aspect of the views on group tools for dealing with racism is that only six respondents (out of 150) mention spontaneously the adoption of race-targeted policies, such as affirmative action, as a solution, while these are widely cited by Black Brazilian respondents. Beginning in the early 1980s, Affirmation Action policies have come under attack and lost ground in the United States—especially as they apply to higher education—following several Supreme Court decisions (Orfield and Kurlaender 2001; Garces 2012). However, at the time we were conducting our interviews in 2007–2008, these policies appeared to be largely taken for granted by our African American respondents. Only a few interviewees voiced familiar criticisms that such policies allow for reverse racism (perhaps from having been frequently exposed to such views at work and in higher education). A 2011 study found that a growing number of whites believe that blacks have gained at the expense of whites, who are now the primary victims of racism (Norton and Sommers 2011).

While redistributive policies were often mentioned by Brazilians, they are not salient among African American respondents. However, previous research has shown that African Americans are more supportive of income redistribution measures than are whites, although their opposition to governmental redistribution has increased in recent years (Bullock 2008; Hochschild and Weaver 2015).

To explore the salience of race-targeted policies, we explicitly questioned our interviewees concerning their opinions about affirmative action.[79] What emerged is a somewhat unified set of attitudes in favor of this policy, with 85 percent of our respondents supporting it (for a variety of reasons, including the continued challenge of racism [35 percent] and the intergenerational transmission of inequality [19 percent]). Support for affirmative action is considerably stronger in the middle class (broadly defined) than in the working class (95 percent versus 76 percent). This is perhaps because the middle class has benefitted more from such policies, notably in higher education, and may also have a better understanding of what these policies entail. Over time, however, statistics show that support among blacks for these policies has declined. According to Krysan (2012: 257–58), "In 1994, 57 percent of blacks favored preference in hiring and promotion; by 2002, this had declined to less than one-half (45 percent), with increases in both 'opposition' and 'strong opposition' (Schuman et al. 1997; analyses by the author)."

In Brazil, the development of racial consciousness is a salient concern, being at the center of media coverage with the implementation of pro-diversity policies in higher education and the creation of a black consciousness movement. In contrast, for US respondents, the development of racial consciousness appears to be a nonissue. Only a few offered responses to our group-tool question that speaks to this topic. This is not surprising, given the level of racial identification and groupness documented earlier. The celebration of black identity, so crucial in the 1960s for mobilization around the Civil Rights Movement ("black is beautiful"), may be so taken for granted that its mobilizing power has either disappeared or is not salient.

Hip hop and other forms of popular culture provide new contexts where the celebration of African American expressive culture is given center stage.

Hope Ahead? Explanations for Racism and Lessons for Children

Our respondents' views on group tools for improving the situation of blacks and best approaches for dealing with racism are undoubtedly tied to how they understand why racism exists and, by extension, whether it can disappear. If racism is explained above all as the result of ignorance and stupidity, it would not be surprising that our respondents believe that educating the racist is an appropriate way to respond to racism.

We find a wide range of responses to the specific question of why racism exists, many having to do with ignorance and stupidity (a response given by 31 percent of the respondents), family socialization (28 percent), and lack of education and exposure to other cultures (21 percent) on the part of the racist. We take ignorance and stupidity as having to do with lack of intelligence and opportunity, which goes hand in hand with narrow mindedness. Such explanations leave only limited room for hope for a change in attitudes. Explanations having to do with human nature (mentioned by 13 percent of the respondents) or "fear of the other" (11 percent) may be even more strongly correlated with a view of racism as a permanent and unchangeable feature of society. Other explanations having to do with competition (mentioned by 20 percent of the respondents) and a desire by whites to protect their privileges (13 percent) also leave little room for social change. Whether respondents believe change is possible will influence what they teach their kids about racism.

Much has changed in the decades since most of our respondents grew up. African Americans have made considerable legal, political, and economic progress, although racial inequality persists across social classes and regions. Across the class divide, standards of child rearing have been revolutionized, and parents have become more attuned to the psychological needs of their children (Hays 1998) and to the damage inflicted by racism (Hill 2006; Hughes et al. 2006). Among the 120 respondents who have children, there is considerably more explicit teaching about how to deal with racism than what these respondents received from their own parents. Only 16 of them say that they did not teach their children anything about racism. Otherwise, the ranges of approaches they promote are quite varied, distributed almost equally across five categories. The two most popular approaches (by a very small margin) consist, paradoxically, in encouraging children to assert their identity and authenticity and reject victimization (mentioned by 21 percent of our respondents who are parents) and to be pragmatic and use deterrents (mentioned by 25 percent). The contrast between these two lessons shows the inherent contradictions parents face in their desire to both protect and enable their kids. Another pair of contradictory approaches is teaching their children to confront (18 percent) and to deflect conflict, that is, to avoid violence and physical confrontation (18 percent)—while yet others tell their kids to treat people fairly and to accept others (14 percent). This diversity in approaches suggests the degree of concern that parents have for the challenges ahead, as racism may not be perceived as being in fast decline.

Mostly likely relevant to what interviewees teach their children about racism is what they learned about racism from their own parents. Surprisingly, given the pervasive presence of racism and segregation in earlier decades, 37 percent of interviewees say their parents taught them nothing concerning how to deal with racism. Many discuss racism as a reality that their parents painfully confronted but said little about, due to the powerlessness associated with such experiences, a shared desire to leave the past behind, a belief in the inevitability of racism, or, more prosaically, due to lack of time or interest. It is possible that adult perceptions that their children were exposed to lower levels of racism than themselves also made preparing them for dealing with racism a less urgent task.[80]

The absence of lessons on the subject is particularly noticeable in the working class, where only 46 percent of respondents said they had received lessons about racism from their parents, compared with 72 percent of middle-class respondents.[81] This suggests quite different class strategies for navigating racism—a pattern that is compatible with well-established class differences in child-rearing styles, with working-class parents being more authoritarian and less oriented toward verbal explanations (Lareau 2003). Compared to the middle class, working-class parents are less educated and have fewer resources that can be mobilized to deflect racism and teach their children how to deal with it. They may also have had less ready access to the therapeutic culture, which encourages using words to express and understand painful experiences (Illouz 2008). However, more recent studies reveal that working-class people are turning to therapeutic language for making sense of their difficulties in the post-2008 era (Silva 2013), at the same time as they are being socialized into middle-class norms of parenting (Daniel 2015). In addition, middle-class parents are particularly concerned with class reproduction and mobility, which shapes the effort they put into protecting their children and structuring and overseeing their experiences at school and elsewhere (Lareau and Goyette 2014). Working class parents are also engaged in a similar project, but they use different strategies to achieve their goals.

Asserting identity and authenticity is a way to claim recognition and is enabled by shared repertoires about what behavior is deemed appropriate in various contexts. Such repertoires contribute to building social resilience

(Hall and Lamont 2013). Respondents who are parents express concern for teaching their children how to maintain their sense of worth in the face of everyday racism. For instance, a contractor taught his daughter to stand up for herself by confronting classmates who told jokes about blacks at school. We coded this instance as a lesson in asserting identity and authenticity and in confronting stigmatizers.

Lessons about assertion of identity often took the form of admonishing children to avoid negative or stereotypical behavior. One mother, a credit analyst, said she wanted to teach her daughter to avoid racism: "I told her the same thing: Don't let it break your spirit, but also be aware that your ways and actions can feed certain stereotypes that you're trying to beat or that you're trying to prove are not so. And that you need to be conscious of that—especially [because] my daughter is still in West Orange school system, which is predominantly white."[82] Thus, parental lessons are shaped not only by the parents' own experiences and acquired wisdom, but also by their understanding of the cultural frames in which their children operate and of the surrounding stereotypes of blacks.

Pragmatism is particularly salient when interviewees who are parents discuss preparing their sons and other young black men to face racism, a topic that concerns the majority of parents (Seventy out of 120 respondents who answered the question concerning lessons about racism expressed an opinion on this topic, 18 of whom were expressly concerned about interactions with the police). A middle-class woman, the vice-president of a nonprofit organization, said:

> I wrote an article for [a mainstream magazine] about what [people should tell their sons about racism]. And my oldest son is now 21, and I am on it. . . . The one thing we tell our children is not necessarily about racism, but we tell them how to react to racist acts. For example, we tell our son when he is driving to not confront, do whatever the police officer says. The police officer says, "Don't move!" don't you move! If he says "Shut up," shut up! I guarantee you that white parents certainly don't have to tell their white children that. I do this because I don't want him to get killed. I want him to come home, and I don't think he has a choice.

Another woman who teaches adult education provides a similar account, urging her son to comply with police officers should he be profiled. When asked if she talks to her daughter about racism, she says:

> Not really, I didn't really have to. . . . But I did talk to my sons, my grandson, yes, he's a boy. He's a black male. [T]hey're most likely to be profiled more, and he has dealt with it, and he has been pulled over, and he did know what to do. [We told him, no matter] what they say, . . .

just do what he says. Don't argue with them because they're crazy, and he's a very pleasurable boy so he's no problem. He wears a seatbelt. He don't drink, don't smoke, he don't do anything that would cause a problem.

The concern for preparing young black men to face the police is hardly surprising, given familiar statistics about the criminalization and incarceration of young black men in America. Racial profiling is a widely available script that reaches deeply into respondents' minds and shapes their responses in significant ways.

Confronting is less appealing when it comes to teaching kids about racism, as parents are concerned with ensuring the security of the youth in the face of potential dangers. This decoupling is worth further exploration, so as to better understand how context enables and constrains responses.

All in all, class differences in lessons taught to children concerning how to deal with racism are small. Access to resources may lead middle-class African Americans to think they have more leeway in responding in theory than they do in practice, where many adopt a pragmatic attitude.

Making Sense of Ideal Responses in Relation to the American Dream

We have seen that the patterns of normative responses to racism identified through questions concerning group tools are largely individual and centered on self-improvement, education, and moral reform. These themes take on their full meaning when we consider the notion of the American Dream and what it enables (Fleming, Lamont, and Welburn 2012). Injunctions of self-reliance, individual responsibility, and competitiveness are part of the omnipresent American Dream, and they have become more salient in the neoliberal era (Hall and Lamont 2013). Their salience is reinforced by an implicit dialogue that African Americans may entertain with prevailing stereotypes, such as black poverty, that can be interpreted as requiring greater investment in self-improvement to overcome. Moreover, this dialogue resonates with the dominant scripts concerning what defines a competent American individual—scripts that stress, among other things, the importance of being proactive, entrepreneurial, oriented toward mobility, and individualistic (Meyer, Boli, and Thomas 1987).

Anderson (1983), Castoriadis (1987), and more recently, Bouchard (2013) have noted the role of collective myths and collective imaginaries in organizing conceptions of symbolic communities and shared sense of possible futures (see also Hall and Lamont 2013). Myths provide ideal representations of what holds the society together, how individuals can gain social membership, and what shared future is possible. Here we focus on the collective uber-myth, the American Dream, defined by Hochschild (1996) as being organized around four tenets: universal ability to participate equally (26), to anticipate success (19), to achieve success through individual action (assumed to be within one's control) (30), and the understanding that pursuing success is virtuous (23).

In many of their idealized responses to racism, respondents appear to be dialoguing with meritocracy and the American Dream, puzzled by what it promises despite the challenges that are thrown in their way as they reach for this ideal. The American Dream is a cultural repertoire that plays a crucial role in enabling the responses we have documented to date.

During the course of our interviews, we questioned respondents about whether they believe in the American Dream and about the meanings they attribute to it. The 108 respondents who defined the American Dream offered definitions that were more diverse and ambiguous than Hochschild suggests, with half using a wide range of definitions (48 percent coded "other"), while 19 percent provided an ambiguous definition. The latter includes the notion of the American Dream as simply "living to your potential. . . . and having fun doing it," "go[ing] to the supermarket and buy[ing] healthy food," "hav[ing] credit cards," "providing for your family," and "the freedom that is afforded to those who know how to get around it [laughter] and those that take advantage of it." Only 17 percent of respondents defined the American Dream using the traditional reference to the middle-class nuclear family: "It's a house, the family, the white picket fence, and a dog." A handful referred explicitly to distinctively African American views of the American Dream (along the lines of Pattillo-McCoy 1999), stating that "the Dream is different things to different people."

While 46 percent affirmed that the American Dream is accessible, a full 49 percent rejected it ("the American Dream is a nightmare"), mentioning that it is unreachable because of inequality (19 percent of respondents), racism (9 percent), or other reasons (26 percent). The middle-class respondents were only slightly more numerous in rejecting it compared to working-class respondents (53 percent versus 45 percent), not enough to confirm that the former are more cynical about the American Dream than the working class (as argued by Hochschild 1996). Conversely, slightly more working-class than middle-class respondents affirmed the value of the Dream (51 percent versus 42 percent), often expressing a desire to acquire cultural membership through consumption.

That a dialogue with the American Dream figures so prominently in idealized responses to racism is not surprising: broadly available negative stereotypes of Africans are a direct violation of this sacred myth, yet many continue to believe in some aspects of the American Dream. This may create a double-bind and work against buttressing the collective resilience of African Americans.

CONCLUSION

This section explained the relative popularity of various responses to stigmatization and discrimination by a range of historical, institutional, and socioeconomic characteristics of American society, as well as by the strength of groupness of African Americans and the cultural repertoires they have access to. Responses are neither haphazard nor idiosyncratic, but rather empowered and constrained by this range of cultural and contextual elements.

One of the most important findings of this section is the predominance of confronting as a response to incidents of stigmatization or discrimination among African Americans. This is enabled by the transformation in race relations in the United States over the past 50 years, and by the Civil Rights Movement in particular, which has empowered African Americans to denounce racism when they encounter it and to believe it is appropriate to educate the racially ignorant when the latter are encountered. Also relevant are institutionalized scripts about racist interactions and their illegitimate character, as well as the strong groupness of blacks and the blatant character of many incidents, which reduces doubts about whether a racist incident occurred and thus encourages confrontation.

The popularity of management of self-responses is connected to familiarity with stereotypes applied to African Americans (e.g., the "angry black") and by high unemployment for blacks, which was accentuated during the 2008 recession, when our interviews took place. The high salience of responses that involve management of the self indicates awareness of the emotional, professional, or material costs of responding too aggressively, and the interviewees' desire to preserve their energy and not organize their lives around fighting racism. Their Brazilian counterparts are more likely to engage in management of self-responses, as they more often view confrontation as incompatible with racial mixture and convivial coexistence across racial groups.

In the United States, working-class respondents engage in management of the self more than do middle-class respondents because of their more vulnerable labor market position. Compared to African Americans, for Arab Palestinians and Mizrahim not responding is the modal response, regardless of whether they are in a precarious labor market position. This may be indicative of Arab Palestinians' hopelessness regarding being able to create change, and of the Mizrahim's low groupness.

We found it surprising that in the neoliberal era, which encourages competitiveness, individual success, and self-reliance, that hard work and demonstrating competence as a means for establishing equality had low salience in responses to actual incidents. However, they figured more prominently in ideal responses, which tend to privilege individual over collective strategies.

More specifically, when asked about the best way for blacks to deal with racial inequality, more than half the interviewees choose self-improvement (particularly through education). While respondents often frame individual and collective improvements as going hand in hand (one stimulating the other), the primary goal of self-improvement is individual mobility and success.

Neoliberal repertoires about mobility and success are intertwined with the repertoires of the American Dream and meritocracy in legitimizing this focus on the individual and reducing collective orientation toward social change among blacks. Moral reform, particularly strengthening the black family, is a salient theme of these individualistic repertoires. In thinking about normative responses, interviewees are constrained by widely held stereotypes about blacks "making excuses," such that their individualist responses are themselves informed by stereotypes. In their ideal responses, a quarter of respondents privilege community tools, such as group solidarity and collective mobilization. At the same time, some deplore the decline of racial solidarity and the crab-in-the-barrel syndrome, referring nostalgically to a time when African Americans were better able to mobilize for collective progress.

The growing inequality between middle- and lower-class blacks does not immediately translate into strong differences in responses across the board. Instead, there are differences of emphasis between classes. In their ideal responses and responses to actual events, the middle class favored confronting more than the working class did. In contrast, the working class respondents responded to actual incidents through management of the self more than middle-class respondents did, although this difference is smaller than expected. The ideal responses are slightly more differentiated across class, with middle-class people valuing collective group tools more than the working-class cohort did. The overall level of similarity in responses across class surprised us and is a clear demonstration that shared experiences of stigmatization and discrimination may diminish differences in social experiences between classes, just as they sustain a strong collective identity or sense of linked fate in the group.

The only types of tools where working-class individuals scored higher than middle-class individuals in frequency of response pertained to self-improvement. With the transformation of the American working class and the decline of solidarity and other central elements of working-class culture, black workers are left to rely on only their personal resources when facing an increasingly challenging market situation. That they rarely mention religion (historically important for the collective mobilization and resilience of black workers) as a group tool is a measure of their isolation and powerlessness at a time when black poverty and unemployment are growing (Cherlin 2014).

When teaching their children how to deal with racism, the middle-class parents emphasize asserting identity and rejecting victimization by a factor of two to one. In contrast, working-class parents are slightly more oriented toward teaching pragmatism and deterring conflict. Thus, the middle class is more aggressive in its responses and less deterred by pragmatic considerations when formulating ideal responses. Middle-class resources may not be so useful when facing the challenge of preparing young black men for the threat associated with racial profiling: given pragmatic constraints, there is a decoupling between what middle-class members do and what they would like to do when it comes to preparing their boys for avoiding the likely threats associated with interacting with the police.

While we have emphasized how neoliberalism is shaping repertoires of responses, we have also considered how the American Dream operates to enable various types of responses. Our interviewees do not share a clear definition of the American Dream, and half of them reject this popular myth, particularly the middle class and women. Most do not believe that the American Dream is realistic. Yet they are in constant dialogue with this myth, including when they formulate their ideal responses. Moreover, progress is slowed by beliefs in meritocracy that legitimize racial and class inequality, the notion that blacks "make excuses" when decrying racism, and stereotypes about blacks. These are all elements that make the drama of race so complex in the American context.

Although aware of racism and other forces that shape their lives, African Americans take responsibility for their fate and, like Sisyphus, aim to push the stone up the mountain against all odds, bolstered by the fragile gains of the past 50 years. But how long can this last? Many African Americans are burning out, and racial disparities in a plethora of areas—including health, education, housing, and occupation—are increasing. Finding the most fruitful response to stigmatization and discrimination remains a collective challenge.

SECTION 2.5: A BIRD'S-EYE VIEW OF THE AFRICAN AMERICAN CASE

Stepping back to assess from a bird's-eye view what we have uncovered, one is struck by the complexity of the human experiences we have described. Dealing with stigmatization and discrimination is a complicated affair, and it requires considerable energy—to an extent that is largely invisible to non-blacks. Many behaviors that culturalists would see as puzzling come to make sense when one factors in the burden of "living while black," that is, the many perils associated with various types of responses, the sheer difficulty of facing scrutiny and stereotypes, and the burden of feeling isolated and misunderstood in the workplace (among other challenges). It is not unreasonable that one would respond to such experiences with anger or disengagement. The costs of experiencing ongoing stigmatization and discrimination add to the "wear and tear" experienced by African Americans as their lives unfold. By shedding light on such experiences, we hope to have contributed to a better understanding of cultural processes of inequality. Thus, the goal of this chapter has been to provide tools and a framework to make sense of what may otherwise seem like disjointed or random behaviors.

Given the legacy of the Civil Rights Era, Black Nationalism, and how African Americans have shown the way to minority rights revolution not only in the United States but beyond (Skrentny 2009), we could have expected a strong predilection for confrontation in our interviewees' responses to racism. And to some extent, this is what we have found. In this sense, our story is not very different from other accounts of responses to racism in the United States. However, our story includes numerous new wrinkles, because we considered various pressures to respond one way or the other that interviewees feel as they dialogue with familiar stereotypes about blacks, while, for instance, aiming to remain true to themselves or gain cultural membership by displaying middle-class attire and lifestyle.

Our account ends with individualism triumphing over collectivism. This stands in contrast to the massive public demonstrations of black solidarity around Black Lives Matter that were unfolding in 2014 and 2015, providing a potent background as we completed this book (see Terry 2015). While our data were collected well before these events, quotidian responses (such as those we studied) away from these events, which were closely followed in the media, should be given more weight when explaining social change than the pronouncements of social movement activists and public policy experts (O'Connor 2001).

In this chapter, we first set the stage for our explanatory apparatus by discussing our approach to groupness. In contrast to standard psychological approaches to racial identity, which contrast in-group and out-group and posit a universal tendency toward self-enhancing behavior, we focused on racial identification and group boundaries to better understand how African Americans hang together as a group. We described the group as having a strong sense of groupness and a pro-universalist outlook. We argued that the strength of their groupness depends in part on the symbolic, social, and spatial boundaries that have been built historically in relation to whites (manifested in the notion of white privilege). While many interviewees embrace a culture of universalism that upholds the notion that we are all equal as human beings, their everyday experiences of stigmatization and discrimination disconfirm this axiom.

Experiences of stigmatization, which may not be as central an object of systematic scholarly attention as discrimination in the sociological litera- ture, are the most common type of ethnoracial exclusion experienced by African Americans as well as by the other four groups we studied. The per- sistence of blatant racism—being openly insulted and called "nigger," for instance—coupled with pervasive subtle racism, clearly suggests that the age of postracial America is still in the distant future. Subtle and not-so- subtle racism continues to coexist with and impact the daily lives of African Americans. It occurs in anonymous relationships as much as in relation- ships with family members, coworkers, and neighbors.

Particularly surprising, in the face of past literature and the growing in- equality among blacks, is the fact that although the middle class mentions more incidents than the working class, the types of incidents mentioned by the middle class and working class are not that different. This suggests that race shapes the lived experiences of African Americans more than class does, at least when it comes to living with racism. The main difference be- tween the two groups is that the middle class mentions being stereotyped as low-income or poorly educated and being underestimated more often. These experiences are most likely enabled by the middle class's expectation that their education and occupation should confer on them a measure of respect that working-class interviewees may not expect. Working-class indi- viduals, for their part, more often say they are subjected to double standards, reflecting their lower level of autonomy in the workplace.

Concerning gender differences, we have argued that men believe more often than women do that they are treated unfairly, misunderstood (almost 20 percent more than women), and stereotyped as threatening. This reso- nates with widely held racialized gender stereotypes. As for age cohort dif- ferences, they resonate with changes in the life conditions of African Amer- icans, with younger people experiencing more racial profiling and older people having experienced more discrimination, double standards, and denied opportunity. What matters here is not only the types of incidents they have been exposed to, which may authorize them to denounce specific types of action, but also their lived experience, which makes various types of unfairness more salient to them.

African Americans most often respond with confrontation in incidents where they believe they were not treated fairly. These responses are empow- ered by historical, legal, cultural, and other elements, including an unam- biguous sense of groupness. But when it comes to ideal responses, they are far more concerned with individual success and demonstrating competi- tiveness and self-reliance than are Black Brazilians and Israelis. While Black Brazilians and some Ethiopian Israelis refer to the United States when de- scribing their views on racism (Mizrachi and Zawdu 2012), African Ameri- cans rarely or never discuss the experience of people in other countries, or transnational dynamics more generally.

Few African Americans offer a straightforward celebration of colorblindness in their responses to stigmatization and discrimination, although they do think about equality in relation to universal referents (religion or human nature: "looking beyond race to what we are as human beings.") Those who, instead of confronting, engage in management of the self typically do not promote strategies of assimilation. Instead, they opt for management of the self stemming from various constraints or because they do not want to confirm racial stereotypes. This is not the same as celebrating colorblindness. Although by some standards, working harder is a colorblind response, few respondents seems to conceive it as such, given the context of high groupness in which their lives unfold. Perhaps working hard functions more as a way to overcome racism while acknowledging challenges that are common across race lines.

This chapter offers several explanations for the phenomena at hand:

- Among the background factors, the history of slavery, segregation, and ethnoracial exclusion, and the resulting racial inequality, all remain dominant factors in shaping the experiences of and responses to racism, as these experiences mediate the strength of groupness among African Americans. They also mediate spatial segregation, the overrepresentation of blacks in low-income groups, racial homophily through institutional segregation (notably through incarceration), and more. Thus for African Americans, the US racial hierarchy remains a powerful determinant in shaping life experiences. Our data do not reveal any support for the argument that we are moving toward a postracial society. Also relevant is the 2007–2008 recession, which weakened African American employment during our research period; the growing inequality among blacks, which explains the concern with class misrecognition (among others); and growing individualism among blacks (Hunt 2007). Finally, the legal legacy of the Civil Rights Era undergirds many of the cultural repertoires about African Americans' full cultural membership that we documented. This will become particularly salient as we contrast the experiences of other groups in Chapters 3 and 4.
- Among the groupness factors, racial identification as well as perceived spatial segregation and homophily feed into the strength of groupness. Pro-diversity cultural repertoires sustain openness among blacks with respect to non-blacks in a cultural environment where universalism is normative.
- Among the cultural repertoires factors, the cultural legacy of the Civil Rights Era, along with institutional scripts about American racism based on past experiences of ethnoracial exclusion, feed belief in the legitimacy of confronting. Finally, meritocracy, the American

dream, and neoliberal cultural repertoires work hand in hand to enable the popularity of an individualist orientation over a collective orientation.

Next we analyze the experiences and responses of Black Brazilians, which will provide us with a unique lens through which to return to the African American case in the book's Conclusion.

CHAPTER 3
BRAZIL

We turn now to the Brazilian case. As in Chapter 1 on the United States, the first section provides background information, which will help place our interviewees in their context. We emphasize historical and institutional dimensions that will be salient in the configurational explanation developed throughout the chapter. This is also true of Section 3.2, which describes Black Brazilians as characterized by blurred groupness, a key dimension to understand how they perceive and react to racism. Section 3.3 explores how Black Brazilians struggle with what they perceive as a subtle or masked racism and how they experience specific incidents of stigmatization and discrimination, often conflating class and race stigmatization. Section 3.4 analyzes how Black Brazilians say they responded to specific incidents and what they view as the best responses from a normative perspective. Finally, in Section 3.5, we discuss how the patterns of experiences and responses can be accounted for. We often rely on comparisons to the US case as well as anticipate a few comparisons to the Israeli case to emphasize how these different contexts enable and constrain how the five stigmatized groups analyzed in this book experience and react to ethnoracial exclusion. We open with a brief overview of the discussions concerning studies about race in Brazil, and the key role of US comparisons in this literature, to help the reader understand our distinctive approach and contribution.

SECTION 3.1: BACKGROUND FACTORS: HISTORICAL AND SOCIOECONOMIC CONTEXT

STUDYING RACE IN BRAZIL

Differences between race relations in Brazil and the United States, the two largest former slave nations in the Americas, have long drawn researchers' attention. In fact, the Brazilian academic literature on race relations has traditionally looked at comparisons with the United States. Most of the explicit comparative studies between Brazil and the United States are based on historical data (e.g., Tannenbaum 1946; Degler 1971; Skidmore 1972; Marx 1998), and survey data (e.g., Telles 2004; Bailey 2009a).[1] They generally emphasize the countries' different historical trajectories but shared (and persistent) ethnoracial exclusion. This book builds on these studies, but it moves beyond them by relying on systematic qualitative evidence from in-depth interviews with blacks in Brazil and in the United States to analyze similarities and differences in how they deal with stigma and seek respect. Such a strategy allows us to grasp how racial boundaries in Brazil are perceived, challenged, justified, or reified in ways distinctive from the American experience, while using the comparison with the United States to better identify the strengths, porosity, and transformations of Brazilian racial boundaries.

Although studies of racial inequalities have been central to the development of both American and Brazilian social sciences, during the second half of the twentieth century social scientists in the United States looked into race much more frequently and intensely than their colleagues did in Brazil. This can partly be attributed to the hegemony of the idea of racial democracy in Brazil, which downplayed ethnoracial exclusion, but perhaps also to the lack of racial diversity in graduate programs (among faculty and students). The few late-twentieth-century studies from Brazilian scholars have recovered Brazilian history as seen through the eyes of the slaves (e.g., Reis 1988) or explored through ethnographies of Afro-Brazilian cultural practices (e.g., Maggie 1992). From a sociological perspective, they have analyzed evidence of the persistence of racial inequality in different realms (e.g., Hasenbalg and Valle e Silva 1988).

Beginning in the late 1990s, American scholars, especially ethnographers, again turned their gaze to Brazilian race relations (e.g., Hanchard 1994; Burdick 1998; Twine 1998). Largely focusing on specific issues (e.g., the black movement, *favela* [slum] residents, and interracial relationships), these studies denounced the existence and persistence of racial inequalities in Brazil. Yet very few studies were concerned with everyday experiences of discrimination and racism among urban blacks (an important exception is Sheriff's (2001) study on race relations in a Rio de Janeiro favela). As Hanchard (1999: 14) stated, "Brazil may be one of the most understudied multiracial polities in terms of everyday racism, given the plethora of literature on Afro-Brazilian culture."

These late-twentieth-century studies could not have anticipated the important changes that occurred in Brazil during the 2000s: the official recognition of racism by the Brazilian state, the implementation of affirmative action policies, and the growing identification as blacks (*negros*) by a large part of the population. As Paschel (2016) comments concerning her fieldwork conducted in the early 2000s, after years of reading in scholarly accounts that ethnoracial issues were silenced in Brazil, she was surprised to find that not only were race-based policies institutionalized by the state, but also discussions of race were at the center of popular discourse on newspaper stands, street corners, and taxi cabs.

Following these important changes, the 2000s witnessed an upsurge in the number of national surveys in Brazil looking into perceptions of race (Bailey 2009a; Loveman, Muniz, and Bailey 2012; Telles and PERLA team 2014), as well as further development of statistical studies analyzing racial inequality based on publicly available official data (e.g., Telles 2004; Schwartzman 2007; Paixão and Carvano 2008; Paixão et al. 2011; Marteleto 2012). In addition, studies of racial quotas and their impact on Brazilian socioeconomic structure and sociability have emerged (e.g., Bernardino and Galdino 2004; Paiva 2010; Cicalo 2012; Schwartzman and Moraes Silva 2012). Even so, scholarship about race relations in Brazil remains far less extensive than in the United States. Studies relying on in-depth interviews with ordinary black people that systematically address issues of stigmatization and discrimination remain few.[2] Thus, we do not engage with as many authors and debates as our chapter on the United States.

Building on Telles's (2004) distinction between vertical and horizontal inequalities, we understand Brazil as a country characterized by strong racial inequalities, which manifest themselves by the persistence of racial inequalities in educational achievement and income. These are coupled with porous racial boundaries in sociability, which manifest themselves by widespread interracial conviviality and high rates of racial intermarriage (especially in lower socioeconomic status groups), as well as by the historical absence of strong collective racial organizations, with no equivalent to the American Civil Rights Movement.[3] Exploring how blacks in Brazil understand and respond to stigma compared with African Americans, we can better capture how this combination of strong racial inequalities and porous racial boundaries shapes the experiences of Black Brazilians, while taking into account the role of history, socioeconomic background, cultural repertoires, and groupness in both countries.

Empirically, we analyze in detail the narratives of incidents of stigmatization and discrimination of our interviewees as well as their responses. As discussed in the Introduction, we seek to make sense of these experiences by analyzing the background conditions that enable and constrain these individuals historically and contemporarily. Socioeconomic and institutional data reveal a mixed picture, with persisting racial inequality in income and educational outcomes, a strong concentration of blacks among the poor and the incarcerated, but medium to low neighborhood and institutional segregation and high interracial marriage. At the same time, the disputes over the idea of racial democracy in Brazil reveal competing cultural repertoires used to frame the black experience: the value of racial mixture, the race-class conflation, and black mobilization/pride. Before exploring these elements, we briefly describe how the black presence, and especially the long history of African slavery, was central in the making of Brazilian society.

THE LEGACY OF SLAVERY AND THE RISE AND FALL OF RACIAL DEMOCRACY

It has been estimated that 4 million Africans entered Brazil between the sixteenth and nineteenth centuries to become slaves, four times the number who entered the United States during a roughly similar period (Curtin 1969).[4] The high figures for Brazil are explained not only by the size and scope of its plantation system, the smaller availability of free labor, and the economic interests of slave traders, but also by the significantly lower rate of reproduction of the slave population. Family dismantling, more frequent in Brazil than in the United States, and extremely adverse labor conditions did not favor demographic reproduction (Curtin 1969). As a consequence, the supply of forced labor had to be constantly renewed. On the one hand, this need for labor helps explain why legal attempts at stopping the African slave trade were opposed by most Brazilian landowners and only succeeded under acute external pressure (Bethell 1970; Conrad 1972). On the other hand, the dismantling of slave families in Brazil in conjunction with the predominance of male colonizers (who came without their families to explore the country) encouraged interracial mixing, sometimes consensual but commonly forced. By 1872, 38 percent of the population was identified in the census as brown (*pardo, caboclo*), supposedly the result of interracial mixing, while 38 percent was identified as white (*branco*) and 19.7 percent as black (*preto*). This same census shows that manumission rates were much higher in Brazil than in the United States, where owners rarely freed their slaves. According to Skidmore (1993), slaves made up 30 percent of Brazil's population in 1819, while in 1872 this percentage was reduced to 15 percent, or 1,510,806 individuals. While among those categorized as browns (*pardos*) 13 percent were slaves, among blacks (*pretos*) slightly more than half (53 percent) were slaves.[5]

Despite the high manumission rates, Brazil was the last country in the Americas to abolish slavery, finally doing so in 1888. By that time, slavery was no longer considered economically viable by a considerable portion of the elite. Many slave owners had voluntarily freed their slaves, and abolition was supported by some sectors of the rural elite (Reis and Reis 1988).

After the abolition of slavery, no blatant segregationist laws were implemented in Brazil. Nevertheless, the 1850 land laws had limited the land-ownership of freed slaves, and the 1890 Penal Code criminalized a number of popular cultural and religious practices largely associated with Black Brazilians. For example, the code defined the practice of *capoeira*, a Brazilian martial art, as a serious crime with severe punishment (earlier it had been considered a serious offense but not a crime). According to Leu (2014), after the enactment of the 1890 code, more than 1,000 *capoeira* practitioners were sent to prison. Similarly, the practice of Afro-Brazilian religions was criminalized, and police often raided houses of Candomblé—one such religion (Moura 1988). In the early twentieth century, some urban reforms, like that initiated by Rio de Janeiro mayor Pereira Passos (1903–1906), sought to "cleanse" popular and mostly black urban spaces, destroying entire neighborhoods (Carvalho 2013).

In addition, in 1891 a federal decree prohibited immigration for people of "the black race" and limited immigration for the "yellow race " (i.e. Asians), while rich states, like São Paulo, were subsidizing (white) immigration from European countries (Skidmore 1993). In academic and political circles, elites openly debated whitening Brazilian society through immigration as the solution for the "racial inferiority of Brazilians" as seen by that era's scientific racism theories (Skidmore 1993). Whitening would take place through the growing presence of European immigrants and by their mixing with the local, darker population. This massively subsidized European immigration further contributed to the exclusion of blacks from opportunities for social mobility. Between 1884 and 1913, approximately 2.7 million white immigrants came to Brazil. Not only did these European immigrants receive tickets from the federal and state governments to come to Brazil, but, in this still mostly rural country, they filled the majority of the new industrial jobs in São Paulo, the new economic center of the country. By 1915, the industrial labor force was 85 percent immigrant and white (Foot-Hardmann and Leonardi 1988). Fernandes (1969) and Andrews (2004) estimate that by 1920, the population of European immigrants in São Paulo was substantially larger than that of Afro-descendants. In contrast, blacks (pretos) and browns (pardos) were (and still are) largely concentrated in the North and Northeast, the poorest and most rural regions of the country. Although there are few systematic studies about subtle or blatant discrimination practices among employers in the Southeast in the early twentieth century (e.g., Nogueira 1954), it is clear even today that this geographical patterning has implications for the distribution of resources and the socioeconomic outcomes of blacks and whites in Brazil (Hasenbalg 1979).

Latin American elites and intellectuals considered themselves to be disadvantaged due to their racial mixing, compared to their North American neighbors. This manifested in the whitening policies just described, which prevailed up to the early twentieth century. These were challenged as an alternative racial narrative started to emerge in the early twentieth century.

The Masters and the Slaves, the 1933 classic work from Brazilian anthropologist Gilberto Freyre, is the most well-known version of this new narrative about Brazilian race formation. He describes the country's history as the marriage of three races—Indigenous, Portuguese, and Africans—each one contributing to the unique Brazilian character (a perspective attributed to the influence of the cultural anthropology of Franz Boas).[6] Instead of a country cursed by miscegenation, Brazil was presented as a nation blessed by racial mixture (*mestizaje*), which was a source of tolerance, malleability, and affection.[7] Racial integration was often illustrated by the absence of segregation policies in the country after the end of slavery, in clear contrast to the US South.

Because there are no survey data on attitudes toward race relations in Brazil in the first half of the twentieth century, it is impossible to know how much the idea of racial democracy was accepted as a reality by most Brazilians, but it was certainly present among intellectuals and in public debates, as discussed in detail by Guimarães (2001). The ideal was also initially endorsed by Black Brazilian intellectuals, even if many viewed this notion as an ideal more than a reality.[8] Brazil's international reputation in the realm of race relations even led UNESCO to fund studies in different regions of Brazil to better understand this "racial paradise" (Maio 1999).

The results of the UNESCO studies, however, became the first systematic scholarly critique of the notion of racial democracy and provided evidence of the persistence of racial inequality in Brazil.[9] The authors came to two important conclusions. First, discrimination and prejudice in Brazil were based not on race defined as ethnic or racial origin, as in the United States, but rather on phenotype: people were discriminated against not because of perceived cultural or ancestral differences, but because of their dark skin (Nogueira 1985). Second, largely influenced by a combination of Marxism and modernization theory, one of the coordinators of the studies, Florestan Fernandes (1969), noted that racial discrimination was slowly being replaced by class discrimination, which was believed to be the main cause of black exclusion by the late twentieth century.

Domestically, however, debates about these studies remained largely restricted to academia.[10] The military coup of 1964 silenced most social and democratic causes in Brazil, including debates about racial inequality. The hegemony of the racial democracy narrative proved efficient in ensuring national unity and stability in the wake of the military dictatorship that would last for two decades.

In the second half of the twentieth century, the idea that racial inequalities were caused by class dynamics became the dominant discourse in Brazilian academia, in government, and in society more broadly. Brazilian academia was largely dominated by Marxist narratives, along the lines of those proposed by Florestan Fernandes (1969), which posed the centrality of class exclusion over racial discrimination. The narrative of the military regime was that Brazil should "make the cake grow before splitting it"—a slogan similar to "the rising tide lifts all boats." Such a narrative denied any particularity to racial inequalities and placed the focus on economic growth and its trickle-down effects as the solution to all social problems. The popular expression "money whitens" illustrates this idea that race was not determinant, suggesting that once blacks are economically successful, they are perceived (and treated) as whites. Racial democracy also became part of the official state discourse (Paschel 2016). Denouncing racism and emphasizing racial identity was seen as unpatriotic not only by the state but by society at large.[11]

However, in the 1970s, some black organizations began openly challenging the description of Brazil as a racial democracy, calling it a myth. Some of these organizations were based on cultural membership and promoted African religion or aesthetics, while others were more politically oriented (and were aligned with political parties). The *Movimento Negro Unificado* (Unified Black Movement), probably the best-known organization, was able to mobilize a considerable number of militants and, more importantly, became visible in public debates (Hanchard 1994).

This new criticism of the racial democracy myth went beyond denouncing the persistence of racial inequalities to show how this idea had in fact contributed to the persistence of such inequalities. It called out the underlying assumption of white superiority in the myth of the three races—illustrated by the silence surrounding the rape of black and indigenous women. It also denounced the persistence of ideals in aesthetics and beauty. Finally, it decried the continuing discrimination against blacks in employment, education, and other valued social resources. As a positive agenda, black movements promoted the right of individuals to organize as blacks and to identify as *negros*, instead of as mixed. For black activists, the idea of racial democracy and its argument that everyone is mixed in Brazil obscured racial inequalities, much as the idea that in the United States everyone is middle class obscures class inequalities in that country.

The consolidation of democracy during the 1990s, after two decades of military dictatorship, allowed for growing mobilization around a number of issues, including race. Race issues became much more visible especially after the 2001 United Nations World Conference against Racism, Racial Discrimination, Xenophobia and Related Intolerance, known as the Durban I Conference. The presence of Black Brazilian organizations at this conference, armed with striking statistics about the persistence of racial inequality, pushed the Brazilian government to officially admit for the first time the existence of racial disparities and to commit to actions promoting equal opportunities, including affirmative action benefiting Black Brazilians (Paschel 2016).[12] The combination of organized social movements, international pressure, transnational cultural repertoires of black rights, and a democratic government provided the final push for the implementation of racial affirmative action in Brazil in the early 2000s (Htun 2004).

With affirmative action, implemented in the form of racial quotas, came heated public debates, manifestos by intellectuals and artists for and against racially targeted policies, and accusations of racism on both sides of the issue. Those against affirmative action were accused of not acknowledging the existence of racial inequalities (or not wanting to remedy them), while those who favored it were accused of wanting to racialize the country, creating dangerous divisions (for a summary of those debates, see Moraes Silva 2007).

The general population also showed mixed feelings toward racial quotas. A national survey conducted in 2008 by Datafolha (a nonpartisan survey company linked to one of the most important Brazilian newspapers), showed that a small majority (51 percent) of White and Black Brazilians agreed on the implementation of affirmative action in the form of racial quotas in universities, but most preferred colorblind socioeconomic quotas (75 percent). Most Brazilians also said they were concerned that racial quotas would increase racism in Brazil (62 percent). In contrast to the United States, there were no strong differences in support for affirmative action across racial groups.

TOGETHER AND UNEQUAL? RACIAL INEQUALITY AND SEGREGATION

According to the 2010 census, when asked about their color or race, 48 percent of the Brazilian population identifies as branco (white), 43 percent as pardo (brown or mixed), and 8 percent as preto (black). The remaining 1 percent identifies with the two remaining census categories of *amarelo* (literally yellow, introduced in 1940 to categorize the Asian population) or *indigena* (indigenous, introduced in 1990 to categorize native Brazilians).[13]

Nevertheless, defining who is black in Brazil today is much more disputed than defining who is African American in the United States or who is

Arab Palestinian in Israel. This is partly because "black" can be translated as preto or negro. Preto is the historical census category that refers mostly to color, which has also been translated as "dark blacks" (Bailey 2009a). "Negro" has become a more politicized term, defended by the black movement to denote that race categories are more than color categories and should be mobilized for collective action. In public debates and social policies, the category negro has been increasingly used to refer to those who identify as pretos and pardos, according to Brazilian census categories. This is justified by numerous studies showing that racial inequality between those who identify as white (branco) and those who identify as dark black or mixed categories (as preto or pardo) is statistically significant on all socioeconomic dimensions. In contrast, socioeconomic inequalities between those who identify as preto and pardo are usually not significant, and the boundaries between these two groups is both contested and contextually variable (Silva 1979; Telles 2004).

Because of our interest in ethnoracial exclusion, we use the term "Black Brazilians" to include all those who identify as preto or pardo, in response to the question we borrowed from the Brazilian census: "What is your color or race question?" This inclusive category comprises 51 percent of the population. In the few instances where we need to differentiate between those who identify as pretos or pardos, we rely on the Portuguese terms.[14]

The pervasiveness of racial inequality in Brazil is confirmed in the 2010 census results. Although enrollment in higher education has substantially expanded in the past decade, the white-black gap has remained strong—16.6 percent of whites 25 years old or older had a college degree versus 6.7 percent of blacks in the same age group. The mean monthly income for Black Brazilians in 2010 was R$724.77 compared to R$1,252.37 for whites. Unemployment rates for Black Brazilians were also nearly 50 percent higher than rates for whites: 9.2 versus 6.2 percent. Finally, the 2010 census also showed that 70.8 percent of those in extreme poverty are black (BRASIL 2011).

Racial inequalities are even more striking in homicide rates. The killing of Black Brazilians, especially by the police, is certainly one of the most notorious cases of what has been called the genocide of the African diaspora (Vargas 2010; Rocha 2012; Alves 2014). Of the 52,264 homicide victims in Brazil in 2010, 71.6 percent were black (Waiselfisz 2014).[15] Blacks are disproportionately killed in confrontations with police—and the Brazilian police force is one of the most violent in the world (Cano 1997, 2000). As in the United States, blacks in Brazil are overrepresented in the growing incarcerated population. In 2012 they represented 60.7 percent of prisoners (whereas they are 50.8 percent of the general population). Pretos are particularly overrepresented: they make up 17 percent of prisoners but only 7.6 percent of the general population.[16]

Another similarity with the United States is the uneven distribution of the black population across the country. Blacks are much more concentrated in the North and Northeast states (where more than 50 percent of the population is black or brown) compared with the South and Southeast states (in most of these states, less than 30 percent of the population is black). As Telles (2004) points out, this regional concentration is an important element in the overall racial inequality of the country and its persistence, since the North and Northeast states are generally poorer, have worse infrastructures, worse educational systems, and less power in national politics than the South and Southeast states.

In the cities, however, Black Brazilians are not as racially segregated as urban African Americans in the United States. As Telles (2004) shows, in 1980 the average dissimilarity rate of blacks and whites (i.e., the percentage of people who would have to move to completely desegregate neighborhoods) in the eight largest cities in Brazil was about half of that in the United States (about 40 percent in Brazil versus 80 percent in the United States). Nevertheless, in cities with a high percentage of blacks, such as Belém (in the North), Fortaleza, Recife, and Salvador (in the Northeast), the isolation (i.e., the percentage of same-race neighbors) of blacks can be as high as in the United States (about 80 percent).

Comparisons between the United States and Brazil of racial intermarriage rates reveal that not only residential but also interpersonal boundaries are more porous in Brazil. Telles (2004), for example, shows that even after controlling for the percentage of blacks in the population, the percentage of intermarriage between whites and blacks in Brazil is much higher than in the United States and has grown between 1960 and 1991.[17] More recent studies show that this trend continued up to 2000. According to Ribeiro and Silva (2009), in 1960 nearly one in ten marriages was between blacks and whites. This compares to nearly one in five (17.4 percent) in 1980, and more than one in four (27.4 percent) in 2000.[18]

Perhaps because of weaker residential segregation and higher frequency of interracial marriage, racial segregation in public spaces (e.g., public schools and public hospitals) and in private institutions (e.g., churches, associations, and unions) is not as striking as it is in the United States. This does not mean there are no purely white or purely black spaces, but that when they are found, such spaces are primarily due not to racial segregation but to regional concentration (given the isolation of blacks in certain regions of the country) or to the socioeconomic exclusion of poorer blacks and whites characteristic of upper-middle-class neighborhoods and institutions. Although this pattern may be similar to what is found in the United States in some respects, we do not find in Brazil black middle-class neighborhoods, and exclusively black associations or churches. This has important consequences for how racial discrimination is experienced, especially for upwardly mobile blacks, as they are often a tiny minority in their middle-class neighborhoods and workplaces, as stated by our respondents (Moraes Silva and Reis 2011).

The black population has largely benefited from the decline of socioeconomic inequality experienced since the early 2000s. This decline was manifested in 2013 by the lowest Gini coefficient ever recorded for Brazil, an outcome widely viewed as resulting from low unemployment rates and the widespread implementation of antipoverty social policies. Most famously, the leading government social policy, *Bolsa Família* (a conditional cash transfer program), benefits 25 percent of the population, most of whom are black families—this group represents 73 percent of beneficiaries, according to government press releases. The new middle class, whose rise has often made headlines in the country and abroad, is also mostly black—but note that its middle classness and degree of economic stability have been contested (Pochmann 2012; Scalon and Salata 2012; Garcia Lopes and de Sá e Silva 2014).[19] The decline of socioeconomic inequality, also characteristic of the entire Latin American region in the 2000s (López-Calva and Lustig 2010), as well as the growth of redistribution policies since the late 1990s, may explain why the negative social and economic impacts of neoliberalism are viewed as less significant in Brazil than in the United States or Israel (Diniz and Boschi 2007).

Nevertheless, in the first decades of the twenty-first century, Brazil continues to be characterized by high socioeconomic inequality. Even though the pervasiveness of inequality has been recognized by poor and elites alike (Reis 1999) and equality of opportunity through education is touted as a solution, only since the late 1990s has access to basic education been guaranteed and higher education become more available.[20] Inequalities in earnings between those with higher education and those without also remain striking: in 2012 the college educated earned more than 5 times the average salary of those without secondary education and nearly 2.5 times more than those with upper secondary education.[21] Maybe more importantly, these gaps are largely perceived as natural, if not appropriate (Scalon 2004). Partly due to this persistent inequality, the black middle class remains small and invisible in the public space—an invisibility that contributes significantly to the experiences of the middle-class respondents in our study.

THE RESEARCH SITE: RIO DE JANEIRO

Interviews with Brazilian respondents were conducted in Rio de Janeiro between 2007 and 2009. Most of the respondents lived in the city, but a few were residents of the broader metropolitan region (Nova Iguaçu, Duque de Caxias, or São Gonçalo). (See Appendixes 1 and 2 for details).

Located in the Southeast of the country, Rio de Janeiro is the second largest city in Brazil, after São Paulo, with 6,320,446 residents in 2010. Even if

Rio's racial distribution generally mirrors that of the country, with 47.4 percent brancos, 39.3 percent pardos, and 12.4 percent pretos according to the 2010 National Census, the experiences of our interviewees are not necessarily representative of blacks in Brazil. In such a large country, regional differences greatly impact how race is experienced. As in Chapter 2 on the United States, we consider these differences by presenting national level survey data for comparison when possible.

As the first hub of coffee production in the country, Rio has historically hosted a high concentration of blacks, especially compared to São Paulo, the largest city with the biggest economy in the country today.[22] In the 1870s, before abolition, the state of Rio had the largest slave population in the country, approximately 300,000 (40 percent of the total slave population), while slaves made up only 10 percent of São Paulo's population (Graham 1970). In addition, in the early twentieth century, fewer European immigrants settled in Rio compared with São Paulo and other cities in the South. Finally, migrants from the Northeast, mostly pardos, have also come to Rio since the early twentieth century looking for better opportunities. Nevertheless, the social mobilization of blacks in São Paulo has been historically stronger than in Rio, even if Rio has been the home of important black organizations, such as the Experimental Theater of Blacks in the 1940s or Black Rio in the 1970s (Hanchard 1994).

Rio was the political capital of Brazil until 1960, and it still has a high concentration of public offices (with public service employment being one of the most important avenues for mobility for blacks in Brazil). Following the partial decline of industries like steel and shipbuilding in the 1980s, Rio's economy, the second largest in the country, has been mostly based on the service sector. Although the city's unemployment rate is below the country average, its reliance on public jobs and services makes it vulnerable to political changes and economic recessions.

As in most Brazilian cities, urban space in Rio is characterized by high levels of spatial segregation across socioeconomic status, with variations in the human development index performance measures, which range from 0.97 in elite neighborhoods (higher than Norway's index) to less than 0.7 in the poorest neighborhoods (a bit lower than the Brazilian average, and close to the index for Belize).[23] Because of this extreme degree of inequality, Rio is called a "*cidade partida*," (Ribeiro 2000), a city divided between its South/rich zone and North/suburban/poor zone, between *favelas* (slums) and *asfalto* (literally, asphalt, referring to access to public services), between areas dominated by the police and areas dominated by drug dealers.

Despite this high degree of class segregation, Rio's division is rarely described in racial terms. And indeed, in his analysis of the 1980 census data, Telles (2004) presents Rio de Janeiro as having one of the lowest racial dissimilarity rates among Brazilian cities.

In one of the few recent studies to directly address racial segregation in Rio, Ribeiro (2007) confirms that the city's segregation of blacks and whites is mostly due to the spatial concentration of whites with high socioeconomic status rather than the exclusion of blacks from middle- or working-class neighborhoods. Ribeiro also reports that Rio has no racialized spatial hierarchy segregating low- and middle-income blacks and whites, even if its high-status areas are mostly white. In short, Rio is a city with strong socioeconomic boundaries, which combines side-by-side racially mixed working-class neighborhoods, majority black *favelas*, and the nearly all-white upper-middle-class neighborhoods, which all share cultural and public spaces (e.g., beaches). In that sense, the city exemplifies the puzzle of Brazilian race relations that we aim to address: how this reality of strong socioeconomic racial inequality but relatively weak racial boundaries in sociability impacts the stigma and discrimination experienced by blacks in Rio de Janeiro.

SECTION 3.2: ETHNORACIAL GROUPNESS

As in the parallel sections in the US and Israeli chapters (Chapters 2 and 4), in this section we construct our understanding of groupness based on (1) the self-identification of our interviewees (as determined by questions concerning self-definition, ethnoracial self-labeling, meanings associated with being black, and perceptions of cultural differences); and (2) the strength of group boundaries as revealed by experiences of spatial ethnoracial segregation, expressed closeness to in-group members (including in dating and friendship), and boundary work toward out-groups (whites in particular).

This section presents a complex and at times contradictory picture of groupness among Black Brazilians. Criticizing research that posits the existence of racial groups as unit of analysis (e.g., in Hanchard 1994; Marx 1998; Twine 1998), Bailey (2009a) argues that the United States and Brazil are characterized by strong groupness and weak groupness, respectively. Drawing on Brubaker and Cooper (2000) and Loveman (1999), he defines groupness as "a scale of racialized population cohesion and subjectivity, high to low" (Bailey 2009a: 20). Although our analysis generally confirms his findings that the groupness of Black Brazilians is relatively weaker than that of African Americans, our comparative approach reveals novel, complex, and contradictory dimensions of groupness. Brazilian interviewees consistently self-identified as black and stated pride in this identification, but, compared to African Americans, they give less consistent meaning to this identity and are much less likely to think of themselves as having a shared culture or as belonging to a distinct group. Moreover, the boundaries that Black Brazilians draw toward non-blacks are more contested than those of African Americans: their sociability crosses racial boundaries at the same time as they commonly combine whiteness and higher socioeconomic status when drawing symbolic distinctions between themselves and whites. In short, even if the boundaries of their group are experienced as more blurred than is the case for African Americans, here again, groupness is contradictory— strong by some criteria (identification and shared sense of group disadvantages) and weaker by others (cultural distinctiveness and boundaries toward non-blacks).

SELF-IDENTIFICATION

As in the United States and Israel, interviews in Brazil started with a general question: "How would you describe yourself?" or "What kind of person are you?" As in the other two countries, nearly all Brazilian respondents answered by speaking of moral attributes. Two-thirds of the Brazilian respondents defined themselves as hardworking, honest, and reliable as friends. They also differentiated themselves from other people along the same lines, making moral boundaries the most salient boundary in their responses to this opening question.

Few responded to this question by mentioning their racial identity—18 out of our 160 interviewees.[24] Thirteen of these understood the question as a request to describe themselves physically, so they mentioned being black together with being tall or short, thin or fat. Only five interviewees relied on race as an important identification/categorization, also mentioning its consequences for their lives, including experiences of discrimination and resilience. One of the five, a 45-year-old female street cleaner, said:

> I feel strong because of the difficulties. I always believe I am capable and never say negative words. Because I am black woman [*negra*], things are more difficult. This color is a burden, even if people say racism does not exist. So, I am always trying to overcome, always trying to do my best, I will not give up on the difficulties of life. I am strong in the face of difficulties. I feel like a strong woman.

In approximately half of the interviews, racial identity was spontaneously mentioned at some point as a salient identification, mostly when respondents spoke about experiences of stigmatization. In addition, when asked specifically about the meaning of their racial identification ("What does it mean for you to identify as black?") in the second half of the interview, most interviewees asserted that their racial identity is important to them. This is in line with the Study on Ethnic-Racial Characteristics of the Population (Pesquisa sobre Caracteristicas Étnico-Raciais da População—PCERP) conducted by the Brazilian Institute for Geography and Statistics (IBGE—Instituto Brasileiro de Geografia e Estatística, responsible for conducting the Brazilian census), which found that 63.7 percent of respondents believe that race or color influences people's lives (IBGE 2011).[25] Some of our interviewees stated not only that their racial identification was important to them but also that they were proud of it. For instance, when we asked Jorge, a 26-year-old male engineer, what it means for him to identify as black, he said it is a reason for pride today, as opposed to yesterday:

A few years ago they [blacks] started to take pride, the issue of negro pride [*orgulho negro*]. Negros have important roles in soap operas; before, they would only have service roles. The value of negros in society today is much more developed. I used to have no role models. A white person is a guy with an attitude, a guy who does the right things, but he does not share your reality—this is the biggest problem. But after you have become aware [*tem a cabeça formada*]. . . . And this is the great importance of NGOs like Educafro, in which I have participated: it is to show that you have value, beyond being black or white, you are a person with rights and duties. This is racial equality.

Self-Labeling: Negro, Moreno, Preto, and Pardo

In contrast to the US literature, writings on racial identification in Brazil have traditionally stressed fluidity over rigidity. The most common arguments presented to demonstrate the fluidity of Brazilian racial identification pertain to (1) the difference between self-classification and hetero-classification (or classification by the interviewer or others) of a person's racial identity; (2) the use of multiple racial terms in Brazilian society; and (3) the existence of a range of terms to describe a color continuum.

The larger difference between self- and hetero-racial identification in Brazil compared to the United States has been documented in ethnographic (e.g., Harris 1964) and survey (e.g., Telles and Lim 1998) research.[26] As discussed by Telles (2004: 91), the consistency between self-classification and interviewer classification of race is nearly 90 percent for those who self-identify as whites, and the discrepancies between self- and hetero-classification are larger for pardos and especially for pretos (29 and 42 percent of inconsistency, respectively, compared to 10 percent among whites).[27]

The multiplicity of Brazilian racial terms was clearly established by a 1976 survey that recorded 135 different terms used by interviewees in response to an open-ended question asking them "What is you color?" Using the same instruments, a 1998 replication of this survey enumerated 145 terms (Schwartzman 1999). Analyzing these surveys, Telles (2004) has demonstrated that the existence of these multiple categories is not significant by showing that more than 50 percent of the responses are concentrated in the traditional census categories (i.e., branco, preto, and pardo). If we also include the category "*moreno*," this percentage reaches nearly 90 prcent.

The Brazilian color continuum is well illustrated by the fact that most non-white Brazilians prefer to identify themselves as *moreno* (literally translated as "tanned") rather than as negro, the more politicized term preferred by the black movement or preto, which emphasizes dark skin color. For example, in the 2008 PCERP survey mentioned above, when asked in an open-ended question about their color or race, 49 percent of respondents chose white, 21.7 percent moreno and 13.6 percent pardo (the census category that denotes mixture, or an intermediate category between black and white), in contrast to 7.8 percent who chose negro. Excluding the individuals surveyed who chose white, nearly 80 percent of non-whites chose mixed-race categories instead of categories more unambiguously associated with being black (IBGE 2011).[28] The use of multiple and mixed-race terms has been interpreted as a whitening strategy used to avoid identifying as black (e.g., Twine 1998).

But as mentioned by Jorge, our young engineer quoted earlier, the usage of the "negro" ethnoracial self-identification has been growing since the 1990s. A survey conducted in 1995 and replicated in 2008 (with similar questions and sampling criteria, but sampling different populations) found that negro identification more than doubled in this period: going from 2.6 percent to 7 percent of the total population. Among pretos and pardos the proportion increased from 12.6 percent to 25 percent (Datafolha 1995, 2008). Even if still a small percentage, negro identification has grown especially among the younger and the more educated, as in the case of our engineer. In Rio de Janeiro, in 2008, nearly 30 percent of preto and pardo respondents identified spontaneously as negros.[29] The growth of the negro identification has been attributed to the increasing prominence of black social movements, the diffusion of transnational repertoires, the implementation of affirmative action policies, and the growing presence of professionals promoting diversity in bureaucratic organizations following the 2001 United Nations World Conference against Racism, Racial Discrimination, Xenophobia and Related Intolerance (Bailey 2008; Paschel 2016).

In our interviews, we asked respondents to identify their race first as an open-ended question ("What is your race?"), and then presented them a list with census categories. Respondents largely identified spontaneously as negros/negras (108 out of 180)—respectively for two-thirds of our middle-class respondents and for half of the working-class respondents,[30] thus diverging considerably from national survey results. Three complementary reasons account for at least some of this difference:

1. While this identification is preferred by the middle class (Sansone 2003; Marteleto 2012),[31] only half of our sample falls in this category, and our working-class respondents have a higher socioeconomic status than the national average for blacks (see Appendix 1).[32]

2. We identified middle-class respondents through snowball sampling (i.e., by asking individuals whom we had interviewed to identify pretos and pardos who would also be willing to be interviewed). The former may have led us to individuals with darker skin.

3. All but one interviewer identified as black, which may have led interviewees to feel comfortable emphasizing their racial identification.

For our interviewees and for the broader population, self-identification as negro does not necessarily translate in racial political consciousness, as has often been presumed by Black Brazilian activists (e.g., Souza 1983). Indeed, as Sansone (2003) discusses in his ethnography of black youth in Salvador (Bahia), the use of this term can be superficial, referring to skin color and appearance, without implying ethnic or group belonging or having shared and distinct customs or values. Similarly, using survey data this time, Bailey (2009a) has found that identifying as negro has little impact on cultural preferences or attitudes toward racial stratification or racial political mobilization. Although we also found that negro self-identification cannot be equated with willingness to mobilize, our data suggest that it often does mean an affirmation of blackness (or a rejection of whiteness) and an awareness of racial identification. In fact, some of the interviewees would change their racial identification from pardo, moreno, or mixed to negro when describing incidents of racial stigmatization or discrimination, as discussed elsewhere (Moraes Silva and Souza Leão 2012).

When asked to specify which official census categories they use to describe themselves, many of our interviewees (70) said they prefer to identify themselves as pardos (browns) rather than pretos (blacks), and this includes individuals who had initially identified themselves as negro (37).[33] A few respondents, however, said they were uncomfortable with the official census categories, commenting that these color categories do not reflect social reality. Six respondents refused to self-identify using the census categories. Nevertheless, some interviewees seem to believe that the census categories are more objective than negro political identification, because they are an unbiased reflection of actual skin tone. Those 37 interviewees who identified as negro spontaneously and as pardo according to the census categories justified their choices by arguing that pardo described the color of their skin (they were not dark enough to be preto) or by the fact that their family is mixed race. For instance, Ana, the journalist cited in the Introduction, said,

"My father was white, technically white. My mother is negra. So I have to identify as parda." Some of the respondents might also choose a census category because it matches what is written on their birth certificate, as is the case for a 59-year-old male university professor, who said: "[the census category pardo] does not and cannot capture reality. I am a negro. But of course, by my birth certificate, I am a pardo."

In our interviews, we also asked people whether they have been labeled with terms different from those with which they identify. Consistent with Sheriff's (2001) findings, many respondents acknowledged that people used different labels to refer to them in an effort to be polite. Some respondents also mentioned facing racial insult (discussed in Section 3.3), for example, being called "pretinho" (a diminutive term that can indicate intimacy or affection but also superiority of the speaker). But, contrary to African American interviewees, Black Brazilians rarely distinguished between labels they believe out-group members should use and those that in-group members can use. Interestingly, some interviewees say that they prefer to be called negro rather than moreno. The statement "I am not a moreno [morena], I am a negro [negra]" was repeated several times in the interviews—showing a clear rejection of the whitening ideology (consistent with Osuji 2013). For instance, a 41-year-old psychologist told us: "When people call me morena, I tell them, I am not morena, I am negra, look at my skin color. . . . People say that there are people who are much darker than me, but I tell them, if you want to know what I am, I am a negra."

To recap, often a single interviewee would identify in multiple ways during his/her interview, illustrating the different and overlapping systems of racial classification in Brazil discussed in detail by Sheriff (2001) and Sansone (2003). Nevertheless, nearly all interviewees affirmed their black identification. In some cases, this involved explicitly denying racially mixed labels in favor of the term negro and stating their black pride. However, while the majority of our respondents are assertive and proud of their black identity, there is little consensus around its meaning.

Meanings of Racial Identity

When asked "What does it mean to you to identify as black?" Brazilian respondents replied in different ways, often showing uncertainty and surprise at the question.[34] This astonishment suggests that categories are not fully institutionalized and taken for granted, especially compared with the way African Americans responded to the same question.

Skin color and black pride were the two most frequently mentioned meanings of racial identity for both middle- and working-class Black Brazilians. When asked what it means to identify as black, a sizable number (more than one-third) of the interviewees said this designation simply refers to the color of their skin and other physical traits. The high frequency with which skin color is mentioned in responses to our question concerning the meaning of racial identification is consistent with results from the PCERP survey: when asked on what basis do they define their color or race and given a multiple choice list, 82.3 percent of respondents said that they define their color or race based on their skin color, while 57.7 percent mentioned that they define it based on phenotype (e.g., hair, mouth, or nose) (IBGE 2011).[35]

The second most common reply to our question about the meaning of racial identity was pride in being black, and this response was often given immediately and with no hesitation (30 percent of respondents). Like Jorge, the engineer cited earlier, some middle-class respondents reported experiencing a growing racial awareness. After suffering discrimination silently during their earlier years, they describe a progressive increase in their racial pride. They commonly associate this change with transnational changes (the Black Is Beautiful Movement) that brought a growing visibility and valorization of a black bodily features (thick lips, curves) and aesthetics (e.g., wearing hair in braids or Afros or wearing turbans). The idea that they were part of a broader, transnational, diaspora also was embraced by a few respondents, even if they had a hard time developing what that meant. Interestingly, a few politically active Ethiopians in Israel replied in a similar way, which might illustrate the diffusion of a transnational black pride movement (Mizrachi and Zawdu 2012). A few respondents explicitly linked their pride to a broader transformation occurring in Brazil, in which a more positive discursive repertoire for describing African features has become available and racial identity has become more salient, as illustrated again by Ana, our 39-year-old journalist:

> My black identity is a construction associated with my adulthood: to let my hair grow natural and long, accept it as kinky, to wear red lipstick on my big mulatta lips, to embrace the culture, to not be ashamed of talking about orixas [Afro-Brazilian gods], to go to samba schools and sweat like the blacks who hear the drums. All this is a construction that for a long time in my life I have repressed. I did not wear lipstick, my hair was always up. So my blackness was slowly fashioned. I learned how to value it.

More commonly, however, interviewees speak of black pride without giving a reason. For example, a 45-year-old male security guard claims "to be black is everything, I am 100 percent black, I feel at ease with being black even if my father is white." Several respondents declared pride in being black but underplayed its importance in shaping their lives. A 34-year-old male economist said, "Black is what I am, how I was born. I am not ashamed, I am proud, but I do not give much value to this question."

Similarly, one-fourth of respondents minimized the importance of race (without expressing pride in being black), explicitly underplaying blackness when asked about the meaning of their racial identification—a position somewhat close to that of the Mizrahim in Israel, for whom ethnic identity is not very salient (see Chapter 4). As put by a male lawyer: "Actually, it does not mean anything special, it's nothing to be mentioned." Those who identified spontaneously as pardos (29 interviewees) were more often uncertain about the meaning of the pardo identity and would commonly use it interchangeably with other labels—such as moreno or *escuro* (dark)—throughout their interview (Moraes Silva and Souza Leão 2012). Again this contrasts strongly with the centrality of blackness for African Americans (see Chapter 2).

Mentions of skin color and black pride were sometimes followed by references to resilience (mentioned by 21 percent of respondents) and stigma or discrimination (mentioned by 19 percent of them). These two descriptors were commonly evoked to express how blacks have suffered and had to work harder to achieve their goals. As put by a 52-year-old female administrator: "I like it [being black]. It is not something that bothers me, I am sorry I have not studied the history of my people. People who were hurt, hard workers who have succeeded after a lot of sacrifice. They were treated unfairly at first, many died.... I like [being black]."

References to history, like this one, were rare in Brazil. Only 20 respondents made a direct reference to history when asked about the meaning of blackness. The disconnect between blackness and history may be enabled by the Brazilian emphasis on racial mixture, a predominant cultural repertoire tied to national identity. Also, slightly fewer Brazilian respondents mentioned having a shared culture (e.g., religion, food, or dress) compared with African Americans (10 percent versus 19 percent). Along the same lines, but relying on survey data collected in Rio de Janeiro state in 2000, Bailey (2009a: 83) found no evidence that negros, pretos, or pardos had distinctive cultural tastes or religious preferences compared to whites, concluding that "it may be difficult to characterize the collective *negro* population (*pardos* and *pretos*) in Brazil as a community of culture." This absence of perceived cultural differences is evidence of porous cultural boundaries between blacks and whites in Brazil, as discussed in the section on group boundaries below.

More evidence of the strength of the racial mixture narrative is the interplay between racial and national identities in Brazil. This issue has not received as much attention in the Brazilian sociological literature as in the United States or South Africa (Moraes Silva 2013). This is largely because, in contrast to the US case, these two identities are generally seen as complementary, as opposed to in tension. This attitude clearly emerges from our interviews and is confirmed by survey data and the secondary literature on the relationship between national and ethnoracial identity, which shows that there is no difference in national attachment between blacks and whites in Brazil. When asked to choose between the two, Black Brazilians give more weight to national identity. Indeed, in the 2010 Project on Ethnicity and Race in Latin America (PERLA) survey, more than 90 percent of Black Brazilians believe Brazilian identity is more important than racial identity (Moraes Silva and Paixão 2014).

To summarize our findings about the meaning of racial identity, most of our respondents view it as an object of pride. This is evidenced by their responses to questions about self-labeling, which reveal a strong preference for the term "negro," a preference accounted for by feelings of "black pride." Nevertheless, respondents typically do not elaborate on the meanings they attach to being black beyond this generic pride, followed by a definition centered on skin color and phenotype. This thinness of meaning (compared to the definitions produced by African Americans) may be due to a relative lack of institutionalized repertoires to describe and account for racial identification that would be comparable to the scripts made broadly available by the Civil Rights Movement in the United States. This thinness may also be due to the symbolic complementarities between black and national identities—which are much more entangled than in the United States.

Nevertheless, our results also show that racial identification in Brazil is not as contested or weak as typically argued in previous studies comparing black identity in Brazil and in the United States (Marx 1998; Twine 1998; Bailey 2009a). Compared to the Israeli cases, we will see that Black Brazilian self-identification falls somewhere between the self-identification found among Ethiopians (who expressed pride in their cultural traditions) and Mizrahim (who also tend to underplay the importance of ethnoracial identity). But racial identification is only one of two dimensions we consider to assess racial groupness among our respondents. When we look at symbolic boundaries, differences between Brazilian and US interviewees are more salient.

GROUP BOUNDARIES

We now turn to perceptions about group boundaries, focusing on experiences and descriptions of racial segregation, whether respondents favor in-group relationships, and whether they spontaneously draw boundaries toward out-group members (especially whites). In our interviews, we found that the symbolic boundaries separating blacks and non-blacks are more porous than in the United States and are somewhat similar to the boundaries between Mizrahim and Ashkenazim in Israel (see Chapter 4). This finding confirms the results of previous studies about weak groupness (Bailey 2009a) and intimate sociability between whites and blacks in Brazil (Twine 1998; Sheriff 2001). Brazil's more blurred symbolic boundaries can be partly attributed to the less racially segregated context in which the Brazilian interviewees work and live, compared with the African American context, as shown in comparative studies relying on national household surveys (Telles 1992). This is also probably shaped by Brazil's historical moral commitment to racial mixture (Moraes Silva and Reis 2012). This commitment, however, does not preclude the existence of tensions in interracial relationships (Osuji 2013), as we discuss in Section 3.3.

Experiences of Spatial Segregation and Integration

In our interviews, we asked respondents to describe the context in which they live. As in the United States, we probed about four types of environments: neighborhood of residence, workplace, schooling (K–12, college, and postgraduate institution), and social interactions (in the context of friendship, community organizations, and religious organizations). In the case of neighborhood and workplace, we considered both past and current settings.

The first striking finding is that more than two-thirds of the Brazilian interviewees (104 out of 160) do not mention racial descriptors when asked to describe the environment where they live or work, or where they went to school. Nevertheless, when asked about incidents of ethnoracial exclusion, one-third of middle-class respondents commented that they were the only black person in their school, college, or place of work. Other studies on the Black Brazilian middle class reported similar findings (Figueiredo 2002; Soares 2004; Praxedes 2006). Often this situation is attributed to structural problems rather than to discrimination—the black middle class is so small and the socioeconomic segregation in neighborhoods and schools so strong that to be black and middle class in Rio de Janeiro is to live in a white world.[36] As a 34-year-old male economist told us, "I see few black people at my position, above me even fewer, but I do not think it is because people do not want to give black people opportunities; it is because a structural filter exists earlier that excludes blacks from opportunities." Teresa, a 49-year-old female medical doctor, elaborated:

> At university, there was only myself and another black, a guy. At [private middle school], I was the only one; even at [federal public high school] there was no one else. We have always been the minority. At the private school, there were only rich people, and I was not rich. So I tried not to stand out. Even today, I sometimes feel that way, because among medical doctors, usually I am the only [black female] one.

Kanter (1977a) associates being a "token" in a predominantly white American workplace with not only heightened visibility but also negative stereotyping and social isolation. This does not necessarily apply to Brazilian interviewees who find themselves in the position of being a "token." A few of them explicitly underplayed the consequences of being the only black around, stating outright that growing up in a mostly white environment was not an issue. For instance, Sonia, a female doctor told us:

It [being one of the few black people] was the same thing at college. My brother, who is a black activist, was always shocked [and used to say,] "In a class of 80 there are only three blacks!" It was only me and two other guys. But I would reply, "What is the problem? I see no problem." I was really good friends with everybody and never heard anything from my friends that showed any type of prejudice.

But these references to white-only spaces are usually perceived as exceptions, mentioned by respondents because such sites stand out. Thus, racial mixture is perceived as the norm, while racial separation is the exception and is unique to elite environments. This is in stark contrast with the US case, where neighborhood racial segregation is generally strong across classes. It is also in contrast to Israel's Mizrahim, who for the most part do not seem to experience a high degree of isolation even in elite environments. The experience of isolation in elite spaces that Black Brazilians describe resembles that of Ethiopians in Israel, although demographically, Ethiopians' underrepresentation in elite environments may be less striking, because they are a small minority and are recent immigrants in their country.

Boundaries and Friendship

We now turn to examining symbolic boundaries, which concern perceptions of similarities and differences, likes and dislikes, perceived inferiority and superiority, between groups. We explored in-group and out-group boundaries by asking the interviewees' opinions regarding interracial romantic relationships and by posing the question: "Do you have friends of all colors?" During our first interviews when we asked "How important is race to you when you choose your friends? (as we did in the United States), Brazilian interviewees could not make sense of this question and were often offended by it, as they perceived it to have racist implications: some mentioned that paying heed to the race of a friend was in itself racist. As discussed below, this is illustrative of important national differences in racial boundaries.

As is the case for African Americans, Mizrahim, and Ethiopian Jews (Arab Palestinians being the exception), Black Brazilians depict group boundaries toward out-groups as relatively porous when they report on their interracial friendships and feelings of closeness with people of other ethnoracial groups. In this regard, the main difference between Brazil and the other cases (especially the United States) is that Brazilians appear to not only be normatively committed to ignoring race in friendships, but to take it for granted. This is well illustrated by the surprise and in some cases, indignation, triggered by the question "Do you have friends of all colors?" Respondents unanimously answered yes and reacted to the question in a much stronger way than did

African Americans, and more emphatically than all groups in Israel. As one 44-year-old female teacher told us:

I have friends of all skin tones ... because Brazilians have different skin tones and identify very differently. So I have friends who are blonde and blue-eyed, and I have friends who are negros but do not see themselves as negros and claim to be morenos, and even two close friends of Asian descent. I do not care, it makes no difference for me. In the broader context of Brazilian society there is different treatment, but in personal relationships there is no difference.

Similarly, nearly all interviewees ignored or vehemently denied the relevance of ethnoracial identity for interpersonal relationship—in contrast to most African Americans. The few respondents (16 in total) who qualified their answers were middle class. They mentioned that most of their friends were white, due to the professional and education circles they operated in, which are mostly white. As a 30-year-old female tourist guide puts it: "Most of my friends are white, but this is due to my academic trajectory: elite schools and universities."

As discussed earlier, most black professionals live in a nearly all-white world both at work and outside work because of the small size of their group and high socioeconomic spatial segregation. This is in contrast to their US counterparts, who may experience mostly white or more diverse environments at work and schools, even if still largely segregated residentially. In that sense, for the Black Brazilian middle class, having white friends is perceived more as inevitable than as the expression of a taste for diversity, as in the US case. In fact, the idea of diversity is not present in the Brazilian respondents' discourses—partly because the idea assumes cultural differences between blacks and whites, which they do not perceive. Nevertheless, like in the US, the middle-class interviewees are quite aware that they are underrepresented in those high socioeconomic status environments, which are perceived as white spaces.

The contrast with the United States is even more evident in the interviewees' responses to questions probing past experiences with interracial dating: nearly all interviewees had been in relationships with whites, and more than half of the married respondents had white partners. These responses resonate with the results of demographic studies described in Section 3.1.

The frequency and normative defense of interracial relationships is largely evidenced in census, survey, and interview data. According to the Datafolha survey of 2008, 90 percent of Brazilians disagree completely (83 percent) or partially (6 percent) with the idea that "people from different races should not get married" (with no difference in frequency across racial groups) (Datafolha 2008).[37] Nevertheless, other surveys have found that people report resistance and sometimes blatant rejection to having negros as sons/daughters in-law (Almeida 2007; Garcia Lopes and de Sá e Silva 2014). Accordingly, a qualitative study of interracial couples in Rio de Janeiro and Los Angeles has also identified racial incidents in interracial couples as common in Brazil (e.g., Osuji 2014),[38] and many of our interviewees experienced incidents of stigmatization in their white spouse's family—in narratives very similar to those of Mizrahim in Israel (see Chapter 4).

In short, interracial friendships and romantic relationships are perceived as natural by Brazilian interviewees, even if they also report dealing with stigma and even blatant experiences of racism in these relationships. Like their US counterparts, they defend interracial relationships normatively, but in stark contrast with African Americans and our three groups in Israel, they reject the assumption of affinities based on racial homophily. The exceptions are the middle-class respondents who depict their circles as mostly white but believe this is largely due to their socioeconomic status and their small numbers. Nevertheless, some of them experience stigmatization or discrimination in these upper-middle-class spaces, as discussed in the next section.

Universalism, Essentialism, and the Absence of Cultural Differences

Nearly two-thirds of middle- and working-class Brazilian respondents believe that racial groups are equal (which is a somewhat similar percentage to what is found among African Americans, where 57 percent agreed with such a statement). Most of their comments are either normative ("we are equal as human beings" or "black and white are just skin colors") or prescriptive ("we should be treated as equal"). Only 11 percent of respondents believe that racial groups are not equal, and they often understood the interview question about blacks and whites being equal as descriptive ("we are not treated as equal"). A 45-year-old female street cleaner summed up the situation as follows: "We are equal, but society does not treat us equally." There were no significant differences between the attitudes of middle- and working-class respondents on this topic.

A similar commitment to universalism, understood as in the previous chapter as an emphasis on similarities or commonalities across groups, is apparent in responses to questions about differences between blacks and whites. Half of the respondents perceive that differences exist, and half said they do not. The first group focused mostly on issues of stigma, discrimination, and racism, which, they argue, make the lives of blacks and whites very different, though they should not be. When asked about the negative aspects of being black, the majority of middle- and working-class respondents point to prejudice or discrimination as the most important disadvantages. The second group, which perceives no differences between racial groups, understood the question as having to do with essential or biological differences and usually replied with a strong commitment to equality: they affirmed that blacks and whites are all human beings, and that the only difference is skin color.

In contrast to African Americans and our three Israeli groups, only a few Brazilian respondents referred to differences in tastes (e.g., food, music), habits (e.g., louder, happier), moral (e.g., family oriented) and attitude towards life (e.g., work ethics). These results are consistent with Bailey (2009a). Relying on a survey conducted in 2000, he found that 68 percent of whites and 64 percent of Black Brazilians in Rio de Janeiro said "there are no differences between customs and traditions of negros and the rest of the population" (Bailey 2009a: 78–79). A 2010 survey asked Brazilians whether there are cultural differences between whites and blacks, differences in how children are raised, and differences in sexual behavior. In all cases, only a minority believed there are differences between racial groups—never more than 25 percent, but on average less than 10 percent (Moraes Silva and Paixão 2014: 197).

This overall perception of similarities, across blacks and whites, also constrains perceptions of essentialized cultural differences as causes of racial inequality. Therefore, arguments about Black Brazilians being culturally or morally inferior were very rare in our interviews and are not salient in the public sphere, in contrast to the United States and Israel.

Weak Anti-white Moral Boundaries

In interviews, Brazilian respondents rarely drew boundaries against whites spontaneously. When they did speak of whites, their statements were consistent with the conclusions of Sovik's (2004) study of Brazilian perceptions about whiteness: "nobody is really white in Brazil." However, when probed about the advantages and disadvantages of being white (one of the questions in our common interview schedule), respondents did state that whites "have it easier" in Brazil, because they are not stigmatized and discriminated against (even if they often qualify their answers by separating poor and middle-class whites).

These findings also resonate with other survey results from Moraes Silva and Paixão (2014), which asked about advantages and disadvantages of being white in Brazil. Perceived benefits of being white related to structural advantages (jobs and opportunities), whereas disadvantages were more stereotypical (worse musicians and worse in sports). In addition, and maybe more important, more than 80 percent of respondents declined to identify any disadvantages related to being white in Brazil. In short, the structural advantages of whiteness seemed to be acknowledged—even taken for granted—by Brazilians of all racial groups (Moraes Silva and Paixão 2014: 210).

Similarly to the mention of a "knapsack" of privileges alluded to in Chapter 2, some respondents, especially from the middle class, pointed to the privilege whites have of not having to think about race or racism. Jorge, our 26-year-old engineer, summarizes this idea:

> Whites in general are conscious of their privileges. Not poor whites, who have no consciousness at all. But a white with a better socioeconomic condition should have more awareness [of his/her privilege]. Yet, usually most people believe there is no racism in Brazil. I have a friend, and we argued. He is an open-minded smart guy, one of my best friends. But he believes it is not like I say. For him, [racism] is something distant, very distant. Really, the issue of blackness is very distant for some people.

As in the quotation above, most references to whites conflate whiteness with high socioeconomic status. Such expressions as "rich whites," and "whites from Zona Sul" were used by the interviewees to differentiate those who were perceived as really privileged from those who were just lighter in skin color.

The conflation of whiteness and high socioeconomic status also reinforces the strength of class boundaries in Black Brazilian narratives. Class boundaries, usually in the form of anti-socioeconomic boundaries, were brought up in different moments of the interviews. Anti-socioeconomic boundaries usually entail the rejection of those who are rich or think too much about money (Lamont 1992). Brazilian respondents commonly mobilized these boundaries to differentiate themselves from people from the upper middle class. Even middle-class respondents tended to distinguish themselves from people who come from elite families or from the most privileged areas of the city (Zona Sul), because the majority of these respondents are first generation college-degree holders and were born and raised in Zona Norte or in other poor suburbs. Black professionals commonly distance themselves from those whom they perceive as rich, describing themselves as "just black people from poor neighborhoods."

Poor whites, in contrast to rich whites, were usually mentioned with empathy to the extent that they share class disadvantages with working-class blacks.[39] For example, when asked for their opinions about racial quotas for access to higher education (the most well-known form of affirmative action in the country), some interviewees voiced concerns about the use of purely racial criteria, because this would exclude poor whites. One of our interviewees, a 29-year-old male chemical engineer, observed, "I think there are many whites who do not have access to education to prepare themselves, like many blacks. Racial quotas are also important as a way of reparation, to correct past injustices, but I do not know about excluding whites." These findings are supported by survey data showing that in spite of widespread approval of racial quotas in Brazil, when asked to choose among several policies, respondents across racial categories prefer the so-called socioeconomic quotas, or quotas based on income criteria, rather than racial quotas (e.g., Datafolha 2008).[40] Indeed, relying on a survey experiment, Bailey, Fialho, and Peria (2015) found that when racial quotas are presented as a zero-sum game between blacks and whites, approval for quotas tends to decline (especially among whites, but also among blacks).

In short, in stark contrast to the United States, where the theme of white privilege is prominent, the strong affirmation of equality and universalism and the even stronger rejection of the notion of cultural differences between racial groups lend support to the existence of porous symbolic racial boundaries in Brazil. Even if interviewees acknowledge white privilege when discussing the advantages (or lack of disadvantage) of being white, anti-white moral boundaries mostly appeared only when whiteness was associated with high socioeconomic status. The conflation of whiteness and high socioeconomic status generally confirms that race alone is not perceived as a basis for moral boundary work between groups. As we will see, this conflation is a key frame through which our interviewees understand their experiences of stigma and ethnoracial exclusion.

CONCLUSION

This section presented a detailed picture of how our Brazilian respondents understand their groupness through two dimensions: (1) their chosen ethnoracial identification and the meaning attributed to it, and (2) group boundaries, including friendship and homophily, and boundaries drawn toward whites. These aspects are influenced by background factors, such as spatial segregation between racial groups, cultural repertoires of racial mixture, and overall patterns of racial and socioeconomic inequality.

Relying on a multilayered definition of identity, our research brings several qualifications to the literature on the strength or weakness of black identity in Brazil. While most previous studies have focused on a lack of racial awareness (e.g., Hanchard 1994; Twine 1998) or the risk of growing divisions between white and Black Brazilians (e.g., Fry et al. 2007; Bailey 2008), our study draws a more nuanced picture, showing (1) Black Brazilians' appreciation of black identification, even if they do not attribute a precise meaning to racial identity and if the latter is not as central or taken for granted as is the case for African Americans; and (2) porous symbolic boundaries against whites, which manifest themselves in the more frequent and taken-for-granted character of sociability between blacks and whites, and by the weak anti-white boundaries Black Brazilians draw.

Respondents asserted descriptively and normatively the porosity of racial boundaries. Half of them are in interracial relationships, and most appear to take for granted that friendship knows no racial bounds—nearly all state that they have friends of all colors. Many African Americans also have white friends, but their closest relationships were reserved for in-group members, while they embraced the ideal of diversity and universalism. Normatively, respondents presented racial mixture as a positive feature of the country and in their lives (Moraes Silva and Reis 2012). This idea of *mistura* (i.e., racial mixture) is an important cultural repertoire that enables certain types of responses to stigmatization while constraining others, as we discuss in Section 3.4.

This positive view of racial mixture does not preclude the perception of white privilege. When drawing boundaries against whites, respondents mostly focus on the latter's economically privileged position.

This adds to the complexity of the Black Brazilians' groupness, which, like that of African Americans, can be characterized as strong by some dimensions and weak by others (and thus contradictory, but contradictory in dimensions distinct from those of African Americans): While identifying positively as blacks, affirming black pride, and perceiving themselves as disadvantaged compared to whites, the Brazilian respondents show less consensus about the meaning of blackness and lead lives that they perceive as more spatially integrated (at least for the working class). At the same time, they more readily engage in interracial relationships and draw weaker antiwhite boundaries than do their African American counterparts.

High socioeconomic inequality and the persistent strength of class boundaries of Brazilian society contribute to weakening the groupness of Black Brazilians, not only because most blacks are poor but also because many whites are also poor. The repertoires of racial mixture—defended as a value and widespread in the practices of interracial marriages—further blur racial symbolic boundaries and present the national culture as mixed and homogenous. In the next section, we explore how groupness, repertoires, and background factors affect how Black Brazilians experience and respond to ethnoracial exclusion.

SECTION 3.3: EXPERIENCES OF STIGMATIZATION AND DISCRIMINATION IN BRAZIL

We now turn to narratives of experiences of ethnoracial exclusion, focusing on both spontaneous narratives of specific incidents and answers to questions about experiences at work and in other realms. As for the US interviews, reported incidents are categorized as stigmatization (assault on worth) and discrimination incidents. Also similarly to African Americans, Black Brazilians mention stigmatization more than discrimination.

Because the very existence of racism and discrimination has been historically challenged through the national myth of racial democracy, it is impossible to understand how our respondents make sense of their experiences without analyzing how they understand this cultural repertoire and how it enables and constrains their interpretation of ethnoracial exclusion. Therefore, before analyzing in detail our interviewees' narratives of incidents, we discuss two issues that were particularly salient in the Brazilian interviews: (1) how they identify incidents of what they see as subtle racism and (2) their constant conflation of race and class in underplaying and often denying racial incidents.

What we term "conflation of race and class" generally refers to the tendency to combine racial identification and socioeconomic status into a composite whole, as if these dimensions were intrinsically linked and impossible to disentangle.[41] We have already seen in Section 3.2 on boundaries toward whites that whiteness and elite socioeconomic status are often used interchangeably when referring to perpetrators of stigmatization. Similarly, being black and being poor are commonly understood as interchangable terms, in particular when referring to reasons for experiencing exclusion and the identification of those who are excluded.

In analyzing the experiences narrated by our interviewees, we find that being stereotyped as low status, poor, or uneducated is the most frequently mentioned type of incident. In narratives coded this way, we observe that the conflation of race and class is itself described by respondents as an incident. It is more often mentioned by middle-class interviewees, who, confident in their high status, also interpret with more certainty an incident as stigmatization. In contrast, working-class respondents are more often uncertain about whether they are stigmatized due to their being black or because they are lower class. Respondents have less hesitation in pointing to ethnoracial (as opposed to class) exclusion when they describe incidents having to do with racial insults, as well as racial profiling and being denied opportunities.

We discuss other differences between middle- and working-class narratives concerning racial incidents. Occasionally, we also refer to gender and age cohort differences—although they are not very salient in our analysis. Finally, we also sometimes contrast Brazilian, US, and Israeli findings to highlight relevant similarities and differences that illuminate our broader analysis of these experiences.

FROM RACIAL DEMOCRACY TO SUBTLE RACISM

Nearly all Brazilians we spoke with acknowledged the existence of racial prejudice in their country. These findings are largely consistent with survey results, which have systematically shown that more than 90 percent of

Brazilians agree that whites have skin color prejudice against blacks (ne-gros) (Datafolha 1995, 2008). Moreover, according to the 2010 PERLA sur-vey, approximately 40 percent of Brazilians of all colors believe that unfair treatment is the main cause of inequality between Black and White Brazil-ians.[42] This explanation was much more frequent than explanations relying on the alleged distinctive cultural or moral traits of blacks (e.g., laziness and lack of self-reliance),[43] which were mentioned by less than 15 percent of respondents of all colors. Interestingly, there are no significant differences across racial categories: nearly half of black and white respondents identify unfair treatment as the main cause of racial inequality.

Survey results also show that Brazilians tend to point to racial discrimina-tion as the cause of racial inequalities more often than Americans do. A Rio de Janeiro state survey conducted in 2000 revealed that 77 percent of white respondents and 86 percent of black respondents attributed occupational racial inequality to racial discrimination (Bailey 2009a: 98).[44] In contrast, 30 percent of white Americans but 59 percent of African Americans attrib-uted US racial inequality to racial discrimination in the 2008 General Social Survey (Bobo et al. 2012: 63). This strong acknowledgment of racism and discrimination among Brazilian respondents also contrasts with Mizrahi in-terviewees, who readily downplay the existence and importance of ethno-racial exclusion. As argued by Telles and Garcia (2013), these survey results indicate a stronger and shared recognition of the structural character of dis-crimination in Brazil (and in other Latin American countries) compared to the United States.

Does acknowledging the existence of racism and racial prejudice in Brazil conflict with the ideal of Brazil as a racial democracy? Bailey (2009a) points out that although references to the myth of racial democracy dominate the literature on race in Brazil, few have examined empirically the topic in de-tail. Guimarães (2001) traced the history of the concept to the 1950s, when it was used to predict that racial mixing would bring about a color-blind society devoid of racism. More recently, some scholars argued that racial de-mocracy is a myth deliberately created to hide racial inequalities (e.g., Mu-nanga 2008); others describe it as a normative ideal to be achieved (e.g., Reis 1996). We do not intend to weigh in the debate concerning whether the ideal of racial democracy is good or bad for Brazilian race relations. Instead, we discuss our interviewees' understandings of racial democracy to capture whether and how this particular cultural repertoire still influences Brazil-ian narratives about racism, especially individual expectations about ideal race relations and reactions to incidents.

When probed about whether Brazil is a racial democracy, the majority of our respondents (70 percent) answered negatively, 19 percent answered positively, and 11 percent were ambivalent.[45] More middle-class respon-dents were critical of the notion, as they view persistent racial discrimi-nation as incompatible with racial democracy. The ambivalent pointed to racial inequality but also to the positive side of Brazilian race relations. As a 54-year-old female doctor said: "There is no racial democracy. But it is a mixed salad and nobody can say 'I'm white.' . . . If you look back, you will find a slave, an indigenous ancestor, and that is why people police themselves [not to be racist]. . . . And that is why the tendency is for things to get better. But of course there is veiled racism." The respondents who regard their country as a partial racial democracy celebrated its racial mixture and compared it favorably to other countries.

We also asked Black Brazilians to compare race relations in Brazil and the United States, and discovered mixed opinions. Half of the respondents consider Brazilian race relations better, more humane and inclusive, which they linked to the value put on racial mixture. For them, the latter explains the lesser violence of Brazilian racism. Even those who acknowledged greater opportunities in the United States see Brazil as offering advantages. In the words of a 33-year-old real estate agent: "Look, in the US, opportunity is for everybody, but even if a black person can make it, things there are worse: the society [there] may give you more opportunities, but the people here are warmer." The other half perceive race relations in Brazil to be as bad or worse than in the United States. Many of these respondents were middle class, and they pointed to the limited opportunities for blacks in Brazil, which constrains social mobility. They also pointed to the greater comfort of middle-class African Americans ("They are used to seeing rich blacks [there].") A 42-year-old female doctor believes:

> [Brazil] is worse. Just look at how few black doctors and lawyers there are. Maybe if things here were more straightforward we would have more opportunities. [Race relations in the United States] are better than this veiled thing. . . . You patronize the little black guy, but you also beat him a little bit. And we are always doing that.

Similarly, many interviewees described Brazilian racism by using a range of terms, such as "veiled," "masked," "camouflaged," "indirect," "subtle," and "subjective," which abounded in the interviews. It is this perception of racism that prompted some interviewees to say they are often unsure whether they are dealing with racism. In their view, racial stigmatization is frequently difficult to discern and requires careful interpretation. In response to our probing, they commonly contrasted the subtlety of Brazilian racism with the more blatant forms of racism in the United States and South Africa. As a 53-year-old male lawyer puts it: "Racism show itself in a non-transparent way. There is nothing like 'you cannot enter this shopping mall because you are black'—and we know there are laws against [racism], it is a crime and all. But from the way people sometimes behave, I think it exists."

Most Brazilian interviewees appear to believe that this veiled character of Brazilian racism, commonly experienced in the absence of overt racist statements, makes it hard to ascertain even if one senses its presence. For example, in the incident mentioned in the Introduction, Ana, the journalist, reported that she could not respond to being stigmatized as a prostitute, because no words were said, whereas some African Americans would not hesitate to qualify this interaction as racist and to react to it.

This perceived veiled character of racism may help explain why, despite the widespread acknowledgement of racial prejudice and discrimination, few Black Brazilians report experiencing discrimination when asked in surveys. For example, in the 2008 Datafolha survey, less than 22 percent of those who identify as blacks (i.e., pretos and pardos) stated ever having been discriminated against. Similarly, in the 2010 PERLA survey, only 20 percent of pretos and pardos stated that they have experienced discrimination due to their skin color. On the basis of a Rio de Janeiro state survey conducted in 2000, Bailey (2009a: 101) found that 24 percent of pretos and pardos surveyed reported feeling discriminated against "at some point."[46] In contrast, in a US survey conducted in 2009, 76 percent of African Americans reported personal experiences of discrimination.[47]

This low frequency of perceived individual racist incidents is puzzling when considered in the light of persistent racial inequalities and their acknowledgment of generalized racial prejudice and discrimination in Brazil. Previous studies have interpreted this low frequency as demonstrating the false consciousness of Black Brazilians concerning the racist character of Brazilian society (e.g., Twine 1998). Our study offers a more complex picture of experiences of stigmatization and discrimination. Although our respondents were at first hesitant to discuss their experiences of ethnoracial exclusion, as the interviews progressed, such experiences were nearly always mentioned, even if their significance was sometimes downplayed.

Narratives of ethnoracial exclusion were generally salient after we questioned Brazilian interviewees about whether they had been treated fairly throughout most of their lives (without the mention of race). Much more often than their US counterparts, they had to be probed about whether they had ever been treated unfairly due to their color or race—which can be partly attributed to the fact that they did not know the interview was about ethnoracial exclusion. As was the case for US and Israeli respondents, they were also queried about incidents at work and elsewhere. Upon probing, nearly all Brazilian interviewees mentioned experiences with ethnoracial exclusion. Nearly all our respondents (142 out of 160, or 89 percent) described at least one incident of ethnoracial exclusion.[48] Only 18 interviewees (or 11 percent) mentioned no incidents, which is much higher than the percentage of African Americans who did not mention any incidents (4 percent) but lower than that for Mizrahi respondents (36 percent).[49]

Consistent with our approach, we inductively identified racialized incidents mentioned by Brazilian interviewees and classified them into two broad categories having to do with stigmatization (or assault on worth) and discrimination. As in the United States, most respondents reported experiencing both types of incidents, but assault-on-worth incidents were more frequently mentioned (by 79 percent, or 127 respondents) than discrimination (mentioned by 60 percent, or 96 respondents).[50] Incidents of assault on worth also represent the majority of the total incidents mentioned in our interviews: 75 percent of the 543 narratives (this is also similar to the US result, where they represented 81 percent). The Brazilian results are summarized by class in Tables A2.3 and A2.4 in Appendix 2.

In the Brazilian case, the conceptual distinction between stigmatization and discrimination helps explain the contrasting results of low reports of incidents in surveys and the high frequency of narratives in our interviews. As we show later in this section, our respondents are more certain about ethnoracial exclusion in situations in which race is directly mentioned or resources are denied (i.e., discrimination), than in situations where they were stereotyped as low status, poor, or uneducated—the most frequently mentioned incidents of stigmatization in their narratives. In the latter case, Brazilian respondents were often uncertain because of their difficulty disentangling socioeconomic and ethnoracial exclusion.

IS IT CLASS OR RACIAL STIGMA?

When queried about unfair treatment, a sizeable number of (mostly middle-class) respondents spontaneously linked unfairness and racism (55 out of 160). These respondents tend to believe negros are nearly always treated unfairly because of their race. This perspective is illustrated by João, a 25-year-old male lawyer who describes how his opinion is often dismissed a priori in professional settings. He says: "Most of the time, I am invisible, but, of course, when I speak some people change [their minds]. They start seeing me in another light. [One] even said I am a 'black man with a white soul.' They [may] begin to accept that I know what I am talking about. This is the worst type of racism, the invisible [kind]."

But approximately half of our interviewees mentioned experiences of ethnoracial exclusion only when probed about race or color. When probed without reference to race or class, 93 out of 160 respondents identified experiences in which they were treated unfairly due to their socioeconomic status, claiming that poor people are never treated fairly in Brazil or that equal opportunities do not exist in the country. As seen in Chapter 2, this is in stark contrast with the United States, where only 29 percent of respondents bring up unfair treatment stemming from class.[51]

This finding is consistent with Bailey's (2009a: 103) survey of the state of Rio de Janeiro conducted in 2000, which revealed that 52 percent of whites and 62 percent of pretos and pardos agreed with the statement: "In Brazil negros are not discriminated against because of their color, but because they are poor." These responses all suggest that class exclusion, not ethnoracial exclusion, is the most salient frame through which unfairness is interpreted in Brazil, even if racial and class exclusion are not perceived as mutually exclusive.

Living in a very unequal society, Brazilians often take class inequalities for granted. The fact that for decades the country ranked highest in income inequality among nations became a cliché. Thus, unsurprisingly, an international comparison of perceptions of inequalities showed that, among all countries surveyed, Brazilians believed inequality was too high but at the same time accepted the greatest of income differentials between professional and nonprofessional occupations (Scalon 2004). As discussed in Chapter 2, Americans have a more ambivalent relationship with class differences and class inequality (Lamont 2000), and they are often oblivious to the stigmatization of poverty (Clair, Daniel, and Lamont 2015).

Across all our Brazilian groups, socioeconomic status and its correlates and signifiers (knowing the right people, being dressed the right way) are often used by interviewees to interpret unfair treatment, underplaying the importance of ethnoracial exclusion. This occurs even when respondents are probed about whether an incident reported was about race or color, as exemplified by Maria, a staff assistant, who described a situation she faced when looking for a job:

> I already had work experience at another clinic, and there was an opening for a receptionist. There was a girl, a young woman, who would put the information into her system to check the [person's] profile.... She was going to include me because it suited my profile. The supervisor called her into a corner [to tell her to not include me].... I thought it was discrimination, but I am not sure it was because I was poorly dressed. I think it was [because I was perceived as poor] because she looked at me from head to toe. It was a nice job, a good salary, all benefits included. The girl who said my profile was good came back with a completely different story, saying the position was already taken and they had not updated the system. It was discrimination. But I did not react because one has to move on [bola pra frente]. It was not the moment to have an attitude.

> Q: But do you think it was because of your color?
> A: I am not sure, maybe. It might have been because of my hair, my clothes. I was unemployed and could not get nice clothes. So I am not sure if it was because of that. I was upset, I was angry, it was the only position and I thought it was for me.

In short, because class discrimination is more readily acknowledged in Brazil than in the United States (where the stigmatization of the poor is so widespread as to be largely taken for granted), respondents more commonly attribute exclusion to class.

The relationship between race and class (generally understood as socio-economic status) has long been debated in Brazilian social sciences. The idea that the problems of Brazilian society should be attributed to class and not to race can be traced back to Pierson's (1942) conclusions that Brazil is a multiracial class society (i.e., a society with economic and social inequality but without social stratification based on race). Marxists (e.g., Fernandes 1969) and theorists of the "mulatto escape hatch" (e.g., Degler 1971) also generally subordinate race to class in their analyses. Statistical studies, from the 1970s on, have showed that regardless of socioeconomic status, race was a determinant factor in explaining social mobility as measured by educational and occupational outcomes (e.g., Hasenbalg 1979; Silva 1979). As mentioned in Section 3.1, debates about racial inequality and discrimination were largely interrupted during the military dictatorship of 1964–1985 and were only discussed in small and isolated academic circles. This may explain why today most Brazilians still view racial discrimination as less important than class inequality, especially when it comes to their understanding of societal problems that should be addressed by public policies (Schwartzman and Moraes Silva 2012).

In the incidents described by our interviewees, the conflation of socio-economic and racial explanations occurs in at least three dimensions: the reason for being stigmatized (their identity as black and poor), the identification of the stigmatizers (white and rich), and the context of stigmatization (elite and white). Interviewees combine blackness and low socioeconomic status when describing the identities of the stigmatized. Indeed, the latter are commonly described as black and poor, black and without an elite surname, black and from poor suburbs, black and from a poor family, and the like. Relying on in-depth interviews with 25 middle-class blacks in Salvador, Bahia, Figueiredo (2002) points out that for middle-class Black Brazilians, being treated as low status is often framed as a misunderstanding (*mal entendido*) of their socioeconomic status instead of racism.

Respondents also commonly view the stigmatizers as both white and elite.[57] They are routinely described as "rich whites," "whites from the South Zone," or "whites who occupy positions of power." This association of Brazilian white stigmatizers with the upper middle class contrasts with the popular (even if academically disputed) association of US racism with working-class whites (Rieder 1987; Kefalas 2003).

This association of whiteness and upper middle class goes hand in hand with the fact that elite environments, such as fancy restaurants and expensive stores, are commonly perceived as places of discrimination. Elite spaces that are perceived as segregated by class are widely defined as white spaces. Given the steep class structure in Brazil, these environments are very exclusive. In such contexts, the dual character of stigmatization (based on blackness and low status) is reasserted. This is illustrated by a 37-year-old female university professor, who describes academia as an elitist environment where people who are like her (i.e., black people from poor backgrounds), are generally excluded:

> I think this issue [of race] comes up in academic life, in certain situations, and therefore in my relationship with my advisor and with the institution. I think it is also related to my socioeconomic condition as a person who lives in the poor outskirts. . . . Being poor, being black creates injustice in the entire society. Our institutions are very elitist. And when we have to share, more is given to those who are seen as belonging to a certain place. My PhD in literature was very elitist. So the place where I come from, my skin color—all have an influence.

This frequent association between blackness and low status might explain why Brazilian middle-class respondents are more certain than working-class respondents that they have experienced racial stigmatization. Thus, fewer than half as many middle-class respondents mentioned no racial incident (5 out of 80) compared to working-class respondents (13 out of 80). Middle-class respondents also mentioned more incidents, more varied types of incidents, and more contexts of incidents. Like their African American counterparts, Brazilian middle-class respondents tended to believe that their class position should protect them from stigmatization. They also can identify ethnoracial exclusion more clearly when it does not, as discussed next.

STIGMATIZATION

Stereotyped as Low Status and Receiving Poor Service

While the previous section describes the uncertainty of interviewees in attributing stigmatization to their alleged racial identity (usually by underplaying ethnoracial exclusion vis-à-vis socioeconomic exclusion), in this section we discuss incidents in which respondents said they were victims of racial stigmatization because others (incorrectly) conflated their being black with their having low status, being low class, or having little education. Indeed, nearly half of Brazilian respondents mentioned incidents in which they were stereotyped as low status, poor, or uneducated (from now on, this will be referred to as "stereotyped as low status"). The high frequency of this type of incident is largely responsible for the overall dominance of stigmatization over discrimination. As mentioned in Chapter 2, this type of incident was much less frequent in the United States, being mentioned by 30 percent of middle-class and 18 percent of working-class respondents.

The higher frequency of mentions of being stereotyped as low status largely stems from Brazilian middle-class respondents. Nearly two-thirds of middle-class respondents mentioned this type of incidents compared with less than one-third among working-class respondents. The former are better able to disentangle what part of exclusion is due to their racial identification than the latter. Given their socioeconomic status, for these middle-class respondents, as for their American counterpart, class stigmatization can be somewhat neutralized by proper presentation of self and by demonstrating their ability to spend and consume. Often the incidents they described occurred in a public space or at work, in contexts where others were not readily aware of their occupational or educational status (e.g., a professor was mistaken for a janitor, a director for a computer technician at work, a doctor for a hospital nurse). As a 39-year-old male economist observes: "[Race] has an influence. You are a person of color, so even if you look like you are a doctor, it will have an influence. Once, when I was in a store, the attendant looked [at me] and a white guy and chose to help the white guy. I knew I had much more money than that white guy, but I just watched and smiled."

If, as is the case with this economist, some middle-class respondents framed such incidents as small inconveniences, many emphasize their emotional impact. Ana, the journalist whose story is told in the Introduction, is a case in point. Denise, a 63-year-old female research chemist who lives in Copacabana (a upper-middle-class neighborhood of Rio) had a different, and more humorous, reaction:

> As I was walking back home, two older ladies stop me and ask, "Dear, do you want a job?" I stopped, placed the bags on the ground and said, "I do. Do you need anyone to work for you?" "Yes," one replied. I then asked, "And how much do you pay?" "Minimum wage, and I have a room for you." I replied, "Madam, minimum wage does not even pay my phone bill. Maybe I can use it to pay the guy who cleans my car. If you pay me 10 or 15 thousand reais, I can work for you. I have no prejudice against any type of work. But with this salary. . . ." One of the ladies realized her mistake, but the other still wanted to argue that it was too much. This is a very prejudiced country. Every time I go to an upper middle class building, they send me to the service elevator.[53] Not anymore, because it is against the law . . . but sometimes I have to call the superintendent!

It is notable that more women than men (40 versus 30) reported feeling stigmatized as low status, poor, or uneducated. This gender difference is linked to the recurrent narrative of black women being mistaken as sexual and domestic workers in middle-class environments, as other studies have also found (Caldwell 2007; Osuji 2013). In our interviews, the stereotype of black women as prostitutes or as oversexualized appeared far less frequently than that of black women as domestic workers. In particular, women in interracial marriages who have lighter skinned children commonly reported being mistaken as nannies, women who open the door of their own houses were often mistaken as maids, and more than a few women were offered domestic jobs while in public spaces, as was the case for Denise, whose experience we just described.[54]

For their part, men more often mentioned being stereotyped as a threat or mistaken for a potential criminal, than did women.[55] For instance, 20 male respondents mentioned instances where women clutched their bags in their presence or where people sat away from them. These incidents are similar to those of male African Americans and will be described later in this section, when we discuss discrimination incidents of racial profiling.

Receiving poor service was the second most frequent type of incident overall, mentioned by nearly one-third of the respondents. It was the most frequent type of incident mentioned by working-class respondents. Interviewees often associate poor service with being stereotyped as poor or low status and with being deprived of full access to consumption—seen increasingly as a sign of citizenship in the expanding Brazilian economy. A previous study of the black middle class already identified poor service as central to the black middle-class experience in Brazil (Figueiredo 2002). The contrast between service offered to whites and blacks, the experience of being ignored when entering a store, and that of being told the price of a consumer good without asking for it, were common narratives.

Ironically, some respondents commented that they deserved good treatment because they have means, just as they seem to assume (conversely) those who cannot afford consuming should not receive good service. This point is made by Miguel, our 30-year-old male economist cited in Section 3.2. He interprets incidents of poor service as resulting from a probability calculus on the part of the salesperson:

> You go to a store, you are poorly dressed. There are two signals there, of course. The salesperson will not give you the same attention he would give to a well-dressed white woman. Is it because I am black? No. It is because I am not buying anything and she is buying half of the store. It is a probability calculus [on the part of the salesman]. Is this racism? If I am better dressed than a white, me a moreno, it is more complicated. But it is still signaling, it is still probability. I have to work a bit to overcome this signaling. I have to dress better to be better treated.

> Q: Do you deliberately think about this?
> A: No, this is natural, it is incorporated. I think it is natural. If we lived in a communist country, with full equality, then you could identify racism, because race would not signal income, and in Brazil race signals income. So I cannot accuse anyone of racism. The guy is a salesman, he gets paid by commission. If he thinks one will buy and the other will not, he will give more attention to the one who will buy. This is clear to me.

Interestingly, even if a third of African American respondents mentioned receiving poor service in their narratives of stigmatization, a few Brazilian middle-class respondents mentioned the United States as a positive example of a place where blacks, especially rich blacks, are well treated. As a 70-year-old male psychiatrist puts it: "The only place I have not felt stigmatized [in an upper-middle-class environment] was in the United States ... [maybe because there] the racial separation is so strong, but if a black man goes to a fancy restaurant it's because he can get in." In fact, a few interviewees also reported being mistaken for Afro-Americans in Brazil (e.g., spoken to in English in check-out lines or restaurants), precisely because they are middle class and black—putting into question the complementarity between black and Brazilian identities discussed in the previous section.

When Race Becomes Salient: Racial Insults and Jokes

Our respondents also reported incidents in which racial motivations were explicit. Racial insults and jokes, taken together, were the second most common type of assault on worth (again, the first being stereotyped as poor, uneducated, or low status). Although Brazil is a country where many downplay racial differences by calling blacks of all shades "morenos," being the object of racial insults and jokes was reported by nearly one-third of our working-class respondents (nearly as frequently as receiving poor service). For their part, one-fourth of middle-class respondents reported being insulted on racial grounds, and one-fifth experienced racial jokes.

Under Brazilian law, "racial offense" (*ofensa racial*), or using racial terms to offend someone's honor, is considered a crime that can be sentenced with up to 8 years in prison. Racial insults against public figures, such as soccer players or actors, often receive widespread media coverage and evoke public outrage.[56] Guimarães (2000) showed that insults were the most common basis for legal action against racism.[57] He finds that racial insults usually involved associating blackness with slavery, dishonesty/delinquency, favelas, immoral behavior, lack of religion, dirtiness, and lack of civilization or education. Most legal actions he analyzed concerned incidents involving strangers, mostly in the workplace (when dealing with clients) or in public spaces. Similarly, Guimarães argues that insults are the way whites react when they feel blacks are challenging a taken-for-granted racial hierarchy—or their sense of group position (Blumer 1958). "More than a conflict weapon, insults seem to be a ritual form to teach subordination through humiliation" (Guimarães 2000: 40). Consistent with this view, some insults reported by our middle-class respondents appeared to have occurred in situations where the victim had the upper hand: they were insulted in traffic for having a better car, at work for refusing to yield to clients' complaints or demands, or in public spaces as a way to settle disputes in which their aggressors were usually wrong.

Although most interviewees find this conduct unacceptable, most also describe them as rare incidents. And although they are concerned with the impact of insults on self-esteem, many treat the incidents lightly. One of the reasons that interviewees downplay these incidents is that many occurred during childhood and at school, and are explained as resulting from a lack of a political awareness among children.[58] It is the case for a 33-year-old female telemarketer who was the only black person in her private school, where she "hardly experienced any prejudice. I had my friends. But I knew there were people who would not talk to me because I was shy. . . . Well, it was the way I was raised. There was a group who would shout "*Neguinha, neguinha* [little black girl]," and I would reply I was a negra. That was the way my mother raised me—I could not say I was white. I was not white. I think it is why this never affected me."

We found that racial jokes were more commonly mentioned in Brazil than in the United States (with 24 percent of Brazilian versus 13 percent of US respondents having experienced them), which might reflect different norms of sociability. More importantly, however, is the different interpretation and reactions to those jokes. In the United States, racial jokes are perceived as either very offensive or as an insult, as illustrated by Joe's reaction when being told a monkey joke in the vignette in the Introduction. In this context, racial humor is typically interpreted as a way to reinforce stereotypes and racial hierarchies (e.g., Park, Gabbadon, and Chernin 2006). In contrast, some Brazilian respondents perceived racial jokes as harmless and inconsequential, as did this 57-year-old male accountant who takes pride in not taking insults seriously. He tells the story of a white man who told him a joke about a black man who dies and is given a funeral. "When his son looks back [toward the tombstone], he sees a vulture on his tomb. When the vulture flies away, he says to his mom: 'Daddy became an angel.' These things exist, right? [The white man] said to me, 'I told you [this joke], because you don't care.' Indeed, I take it fine, I do not overreact."

Some respondents attributed racial jokes to intimacy and the easygoing character of Brazilian sociability. Indeed, jokes were more commonly reported as occurring in personal relationships rather than in anonymous interactions. Similarly, in her comparison of interracial couples in Los Angeles and Rio de Janeiro, Osuji (2014) found that jokes were much more frequent among couples in Rio.

Relying on ethnographies conducted in Mexico and Peru, Sue and Golash-Boza (2013) found a similar pattern of responses to racial jokes: blacks and indigenous peoples often laughed with the joke teller, underplaying its importance. These authors argue that although people feel harmed by those jokes (even if they do not acknowledge it), positive social sanctions silence objections and legitimize racial jokes. According to them, "going along" reproduces racial hierarchies while framing racial humor as benign and using laughter to soften racism. We will return to this point when we discuss responses to incidents, especially the higher incidence of nonresponse in Brazil, in the Section 3.4.

Finally, and also consistent with Guimarães' (2000) findings, instances of gratuitous racist insults were reported, which contradicts the image of Brazil as a society where racism is rarely salient. For instance, 45-year-old male economist told us that he was randomly called "*Crioulo*" (a pejorative term for blacks), one day when he was standing on the street—very well dressed, he stressed. Next to him stood an old man who mumbled under his breath: "not long ago you were at the rack [the tree trunk to which slaves were tied to be beaten], and now you are there standing like a prince." Similarly, a 48-year-old administrative worker reports that one day when he was sitting at a bar, an old lady came to him and said: "It is your lucky day, you were supposed to be at the rack." Although there were not many such cases, the violence and bluntness of these two narratives contradicts the notion that racism in Brazil is typically subtle (in a context where less than 1 percent of the population sees themselves as racist).

Other Types of Assault on Worth

Being underestimated and treated as exceptional are two other types of assaults on worth that were salient in Brazil (although they occur less often than racist jokes and insults). They are more frequently mentioned by middle-class rather than working-class respondents; being underestimated was mentioned by one-third of middle-class respondents, and nearly a third reported being treated as exceptional (versus 14 percent and 10 percent for these categories among working-class respondents). Being underestimated usually involved having your technical, professional, or intellectual ability questioned because you are black. Being regarded as exceptional involved being described as better than most blacks, in statements such as "you are a white person in a black skin." In such incidents, respondents are made to feel the slight of low expectations.

Most of these incidents happened at work or at school, contexts where the stereotypes of blacks as incapable, less competent, or less intelligent than whites seem to be activated. For instance Jorge, the young engineer quoted in Section 3.1, laments that in his work environment, blacks are often expected to fail—people think "Will he be able to do it? Will he do it that way?" He recounts a recent international meeting of his firm where he was the only black person in attendance, and he made a presentation ."But I did not realize until the moment I entered the room that I was going to be the only black person there.... Everybody, even me, was waiting for me to fail at one point. But I had exhaustively prepared my presentation.... You can see that people expect you to fail. Because I am black, I can sense some mistrust."

Conversely, those who succeed feel they are regarded as exceptional. This is accentuated by the fact that our middle-class respondents are often the only black person in their position at work. As a middle-aged male physician puts it, people around him wonder "What is a black guy doing here? But they also realize that there must something special—that person must be at their level." He recalls that a Catholic nun he worked with aimed to compliment him by saying "'You are a black person with a white soul.' . . . I replied, 'Look, sister, I am not sure if souls have color, but if they do, I would rather that mine is the same color as my skin.' She stared at me like someone who could not understand." When treated as exceptional, respondents typically dismiss the stigmatization and pardon the aggressors. Even such comments as "you are a black person with a white soul" are downplayed as ignorance on the part of the stigmatizer.

Interestingly, being treated as exceptional was not mentioned by US and Israeli respondents. As in the case of being stereotyped as low status, the greater frequency of such cases in Brazil is probably related to the invisibility of the black middle class and the strong association between blackness and manual labor. But unlike being stereotyped as low status, in these cases the stigmatized person's occupational position is usually known to the stigmatizer, making the incident more blatantly racial.

Other types of incidents of assault on worth—such as being excluded from social networks (i.e., not included in social events, being made to feel unwelcome in the family of one's spouse or friends), being ignored, and being misunderstood—were mentioned by less than 20 percent of respondents in both class groups. A question about being misunderstood specifically by whites was asked in both the US and Brazilian surveys. Half of US respondents reported having experienced that type of incident, compared with only 11 percent of Brazilian respondents. In fact, most Brazilian respondents viewed the question as nonsensical. The different reaction to this question in the United States and Brazil can be partly attributed to the different group boundaries between blacks and whites in the two countries, as described in Section 3.2, especially to the more porous cultural and moral boundaries toward whites in Brazil.

Only a few respondents mentioned more violent incidents, such as physical assault, being threatened, and vandalism. Differences between male and female respondents for this type of incident were generally not significant. Unlike the US case, where physical assault was mostly mentioned by men, in Brazil only women reported experiencing physical assault and vandalism, and the three such incidents mentioned were all related to sexual assault— indicating another gendered dimension of stigmatization.

DISCRIMINATION

Sixty percent of our respondents identified at least one incident in which resources were denied to them due to their racial identification. Class differences in reported incidents of discrimination are not as striking as in the case of assaults on worth. Respondents seem to be much more certain when identifying discrimination rather than stigmatization. That nearly two-thirds of the respondents could identify discrimination in a context in which racism is constantly challenged suggests the need to reconsider its impact on the structures of opportunities. It also highlights the analytical advantage of our conceptual distinction: while public debates in Brazil focus mostly on stigmatization and its possible consequences for discrimination, Black Brazilian respondents also perceive discrimination without stigmatization (i.e., situations in which they were excluded from resources without openly being mistreated or offended). Here we discuss the three most frequently mentioned types of racial discrimination incidents: (1) being denied job or promotion opportunities; (2) being segregated or excluded from public spaces, networks, or service; and (3) being racially profiled.

Although most incidents reported by Brazilian interviewees are cases of assaults on worth, the second most common incident is "being denied opportunity," which we consider a form of discrimination. It was equally frequently encountered by both class groups (57 respondents, or a little more than one-third of respondents in each class group). In many instances, individuals refer to not getting a job because they are black. For example, some mention sales jobs that were given to white applicants, even if the latter were less or equally experienced than them. Others mention cases where they were overqualified and passed over. For instance, a 57-year-old female administrative staff member describes a case where a white applicant was preferred to three superior black applicants who had done better on a written test. Also, an investment bank informed an economist that he was overqualified for a position after having scored 100 percent on a test.

Other interviewees mentioned incidents in which race was openly used to exclude applicants. There is the case of a 30-year-old female administrative staff member who tried to get a job as a waitress but found out the restaurant was known for hiring only white waitresses. And that of a young female working-class respondent who was hoping to work as a Santa Claus assistant in a mall before learning that she was too dark for the role. In another case, on learning that he did not get a job because of his race, a 29-year-old accounting technician concludes "Now every time I see a job posting that asks for a picture, I do not even bother applying."

With regard to posting pictures for job applications, another interviewee, a young female economist, unintentionally conducted a discrimination field experiment. A recent graduate looking for a job, she posted her CV on two headhunter websites. On one of them she managed to upload her picture, while on the other she could not. While she got fewer and worse offers from the website that had her picture, on the other, she received many calls but was not offered a position. In one case, "A guy called me five times to schedule an interview. . . . He really [wanted] me to come, because he had liked my CV. When I got there, he interviewed me like he was not really interested. I am not sure why he never called back. Maybe when they saw that I am black [they decided not to hire me]."

Exclusion was mentioned by 18 percent of respondents, the same percentage as in the US, but in Brazil it was more cited by middle class (23 percent) than by working class (13 percent)—while in the US it was evenly distributed across classes. The incidents reported involve striking narratives of blatant discrimination in shopping and dining (or other public) spaces (mentioned by nearly one-fourth of middle-class respondents). This is surprising in a country where the narrative of racial democracy prevails. For example, in one of the few mentions of exclusion from housing opportunities, a 59-year-old social worker describes an instance where she wanted to visit an apartment that was for sale, but did not succeed, as the doorman falsely informed her it was no longer available. She discovered the lie after her (white) father went to visit it shortly afterward and was told by the doorman: "Just now, there was a *neguinha* [a pejorative term for black woman] to see the apartment. How can she dare? Those people do not know their place." The interviewee arrived right after, greeted her father, and told the doorman she could put him in jail for discrimination. But she did not sue him, because, in her words, he was just an ignorant migrant from the northeast who also suffered because of discrimination.

Finally, racial profiling was mentioned by nearly one-third of the interviewees, more often by middle-class respondents, and more frequently by men. As mentioned earlier, these incidents usually happened in conjunction with being stereotyped as a threat: black men are often perceived with suspicion, and therefore receive close scrutiny when shopping. Banks were also commonly cited as sites of profiling. Black people are often stopped, while other people pass through security doors without worry. A 28-year-old male accountant describes how he recently yelled at a security guard who was following him in a supermarket: "I started shouting: 'Why are you following me?' He replied it was his job. . . . I asked him, 'Do you think I will steal anything? My monthly income is six times yours.' Fuck it! I was so mad, I just thought I had to humiliate him."

But the most violent incidents of profiling happen in interactions with the police. Respondents commonly describe situations in which they were stopped and searched by the police. For instance, a 43-year-old male journalist explains: "With the police it is always like that: when I am in a bus and they enter to search, they always come to me. The police make you stand up and search you, ask you to open your bag. They do not even bother to ask for your ID."

The higher rate of police violence against black men is confirmed by the high mortality rate of black men in confrontations with police. According to a 2005 United Nations Development Program (UNDP) report, blacks are killed far more frequently by the police than are whites in the state of Rio de Janeiro,[59] which has led some scholars to argue that we are witnessing a

Black Brazilian genocide (Vargas 2010; Rocha 2012; Alves 2014). Although these numbers are widely disseminated by the media, they rarely cause concern, not because blacks are seen as more prone to criminal activities, but because they are poorer, and poor people tend to be viewed as the usual suspects by a police force known to shoot without asking questions (Cano 2000). Incidents similar to the killing of Trayvon Martin and Michael Brown in the United States happen frequently in Brazil but do not make headlines.[60]

CONCLUSION

While nearly all of our Black Brazilian respondents described incidents of ethnoracial exclusion, they were more hesitant to state that such exclusion had occurred than were African Americans. Survey results demonstrate that Brazilians (white and black) are certain about the existence and importance of racism and discrimination in shaping racial inequality (even more so than US whites and African Americans, according to national surveys), but they also show that Black Brazilians are much more uncertain when it comes to reporting personal encounters with racism or discrimination. Moreover, we find that (1) Black Brazilians do not agree that Brazil is a racial democracy but tend to experience Brazilian racism as subtle or masked, especially compared to that encountered in the United States, and (2) they often express uncertainty in pointing to race as the cause of their stigmatization and commonly conflate racial identification and socioeconomic status as causes for being treated unfairly. In fact, when not probed about whether unfair treatment was due to their racial identification or skin color, most respondents (more than half) spontaneously attribute this treatment to their lower socioeconomic status.

Relying on our conceptual distinction between assaults on worth (or stigmatization) and discrimination, we found that uncertainty about experiencing ethnoracial exclusion is stronger when our interviewees describe incidents of stigmatization—which might be one reason Black Brazilians generally have low frequencies of response in surveys that aim to measure everyday racism with questions about personal experiences of discrimination. As shown in Section 3.1, Brazil is a country that historically has been dominated by the national myth of racial democracy, where race and racism are rarely discussed. This historical silence about racial discrimination seems to constrain narratives about racial stigmatization in everyday interactions. In contrast, socioeconomic inequality seems more openly acknowledged in Brazil than in the United States—where traditionally, many self-identify as being middle class. Brazilians are aware that they live in one of the most unequal countries in the world, especially compared to countries with a similar GDP. This enables them to identify their experiences as socioeconomic exclusion. As Guimarães (2006) puts it, in Brazil, race discrimination is seen as unacceptable, but class discrimination is viewed as natural.

What we call the conflation of race and class shapes how interviewees interpret experiences of ethnoracial exclusion at different levels. First, respondents often conflate blackness and low socioeconomic status as the reason for being stigmatized or discriminated against. This conflation is enabled by the fact that most blacks are poor and the black middle class in Brazil is largely invisible, as discussed in this chapter's background section. Second, the salience of socioeconomic boundaries also leads interviewees to conflate whiteness and high socioeconomic status when identifying stigmatizers—rich whites (but not poor whites) are often presented as the source of Brazilian racism. This conflation is enabled by the blurred symbolic boundaries between blacks and whites described in the previous section, in which our respondents distance themselves from rich whites while feeling closer to poor whites, with whom they share disadvantage. Third, elite middle-class spaces (shopping malls) are represented as white and as the most important locus of ethnoracial exclusion. In fact, as discussed in Section 3.1, these are the spaces that are most racially segregated but also most socioeconomically exclusive in the country. Finally, conflation of race and class also shapes the most frequent type of incident mentioned by Brazilian interviewees: being stereotyped as low status, poor, or uneducated. Middle-class interviewees, in particular, commonly mention incidents in which others (incorrectly) conflated racial identification and low status, class, or education when interacting with them. In Section 3.4, we will see that the conflation of race and class also appears in responses to ethnoracial exclusion, in the form of signaling class to deflect racist stereotypes.

The centrality of class over ethnoracial identification is similar to what we will see for Mizrahim in Israel, perhaps related to the strong demographic presence of both groups in their countries, especially in the working class. For Black Brazilians and for Mizrahim, ethnoracial stigmatization and stereotypical association with the low-income, uneducated, and low-status group go hand in hand. If blackness and poverty are also associated in the US context, the strength of African American groupness and the civil rights gains and related policies (e.g., affirmative action) enable interpretations based on racial exclusion across class lines.

We also found that middle-class Black Brazilian respondents more commonly identify ethnoracial exclusion of different types and in different contexts than do working-class respondents. Because they are able to move upward across class lines, they can more clearly identify their exclusion as rather racial than socioeconomic. That they do not always reap the benefits of their class position in such an unequal society (in which the distance from the top to the bottom is very large) probably makes exclusion even more salient. While the Brazilian working class tends to attribute stigmatization more often to class, the middle class more often mobilizes a racialized explanation. The middle class's ability to disentangle race and class as causes of stigmatization also helps explain why class differences are more striking in Brazil than in the United States, where racial frames are salient across classes.

Another stark contrast with African Americans (and a similarity to Ethiopians and Mizrahim) is that many Brazilian interviewees underplay the importance of racist insults and jokes. Also, very few respondents identified situations in which they were misunderstood or felt disrespected by whites (even when they were probed on this). But there are also important similarities between African Americans and Brazilian interviewees: in both cases, some black men often mentioned being stereotyped as a threatening, and exclusion from opportunities is frequently reported. In addition, racist insults were frequently mentioned as a type of incident in both countries. Finally, cases of police violence, like those of Trayvon Martin and Michael Brown, are tragically familiar to Black Brazilians.

Overall, despite often hesitating when identifying instances of ethnoracial exclusion, and despite the conflation of race and class, a significant number of Brazilian respondents did clearly identify situations of both stigmatization (assault on worth) and discrimination and usually thought this treatment is unacceptable. Next we discuss how they reacted (or thought they should react) to these situations.

SECTION 3.4: RESPONSES TO STIGMATIZATION AND DISCRIMINATION

There are few studies of responses to ethnoracial exclusion in Brazil. Most of them focus on the historical resistance by slaves (e.g., Reis 1988), black movement organizations (Hanchard 1994; Alberti and Pereira 2007; Domingues 2007), the adoption of antidiscrimination laws (e.g., Guimarães 1998; Racusen 2004), and recently implemented affirmative action policies (Teixeira 2003; Bailey 2009a; Bailey, Fialho, and Peria 2015). Again, our study breaks new ground by focusing on the normative and idealized responses mobilized by ordinary people, including by asserting equality and searching for respect.

As for our US respondents, in most cases, interviewees included their responses in their description of actual incidents.[61] How they say they reacted reveals how they understand who they are, how they make sense of their experiences, and how they legitimize their actions. It also reveals how they justify their actual responses (Boltanski and Thévenot 1991; Boltanski 2011).

We also analyze ideal responses or normative views on how to respond to stigmatization and discrimination by focusing on questions concerning (1) the best tools to reduce racial inequality, (2) the best way to deal with racism, and (3) views on different strategies, such as affirmative action, racial democracy, and black movements. Our aim is to explore how respondents understand the collective capabilities of their group or what they believe members of their group can do, either alone or together, to gain respect.

Although respondents in Brazil and the United States tend to converge in the way they confront and engage in management of the self in responses to stigmatization and discrimination, Brazilians more often choose to ignore those incidents. Also, Brazilian and American interviewees diverge more in their ideal responses, with Brazilians focusing more on universal policies (e.g., improving the quality of the educational system or income redistribution) and educating the ignorant, rather than on strategies of confrontation that may deepen racial boundaries between blacks and others. We also found Brazilian respondents are still divided about the relative merits of various institutional responses to racism, such as affirmative action and whether collective mobilization (joining the black movement) is desirable.

We looked for and did find significant differences in the ways middle- and working-class blacks respond to ethnoracial exclusion. The middle-class interviewees are both committed to color-blind policies and to increasing awareness of racism, whereas workers are more consistent in defending color-blind strategies only. These results resonate with the approach of middle-class African Americans, who value racial mobilization more than their working-class counterpart does.

ACTUAL RESPONSES TO INCIDENTS

Confronting

In Brazil, confrontation is one of the most frequent responses to ethnoracial exclusion, just as it is in the United States and Israel. It includes responses to a situation in which the interviewee speaks out or reacts, whether politely, formally, or violently, to bring racism to light. Confrontation is also present as an ideal response, as Brazilian respondents stress the importance of making incidents of racism more visible. As a response to incidents, confronting is more frequent among middle- than working-class respondents: nearly two-thirds of middle-class and half of working-class respondents reported confronting in response to an actual incident. As an ideal response, confrontation was also mentioned by approximately half of all respondents. Although we acknowledge that a desirability effect may inflate the prominence of confronting as a response everywhere (Nederhof 1985), representations of legitimate and appropriate responses are nevertheless an important object of study.

Most Brazilian respondents understand confrontation to mean denouncing stigmatization or discrimination by speaking out. Such a strategy is consistent with the perception that racism in Brazil is subtle, discussed in Section 3.3. As a male civil servant suggests, an appropriate response is to unmask racism:

> is to say openly that it exists. People here do not admit it, but they do have prejudice. We have to discuss it, see what happens in reality, statistics, recognize that this is not only about class. Education might allow future generations to understand [that] there is no race, [that] we are all equal, [that] there is no significant difference that justifies an aparteid, even if dissimulated, as it exists here. The current generations, they need to accept that they are racist and work on it.

A few respondents suggested that the best way to confront racism would be massive public interest campaigns or civil education at school. Indeed, Brazil has had a few initiatives, usually partnerships of black organizations and the federal government, to raise awareness of racial prejudice. Before the census of the population was conducted in 1991, the federal government, in conjunction with the black movement, launched a campaign for Brazilians to declare their blackness, relying on a motto with a double meaning: "Do not let your color pass in white: respond with good sense" (*não deixe sua cor passar em branco, responda com bom s/censo*).[62] The early 2000s saw another campaign to encourage discussions of racism, promoted with the provocative question: Where do you hide your racism? (*onde você guarda seu racismo?*) (Heringer and Lopes 2003). Eight of our respondents mentioned these awareness campaigns when they were asked about the best way to deal with racism. For instance, a 54-year-old female executive secretary replied thus: "[By] talking about it, looking for racism inside us. There is even a campaign ..., 'Where do you hide your racism?' We should not hide." More commonly, however, interviewees were in favor of denouncing racism in individual interactions, as it happens. As Denise, the researcher cited in Section 3.3, puts it:

> We cannot openly fight [*partir para a briga*] because people are ignorant. What I try to do is to show that it is wrong, that skin color is not the problem, and that I will take the social elevator and nobody is going to stop me.... [You] cannot let it slide because [this would] give the impression that you agree. And some people agree because they have low self-esteem and think they should be treated that way.

Brazilian interviewees commonly stressed that confrontation should be done politely (a point rarely raised in the United States). This was the case for the physician cited in the previous section who, on being told that he is "a black man with a white soul," replied calmly. As he pointed out, he wanted to be very polite while also making the stigmatizer reflect on her racist comment.

The emphasis on politeness goes hand in hand with the view that people should be educated against racism. This is the ideal response most often mentioned by Brazilian interviewees when asked about the best way to deal with racism. As in the United States, the response focused on educating the racist pertains to both convincing offenders that racism is wrong and of the need "to re-civilize people and teach them we are equal," as a 41-year-old female teacher put it.

While defending polite confrontation and moral education, Brazilian interviewees commonly described violence and aggression (including verbal aggression) as wrong. As a civil servant said: "To create a polemic is not going to get you anywhere. You need to compromise." In some interviews, tension emerged between confronting—or, in their words, "asserting" yourself—and creating divisions. As a 25-year-old driver puts it: "You should assert yourself, defend your race, but not exclude whites. Just show them it is not because they are white that they have the right to everything. Black and white can be together." Asserting oneself is also associated with affirming black identity. In fact, black consciousness, or embracing and asserting a black identity, was mentioned by a few respondents as a way to respond to racism and gain respect. But it was also explicitly rejected by others as a form of reverse racism. In most cases, respondents express a concern that by denouncing racism, they may deepen the divide between racial groups. This concern is not nearly as prevalent among African Americans. This contrast is one of the main differences in actual responses between the two groups.

Because "race talk" has been silenced for so long in Brazil, as discussed in Section 3.1, "naming race" might more readily be perceived as overly aggressive (or impolite) in this country compared to the United States. Therefore, hesitation to "name race" or to point to or denounce racism can be traced to a desire to avoid being viewed as paranoid, being accused of reverse racism, and being perceived as creating unnecessary social divisions—especially in the absence of incontestable proof of racism. Such hesitation may also be motivated by fear of reprisal. Although these motivations appear more clearly in responses we categorized as "management of the self" and "no response," they are probably also a driving force behind this common emphasis on politeness and nonaggressiveness.

Another major difference between Black Brazilians and African Americans is that using the law to confront was mentioned by only 20 interviewees in Brazil, far fewer than in the United States, where formal complaints and lawsuits were mobilized by one-third of interviewees (see also Roscigno 2007). Nevertheless, several Brazilian respondents mentioned that racism is now a crime in Brazil. Since 1951, racism has been considered unlawful under the Afonso Arinos Law (named after the lawyer, university professor, and congressman who proposed it). This law defines discrimination narrowly and includes acts of blatant discrimination, such as blocking the entrance of blacks to a facility or refusing service. In part, because Brazil has not had an official racial segregation policy since the end of slavery, such incidents are seen as rare and as more frequent in the United States than in Brazil (although no clear evidence supports this perception). Only in 1988, under a new democratic Federal Constitution, did black activists succeed in upgrading racial discrimination from a misdemeanor to a crime (Law 7.716, promulgated in 1989; BRASIL 1989). The new law expanded the 1951 definition of racial discrimination to include denial of access to public transportation, public buildings, and elevators (the latter to avoid the common practice of sending blacks to service elevators). As in Israel, the use of the law remains somewhat marginal in Brazil, even if the number of complaints filed is growing. According to the Brazilian Presidential Office of Promotion of Racial Equality (SEPPIR), between 2011 and 2014, there were a 1,500 formal complaints of racism or racial offence. This is four times more than between 2007 and 2010 when the total number of complaints was less than 400.[63] Most of these complaints tend to be dismissed or abandoned (Machado, Santos, and Ferreira 2014).

Based on an analysis of more than 300 filed police reports, racial discrimination complaints, and other documents from the 1990s, Racusen (2002) found that the most common type of complaint filed concerns instances where the plaintiff had been insulted by a neighbor or coworker. Nevertheless, most law officials tended to understand accusations of racism as *injuria*, a lesser misdemeanor of verbal injury to one's honor, which is considered a personal problem—not a racist crime. Comparing studies about the US legal system and how it deals with cases of racism, Racusen argues that verbal insults trigger closer court scrutiny in the US context. He also found that in these legal cases, Brazil defendants often claimed to be nonracist by pointing out that they are mulatto (or racially mixed) or married to a non-white partner—evidence that was often accepted by judges. Rather than inferring causality from timing or logic, judges rarely put the burden of proof on the defendants (see also Racusen 2004). These are the reasons very few people in Brazil have been convicted of racial discrimination as a crime (Guimarães 1998).[64]

Our interviewees hesitated to take legal measures even when racist comments were blatant, because they were skeptical about the outcome. This is illustrated by Rita, an administrative staff member who decided to not sue her employer after facing what to her seemed to be a blatant racial incident, in which she overheard someone calling her an illiterate black. She explained to her colleague that she did not want to sue, because witnesses would deny the incident had happened. And indeed, "The next day, they said: 'Nobody said that, you are not even black. You are seeing discrimination in your own head. Now everything is discrimination?' I had to hold myself . . . I was hurt. I called my manager and spoke to him, but he said to let it go. I told him exactly that—I told him they would say 'she never said that.'" While such hesitation is also present in the United States (Nielsen and Nelson 2005; Roscigno 2007) and data are not available to establish the relative frequency of such reluctance, our interviews suggest that African Americans do mobilize the law more readily.

Finally, very few interviewees mentioned using intimidation or responding physically to incidents of stigmatization. In one case, a doctor reported that in her schooldays she fought with a girl who had called her a monkey. Interestingly, intimidation usually took the form of asserting class status (with or without the threat of legal or administrative measures). This is illustrated by Nina, a physician who threatened a shop attendant after hearing her make racist comments. She said to her: "Look, dear, you work with the public. . . . I could go speak to your boss, and you would lose your minimum wage salary because I am upset. I am a physician and make much more money than you. But in order not be an asshole, I will let it slide." The high visibility and strength of class boundaries is likely to enable such class-based responses.

In short, confrontation is common in responses to actual incidents of ethnoracial stigmatization among Black Brazilians, just as it was among the other groups considered in this study. However, for them, the normative response aims particularly at educating the ignorant and often involves navigating an uneasy balance between making racism visible and not creating unnecessary social divisions or tensions. This tension sums up the challenge that Black Brazilians face when dealing with exclusion in a context where racial boundaries are blurred and where racism is often perceived as veiled.

Management of the Self

As in the other chapters, we refer to management of the self as instances in which respondents believe stigmatization or discrimination is occurring but they decide not to react directly, because the cost is too high, or they wish to preserve energy or maintain their emotional composure. In the Brazilian case, this also includes signaling class status to indicate that one should not be stigmatized—what we call "acting against stereotype." Confrontation is the most frequently mentioned type of response in the United States and Israel, whereas it is mentioned as frequently as management of the self and no response in Brazil.

For Black Brazilians, a key distinction between confronting and management of the self is that the latter often involves a deliberate effort not to make race salient in the interaction. This is of particular concern for Black Brazilians, given the great emphasis put on interracial civility, avoiding social balkanization, and the downplaying of racial differences discussed above. Many say they go to great pains to do so, although this is not always an easy task, as expressed by André, a journalist we met in the previous section. He describes a situation where he was checking in at the business class counter at the airport. After the clerk told him to move to the economy line, he stated that he belonged in this line and that he could have her fired for not first asking him whether he had the documents needed to be in this line. When probed by the interviewer, he explained that he did not make race salient in his response:

A: She understood what I was talking about, she knew what she was doing.
I: But why did you not mention race? Is there a reason?
A: I am not sure. I think it has to do with things that are not said. How can I accuse you of something I cannot prove? And she can say I accused her of a crime she did not commit, because racism is a crime. So because she was not explicit, I was not either.

As discussed in Chapter 2, to an outsider this type of strategy might seem equivalent to not responding, but in contrast to the "no response" code, here the individual reflects on the best way to respond to a specific incident, the costs and benefits of various types of responses, the pragmatic constraints that should shape the response, and so forth. As in the United States, the decision is often guided by the desire to preserve one's emotional energy. In the words of Eduardo, a young professor, "Confronting is really tiresome [chato]."

Management of the self is mentioned by equal numbers of middle- and working-class respondents. Whereas preserving energy was the most common reason offered by working-class respondents for managing the self (mentioned by a third of them), countering stereotypes about blacks was the most common strategy cited by middle-class respondents (a third of them).

Because the most salient stereotype mentioned by Blacks in Brazil is being poor or low status, acting against the stereotype means signaling high status and class. As was the case among African Americans, some middle-class respondents told us they would dress up when going certain places, to signal their occupational status as a preemptive strategy. For example, 49-year-old Teresa, a women physician, states:

Most of the nursing staff thinks I am a nurse because I am not blonde. So sometimes you have to assert yourself. I have a friend, Vera, who is

darker than I am, and she would always arrive at a hospital and immediately introduce herself: "My name is Vera. I am a doctor who will
work today" [to avoid being mistaken for a nurse]. So I thought that
was a good idea [and started doing this].

Similarly, Eduardo, the university professor, says he puts on classical music on his car stereo when stopped by the police. "This would always puzzle
them—how can a big black guy be listening to classical music?"[65]
Another common example of acting against the stereotype, mentioned
more often by working-class respondents, was consuming. For example, when
receiving bad service or being ignored by a salesperson, some reported buy-
ing even more to demonstrate their socioeconomic status. A 52-year-old female administrator described how the attitude of a uncooperative furniture
store salesperson changed after the clerk realized that she could afford a
large bookshelf she was looking at. Instead of confronting the salesperson, she
explains her strategy as follows:

I always try to show the person that she is wrong, one way or another.
You do not need to fight, . . . you just need to have an opportunity, patience. When she started to collect my information and realized I worked
at [a large Brazilian firm], she changed her attitude. That is what I say:
just have patience and you will get there! Show her that her attitude is
useless.

These examples demonstrate, once again, how phenotypes often lead out-
group members to misinterpret class status in Brazil, and how respondents
signal class identity to deflect ethnoracial exclusion.
Humor is also a common strategy to manage the self, apparently more
so than in the United States and Israel. Management of the self through
humor is exemplified by Denise, the nuclear chemist cited in Section 3.3,
who was offered a job as a maid and responded that this would require the
stigmatizer to pay her more than her current salary. Like the option of speaking out (as a form of confrontation), this response is seen as socially acceptable, because through humor one educates, and demonstrates wit and the
capacity to make fun of the stigmatizer. Another example is that of an off-
service naval official in his thirties who was congratulated for his dapper attire with the comment "Are you dressed as a white?" "I just smiled, did not
say anything at first, but he was dressed as a *funkeiro* [performer of popular
music commonly associated with favelas]. I just asked, 'And are you dressed
as a black?' They laughed a lot. I was cool. I was not offended by that. I just
took it naturally."
Like their African American counterparts, by managing the self, respondents in Brazil hope to gain respect without having to bear the costs of direct confrontation. Strategies that signal class status or counteract low-status
stereotypes were particularly common in Brazil, illustrating once more how

Brazilian respondents believe that signaling their class status can (or should) trump racial stigmatization.

Not Responding

Here we are considering cases where interviewees reported that they did not respond because of shock, passivity, feeling they had no choice, or not recognizing the significance of the incident. If confronting is considered a socially desirable response, because it shows agency and capacity to react, not responding—often associated with a passive stance, low self-esteem, or acceptance of stigmatization—may be seen as the least desirable response. It is also hard to consider it as a strategy to redress racial injustice.

Nevertheless, more than half of our respondents (middle and working classes combined) mentioned not responding to incidents, because they were taken by surprise, they were shocked, or they could not do anything about it. Especially in incidents of police racial profiling or discrimination while seeking a job, not responding is perceived as resulting not from a deliberate decision (a choice, or management of the self) but from constraints.

Brazilian respondents also mentioned the inability to prove racism as a reason for not reacting. An example is the story of the journalist mistaken for a prostitute, which was presented in the Introduction. The perception of Brazilian racism as subtle appears here in its most perverse dimension. We saw that the legal burden of proving racism in Brazil is placed on the stigmatized individual. Responding to cases where the stigmatizer does not make race salient is challenging, because assuming that racism occurs is widely viewed as an illegitimate (paranoid, antisocial) response. As a psychologist puts it, "The myth of racial democracy limits the possibility of taking action even when you know you are being harmed in a situation."

The higher frequency of no response in Brazil compared to the United States may also be due to Black Brazilians' having a smaller repertoire for dealing with racism. Some respondents mentioned they did not expect to be discriminated against personally, either due to their class or because they do not think about racism frequently. André, the journalist quoted earlier, explained why he had not reacted to a particular situation:

> Racism is cowardly. . . . It is like when you are walking on the streets of Rio: you walk in Rio, and you know Rio can be dangerous, [as] there is urban violence. But eventually, you go out and get home on your own. Walking, you know you can be a victim of violence, but when it happens, it always gets you by surprise. Racism is the same: when it happens it is like someone hitting you from behind.

But reactions coded as "no response" also include cases in which respondents ignore the incidents, because they view them as minor or insignificant. Some interviewees, especially from middle class, presented themselves as unfazed by these incidents, as if they were the problem of the stigmatizer, not theirs. In justifying ignoring an incident, working-class respondents rely more often on a religious or moral repertoire to justify their non-responses. They may regard not responding as a way to retain moral superiority by showing their capacity to forgive.[66] This is suggested by a 50-year-old municipal security guard who comments about racist jokes:

> When there was a joke, a joke about black people always comes up. And when you are black, it is always upsetting—like a Portuguese would be upset about a joke about Portuguese, or the blonde. . . . I forgive. I had a brother, not biological, and sometimes he would make jokes. There was also this family that used to come to my place, and although they really liked me, it was obvious they were racist. I just forgave them. I would not go to war, I would not argue.

Black Brazilians also commonly identified not responding as an ideal response. About one-fourth of respondents mentioned that the best way to deal with racism is to ignore it, underplay it, or forgive it. Interviewees justified this response with the same reasoning working-class respondents used to justify deliberately not responding to actual incidents: by displaying a superior behavior, blacks can show they are as good as or better than the racists. From an action perspective, this strategy is the opposite of racial consciousness, as it posits that to reduce racism one should not talk about it or should act as if it did not exist. Along these lines, a 31-year-old male private security guard commented:

> I think people should not give it [racism] too much importance—that is the best way to deal with it. Or, when you get somewhere you know you will have to face it, you have to be prepared. If anyone tries to put you down, you should not feel inferior. You know it, you should be proud, regardless of what people are thinking, you are not doing anything wrong. If they say you are black, you should say they are white, what is the difference? The person has to be prepared for it.

When the interviewer probed further, asking whether he felt prepared, the man responded, "Yes, racially, socially, and financially. If they try, and they might get you one day when you are feeling down, they might hurt you. But it normally does not hurt me."

Nevertheless, the fact that not responding figures significantly as an ideal response illustrates the lasting prominence of the notion that racism will progressively disappear on its own, as it is the result of a cultural lag or a product of ignorance. Yet, as argued by Sue and Golash-Boza (2013), not responding may signal acceptance, thereby legitimizing and encouraging the reproduction of racial stigmatization. From this perspective, while confrontation makes racism visible, not responding may contribute to making it invisible.

IDEAL RESPONSES

Universal Policies versus Affirmative Action

Because black identity is not foremost for our Brazilian interviewees (unlike their US counterparts), we did not ask them about the best tools blacks have at their disposal to improve their situation. Indeed, our pilot interviews revealed that they viewed this question as nonsensical.[67] Instead, we asked respondents about their views concerning the best tools to reduce the racial inequality between blacks and whites, as well as about specific strategies, such as affirmative action and joining black organizations (or black movements, as they are referred to in Brazil). By analyzing their responses, we discovered how their perceptions of racial inequality are rooted in structural features of Brazilian society (e.g., the low quality of public education, the large informal job market). We also captured how they understand the driving forces behind racial inequality.

As discussed earlier, national surveys reveal that Black and White Brazilians are highly aware of racial inequality as a defining feature of their society (Bailey 2009a). This also applies to our respondents. More specifically, when probed about racial inequality between blacks and whites, all but five interviewees acknowledged its existence, pointing to such evidence as "most poor people are black," or "[Racial inequality] is in the statistics."[68]

The question about racial inequality was followed by exploring their views concerning the best tools available for reducing it. As in the United States and Israel, education was the most common answer. Probing further into the meaning of this response, we discovered that respondents generally point to policies to improve the Brazilian system of education, in particular, public and free education as a universal policy that makes opportunity available to all (in Portuguese, *investir na educação pública*). This valorization of public education shows a common understanding that if the government develops public policies and invests funds to reduce overall inequality (what we term universal policies), racial inequality will be reduced as well. Therefore, respondents link universal education to an overall redistribution of resources and more equality of opportunity—illustrating, once more, how they believe that racial inequality should be addressed by reducing socioeconomic inequality. This position was explicitly defended by more than one-third of the respondents and was more frequently mentioned by middle- than by working-class interviewees. As stated quite explicitly by a university professor:

I think that to reduce racial inequality we have to reduce overall inequality, socioeconomic inequality, and allow everybody to have, in practice, equal opportunity. In a class society, blacks occupy the lowest positions in the class structure, so we have to make them equal, distribute income and opportunities. [Class inequality] affects blacks but also other groups in society: women, migrants from the northeast, and people from lower economic backgrounds. A more egalitarian society would solve the issue of blacks.

Brazilian respondents put less emphasis on the role of individual strategies for reducing racial inequality (hard work, gaining formal education, moving up) compared to their US counterparts. Self-reliance is less central to them, perhaps because inequality and structural barriers are given prime importance, and success is more often attributed to luck than to hard work (Scalon 2004). Moreover, as discussed in Section 3.1, neoliberal cultural repertoires (e.g., the privatization of risk and market fundamentalism, discussed in Chapter 2), are less prevalent in Brazil, where the state (compared to the market) plays a more central role in coordinating society than it does in the United States. The idea that the state is responsible for eliminating poverty and inequality is widespread, even among elites (Reis and Moore 2005).

As normative responses, neither policies of universal access to education nor self-reliance emphasize racism and discrimination as the cause of racial inequality, as both see correcting class inequality or valorizing individual efforts as the solution. The 2010 PERLA survey provides consistent evidence: when asked why blacks are poor, Brazilian respondents put slightly more weight on the poor quality of schools and their low educational level than on unfair treatment and discrimination (45 percent versus 40 percent; Moraes Silva and Paixão 2014: 209).[69] In contrast, we saw that in the United States, individualist (moral) explanations are increasingly favored over structural explanations.

While some respondents view universal access to education as incompatible with affirmative action policies, others argued that these should be coupled to help equalize opportunities for blacks. Eleven respondents spontaneously mentioned racial quotas as the best way to reduce racial inequality.[70] For them, equality of conditions is more important than equality of opportunity; they view affirmative action policies as an essential tool to reach this goal. In the words of an administrative staff member in her late twenties:

> [The reduction of racial inequality] has already started, in many sectors in the workplace. Because there is discrimination, if a black person and a white person go looking for a job, the probability that the white candidate will be chosen is much higher.... There is still a lot of room for improvement, but [reduction] has already started. Racial quotas are a great victory.

The greater salience of spontaneous mentions of affirmative action and racial quotas in narratives about ideal responses in Brazil as compared to the United States may be due to its more recent implementation (in the 2000s) in Brazil and its strong presence in the media. As in the United States, the most visible cases concern affirmative action in access to higher education. In this country, affirmative action policies based on racial quotas or the use of different entrance scores for minority students are illegal, whereas the Brazilian supreme court established their legality in 2012. As mentioned earlier, a small majority of Brazilians approve of such measures (e.g., 50.8 percent of the respondents to the Datafolha 2008 survey were in favor versus 39.5 percent against), and this approval has slightly increased in recent years. Nevertheless, as also mentioned earlier, when probed concerning their views about different types of policies to increase access to public and private universities, national surveys reveal that most Brazilians prefer quotas and universal policies based on socioeconomic criteria, which are perceived as addressing class inequality directly. Less than 10 percent of those surveyed prefer racial quotas when presented with a class-based alternative (e.g., Santos and Silva 2005).[71]

White and black attitudes toward racial quotas are more similar in Brazil than they are in the United States: as pointed by Bailey (2009a: 159), national surveys have found that differences across racial groups are small, and even insignificant, in Brazil, whereas the 1986 American Election Study showed that 29.7 percent of whites and 79.7 percent of blacks approved of racial quotas at universities, and that 15.4 percent of whites and 67.7 percent of blacks approved of racial quotas for jobs.[72] While college graduates are more supportive of racial quotas or other types of affirmative action in the United States (especially among whites), the opposite is true in Brazil, with college graduates rejecting affirmative action more often than do those without a degree.

In contrast to surveys results, our middle-class respondents approve of racial quotas in higher education slightly more than their working-class counterparts, with half of them in favor and the rest equally opposing them or expressing ambivalence. Arguments in support of racial quotas concerned the need to create more opportunities for blacks and to make the black middle class more prominent. Among working-class respondents, slightly more than half oppose this policy, criticizing it for not being meritocratic, for discriminating against poor whites, and for implying that blacks are not as meritorious as whites. This is consistent with the fact that many Black Brazilians believe the main obstacle to their social mobility is socioeconomic inequality, not racial discrimination. However, nearly half of working-class respondents support racial quotas, largely on the basis that it creates equality of opportunities for social mobility in a country where educational opportunities are very unequally distributed.[73]

More consistent with survey results that show a preference for class-based affirmative action policies over racial quotas, a large majority of our respondents across classes preferred policies that combine racial and class criteria, such as quotas for public schools that include poor black and white students. Thus, affirmative action policies are viewed as a remedy to reduce both racial inequality and overall socioeconomic inequality—once again revealing that the former is viewed as depending on the latter.

Nevertheless, some expressed the opinion, also mirrored in national surveys, that affirmative action policies may feed racism. Many fear that categorizing people as white and black may strengthen racial boundaries, which is indicative of their commitment to racial mixture and porous symbolic boundaries between blacks and non-blacks—a concern far less salient in the United States. This fear influences their views on the black movement, to which now we turn.

Collective Mobilization: Ambivalence toward the Black Movement

As is the case for African Americans, collective mobilization was rarely mentioned spontaneously by Black Brazilian respondents. Thus, we directly probed their views of the black movement.[74]

Black mobilization in Brazil dates back to the seventeenth century slavery revolts (Reis 1988). Frente Negra Brasileira (FNB), the first but short-lived black political party, was created in the 1930s and abolished in 1937 with the Vargas dictatorship. FNB is usually described as proposing an assimilationist agenda (Barbosa 1998; Andrews 2004). It was followed in the 1950s and 1960s by social and cultural movements promoting black consciousness (e.g., TEN, the Experimental Negro Theater). Movimento Negro Unificado, founded in 1978, became the most well known of these movements and mobilized large numbers of blacks around its antidiscrimination agenda (Hanchard 1994; Covin 2006). Since democratization in the 1980s, new black organizations have appeared, and some became institutionalized as nongovernmental organizations. All these historical movements and recent organizations—which the literature broadly terms the "black movement"—have contributed to the increased visibility of racial issues and have collaborated with the Brazilian state to implement racial quotas.[75] Despite this success, students of this movement in Brazil agree that it was never a mass movement (e.g., Paschel 2016).

Racial political mobilization is a topic of relevance that has attracted limited scholarly attention in Brazil. In his pioneering work, de Souza (1971) asked three basic questions that still guide this small literature: (1) Is there a relationship between race on the one hand and political attitudes and behavior on the other? (2) Can shared racial political attitudes generate collective political behavior? (3) Are there any obstacles to political organization on the basis of race? Here we revisit recent answers to these three questions.

Regarding the first question, studies have generally concluded that racial identity has an independent influence on political behavior, even if mediated by class (e.g., de Souza 1971; Soares and Silva 1987; Bueno and Fialho 2009; Mitchell 2009). Regarding the second question, the response has largely been negative: although Black Brazilians may take race into consideration when voting (Bailey 2009b), they are not strong supporters of black politicians, and few are elected to congress (e.g., Santos 2000; Campos and Machado 2015). Regarding the third question, the weak collective mobilization of blacks has been explained by the discriminatory actions of the state, exemplified by its active role in the symbolic inclusion of blacks through racial democracy ideas coupled with its passive role in their socioeconomic exclusion (e.g., Marx 1998). But little is known about how ordinary people perceive the potential and limits of black mobilization—a topic we attend to through in-depth interviews.

Bailey (2009a: 144) explored through survey research how Brazilians evaluate black movement and antiracism organizations, and our findings support his conclusion that there are "overwhelmingly positive attitudes toward the movement" and that it is a mistake to assume "that the lack of more active antiracist organizations in Brazil stems from public apathy." He showed that 81 percent of the residents of the state of Rio de Janeiro surveyed in 2000 agree that "the black movement is right when it claims that there are a lot of racial prejudice in Brazil and that it should be fought against;" 94 percent of them agreed that "negros in Brazil need to organize and fight to have their rights respected;" and 90 percent supported the view that "the situation of negros in Brazil is only going to get better if they organize to fight for their rights" (Bailey 2009a: 127). Also, 55 percent reported that they would participate in some activity to combat racism; and 54 percent said they would consider becoming a member of an organization to fight against racism (Bailey 2009a: 128). Although those who identify as pretos are somewhat more supportive of these statements than are other groups, the difference across racial categories never reaches more than 10 percent.[76] Nevertheless, and most surprisingly, 86 percent of participants in the Rio de Janeiro state survey conducted in 2000 and 65 percent of the 2010 PERLA national sample had never heard of any organization to defend or protect the interests of blacks (Moraes Silva and Paixão 2014: 199).

Among our interviewees, although 23 claimed not to know anything about black movement organizations, most had opinions about them. Their evaluations, however, were split. Nearly half of all respondents supported the black movement and saw it as an important tool to address racism, preserve black culture, or improve the conditions of blacks. Many saw the movement as following the US model of Civil Rights Movement, seen as successful on the eve of the election of the first African American president in the United States, when most interviews were conducted.

Of our respondents, approximately 15 percent (or 27 respondents), most of them middle class, have been or are currently involved in black organizations—consistent with previous findings about the greater presence of middle-class blacks among black militants (e.g., Hanchard 1994). The organization mentioned most often was the Pré-Vestibular para Negros e Carentes, which offers preparatory courses to poor and black students who cannot afford private preparatory classes and are seeking university admission. This organization also offers courses that teach about racial pride and racism in Brazil. Such organizations have invested in mobilizing blacks and have mostly gained traction in the middle class (Paschel 2016).

If, consistent with survey results, most of our interviewees expressed overall sympathy for the black movement and the need for blacks to organize the fight against racism, nearly half of the interviewees also had strong criticisms of it. Some complained that browns were excluded from the movement for being light skinned, while others viewed the movement and black organizations in general as controlled by a few self-interested individuals. This latter statement is consistent with Bailey (2009a), who found that 38 percent of those surveyed (and 43 percent of pretos) believed that black movement organizations are most concerned with defending only the interests of their members.

Finally, some interviewees said they feared these organizations expressed black anti-white racism. Interviewees denounced vehemently what they perceive as the most extreme form of this radicalism: encouraging black people to marry black people only. A critique of this isolationism (attributed inaccurately to the black movement) is articulated by a psychologist. Discussing her cousin, who is an intellectual of the black movement and believes that blacks and whites should not intermarry, this interviewee describes his perspective as untenable. "I was offended. . . . It is a type of thought I do not agree with." Ana, the female journalist quoted in the introduction to this book, voiced a similar view while favoring racial mixture:

> Sometimes I think that the Brazilian black movement encourages reverse racism [*racismo as avessas*]. I am not for segregation even if it comes with equality of opportunity. I am for equality, for diversity, for mixture. This bothers me a lot. I am a *negra* who dates white men. Black Brazilian men never hit on me, but there is one I would love to date [laughing].

In these common (even if inaccurate) criticisms of the black movement, racial mixture reappears as one of the most positive aspects of Brazilian race relations. Relying on the same interviews, Moraes Silva and Reis (2012) show that racial mixture is not understood by interviewees as whitening or as the solution to racism and discrimination, but is simply valued and taken for granted as an orientation that favors more open racial relations and a more fluid view of racial identities. Even if they acknowledge the reality of racism, these respondents value racial mixture as a characteristic of the country and of Brazilians themselves. This is illustrated by the following opinion of an economist who supports the black movement. Even if he believes that miscegenation is not a solution to racism, he captures the association between mixture and accepting racial differences:

[A good thing about Brazil] is our miscegenation. It can be viewed negatively through some frames, such as subtle prejudice. Brazil is made of new people. Although there is hidden racism, we are open, especially in places like Rio de Janeiro, and I think it is getting better. From what I had in my childhood to what my daughters have today, Brazil has improved a lot on this issue.

These findings indicate that resistance to the black movement may be due to its perceived racial exclusivism rather than to a refusal to mobilize around racial identity per se. This is confirmed by results from a 1986 São Paulo survey, in which 11.3 percent of those surveyed expressed support for organizations limited to blacks or mulattos, while 75.3 percent expressed support for multiracial organizations (which blacks, mulattos, and whites could join) (Hasenbalg and Valle e Silva 1999: 173).

To recap, although few people believe that contemporary Brazil is a racial democracy and most show support for black organizations, they value racial mixture and are concerned that the growth of black mobilization might threaten the porous racial boundaries of Brazilian sociability.

CONCLUSION

This section presented a complex picture of responses to stigmatization and discrimination among Brazilian interviewees and revealed two overall competing types of responses, one of them colorblind and the other favorable to bringing race to the center of the debate. When defending different types of actual and ideal responses, interviewees relied on both narratives to try to reconcile their critique of ethoracial exclusion with the preservation of porous racial boundaries.

As for the other four groups analyzed in this book, confrontation was commonly presented as a response to incidents of ethnoracial exclusion and defended as an ideal response, but Brazilian respondents more frequently expressed fear that it might rigidify the racial boundaries and create "dangerous divisions" (in the words of those who oppose racially targeted policies; Fry et al. 2007). Management of the self is often mobilized, especially by signaling middle-class status—which once again we take to be evidence of the strength of class boundaries in Brazil. Not responding is a more frequent response in Brazil than in the United States, and to some extent, Israel. There is special concern for "naming racism" when it cannot be clearly demonstrated for fear of seeming paranoid and overly divisive, or for not being able to establish that racism had occurred. Black Brazilians often saw themselves in situations in which they felt it was impossible to react to incidents and, sometimes, they downplayed the latter's importance and opted to ignore them. Nevertheless, the consequence of not talking about race and racism is to make these concerns invisible, especially in a context in which their consequences are contested (Sue and Golash-Boza 2013).

Both as a response to incidents and as an ideal response, not responding is more frequent among working-class respondents, perhaps because they are more vulnerable and attuned to the possible negative consequences of responding or because, compared to middle-class respondents, they may be more committed to colorblind class discourses. Their solidarity with poor whites in responses about racial quotas can be interpreted as evidence of the latter.

The ideal responses most commonly mentioned are making education more widely available and redistributing socioeconomic resources. Although some support affirmative action in the form of racial quotas, alongside these redistributive policies, others see those two strategies as incompatible. The most frequent reasons for supporting affirmative action (mostly in the middle class) is a belief in the importance of recognizing the reality of racial stigmatization independently of class inequality and the concentration of blacks in the lower class. Nevertheless, consistent with regional and national survey results, many respondents defend the conciliatory strategy of promoting affirmative action policies that consider both class and racial disadvantages.

Finally, the paradox of acknowledging ethnoracial exclusion while not embracing black organizations can be partly attributed to the continuous influence of racial mixture as a societal ideal of intrinsic value that ensures the persistence of weak racial symbolic boundaries. Even when strong socioeconomic inequality between racial groups is acknowledged, strengthening symbolic boundaries between blacks and whites (or making racial divides more salient) remains unacceptable for some respondents.

Nevertheless, for some middle-class respondents, there is a trade-off between reducing socioeconomic inequality between blacks and whites and the need for blacks to organize as a group and work against racism, which requires developing stronger groupness. Often looking to the United States for historical lessons, these individuals believe that black mobilization is the best way to improve their situation, yet they also view mobilization as possibly leading to greater racial tensions. We return to this issue in the next section, the chapter's conclusion.

SECTION 3.5: THE BROAD PICTURE
FOR BLACK BRAZILIANS

This chapter analyzes experiences of ethnoracial exclusion of Black Brazilians in the context of Brazil's historical and socioeconomic background, competing cultural repertoires, and their sense of groupness. Explaining our findings requires taking into consideration multiple and sometimes contradictory forces that are shaping Black Brazilian experiences of ethnoracial exclusion. We now provide a broad picture of the main findings while focusing on the explanatory factors that have been highlighted throughout this chapter.

Groupness. In contrast to African Americans and Arab Palestinians (but similar to Ethiopians and Mizrahim, as shown in Chapter 4), the ethnoracial exclusion experienced by Black Brazilians occurs in a context where color-blindness has historically operated as official national myth. As discussed in Section 3.1, racial democracy became the official state narrative in the mid-twentieth century.

Our analysis suggests that racial democracy certainly still shapes how black groupness is conceptualized and understood in Brazil today. Even if Black Brazilians clearly stated awareness and even pride in their racial identification, they do not view themselves (nor are they viewed) as having a distinct culture—this is in stark contrast to African Americans and the Israeli groups.

The Brazilian case is also very different from the US and Israeli cases, in that spatial integration of Black Brazilians is higher than that of the other groups under consideration, with the possible exception of the Mizrahim in Israel. Interracial friendships, dating, and marriage are also widespread. Indeed, members of this group commonly live in racially mixed neighborhoods and socialize with white relatives in their multiracial families. They also experience integrated institutional settings (e.g., in many elementary public schools). As Telles (1999) puts it, in Brazil most blacks and whites are not separated but are very unequal.

Although the groupness of Black Brazilians is more porous than that of African Americans, it is not as contested or weak as typically argued in previous literature on race in these countries. Our Black Brazilians were proud of their black identification and, when probed, claimed it as an important element of their lives. Important institutional and political transformations have occurred since American social scientists wrote about a "lack of racial consciousness" among Black Brazilians (e.g., Hanchard 1994; Twine 1998) or their weak groupness (Bailey 2009a). As discussed in Section 3.1, since the beginning of the 2000s, governmental policies with regard to race have changed substantially, partly in response to pressure from the black movement (Paschel 2016). This is exemplified by widespread implementation of race-based affirmative action policies in education and the public sector.

Of course, globalization also plays an important role in the diffusion of new ideas concerning diversity and multiculturalism as well as antiracism policies. But these foreign ideas cannot survive without domestic actors who mobilize them. Changes have occurred in the context of democratization (post-1980s), with the growing presence of social movements, including the black movement, pressuring the state and left-wing governments for change and redistribution (Paschel 2016).

Finally, a growing black middle class has also raised new challenges to traditional understandings that upward mobility would "whiten" Black Brazilians. Quite the contrary, our data indicate that those who are higher in the social structure have stronger racial identification.

Stigmatization and Discrimination. Compared to African Americans, however, Black Brazilians are much more hesitant to point to incidents of ethnoracial exclusion, often explaining such incidents by class instead of racial stigmatization. This is due in part to the greater availability of repertoires of class disadvantage as compared to racial disadvantage. Not so in the United States, where repertoires about racial injustice are readily available to African Americans.

This does not mean that Black Brazilians believe their society is a racial democracy. Nor are they blind to structural racial inequality and discrimination. As shown in Section 3.2, they perceive that most high socioeconomic status positions are occupied by whites, even if they feel closer to poor whites. This is evidence of the porous racial boundaries and of the salience of class as a divider in Brazilian society. In this context, they are often at pains to determine whether the stigmatization they experience is due to their low class status or to their being black (what we termed conflation of race and class). This partly explains why some respondents would "name racism" only when facing explicit racial insults or blatant instances of racial discrimination in employment or elsewhere.

Capturing this greater hesitancy helps us make sense of the fact that Brazilian respondents report fewer incidents than do their American counterparts in standard surveys about experiences with everyday racism. Yet, after probing, we also found that incidents that were at first perceived as being due to class stigmatization were often described as due to racial stigmatization as well. Narratives of blatant or subtle discrimination incidents were also quite frequent, which might be surprising in a country where less than 1 percent of the population sees itself as racist.

Porous groupness, in particular weaker symbolic boundaries, also shapes Brazilian interviewees' perception of stigmatization. For example, the low perception of cultural differences also explains why Black Brazilians rarely reported feeling misunderstood by whites and reported few incidents in which they felt stereotyped culturally or morally. Similarly, the normative defense of interracial marriage and racial mixture more generally may be leading respondents to minimize common experiences of stigmatization in families and preference for white partners (Osuji 2013).

Responding to Ethnoracial Exclusion. This valorization of porous groupness, partly a consequence of the racial democracy myth, also constrains patterns of response to racial stigmatization. As is the case for the four other groups under consideration in this book, Black Brazilians often deal with stigmatization and discrimination through confrontation. However, they are as prone to not respond and to engage in management of the self. That respondents value racial mixture may mean that they often see a trade-off between preserving the latter and confronting racial stigmatization—which also partly explains their ambiguity toward the Brazilian black movement.

Even when confronting racism, our Black Brazilians interviewees favor peaceful confrontation through such strategies as engaging in moral education or educating the ignorant. In response to incidents, they often engage in management of the self, since they hesitate to confront when not facing explicit racism—a pattern that may contribute to the reduced visibility of racial stigmatization in the Brazilian context. Finally, both as an actual and an ideal response, not responding is also more common in Brazil than in the United States and Israel. It occurs sometimes because interviewees underplay stigmatization and sometimes because they believe they cannot do anything about racist incidents due to structural constraints. The historical silence about race in Brazil also may have limited the cultural repertoires available to respond to such incidents. Regardless of the reasoning behind not responding, the consequence is that incidents of stigmatization and discrimination often remain largely invisible. Nevertheless, the assumption that stigmatized groups always have to respond adds to the burden of these groups. Perhaps the responsibility of responding should be shared between them and members of nonstigmatized groups, who often do not take an active stance in denouncing ethnoracial exclusion.

The greater availability of repertoires of class disadvantage and scripts of socioeconomic exclusion and the conflation of race and class also shapes Brazilian ideal responses to stigmatization and racism. The most frequently mentioned ideal response in Brazil was universal (and color blind) policies to redress socioeconomic inequalities. This preference is based on the assumption that if socioeconomic inequality is reduced, racial inequalities and ethnoracial exclusion will decline. Although universal policies may be key to redistribution in an unequal country such as Brazil, they may also contribute to the silencing of racism as an engine of inequality. That Black Brazilians do experience stigmatization and discrimination is proof that socioeconomic achievement is not a remedy for ethnoracial exclusion.

Class Differences. Differences between black middle- and working-class respondents are generally starker in Brazil than in the United States. Black Brazilian middle-class interviewees were more certain when describing personal experiences of racial as opposed to class discrimination and stigmatization, identified more incidents over a broader range of types and contexts, and relied and deployed a broader range of responses to ethnoracial exclusion.

Although it has been growing in size in the past decades, the Black Brazilian middle class is still small compared to its African American counterpart. Black Brazilians are widely underrepresented in a middle class that is relatively small as a proportion of Brazilian society. In addition, whereas middle-class African American often live in African American neighborhoods that include blacks from various classes (Pattillo McCoy 1999), middle-class Black Brazilians typically have to live in all-white neighborhoods if they want to reside in middle-class areas; even if they may prefer to live in a racially mixed neighborhood, black middle-class neighborhoods do not exist.

Ironically, this spatial integration of middle-class blacks has been interpreted as evidence of the lack of racial barriers in Brazil or the proof that "money whitens." But our middle-class respondents mentioned numerous experiences of being mistakenly perceived as maids, repairmen, security guards, and other low-status occupations when moving through their neighborhoods. Being stereotyped as low status, poor, or uneducated was the most frequent incident among middle-class respondents, mentioned by two-thirds of them. If they often explain these experiences as driven not by racism but by a simple misreading of their class positions, they less often hesitate to point to their race as a cause of incidents than do their working-class counterparts.

The conflation of class and race also shapes how middle-class interviewees respond to being stereotyped as low status, the most frequently mentioned type of incident in Brazil. They often engage in exhausting battles for the affirmation of their middle-class status—a struggle largely invisible to middle-class whites: they try to prove or make evident their middle-class status through conspicuous consumption or by referring to their occupation, so as to disprove the view that they belong to the large group of blacks who are poor. Although this fear of class misrecognition is also present among African Americans, it is more salient in the narratives of middle-class Black Brazilians. This may be because the social distances between the middle class on the one hand, and the working class and the poor on the other, is greater in Brazil than in the United States.

Middle-class respondents also relied more often on transnational repertoires of blackness and were highly critical of the racial democracy narrative—even if they often expressed ambivalence toward black movements. The experiences and attitudes of these black middle-class respondents are particularly illustrative of how the dominant cultural repertoire of racial mixture is being simultaneously challenged and reproduced in Brazil today. But the situation is changing rapidly: many interviewees identify as negros and denounce stigmatization and discrimination. Moreover, racial inequality is now acknowledged as a public problem by the government and is addressed through race-targetted affirmative action policies. However, we also find continuing resistance to targeting racism, as demonstrated in the widespread and growing preference for using income criteria over race for setting quotas in higher education. Interviewees also largely resist what they perceive as the black exclusionism of the black movement. Finally, the national myth of racial democracy continues to exercise a certain appeal, as revealed by the large number of respondents who mobilize racial mixture as a valued cultural repertoire.

It is beyond the scope of this book to evaluate whether Brazilian blurred groupness and repertoires of racial mixture do more harm (by making mobilization around race difficult) than good (by facilitating interracial sociability and minimizing racial residential segregation). We also refrain from predicting the future directions of these changes, because cultural processes are historically contingent (Lamont, Beljean, and Clair 2014). Our interviewees, however, spoke of how they are experiencing these changes. André, the 40-year-old journalist cited earlier, recalls his own childhood experience with racism. We close this chapter by quoting him as he expresses the hope that his son will be better able to pursue his dreams and ambitions. This quote also reminds us that despite the national differences discussed in this book, race is a transnational social construction. In the Brazilian context, exchanges with the United States remain significant and ongoing:

> I was the best student of history in sixth grade, and we were doing Brazilian history. At one point, I said, "Ah, teacher, if I were the Brazilian president, I would go to Portugal to try to recover everything they took from us." The other students started giggling in the back. . . . [The teacher] said, "What's going on here?" Someone replied, "Teacher, who has ever seen a black president?" That was such a shock to me. I started crying, the teacher scolded the boy, then I cried of shame [because] I was embarrassed to cry and such. But today my son's schoolmates would not say this to him. I think the boy's logic was right: he had never seen, and he did not know [that there could be a black president]. But today [after Obama's election], my son will probably not hear that type of comment.

CHAPTER 4
ISRAEL

The Israeli case is the third and final one in our comparative journey. As in the previous two cases, we begin in Section 4.1 with a concise sociohistorical background of the three Israeli groups: Arab-Palestinians, Mizrahim, and Ethiopians. Contextualizing everyday experiences of our interviewees in wider historical, political, and socioeconomic contexts underscores these groups' different positions with regard to the Zionist national narrative. We suggest that this is a crucial factor in explaining stigmatization and racism in Israel. It is also highlights some taken-for-granted assumptions with respect to national belonging in the United States and Brazil. In Section 4.2, we examine the multidimensional facets of groupness among these three groups: the strong national groupness of Arab-Palestinians, whose sense of group identity is shaped through the historical lenses of the enduring Israeli-Palestinian conflict; the dissonant racial groupness of Ethiopians, who are stigmatized largely due to their skin color, even though they construct their self-identification as full members of the Zionist project; and the weak sense of ethnic groupness of Mizrahi interviewees, who for the most part downplay their ethnic self-identity. Section 4.3 analyzes these groups' experiences of stigmatization and discrimination, and Section 4.4 describes how they react to such incidents in situ, as well as their views about the best ways to deal with social exclusion. In Section 4.5, we summarize our findings and situate them at the intersection between historical background, groupness, and available repertoires of exclusion, incorporation, and national belonging.

SECTION 4.1: BACKGROUND: HISTORICAL AND SOCIOECONOMIC CONTEXT

ZIONISM AS CONSTITUTIVE LEGACY

The historical roots of the three groups at the center of our analysis in Israel cannot be traced back to slavery, unlike African Americans and Black Brazilians. Instead, the primary legacy that shapes these groups' experiences is the establishment of the state of Israel in 1948. The modern state of Israel is the realization of the Zionist movement's vision to reestablish a sovereign Jewish state. Zionism, one of the nationalist movements that emerged in Europe in the nineteenth century, was founded by secular Ashkenazi Jews (i.e., Jews from Central and Eastern Europe) in response to rising European anti-Semitism, exemplified by the Dreyfus Affair in France and the anti-Jewish pogroms in Czarist Russia. This nationalist political movement, formally established by the Austro-Hungarian journalist Theodor Herzl in 1897, encouraged Jewish migration to Ottoman Palestine. After defeat of the Ottomans in World War I, the League of Nations mandated authority over the future territory of Israel to the British government. The terms of the mandate called for the creation of a Jewish body to advise British authorities in matters related to the Jewish homeland. In 1920, the mandatory government officially recognized the Jewish community in Palestine as a legal entity. In the wake of World War II, the United Nations terminated the mandate and adopted *The United Nations Partition Plan for Palestine*, which recommended territorial partition of the territory into Jewish- and Arab-controlled areas. On November 29, 1947, the UN General Assembly adopted a resolution recommending adoption and implementation of the Plan. A war between the newly declared state of Israel and its Arab neighbors erupted immediately thereafter.[1] Alongside the Israeli declaration of independence in May 1948, a new contested social category emerged: Arab Palestinians citizens of Israel, who are at the center of the Israeli case.

With the establishment of the state of Israel, Jewishness became the official factor informing national identity. Indeed, the Law of Return, passed in 1950, declared the right of all Jews, wherever they reside, to immigrate to Israel and have Israeli citizenship.[2] A census conducted shortly after the end of the war in 1948 counted about 800,000 inhabitants of the new state of Israel, of which 18 percent were Arabs and 82 percent were Jewish—80 percent of Ashkenazi origin and 20 percent Mizrahi (Rebhun and Malach 2009). In the next 18 months, the Jewish population doubled to 1,300,000, and reached 1,550,000 a decade after independence, due to immigration.

One of the major outcomes of this massive population increase was the dramatic transformation of the country's ethnic makeup. In the late 1950s only 44.5 percent of post-1948 immigrants were Ashkenazi (i.e., of European and North American origin), whereas 53.4 percent were Mizrahi (i.e., from Middle Eastern and North African countries). As a result, by 1960, the Ashkenazi proportion of the Jewish population had decreased to 58 percent (from 80 percent), whereas the Mizrahi proportion had risen to 42 percent (from 18 percent). The higher birth rate among Mizrahim has increased their proportion of the total Jewish population, such that they are now a narrow majority of all Jewish Israelis. For their part, Ethiopians arrived in two waves in the mid-1980s and early 1990s, totaling about 100,000 new immigrants. The 1970s and 1990s also witnessed immigration from the former Soviet Union and Eastern Europe, which brought in almost 1,000,000 Jews who are classified as Ashkenazi.

As spelled out in the Introduction, this chapter compares three groups, Arab Palestinian citizens, Ethiopians, and Mizrahi Jews, in the same contested political space and draws on 40 to 50 interviews per group (see Table A1.4 in Appendix 1). Smaller sample sizes for each of these groups (compared to those described in Chapters 2 and 3) mean that we cannot reasonably draw conclusions about class, gender, or age differences in each group, although our interviewee population was deliberately sampled to be heterogeneous in these dimensions. We thus rely less on numerical comparisons to parse out in detail the similarities and differences in experiences and responses among our respondents than in the other chapters, emphasizing instead a thematic interpretation of the main trends and stark contrasts in our interviews. Also, given space limitations, we cannot go into the same depth or detail about each group. Instead, we focus on Arab Palestinians and highlight key points of comparison with Ethiopians and Mizrahim in each section (for a fuller discussion of the Ethiopian and Mizrahi cases, see Mizrachi and Zawdu 2012; Mizrachi and Herzog 2012). Although all three groups share Israeli citizenship, only Ethiopians and Mizrahim consider themselves as belonging to the Jewish nation. By and large, our internal comparison highlights the role of Jewish national belonging as a basis of groupness, one shared by all Jews, irrespective of their particular ethnic and racial identities. In the rest of this section, we illuminate the historical background and current situation of Arab Palestinians, Ethiopians, and Mizrahim in Israeli society.

ARAB PALESTINIANS AND THE JEWISH POLITY

Arab Palestinian citizens experience the most exclusion of the three Israeli groups, based on several parameters. It is worth repeating that we are concerned only with Palestinians who are citizens of Israel, a group distinct from Palestinians living in the West Bank and Gaza Strip, as well as Palestinians in East Jerusalem who have been granted Israeli residence but not citizenship. The group that concerns us comprises Arab Palestinians who live on Israeli territory, are members of the Jewish state, but are not full participants in the Jewish polity because they are not Jewish. For example, they are not required to serve in the army. Military service is a crucial symbol of cultural memberships in the context of a national society that has been perpetually at war since its creation in 1948, and military service provides access to important social networks and job opportunities. This is but one manifestation of Arab Palestinian marginalization and segregation, other aspects of which we discuss later in this section.

These Palestinian citizens of Israel are designated as "Arabs" in reference to their culture, mainly their language, which they share with the wider Arab world. This Arabic-speaking population includes Muslims, Christians, Druze, and other religious traditions, but not Jews.[3] Thus the term "Arab" refers to a group that is highly varied in terms of region and religion, as it includes Muslim Bedouin tribes living in the North and South of Israel, Christian Arabs living in large cities, and Druze in the north, among others.

Members of this group also vary in terms of national self-identification: not all Arab citizens of Israel self-identify as Israelis or as Palestinians, with the latter being a politically loaded attribution. For years, Arab Palestinian citizens of Israel were referred to colloquially as "Israeli Arabs." While still in use, this term has been replaced for the most part by what is viewed as the group's own preferred designations—Palestinian citizens of Israel, Palestinian Arabs, Palestinians of 1948, or Palestinian Israelis (Rabinowitz 1993). These terms are also contested, because they require recognition of Palestinian nationality, which is more of a political than an ethnic status: it refers to Palestinian national identity that many view as defined in opposition to an Israeli identity. In contrast, "African American" is not viewed as being incompatible with the term "American."

Our use of the term "Arab Palestinian citizens of Israel" (or "Arab Palestinians," and sometimes simply "Arabs" or "Palestinians") complies with the preferred self-identification of two-thirds of the Arab population in Israel (Smooha 2013). In addition, we apply this term inclusively here to sidestep and downplay variations in how various subgroups included in this broader community understand their national belonging.[4]

Smooha's (2013) important recent survey of this population revealed that despite the hardening of attitudes toward Israel and its more frequent overt protests, overall, Arab Palestinian citizens hold a pragmatic view of their status as a minority in Israel: 56 percent of the Arabs surveyed have "reconciled themselves to Israel as a state with a Jewish majority," 61 percent as "a state whose language is Hebrew," and 53 percent as "a state with an Israeli-Hebrew culture" (Smooha 2013: 12). Moreover, 55 percent of Arab respondents would prefer to live in Israel than in any other country in the world. To quote Smooha's (2013: 12) interpretation of his results at length:

> Reconciliation with Israel's Jewish character does not mean preference, as the Arabs prefer a binational state to a Jewish and democratic state, nor does it imply justification of the status quo, since 69.6 percent of the Arab respondents think that it is not justified that Israel maintains a Jewish majority [in its population]. In addition, the Arabs show a strong commitment to coexistence grounded in acceptance of Israel within the pre-1967 borders, management of relations according to democratic procedures, and relationships based on choice. For example, 80.5 percent of the Arabs agreed that among the kinds of relationships "between Arabs and Jews [there] should also be relationships that people voluntarily choose such as personal friendship and activity in joint organizations."

Unlike African Americans and Black Brazilians, Palestinian citizens of Israel are not phenotypically marked. They are physically similar to the Jewish population, whose majority, the Mizrahim, similarly trace their geographic origins to neighboring Arab states, such as Iraq, Yemen, and Morocco. They can often be identified as Palestinian when they speak Arabic in public, speak Hebrew with an accent, or wear religious clothing (e.g., a headscarf for religious Muslim women). Unlike their counterparts in the United States and in Brazil, Arab Palestinian exclusion is not a function of phenotype but a matter of their position outside the imagined community of the Jewish nation-state of Israel (Anderson 1983). Their national identity (as Palestinians) and their negatively defined religious heritage (as non-Jews) provide the foundations for the social and symbolic boundaries defining Arab Palestinians as a group.

Furthermore, in their case, the legal boundary of citizenship (as Israelis) and the symbolic boundary of national belonging (as Palestinians rather than as members of the Israeli nation) are in historical tension, given the conditions under which the modern nation-state of Israel was created. Furthermore, an Arab party has never been invited to join the ruling coalition, and the idea of an Arab prime minister remains utterly inconceivable to most Jewish Israelis (Ghanem 2001). Although the Israeli government has repeatedly described itself as a liberal democracy, the preferential status given to Jews under Israeli Republicanism and the systematic legal and political marginalization of Arab Palestinian citizens of Israel have been widely documented (Lustick 1980; Peled 1992; Shafir and Peled 2002; Yiftachel 1997, 2006). The depth of the Jewish-Arab divide is revealed in the Israel Democracy Index, a nationally representative social survey that since 2003 has collected data on a wide range of issues related to life satisfaction, attitudes toward the government, and political beliefs. The 2014 Israel Democracy Index showed that while 43 percent of Jewish respondents said that they very much "feel a part of the State of Israel," only 17 percent of Arab Palestinians felt similarly (Hermann et al. 2014).

Moreover, although Arab Palestinians have citizenship rights, they suffer from systematic discrimination. Their social and political participation is greatly constrained, as manifested by their lower social and economic status, their geographic isolation, and their limited and often segregated institutional access (Shafir and Peled 2002; Kimmerling 2004; Mizrachi and Herzog 2012). As mentioned above, unlike Jewish Israelis, Arab Palestinians are not conscripted into the army, which serves as a crucial engine for social integration and the acquisition of human, social, and symbolic capital in Israel.[5] This exceptional status is associated with and reinforces widespread views of this group as being "untrustworthy" (Shafir and Peled 2002). More generally, the symbolic exclusion of Arab Palestinians is also based on a widespread belief that their political allegiance to the Israeli state is questionable, which is derived from their presumed allegiance to the perceived enemy in the Palestinian-Israeli conflict. Evidence of this stigma is found, for example, in a bill proposed by right-wing parties in 2010, which required all Arab Palestinian citizens to take an oath of allegiance to Israel as a "Jewish and democratic state," and which would have punished a refusal to do so by loss of citizenship.[6] As we describe below, the experiences of exclusion of Arab Palestinians, and their specific responses, are shaped to various degrees by the vicissitudes of the broader Israeli-Palestinian conflict.

Yiftachel (1997, 2006) has proposed the term "ethnocracy" to capture the character of Israel as a regime in which a dominant ethnicity (Jews) aims to preserve or extend its disproportionate control over a contested multiethnic territory. He argues that geographic location and ethnic segregation has created an ethno-class regime that systematically favors the Jewish population. For his part, Smooha (1990, 2002) has labeled this type of democratic regime an "ethnic democracy," while Connor (1993) uses the term "ethnonationalism" to describe national identity based on a common language, culture, ancestry or—as in the case of Israel, religion. Brubaker (1996, 2009) has written on forms of nationalism that distinguish between formal citizenship and national identity. Irrespective of these perspectives and labels, social scientists have yet to consider how such regimes of ethno-national distinction are experienced by ordinary Arab Palestinians, an approach that is rectified by the research reported in this chapter (see also Guetzkow and Fast 2016). By considering Arab Palestinians in relation to African Americans and Black Brazilians, the Israeli case casts light on national identity as a powerful force driving stigmatization and discrimination. Our research into the role of national identity in shaping ethnoracial exclusion is particularly timely, given the increasingly multinational character of Western (and other) liberal democracies (Connor 1993; Kymlicka 2007; Vertovec 2015).

While the scope of the civil rights available to Arab Palestinians has improved since the 1990s (Shafir and Peled 2002), for example with the passing of antidiscrimination legislation, suspicion and mistrust between Arabs and Jews remain entrenched (Smooha 2013: 50–56). These feelings have been reinforced by events surrounding the group's growing politicization since the late 1970s. Arab Palestinians have increasingly sought active participation in national political institutions in the wake of two major confrontations. The first, which occurred on March 30, 1976, is annually commemorated as Land Day. On that day, as an expression of solidarity with Palestinians in the occupied territories, a general strike and marches were organized in Arab Palestinian towns in response to Israeli government plans to expropriate thousands of acres in the West Bank for security and settlement purposes. In the ensuing clashes with the Israeli army and police, six Arab Palestinian citizens were killed, almost 100 were wounded, and hundreds were arrested. In the second event, which took place in October 2000, 12 Israeli Palestinian citizens were killed by Israeli police during demonstrations held in support of the Second Intifada.[7]

Rouhana (1989: 55) argues that "the Arabs in Israel have grown [in number] to the point where they can no longer be ignored by either Israelis or Palestinians." At the same time, this group is experiencing contradictory pulls and pushes. Indeed, recent research on Arabs living in Israel has focused on their "Palestinization," that is, a growing consciousness of a separate national identity, concurrently with pressures for "Israelization" (Rouhana 1997; Ghanem 2001). On the one hand, the trend toward "Palestinization" is suggested by survey data, which shows that the notions of "homeland" and "Palestinian people" are two of the core components of Arab Palestinian collective identity (Rouhana 1997: 132). On the other hand, signs of "Israelization" are also present. Based on a recent survey of Arab Palestinians and Jews, Smooha (2013: vi) concludes that "in Arab eyes, integration [into the Israeli polity] would increase their access to resources and to a less traditional way of life without them having to assimilate into the Jewish population."

The presence of these contradictory pushes and pulls is revealed by other studies that uncover multiple avenues to being a "Palestinian living in Israel" that do not accord with rigid acceptance of the Jewish/Arab division. Internal segmentation is increasing the salience of other dimensions of identity, including religion, region (e.g., cities, farms/villages, and Bedouin settlements), class, gender, and political affiliation (Herzog 1999, 2007; Kanaaneh 2002; Bligh 2003; Kanaaneh and Nusair 2010).

These internal contradictions in the Arab Palestinian community also manifest themselves at the level of social science knowledge. Research on

Arab Palestinians had previously been within the purview of professional Orientalists, who approached the group only in terms of security considerations (Eyal 2006). Arab Palestinians have been included in public opinion surveys since the 1990s, and it is only recently that they have started depicting this group on multiple dimensions. Documentation of Arab experiences of marginality has led to the multiplication of studies based on in-depth interviews focusing on Arab, Bedouin, and Druze women (Herzog 1999, 2004; Abu-Rabia-Queder 2007; Abu-Rabia-Queder and Weiner-Levy 2013), the younger generation (Rabinowitz and Abu-Baker 2005), Arabs living in mixed Jewish-Arab cities (Monterescu and Rabinowitz 2007), and Arab intellectuals (Ghanim 2009). Our study focuses on relatively understudied groups, that is, ordinary middle- and working-class Arab Palestinians.

Arab Palestinian citizens of Israel, who make up approximately 17 percent (about 1.5 million people) of Israel's current population, are concentrated in 112 homogeneous localities (8.6 percent) and 8 mixed cities (about 8.4 percent) (Khamaysi 2011: 14, 86). The majority are Muslim (about 82 percent), with sizeable minorities of Christians (about 9.4 percent), and Druze (about 8.6 percent) (Khamaysi 2011: 86). Due to land expropriation in the wake of Israel's establishment, nearly all Arab small land-owning farmers and peasants have been proletarianized (Rosenfeld 1964); this group currently occupies the lowest strata in Israeli society (Lewin-Epstein and Semyonov 1993; Haberfeld and Cohen 2007). In 2010, the average income of Arab households (New Israel Shekel [NIS] 9,232) was about 40 percent below that of Jewish households (NIS 15,312). A large percentage of Arab households currently live below the poverty line (48.7 percent), with that percentage increasing slightly in recent years (45.3 percent in 2001, 47.6 percent in 2007; Gharrah 2013).

Large differences are likewise found in average personal income. While average income for Israel's total population was NIS 9,030 in 2013, average income for Arabs was NIS 6,076. During the preceding decade, the Arab-Jewish wage gap had widened—Arabs earned 73 percent of the Israeli average wage in 2003 (Jews and Arabs combined) but only 67 percent in 2013 (Swirski, Connor-Attias, and Ophir 2014). Unemployment is also higher among Arabs than among Jews, although fluctuating over time (Gharrah 2013).

The marginal position of Arab Palestinians is intensified by spatial segregation (Yiftachel 1997, 2006). In the early 1990s, approximately 85 percent of Arab Palestinian citizens of Israel resided in purely Arab communities (Lewin-Epstein and Semyonov 1993); this percentage rose to 90 percent by the first decade of the twenty-first century (Gharrah 2013). Arabs tend to reside in smaller towns and villages than does the Jewish population: as of 2010, only about 40 percent of the Arab population resided in cities, compared to 81 percent of Jews. Also, while 52 percent of Arabs resided in small communities,[8] this figures is 8 percent for Jews (Gharrah 2013). Another approximately 8.6 percent of Arabs live in so-called mixed cities (Falah 1996).[9]

This spatial segregation has affected income inequality because of the limited employment opportunities available in Arab residential areas (Lewin-Epstein and Semyonov 1993). These areas are characterized by little job diversity and high person-to-job ratios (2.85 in Arab communities compared to 2.25 in Jewish ones). Among working-aged Arab Palestinians (aged 25–64), employment reached only 49 percent (72 percent for men and 26 percent for women, the latter comparable to the figures for the Jewish population; Gharrah 2013).

Spatial segregation is known to encourage institutional segregation, especially in the school system (Arar 2012). Similar to Québec, which funds both French- and English-speaking schools, the Israeli state supports two parallel school systems, an arrangement valued and desired by the majority of Arab Palestinians (Smooha 2013). In 2013, out of 1.6 million pupils enrolled in the Israeli educational system, only 5,000 Arabs attended Jewish (Hebrew) schools, while 177 Jews attended Arab schools (Shwed et al. 2014). Among all the Israelis who graduated from high school in 2005, 35 percent entered an academic degree program in a college or university by 2013. This figure included 39 percent of all Jewish high school graduates and only 20 percent of their Arab peers (Swirski, Connor-Attias, and Ophir 2014).

Arabs are also overrepresented in Israeli prisons, as they make up about 35 percent of the criminal prisoner population, with the ratio between Jewish and Arab incarceration rates dropping slightly from 3.15 in 1970 to 2.3 by 2001 (Korn 2003). The first decade of the twenty-first century has seen an increase in Arabs imprisoned, to 42 percent of all prisoners in 2010, or more than twice their share of the general population (Illuz-Eilon 2011).

ETHIOPIANS AND MIZRAHIM: IN THE PINCERS OF ETHNO-NATIONAL IDENTITY, EXCLUSION, AND INCLUSION

Whereas the Arab Palestinians were considered outside the Zionist project from its beginning, the two other groups, Mizrahim and Ethiopians, found themselves in the purview of the Zionist mission. Although Israel's Declaration of Independence mentions commitment to universal, democratic ideals, such as social equality regardless of race, religion and gender, in practice equality is often questioned in reference to Arab Palestinians and, to a generally lesser extent, to the two Jewish groups discussed here. Moreover, the Zionist Movement aspired to create a "new Jew"—modern, liberal, and secular—suited to the Western democratic order and its industrial economy (Mizrachi 2004; Sasson-Levy and Shoshana 2013). This goal was challenged by another Zionist mission: "the ingathering of the exiles," that is, bringing to Israel Jews from the global diaspora. In the early decades of the state, immigrants poured into the country from a wide range of European, Middle Eastern, and North African countries. Some of these Jews were far removed from this European ideal cultural model of the new Jew. Conforming to the modernist-secular prototype of the new Jew is arguably more viable for Mizrahi Jews than for Ethiopians: while the main obstacle to Mizrahi assimilation is being perceived as culturally backward, Ethiopians face the same burden in addition to being strongly marked phenotypically.

Ethiopian Jews. The very real diversity of the Israeli population has consistently challenged the Zionist melting-pot ideology and policies adopted by the state of Israel since its establishment in 1948; the arrival of Ethiopian Jews added racial phenotype to the ethnic mix. In 1973, Israel's chief rabbis declared that as descendants of the biblical Jewish tribe of Dan, Ethiopians were entitled to immigrant status. In 1984, 15,000 Ethiopians were airlifted to Israel in a secret operation that involved passage through Sudan. In the early 1990s, another approximately 35,000 Ethiopians arrived, with smaller numbers entering periodically since then. All told, about 125,000 Israelis of Ethiopian descent currently live in Israel, accounting for 2 percent of the total Jewish population (Israel State Comptroller's Report 2013).

Ethiopians share with Mizrahim the stigma of cultural backwardness, compounded by the stigma of blackness and doubts over the authenticity of their Jewishness (Kaplan and Rosen 1993; Weil 1997; Homel 2012). Moreover, the stigma surrounding Ethiopians is stronger in part due to their status as recent immigrants. Despite repeated declarations by politicians and public officials affirming their full membership in Jewish Israeli society, members of this group continue to experience exclusion based on phenotype (Ben Eliezer 2004). Thus it is not surprising that the media and public intellectuals reccuringly denounce the racism experienced by members of this group.

The ethnoracial exclusion experienced by Ethiopians is due to their phenotype, accentuated by their relatively recent arrival, and additional challenges tied to immigration and acculturation, such as lack of fluency in Hebrew. These last two aspects distinguish them from African Americans and Black Brazilians. But as we shall see, this distinctiveness does not prevent Ethiopians from exhibiting a sense of national belonging and full self identification with the Israeli Jewish polity, which is comparable to that found among Mizrahim.

Although state authorities and the public alike have framed Ethiopian migration as an episode in the heroic Zionist narrative—that of the ingathering of the exiles and the return of the lost tribe, this "return" has been accompanied by skepticism regarding their Jewish roots and religious culture (Homel 2012), which has added to the debate over their racial otherness and presumed cultural "primitiveness" as immigrants from Africa (Weil 1997; Samon 2003;

Ben Eliezer 2004). Nevertheless, as has been the case for other immigrant groups, Ethiopian Jews have benefited from integration-targeted programs provided in state-sponsored immigrant absorption centers that also offer temporary living quarters, intensive Hebrew classes, and basic information about life in Israel, all meant to "provide a soft landing and supportive framework, tailored to the [immigrants'] needs."[10]

For Ethiopians, as for the earlier generations of Mizrahim, the government interpreted their "needs" through an assimilationist agenda. For example, as soon as their airplanes landed, the immigration officials welcoming them provided Israeli names for their children (Ben-Eliezer 2008). This is only the most blatant element of what some scholars have described as a broader state project of cultural and educational acculturation, designed to "whiten" Ethiopians (Ben Eliezer 2004). Governmental agencies placed them in low-income neighborhoods and developing towns on the geographic and economic periphery. Today they are concentrated in a small number of de facto segregated neighborhoods and towns, with 70 percent of this population living in 17 mostly low-income communities. As newcomers, Ethiopians found themselves at the bottom of the socioeconomic ladder (Ben-Eliezer 2008). There is now broader recognition of their low position in the Israel social structure (Hendels 2013).

Social scientists began investigating the meaning of the emerging category of race in the Israeli public discourse after a major influx of Ethiopian immigrants in the 1990s. Although the term "racism" was for many years taboo in Israel due to its association with the Holocaust, it entered the public discourse in the mid-1970s, when Palestinian movements began equating Zionism with racism, a rhetorical link sanctioned by international organizations, such as the United Nations (Herzog, Sharon, and Leykin 2008). Social scientists have also studied this group's structural marginality (Swirski and Swirski 2002), its adjustment to Israeli society, and institutional responses to this group of new immigrants (Kimmerling 2004: 441–457). State institutions have often perceived Ethiopians as a problem (Hertzog 1998), given the questions surrounding their status as Jews (Kaplan 1988; Goodman 2008) as they experienced the racialization (Samon 2003) of their lifestyle and identity (Shabtai 1999, 2001), together with their acculturation (Kaplan and Rosen 1993; Kaplan 1997). Although some scholars have studied Ethiopians' reactions to racism in institutional and non-institutional environments (Shabtai 1999; Ben Eliezer 2004; Shabtai and Kagen 2005), there remains a paucity of grounded research, which our study aims to redress.

Because spatial concentration of Ethiopians caused property values to drop in their neighborhood, moving out and up has become more difficult (Swirski and Swirski 2002).[11] Many Ethiopian children were placed in special absorption centers on their arrival in Israel, and large numbers remained isolated from the general population. In 2003, only a third passed their high school matriculation (*Bagrut*) exams—compared to 52 percent in the general Jewish population (Kaplan and Salamon 2004). Although employment rates have improved, a lower percentage of Ethiopians (as opposed to the general Jewish population) actually work: 55 percent of those aged 22–64 compared to 75 percent for the entire Jewish population of the same age (Kaplan and Salamon 2004).

Differences in educational attainment partially explain this gap (Kaplan and Salamon 2004). In 2007, the percentage of Ethiopians working in non-professional jobs was 37 percent—more than five times the rate for the general Jewish population (7 percent; Offer 2004). Only 10 percent of Ethiopians are in academic, professional, or managerial occupations, compared with 40 percent of the general Jewish population (Habib et al. 2010). Conversely, the percentage of Ethiopian families living below the poverty line was more than three times greater than that of the general Jewish population, at 52 percent and 14 percent, respectively.

In the political sphere, Ethiopians have almost no representation in elected bodies at the local and national levels. While they are drafted into the army, their desertion rate is the highest among all groups enlisted, mainly because their families need their financial support through paid work. In 2006, adult Ethiopian immigrants represented 8.5 percent of convicted criminals, more than four times their percentage in the population, with these numbers rapidly growing (Habib et al. 2010). An astounding 42 percent of all detained teenagers held in Israel's only juvenile detention facility are of Ethiopian descent.

Mizrahi Jews. The arrival of almost half a million Jews from Arab and North African countries in the 1950s and 1960s prompted creation of the category "Mizrahim," an umbrella term covering a range of social types and ethnic identities.[12] Using region of origin to distinguish the veteran Ashkenazi (Westerners coming mainly from Europe) residents from the new Mizrahi immigrants ("Easterners" originating from predominantly Muslim and Arab regions) served to signify each group's place in the diversifying social hierarchy (Herzog 1985). Some parallels can be found between the use of the term "Mizrahi" with the terms "Hispanic" or "Latino" (in the United States) as labels designating subgroups of people with different national origin or ancestry (Rumbaut 2009; Mora 2014). As a social category/identity, the term "Mizrahi" has been culturally and politically contested from its inception (Herzog 1985, 1990a). Until 1990, being Mizrahi was largely considered a temporary condition, synonymous with Orientalist stereotypes about the backwardness and inferiority of less developed, non-Western cultures (Said 1978), which was expected to disappear with assimilation into modern Israeli society. Such views fueled the stigma associated with Mizrahi identity until fairly recently, when it became a basis for making claims in the framework of identity politics (Mizrachi 2004; Shenhav 2006).

In the 1950s, the government of the new state encouraged immigration by Jews from Arab countries with the explicit aim of increasing the Jewish population. This created a new challenge for social integration, given that Western Zionists often viewed Mizrahi Jews as vulgar, premodern, and even primitive (Shiloah and Cohen 1983).

From their initial arrival in Israel beginning in the early 1950s, Mizrahi immigrants were typically considered to be composed of backward, non-modern, and by definition, non-Western ethnic groups, and these Oriental-ist stereotypes remained entrenched for years (Shohat 1988, 1999; Hever, Shenhav, and Motzafi-Haller 2002; Mizrachi 2004). Various state policies contributed to their marginalization in the economic-political (Grinberg 1989), educational (Shavit 1984), and cultural spheres. To make them "fit" for the modern nation-building project, these immigrants were thought to be in need of moral, cultural, educational, and psychological reform (Khaz-zom 2003; Mizrachi 2004; Shenhav 2006).[13] For instance, the state predomi-nently settled new Mizrahi arrivals in geographically peripheral towns and encouraged their integration into lower-class occupations (Swirski 1989). To this day, the term "periphery" is closely associated with Mizrahim. Since the 1990s, the socioeconomic inequality they experience has lessened as they have achieved upward mobility, mainly through education (Dahan 2013). These changes have also been associated with increased political representa-tion (Rahat and Itzkovitch Malka 2012). Nevertheless, Orientalist attitudes and stereotypes have remained entrenched, and Mizrahim remain underrep-resented in the elite and overrepresented in the lower classes (Cohen, Ha-berfeld, and Kristal 2007; Haberfeld and Cohen 2007).

Although the Zionist ideology of the melting pot constitutes a power-ful inclusive and unifying repertoire that favors assimilation, Mizrahim can sometimes be identified through specific markers. These include mentions of their place of residence ("the periphery," which is a strong marker) mixed in with specific class and ethnic habitus, which are expressed through a dis-tinctive accent, "look," and sets of cultural practices, such as musical tastes and typical sonic cues (Katz-Gerro, Raz, and Yaish 2007; Schwarz 2015). The existence of a distinctive and recognizable (albeit stigmatized) group style and their emerging political claims are a challenge to the cultural cohesive-ness needed to construct a unified national identity (Herzog 1984). Hence, the term "Mizrahim," remains understood by many Israelis as a stigmatized identity or degrading social label (DellaPergola 2007).

At the same time, the majority of the Mizrahi population embraces the Zionist ideal of the Jewish melting pot without adhering to a shared iden-tity with a distinct collective narrative of group disadvantage and marginal-ization. Their identification with the Zionist narrative distinguishes them from African Americans, who have a highly institutionalized historical nar-rative of oppression and discrimination and sense of linked fate, and Black Brazilians. Hence, the very meaning of Mizrahi identity remains largely amor-phous and blurred in its articulation (Herzog 1984).

Mizrahim and Black Brazilians are similar in that they both identify with the majority culture and are reluctant to accentuate the distinctive features of their group (which could lead to balkanization of those sharing national identity). However, Black Brazilians have come to express greater group pride and self-awareness, especially in recent decades. In both Israel and Brazil, social movements have aimed to mobilize these stigmatized groups, but with mitigated success.

Another difference between our three cases is that while Mizrahi history is not part of the school curricula, African American and Black Brazilian historical narratives of slavery are considered legitimate and are taught in the schools. Efforts made by Mizrahi intellectuals and activists to increase group self-awareness and politicization have not been embraced by working-class Mizrahim (Mizrachi 2011). This liberal form of identity politics, shared by liberal elites, remains alien to them (see the discussion on liberal isomorphism in Section 4.2).

And yet, while remaining a cultural minority in Israel due to the dominance of Ashkenazim in the sociopolitical and cultural spheres, Mizrahim currently constitute a demographic majority among Israel's Jewish population: As of 2008, they made up 38.4 percent of the Jewish population,[14] compared to 25.8 percent for Ashkenazim, 14.6 percent for third-generation and mixed groups, and 21.2 percent for new immigrants (Cohen 2015).[15] The majority of all Israeli Jews now have, in fact, some Mizrahi ancestry (Central Bureau of Statistics 2014).[16]

Inequality between Mizrahim and Ashkenazim likewise persists despite substantial mobility among educated Mizrahim and the blurring of social boundaries through intermarriage, with 35 percent of all Jewish marriages being inter-ethnic (Steir and Shavit 2003). Income disparities between Ashkenazi and Mizrahi Jews[17] remained fairly constant throughout the first decade of twenty-first century, with Mizrahi Jews slowly gaining in income. Educational inequality is even more striking: By 1995, 32 percent of male and 40 percent of female Ashkenazi Jews were college graduates, compared to only 10 percent of male and 13 percent of female Mizrahi Jews (Swirski, Connor-Attias, and Ophir 2014). During the 18-year period between 1992 and 2010, the number of second-generation Mizrahim holding academic degrees and belonging to the middle class rose from 51 percent to 67 percent. In contrast, a moderate decline was observed among second-generation Ashkenazim,[18] from 74.0 percent in 1992 to 70.2 percent in 2010.[19] According to a report issued by Swirski, Connor-Attias, and Ophir (2014), Mizrahi households exhibited greater upward mobility than any other Israeli households during 1990–2010 (see also Dahan 2013). This rate of change greatly exceeds that observed among immigrants from the former Soviet Union as well as among Arab Palestinians, and it indicates a narrowing of the gap between Mizrahim and Ashkenazim in absolute terms.

THE RESEARCH SITE: TEL AVIV–JAFFA

Most of our interviewees live in the Tel Aviv–Jaffa metropolitan area, known in Hebrew as *Gush Dan*. Located in the central western part of the country along the Mediterranean coastline, this is Israel's largest and most densely populated metropolitan area. Its estimated population of 3,464,100 residents constitutes 42 percent of Israel's total population; 95 percent (3,286,500) are Jewish and the rest are Arab Palestinians (Central Bureau of Statistics 2014).

Founded in 1909 during the pre-state era, Tel Aviv is Israel's first modern Hebrew (Jewish) city. The city began as a suburb of Jaffa, the former Arab metropolis commonly referred to as the "Bride of Palestine" (to denote its central location in the Arab space) or the "Bride of the Sea" in light of its role as an international port and trade center. After 1948, Jaffa lost its autonomous status and was annexed to the Tel Aviv municipality. As a result of the mass immigration of Jews from Europe and Arab countries, and the displacement of Arab Palestinians to other cities or outside Israel's borders, only 5 percent of the original Arab Palestinian population remained in Jaffa. This city was thus transformed from a cosmopolitan port town with roots in antiquity to a place of refuge in recent years, primarily for poor foreign workers and Palestinians from the West Bank and Gaza. With the gentrification of Jaffa since the late 1990s and the entry of middle-class Jews into the area, poor Arab Palestinians are leaving Jaffa. Their destinations tend to be neighboring, but poorer, Jewish-Arab mixed cities, such as Ramla and Lod.

The Arab Palestinian population in Jaffa is 70 percent Muslim and 30 percent Christian (Monterescu 2006, 2007). To ensure more diversity in our study, we interviewed some Arab Palestinians from neighboring Arab towns that do not formally lie in the Tel Aviv metropolitan area, but whose residents frequently work there. For their part, nearly all of the Ethiopian interviewees were from the Tel Aviv metropolitan area. Most were second-generation Ethiopians born in Israel or who had immigrated to Israel with their parents at a very young age. Mizrahi interviewees resided, for the most part, in several suburban towns (Bat-Yam, Holon, and Petach-Tikva) that are heavily populated by middle- and working-class Mizrahim that are part of the Tel Aviv metropolitan area.

It should be noted that this area is far more secular than the rest of the country, with most of our interviewees either secular or mildly observant. No ultra-Orthodox Jews were included in our sample. This fact is an important limitation of our study, as this subsection of the Israeli population, which makes up approximately 9 percent of the Jewish population (Central Bureau of Statistics 2014), is growing and politically influential. Our decision not to include ultra-Orthodox Jews rests on this group's tendency to live in homogeneous enclaves and maintain very few daily social contacts with the wider society. Furthermore, the meaning of ethnicity in the Jewish population tends to vary with degree of religiosity and political ideology, factors that influence intergroup relations in every social sphere. More specifically, in ultra-Orthodox communities, Mizrahi-Ashkenazi segregation in particular is strongly institutionalized through separate schools and synagogues (Bitton and Glass 2016) and by strictly enforced norms against intermarriage. As such, we believe the stigmatization of ultra-Orthodox Mizrahim deserves a separate study. Here we concentrate on the far less institutionalized boundaries that are found in the more secular parts of Israeli society inhabited by the majority of our Jewish respondents, as well as the majority of the country's inhabitants.[20]

Our decision to conduct interviews in the Tel Aviv area (*Gush Dan*) prevents us from capturing the full range of experiences and responses to ethnoracial exclusion by the Palestinian population. This is certainly the case, as Arab Palestinians who reside in isolated villages may understand stigma and discrimination very differently than do the urban dwellers we spoke with. We did, however, have several interviewees who live in smaller villages but worked in the Tel Aviv area. Hence, although our data-collection strategy could not encompass Israel's entire social landscape, it did capture narratives of ethnoracial exclusion for a sizable number of the groups situated in a core area of Israel.

SECTION 4.2: NATIONAL BELONGING, RACE, AND ETHNICITY IN THE FORMATION OF GROUPNESS

In this section we compare Arab Palestinian citizens of Israel, Ethiopian Jews, and Mizrahim along several dimensions of groupness. We pay particular attention to the meaning of group identity for our interviewees and the strength of group boundaries as experienced through perceived residential and institutional segregation, as well as experiences with intergroup socialization and marriage. However, our discussion differs from the US and Brazilian cases in a few respects. To begin with, we did not ask our respondents about which racial label they used to refer to themselves, as we saw early on that respondents were confused by this question: irrespective of the many overlapping cultural, ethnic, religious, and political distinctions found in Israel, Israelis typically do not describe themselves in terms of race. Even Ethiopians tend to self-identify as Ethiopian rather than black. Second, our discussion of boundary work against other groups is complicated by the fact that each of the groups we studied defines itself and is defined in relation to a different reference category: Arab Palestinian groupness is defined in reference to Jews; Ethiopian groupness in reference to non-Ethiopian Jews (both Ashkenazi and Mizrahi), and Mizrahi groupness in reference to Ashkenazi Jews. Our interviewees drew comparisons to these reference groups most clearly when discussing the meaning of their group identity, and so we locate our discussion of boundary work against out-groups in the section where we discuss the meanings that our group members attached to their group identity. Finally, we did not ask our respondents' opinions directly about equality of groups. Instead, we asked them to offer a map of Israeli society. Our interviewees painted a complex picture of multiple overlapping social divisions along lines of nationality, ethnicity, race, class, and religion as the basis for social inequality. Their views on universalism and multiculturalism come across in their answers to this and other questions.

Before launching into our analysis, we offer a brief overview of our findings to guide the reader through the complex terrain of groupness in our three cases. Table 4.1 summarizes the key elements of groupness in the three Israeli cases, along with historical, political, and demographic characteristics of the groups as described in Section 4.1. Many of these features can also be found in Tables 1.2–1.4 in Chapter 1.

The meaning of group identity for most of our Arab Palestinian respondents was defined in terms of nationality. Here they drew on a shared historical narrative of national dispossession and catastrophe that occurred as a result of the 1948 war and resulted in the foundation of Israel. Group identity was frequently defined in terms of differences in religion, traditions, dress, and language. Residential and institutional segregation was experienced as almost total, and our interviewees described interacting with Jews mainly at the workplace or, for those with more education, in college. Friendships between Arabs and Jews were not uncommon, but for the most part they rarely reached deep levels of intimacy (Bronshtein 2015) and depended on a bracketing of the broader Israeli-Palestinian conflict.

Ethiopians' groupness can be described as dissonant: they experienced a sharp divergence between their self-definition as Jews and Israelis and their perception of being stigmatized on the basis of their skin color and immigrant status. They defined the meaning of their group identity mainly in terms of differences in traditions and, for some, language. Their experience of residential and institutional segregation, especially in terms of neighborhood and schooling, was quite striking, but it was not a significant feature of their army service or work experience. Friendships with non-Ethiopians were fairly common, yet for many of our interviewees their closest friends were fellow Ethiopians. Marriage with non-Ethiopians is still relatively rare, but it is not something that is considered taboo. For the most part, Ethiopians

TABLE 4.1. GROUPNESS AND BACKGROUND ELEMENTS FOR THE THREE ISRAELI GROUPS

ELEMENT	GROUP		
	Arab Palestinian citizens of Israel	Ethiopian Jews	Mizrahim
Religion	Non-Jewish	Jewish: externally contested	Jewish: uncontested
Position vis-à-vis Jewish polity	Outside	Inside but occasionally contested	Inside
Group boundaries	Impermeable	Rigid but not impermeable	Permeable
Residential and institutional segregation	Total	Almost total	Partial (depending on socio-economic status)
Percentage of total population	19.0	1.8	26.5[a]
Immigration status	Non-immigrant: native	Immigrant	Nonimmigrant by generation
Socioeconomic status	Low vis-à-vis Jewish society; internally diversified	Generally low	Unevenly distributed
Primary reference group	Jewish Israelis	White Jewish Israelis (Ashkenazim and Mizrahim)	Askenazi hegemonic elite
Self-identification vis-à-vis the primary reference group	Unambiguous (i.e., Arab Palestinian)	Unambiguous (Jewish; generally downplaying blackness)	Unambiguous (Jewish; generally downplaying Mizrahi identity)
Sense of linked fate	High	Partial	Generally none; diversified among activists and subgroups
Ease of recognition by external markers (e.g., skin color, dress, accent)	Occasionally ambiguous	Unambiguous	Sometimes ambiguous
Phenotype	Ambiguous	Unambiguous	Ambiguous
Language	Arabic and Hebrew	Amharic and Hebrew	Hebrew
Accent	Unambiguous (when speaking Hebrew)	Increasingly ambiguous by generation and class	Ambiguous by generation and class

Notes: [a] See Cohen (2015). This figure represents individuals born in an Arab or North African country or having at least one parent born in an Arab or North African country. It does not include third-generation Mizrahim, who are classified as Israelis. By 2008, Mizrahim comprised 38.4 percent of the Jewish population, compared to 25.8 percent for Ashkenazim; in addition, third-generation and mixed groups made up 14.6 percent and new immigrants 21.2 percent (Cohen 2015). Mizrahim are currently the largest ethnic group in the population. A majority of all Israeli Jews now have, in fact, some Mizrahi ancestry (Central Bureau of Statistics 2014).

make their claim for equality not on the basis of universalism but rather on the basis of their Jewishness.

Our Mizrahi interviewees' groupness was weak, and they engaged in what we refer to as "contingent detachment:" they were reluctant to define themselves as Mizrahi and detached themselves from this categorization, but at the same time they were able to attach meaning to the Mizrahi identity, mainly in terms of cultural differences between Mizrahim and Ashkenazim (Mizrachi and Herzog 2012). The experience of segregation is patterned by generation and class background: first-generation and working-class Mizrahim are more likely to live in geographically isolated towns or neighborhoods with high concentrations of Mizrahim, whereas younger, middle-class Mizrahim do not live in highly concentrated or segregated areas. Like Ethiopians, Mizrahim do not claim equality based on universalism, nor do they claim recognition of their differences. Instead they make claims to equality on the basis of their Jewishness.

SELF-IDENTIFICATION, SELF-LABELING, AND THE MEANINGS OF GROUP IDENTITY

Arab Palestinians

We opened our interviews by asking the interviewees to describe themselves. As with the US and Brazilian groups, Arab Palestinians rarely used group identifiers to do so; altogether only five of them (or 10 percent) spontaneously used the term "Arab" or "Palestinian" when asked to describe themselves. Instead, they preferred to describe themselves in terms of personal traits and qualities (e.g., tenacity, honesty, meticulousness, and positivity), together with self-descriptions, such as "I like to work," "I like spending time with my family," "I like people," "I like life," and "I like to live for the moment." They often used the term "ordinary person" with respect to themselves.

Nevertheless, further questions and probing revealed that their self-identification as Arabs, or Palestinians, is unequivocally based on their distinctiveness from Israel's dominant group, the Jews. While skin color and class played almost no role in these processes (in sharp contrast to African Americans and Black Brazilians), historical narratives of national dispossession loomed large, as did culture and religion (Amara and Schnell 2004). Arab Palestinians have a strong sense of linked fate (i.e., they perceive their life chances as connected to those of other group members), which is framed primarily by the Palestinian side of the Janus-faced narrative about the 1948 war, with its counterpart being the Jewish Israeli Zionist narrative. Thus, Palestinian communities today tend to commemorate the Israeli Day of Independence as the *"Nakba,"* which means catastrophe in Arabic. More broadly, they do not share in, and are even typically profoundly alienated from, the civic and religious symbols and ceremonies associated with this celebration of the Jewish state, a fact that heightens their sense of groupness.

This perceived national divide was somewhat reflected in our interviews, where a small majority of our Arab Palestinian respondents outlined a highly politicized identity when describing what it means to be Arab: 56 percent referred to their collective history and national identity, and only 28 percent referred to the discrimination they faced as Arabs in Israel (some referred to both). Also our interviewees differed somewhat in how they described their experience of domination and subjugation. While many described their estrangement from the Jewish polity ("I don't feel Israeli even though I have an Israeli ID;" "I am Palestinian, nothing connects me to Israel . . . what connects me to the Palestinians is blood, nationality, and language"), others expressed more explicit political claims ("I'm an Arab [living] under occupation;" or "I am the *real* native"). However, a sizable minority of interviewees did not express these feelings of alienation or did not express a strong sense of identity beyond describing their distinctiveness simply as being Arab or speaking Arabic.

Despite having Jewish friends and having attended high school in a Jewish town, Sayid, a young social activist from Jaffa, expressed his alienation from the polity in stark terms: "I was born Arab in this country, and I do not feel like it belongs to me—not the flag, not *HaTikva* [Israel's national anthem, meaning "the hope"], and not their [the Jews'] state." He described his political awakening in these terms:

When I was young I was not aware of my identity. I studied in a Jewish school. . . . It was only in college that I met other Arabs, faced racism, and began to learn from my friends about my roots and my history. . . . In the first elections I voted for a Zionist party. But in time, as I became more aware of my belonging, I became an activist in Balad [a nationalist Arab party].

He tells a story of emerging personal identity that is deeply connected with his national identity:

Being an Arab is very limiting in many ways, and it really influences my character as an ambitious person because it causes depression and [I] retreat from the goals I want to achieve. . . . Being an Arab in Israel makes me proud; it's my origin and what I am. But being an Arab in Israel means being considered a second-class person and gives you no advantages.

That he describes himself as an Arab in Israel, instead of an Israeli, is meaningful, because the phrase indicates pride in his Arab identity rather than his Israeli one. Many of the Arab Palestinians we interviewed spontaneously used "Arab citizen of Israel" or similar language to symbolically denote their separation from the Jewish polity. The use of the term "citizen" underscores the demarcation between their legal civil status and their sense of national belonging. A similar distinction does not appear (and certainly would not make sense) for members of the other two groups we interviewed in Israel, nor among interviewees in Brazil and the United States. Whereas African American interviewees were often critical of American race policies, Arab Palestinians were concerned with nationalistic, not race-related, policies, although they often used the language of racism to define discriminatory nationalist policies.

While their sense of groupness was very clearly and sharply defined in relation to Jewish Israelis, our interviewees nevertheless had difficulty carving out a coherent identity vis-à-vis the larger Arab world. For some, self-identification as Arabs meant solidarity with other Arabs both in Israel and in the wider Arab world. Others viewed their Palestinian national identity as distinct from an Arab identity. But they also experience conflict between being Arab and being Israeli. For instance, in response to the question of what it means to be Arab, Fatma, an unemployed woman from Jaffa, said:

> Since I was born, I knew myself as an "occupied Arab" [*Aravia kvusha*], what is known as the "1948 Arabs" [i.e., a Palestinian who remained in Israel], who were originally Palestinians, are [now] under Israeli rule and carry an Israeli ID. . . . I'm not proud of having an Israeli ID but I am proud of having rights that I wouldn't have in other Arab countries. It is humiliating in an Arab country that I am Israeli,[21] and here, it's humiliating that a Jew looks at me as [if I were] an Arab terrorist.

Fatma expresses dismay at belonging to an "occupied" minority in her own land, yet as a woman she appreciates the benefits of living in Israel compared to Arab countries. Whatever the political meaning Arab Palestinians gave to their group identity, the centrality of that identity is evident, as is their valuing of Israeli citizenship and the benefits that come with it. This presented our interviewees with a dilemma in terms of how to label themselves. Some preferred to use the more politically charged term "Palestinian" during our interviewees, whereas others created distance by referring to themselves as "Arab" or in some cases, "Arab Israeli." In his national survey of Arab Palestinians, Smooha (2013) found that 32 percent of those questioned said they preferred to call themselves Israeli Arabs, 45 percent call themselves Palestinian-Israelis, and 22 percent drop the Israeli moniker altogether and refer to themselves as Arab-Palestinians. Only 12 percent viewed Israeli citizenship as their most important affiliation, compared to a majority who viewed their affiliation as Palestinians or according to their religion as more important.

On the whole, our interviewees vary in how central political narratives are in informing their sense of group identity. This is in line with existing research on Arab Palestinians' political orientations, which points in two different directions. Rabinowitz and Abu-Baker (2005) identified a trend among Arab university students to strongly identify with the Palestinian cause and to express pride in their distinctive national identity as Palestinians. Smooha (2013), in contrast, points to a more pragmatic attitude, where despite issues around self-labeling and feeling alienated from the state, Arab citizens of Israel on the whole favor integration into Jewish Israeli society—within limits.[22] We discuss these competing interpretations later in this section, where we consider the differences in attitudes and approaches between young, educated, and politically active Palestinians and the general population.

We found that many Arab Palestinians also wrestle with an identity located between mutually hostile worlds: they are perceived as marginal both by Israel's Jewish majority and by other Palestinians, Arabs, and Muslims outside Israel. Indeed, one respondent described the associated feelings and the problems it creates with attempts at developing a coherent sense of identity and self-labeling:

> When I'm abroad, I say I'm Palestinian. They ask me whether I'm a 1948 Palestinian. . . . They say the Palestinians are the ones who left. We feel bad for them. And I say: "Well, why don't you feel bad for me? We're the ones who stayed in Israel and have continued to struggle. I'm a religious woman who fights every single day for the land that your parents left because we, Israel's Arabs, are the most downtrodden people in the world. I appreciate it that you don't like Israelis, but I'm not going to lie to you, I'm an Israeli because I was born within the borders of the State of Israel."

Fatma's narrative expresses the fractured character of Arab Palestinian identity—the condition of having identities that are cross-cutting, conflicting, and mutually exclusive (Rabinowitz 2001). Other Arab Palestinian respondents often echoed Fatma's views of her experience. Many made statements such as the following:

> You have the Jews to deal with, who always look at you as different. On the other hand, you have the Arabs who want you to be Muslim and also want you to be Palestinian. I am neither one nor the other. . . . I like Israel and I like living here, and I look at the Palestinians and I think that it is sad that they are not my people. I am Israeli, even though I am Arab.

Not all of our interviewees talked about what it means to be Arab exclusively or even primarily in political terms: about half mentioned cultural aspects. They contrasted Arab and Jewish "traditions" and "mentalities," pointing to cultural distinctiveness to enhance the moral worth of their own cultural values, norms, and attitudes (Lamont 2000; Lamont, Morning, and Mooney 2002). For example, a young construction worker from a small village described cultural forms of communality—taking care of the sick, responding to those who ask for help, and so forth—as morally superior to behaviors found in individualistic Israeli society. Another feature of Arab culture mentioned was language: Arab Palestinians speak Arabic at home and are educated in a separate school system where Arabic is the language of instruction. For them, Hebrew is a second language, and most Arab Palestinians find it difficult to speak Hebrew without an accent.[23] One of our interviewees was asked what makes him Arab, and he replied, "I was born an Arab, and I speak Arabic." He later talked about how the Arab language makes him feel culturally unified with other Arabs around the country. Speaking a different language from the majority group thus contributes to a strong sense of groupness among Arab Palestinians.

A small minority also criticized cultural aspects of their group, as when a 30-year-old Muslim lab assistant described how Jewish tradition does not favor men over women as much as her Muslim tradition:

> I personally don't think that religion states that a woman can't go out and work. . . . Fathers and brothers have to supervise their sisters and their aunts and female neighbors so that they don't mess around. . . . Tradition always favors men. This is less true among the Jews.

Some referred to their national identity by mentioning their town or place of residence (Mi'ari 1987), thus underscoring their social distance and geographical segregation from Jews. Local identity is an especially important component in the identity of Arab Palestinians in Israel; it is connected to a strong tradition of localism and relatively low geographical mobility (Mi'ari 1987; Bishara 2000). This is reinforced by their exclusion from Israel's centers of power and by the state's distrust of them as Palestinians (Herzog and Yahia-Younis 2007; Yahia-Younis 2010).

In sum, Arab Palestinian citizens of Israel draw distinct symbolic boundaries between themselves and the Jewish majority when defining who they are. These boundaries and sense of linked fate are reinforced by a collective historical narrative of national dispossession and the ongoing sense of exclusion from the Israeli polity. Thus, in contrast to the other minority groups in this study, Arab Palestinians can be characterized as an unassimilated minority. While many of our interviewees articulated their self-identification in language that was self-consciously defiant and critical of the Israeli state, others expressed their symbolic separation more subtly and more in terms of cultural differences. They also described the difficulty of constructing a coherent identity due to being treated as outsiders both in Israel and the broader Arab world. However, alongside feelings of alienation, they also expressed cultural pride in Arab language, culture, traditions, customs, religion, mutual assistance and responsibility, family ties, and family honor.

Ethiopians and Mizrahim

Ethiopian Jews. Although Ethiopian immigrants come from varied geographical, cultural, and class locations in their country of origin, Israeli governmental authorities and the public conceive of Ethiopian Jews as a single social category marked by skin color (Ben-Eliezer 2008). In Chapter 1, we characterize their groupness as *dissonant*, because it is structured by their self-identification as Jews participating in the Zionist project and their external categorization as black by Israelis coupled with strong social boundaries. This tension shapes their lived experience and perceptions of linked fate. By drawing on the Zionist narrative of the ingathering of the exiles and the repertoire of the Jewish melting pot, which idealizes the incorporation of successive waves of Jewish immigrant groups (e.g., Jews from North African countries), they frame their racial exclusion as temporary (Mizrachi and Zawdu 2012). Despite their experience of persistent stigmatization and discrimination in multiple spheres of life, they often compare themselves to previous waves of Jewish immigrants who were initially stigmatized but were eventually incorporated into the polity. In this, they resemble some African Americans who strongly self-identify as Americans despite experiencing American racism. And, in contrast to Black Brazilians, Ethiopians view themselves as having a distinct culture. This is hardly surprising, given their relatively recent arrival as immigrants.

Most of the Ethiopian interviewees referred to their skin color as a distinctive marker that separates them as a group within the Israeli polity. As one of our interviewees put it: "You are seen and judged first and foremost as a black Ethiopian." However, because this categorization is in tension with their self-identification as Jews on their way to assimilation, the majority rejects identifying themselves based on their "blackness," which as a distinct, core identity could serve as a basis for making claims for equal participation (Mizrachi 2014). Still, mobilizing a global racial discourse, a small minority of highly educated middle-class Ethiopians has begun making political claims based their desire to retain their distinct identity (Mizrachi and Zawdu 2012). In our sample, only a small group (12 percent) of our Ethiopian interviewees self-identified as Ethiopian, while an additional 10 percent mentioned their immigrant status.

When asked directly about what it means for them to be Ethiopian, a majority (55 percent) mentioned a shared culture and 18 percent mentioned their common history. Nearly half stressed the salience of skin color in shaping a strong sense of groupness. For instance, a young Ethiopian secretary in a law firm, married to an Ashkenazi man, described her growing racial self-awareness, which she states as coming from the "outside":

> First of all, I see myself as a woman.... Second, I see myself as Sara, Sara the Ethiopian.... That's an awareness that was forced upon me.... As I was growing up and people started to notice my color and the difference in me because of that color. They pointed it out to me.

Similarly, Yisrael, a maintenance worker, who was a year old when his family arrived in Israel, views himself as an "Israeli pure and simple" despite noting that "no matter what, your skin color gives you away." Again, the dramatic tension between self-identification as Israeli and Jewish, and external categorization as black and an immigrant, are central for many, as illustrated by a young woman who mocks the surprise of ordinary Israelis at her perfect Hebrew: "Wow, the Ethiopian woman [has] no accent at all!"

When describing a shared culture, many described eating traditional foods, like injera bread, or speaking and reading Amharic, the Ethiopians' mother tongue. They also talked about sharing what they described as an Ethiopian or African mentality. Key elements of this mentality, which also served as a way of drawing moral boundaries against other Israelis (by which they meant Ashkenazi and Mizrahi Jews), were a respect for and deference to elders and caring for one another. For example, one of our interviewees talked about how it is important to greet people who are older on the street, listen to them, and get their advice. She contrasted this with how "Israelis" treat older people disrespectfully, illustrating it with a story of seeing young people on a bus refusing to give up their seat to an older person. Also salient is the way in which people care about one another. One woman, for instance, described how much she appreciates her community's solidarity, expressed at events such as funerals and memorial services: "People come from all over the country. They may not even know exactly who the person was, [perhaps] a relative of a relative, but everyone comes and pays their respects." Another worries that the Ethiopian community is "forgetting Ethiopian society and getting into the Israeli mentality, where you don't care about your own brother, so to speak."

Mizrahi Jews. Whereas Ethiopians all originate from a single country, Mizrahi Jews hail from a multitude of Middle Eastern and North African countries, such as Yemen, Iraq, Tunisia, and Morocco (recall that "Mizrahi" simply means "Eastern" in Hebrew). They arrived in Israel without having a shared culture, norms, traditions, or even language (even if most spoke Arabic, they were often in mutually unintelligible dialects). Yet the label "Mizrahi" was used to distinguish this heterogeneous group from the Ashkenazi immigrants from European countries (who also came from a wide range of different countries), and it came to mark this diverse group of immigrants under a common group identity.

On the whole, our Mizrahi interviewees have a weak sense of groupness based on ethnicity and engage in what we call "contingent detachment" (Mizrachi, Goodman, and Feniger 2009), meaning that although they generally detach their self-identification from "Mizrahi" as a stigmatized group identity (and may even reject the existence of the category itself), they are nevertheless able to discuss Mizrahim as a social category and even, in some contexts, identify with the category, especially in terms of its positive meaning. Mizrahi respondents generally denied experiencing any barriers to their full integration—despite research documenting the undeniably strong educational and occupational barriers that they still face. Instead, they emphasize their Jewishness or Israeliness to downplay symbolic boundaries that would distinguish them as an oppressed or stigmatized group (Mizrachi and Herzog 2012). For example, when asked how they define themselves, one of our interviewees remarked: "I view myself as an Israeli of no color at all." When asked what it means for him to be Mizrahi, another replied: "First of all, in terms of my identity, I am a Jew. . . . I don't listen to Yemenite music [and] I've never felt Mizrahi." Another claimed that the only importance of being Mizrahi was to "know some background, what culture they came from. In this sense it is important to me. But it does not define me, except that I was very lucky that I didn't have to grow up eating Polish food. But everything else? No, it doesn't matter." Only one of the interviewees spontaneously self-identified as Mizrahi. A handful of respondents went so far as to say that there was no meaning to the term, whereas none of our Arab Palestinian and Ethiopian respondents made this claim for their respective labels.

And yet, even though most did not define themselves as Mizrahi, they nevertheless found it easy to define the meaning of Mizrahi identity when asked to do so, almost always mentioning food and music and describing a family-oriented, warm culture that preserves communal and religious traditions: "it's the food, the family, the clan, the commotion," as one of our interviewees put it. A third of our respondents mentioned these kinds of cultural features when asked to define what it means to be Mizrahi; 20 percent mentioned phenotype differences in terms of having a darker skin color; and 12 percent mentioned discrimination against Mizrahim, with virtually all of them describing it as a thing of the past. When asked what it means for them to be Mizrahi, almost all of the respondents slipped into discussing a particular national culture, whether it be Moroccan, Persian, Yemenite, and so on. In other words, they closely associate the term "Mizrahi" with their particular national heritage, another indication of the lack of identification with the group identity.

Mizrahi respondents drew moral boundaries between themselves and the Ashkenazi majority by contrasting Mizrahi warmth and familiarity with Ashkenazi selfishness and individualism: "They [Ashkenazim] will not hesitate to put their parents in an old-age home; for us it is unthinkable—they will stay at home and move about between members of the family." "With the Ashkenazim, the relationship between parents and children revolves around money, not around respect like in our case." "The Ashkenazim are condescending while we are more modest."

Mizrahi interviewees also deflect the stigma attached to their ethnic identity per se by referring to the stigmatization of their place of residence (center versus periphery,[24] good versus bad neighborhoods) and lifestyle (e.g., musical preferences, clothing styles). For instance, Liron, a resident of Tel Aviv, describes her experience of ethnic identity through the stigmatization of place:

> First, people have a tendency to categorize: You meet a person and the first question is "What ethnic group do you come from? Where were you born?" The question of where you were born—that's my weak point. . . . Because I grew up in Lod [a poor mixed town of Jews and Palestinians in the center of the country], which is considered so bad, with so many stigmas, that as soon as I am asked where I was born I shrink inside because I know what the reaction will be.

When economic inequality between Ashkenazim and Mizrahim was mentioned, interviewees typically described it as a thing of the past, or as due to individual or regional differences. When asked to map Israeli society, if they mentioned the Mizrahi-Ashkenazi economic gap, they lumped it together with other social divisions, along with rich versus poor, Tel Aviv versus the rest of the country, men versus women, Arabs versus Jews, good versus bad citizens, and so forth. These findings are consistent with other research showing that Israelis describe social differentiation and hierarchy with the aid of multiple dimensions of social division and stratification (Smooha 1999; Kimmerling 2004).

To summarize, skin color is the main marker for Ethiopian Jews, coupled with their status as new immigrants. Despite the tension between their self-perceived Jewishness and external definitions, they strongly self-identify as Israelis. Their groupness is dissonant due to their skin color, African origin, and alleged backwardness, immigrant status, and the lack of consensus about their Jewishness. As much as they desire to assimilate, they feel strongly stigmatized by both Ashkenazi and Mizrahi Jews. With the exception of a small elite, they do not engage in political claims-making based on their distinctiveness (Mizrachi and Zawdu 2012; Mizrachi 2014), contrary to expectations that a transnational diffusion of a universalist discourse on racism would lead them to do so (Bourdieu and Wacquant 2001a). Even the discourse surrounding the wave of demonstrations by Ethiopians in the spring of 2015 focused primarily on the notion that Ethiopians are Israelis and should be treated as such, although the protests themselves indicate that identity politics may be gaining ground among Ethiopians as their hopes for fuller integration languish. Still, despite the dissonance between their Jewish-ness and racial otherness, Ethiopians generally embrace their Jewish and national identity, which is the primary repertoire they draw on to make claims for equality and incorporation.

In this they resemble Mizrahim, who similarly embrace both Jewish and national identity as Israeli but without sharing the racial stigma that Ethiopians face. Both groups nonetheless share a stigmatizing trait in relation to the Zionist project: their origins in African and Middle Eastern countries have led to both being stereotyped as culturally backward. The two groups diverge, to different degrees, from the "new Jew," an idealized figure promoted in Zionist discourse: an individual who is Western, secular, modern, and rational (Mizrachi 2004). As such, they may be viewed as somewhat unfit for liberal democracy and the global market economy. Even so, Mizrahim and Israeli Ethiopians are, symbolically and in terms of self-definition, full members of the Israeli polity, unlike the Arab Palestinians. They unambiguously self-define as Israelis, not as "citizens of Israel." As we will see, this profoundly influences how they experience and respond to stigma and discrimination.

GROUP BOUNDARIES

The structural and institutional conditions described in Section 4.1 play a major role in shaping the formation of social boundaries and intergroup interaction in Israel. Here we consider in greater depth the ways in which the three Israeli groups experience residential and institutional segregation. We also consider group boundaries through perceived friendships and marriage patterns with out-group members.

Arab Palestinians

The social and symbolic boundaries standing between Arab Palestinian and Jewish citizens of Israel are deep and pervasive, and they reinforce groupness among Arab Palestinians. These boundaries manifest themselves in perceived institutional and residential segregation and inequality in all spheres of life as well as in the perceived role played by the Israeli state in perpetuating group differentiation and hierarchy.

Institutional segregation between Palestinian and Jewish Israelis is entrenched and taken for granted by both groups in education, the army, and the labor market. While there is almost total segregation in primary and secondary education, only at the university does a small minority of Israeli Palestinians live side-by-side with Jews. As for the army, service is required for Jews but not for Arabs (except Druze), and very few Palestinians volunteer

for it (or for national service), as they typically do not identify with state institutions. Finally, the workplace is one of the few spheres where Jews and
Palestinians can interact more frequently.

The residential segregation of Arabs in Israel is more severe than for
blacks in the United States, but it is largely taken for granted and rarely contested (unlike the American case). Half of Arab Palestinians live in towns or
villages that are exclusively Arab. Even in mixed towns, the lines between
Jewish and Arab neighborhoods are clearly drawn, which suggests that the
two groups do not wish to live together (Amara and Schnell 2004; Bernstein
2007; Monterescu and Rabinowitz 2007). In his national survey of Arab Palestinians, Smooha (2013) found that 42 percent of those interviewed favor
living in Jewish neighborhoods, and 37 percent want their children to
attend Jewish high schools. However, these attitudes should not be interpreted as indicative of a desire to assimilate but as expressing a desire to
improve their standard of living and access to resources, such as jobs and
schools.[25]

Arabs seeking to live in Jewish neighborhoods routinely face (often
open) discrimination from real estate agents and landlords. While there
have been a handful of exceptional court cases in which Arabs sued over
residential discrimination, there is no law forbidding private owners from
discriminating when selling or renting property. Some effects of this high
level of spatial segregation are decried by Sanin, a museum tour guide, who
explained that the average Palestinian meets Jews only when he or she goes
to college or enters the labor market: "Only at this age are we exposed to
Jews, and vice versa. This gap and this distance from the other side create and
deepen the stereotypes acquired at home."

Arab Palestinian respondents who live in integrated neighborhoods or
Jewish towns face significant challenges when trying to integrate their children into the Jewish school system. Two describe similar experiences when
attempting to register their children at local schools: One, a single woman
with children, was "advised" to turn to an Arab-language school to avoid discrimination, which was clearly impractical, as the nearest Arab school was
located in a different town. The other, a manager of a post office, was turned
away when she tried to enroll her child in a local Jewish kindergarten.
When explaining the decision, a local council's clerk asked her: "You're
not afraid that some kid will come and say to your son: 'Dirty Arab'?" This
strongly contrasts with the dominant norms of universalism that prevail in
the American context, even in the midst of pervasive racism.

Boundaries and Friendship. For Arab Palestinians, spatial segregation
is the result of combined state actions and self-segregation, motivated by
private and collective insecurity and by a desire to protect the group's well-
being, collective identity, and memory. Thus, for Arab Palestinians, vigi-
lantly guarding group boundaries has become particularly important (Sa'di

and Abu-Lughod 2007). The nature of segregation is dual, with each group having its own reasons for policing strict social boundaries. As a result, the Arab Palestinians often exist as an unassimilated minority amidst Israeli society.

This is especially evident in the realm of personal relationships, particularly regarding marriage. When probed about intergroup marriage, all our Arab interviewees expressed negative views, in strong contrast with American and Brazilian respondents. Although the absence of civil marriage in Israel may be viewed as contributing to a low level of intermarriage, other social forces contribute to maintaining social boundaries. Indeed, many of our interviewees expressed their desire to maintain boundaries between Jews and Palestinians on the basis of cultural differences, customs, religious prohibitions, the need for families and communities to exercise oversight of women, and a concern for reputation ("What would people say?"). Mixing is considered problematic, as described by one interviewee whose brother "married a Jewish Russian woman who converted to Islam for him. It caused a lot of trouble at home for us and for her. My parents were really not happy about it, and certainly her parents weren't, either." This interviewee concluded that although he sometimes dated Jewish women, he would not marry one.[26]

As observed in many other national contexts (Yuval-Davis and Anthias 1989), women in Arab Palestinian society serve as markers of group boundaries (Kanaanch 2002; Kanaaneh and Nusair 2010b). Constant supervision of intersex social relations in Arab Palestinian communities, particularly women's behavior, has been well documented (Hasan 2002; Yahia-Younis 2010) and was repeatedly mentioned by interviewees. This practice is perceived by many as worthy of preservation, as indicated in the following remark, which was echoed by some of our interviewees: "We are a more conservative society, especially in regard to women.... Jewish women have more opportunities to work and study than Arab women, but our Arab women take better care of their families." Saed, an educational counselor, noted: "The most important thing is that [Arab Palestinians are] in a constant struggle to maintain their identity as distinct and different from other groups." This task of protecting identity thus can be viewed not simply as an outcome of state oppression, tradition, and culture but also as a collective project of strengthening solidarity and groupness.

Arab Palestinians interviewees who live in the greater Tel Aviv metropolitan area are distinctive in that they are employed mainly in workplaces owned and staffed by Jews. The workplace was therefore the primary site where they could and did form social ties with Jews, but with an important class difference: while working-class interviewees almost never declared having Jewish friends, those who had such relationships mostly described them as confined to the workplace. Only two of our interviewees claimed to have a deep friendship with their Jewish employers, which even extended to their families. These connections provide protection against discrimination and racist insults at work. Respondents stated that what made these friendships possible was separation between the personal and the political—that is, avoidance of any mention of the Palestinian-Israel conflict.[27]

A handful of middle-class interviewees described circles of friendship that included Jews encountered outside work, at times in connection with political activism. However, these relationships were rarely described as deep or as extending to private life. In some cases relationships were predicated on having similar political views, but in others they exist (again) because individuals avoid talking politics. Omar, a medical student, reported extensive intergroup student activities on his campus. He recounts something that happened on an internet forum for one of his classes:

> An Arab student collected pictures of the destroyed houses in Gaza and the children and put them up on the forum under the heading "For empathic future doctors." The topic took on a life of its own, and there were comments made by both sides . . . until someone from the class committee came and said that we are all students here, and that is what is special about us and that the forum is for the exchange of files, exercises, and lectures, and it is forbidden to hold [political] debates like that. . . . The topic was closed but the scar remained.

This incident illustrates how politics remains a contested terrain, with intergroup relations subject to quick deterioration, especially during times of heightened tension. This is not entirely one sided: as one woman put it: "There are Jews who aren't prepared to have a conversation with Arabs, and there are Arabs who aren't willing to speak to Jews." This is partly because "Arabs are proud of their history, their heritage, their past." National pride is connected to what one middle-class interviewee described as resistance to "educational, cultural conquest." A weakening of group boundaries is thus only possible when the broader political conflict is bracketed.

A Restricted Discourse on Universalism and Multiculturalism. A handful of interviewees transcend the national divide by mobilizing a global transnational discourse of cosmopolitanism and universalism and a modernist view of cultural hierarchies and progress. Nevertheless, this discourse is in tension with a desire to preserve Arab culture. For example, Omar, an Arab Palestinian medical student, reaffirms modernist views of cultural progress, in the framework of which Arabs are regarded as backward. He thus depicts Jews as modern and Arabs as "a closed society, living in the past." Reflecting on the challenges of progress, he states: "The West can be compared to the sun; if you go too near you get burnt, [but] if you keep far away you remain in the shadows, the dark. A certain distance must be maintained— learn from the West their diligence, thought processes, but not everything."

Omar's idealized view of the West appears to be in line with trends observed in the general Arab-Palestinian population in Israel. According to a 2015 survey conducted by Sammy Smooha, when asked whether Israel should be integrated within the Arab zone or the West, 60 percent of Arab Palestinian respondents chose the West, compared to just 45 percent in 2013 (Smooha 2016). Smooha attributes this increase to disillusionment with the Arab Spring as well as the rise of Islamic fundamentalism. At the same time, Omar's concern about preserving his own culture speaks to his cultural ambivalence, which may be understood in terms of his unique social position as a highly educated member of the Arab elite.

Other manifestations of this ambivalence were expressed in the context of life in Israel where universalism and modernization were sometimes conflated with "Israelization" (becoming more like Jewish Israelis). Some Arab Palestinian respondents describe breaches of symbolic boundaries as attempts to mimic Jewish patterns of behavior. Members of this minority, mostly young people, appear to be modeling themselves on the majority (see Alexander 2001). As one of our interviewees remarked, "The younger generation is very much influenced by Jewish society . . . the way they talk, the way they dress, the music they listen to. . . . There are young Arabs who speak more Hebrew than Arabic." This crossing of boundaries is often met with criticism.

At the same time, some respondents suggested that these boundary-crossing behaviors are a way for Arab Palestinians to participate in a shared public sphere and a more multi-ethnic Israeli culture. Abed, a teacher and graduate student who chose to live in Jaffa because of its ethnic diversity, is critical of the fact that traditional Arab lifestyles are being displaced by Jewish Israeli lifestyles. He nevertheless suggested that "Israeli culture is being formed. Arabs and Jews and even Russians are beginning to adopt similar social patterns and to draw from one another, and this is creating a kind of common culture." He appreciates the solidarity in Arab society but is critical of the reluctance of Arabs to change, "to adapt to the developments around them. Maintaining their uniqueness meant becoming immobile and living in the past." He presented himself as someone who does cross boundaries:

> I am always in contact with Jews, at work and in my studies. Usually we have a common language because I meet with educated people with whom a serious businesslike conversation is possible even though there are some who do not accept my opinions. . . . I am a multicultural person. Sometimes I even feel closer to a Jewish or Christian person than to an Arab.

He emphasized that the learning should be mutual—Arabs from Jews, and Jews from Arabs. Using multiculturalism as a strategy for integration (Alexander 2001), this individual alludes to how a weakening of group boundaries through the embrace of cosmopolitanism may occur for Arab Palestinians. We should bear in mind, however, that his perspective is shared by only a small number of interviewees.

Ethiopians and Mizrahim

Ethiopian Jews. In terms of their experience of residential and institutional segregation, Ethiopians occupy a position that is somewhere between Arab Palestinians and Mizrahim. The overt residential segregation of Ethiopians, as noted in Section 4.1, can be readily observed in the poor neighborhoods and development towns where most members of this group live (with 70 percent residing in just 17 communities). These neighborhoods tend to be much more highly segregated than those populated by Mizrahim. But unlike Arab Palestinian segregation, Ethiopians experience their residential segregation as being imposed (as opposed to chosen), unfair, and stigmatizing. This has led to their situation receiving considerable attention from the media and public policy makers.

As a result of this spatial segregation, Ethiopians are subject to higher levels of institutional segregation, especially in schooling, which reinforces their sense of groupness as a product of external categorization. This is exemplified by the experience of a police officer who encountered refusal when attempting to register his daughter at a local school, which he ascribes to perceptions of Ethiopians as recent immigrants: "[T]hey're afraid. Because when they see Ethiopians they think of new immigrants. They don't think that my daughter is a native-born Israeli. Understand? She was born here, but they say, okay, they're Ethiopians and they'll . . . lower the level of all sorts of things . . . so they don't want us."

Although virtually all of our interviewees live in neighborhoods with high concentrations of Ethiopians, most of them work in integrated spaces, mainly as service providers. Yet their immigrant identity and skin color immediately act as clear markers, which reinforces a strong sense of groupness. Orit, an Israeli-born Ethiopian woman who studied in an integrated school and does not speak Amharic, described her reaction when working in a supermarket where some of the staff mistreated another Ethiopian employee: "Suddenly lines between 'us' and 'them' [the non-Ethiopians] were created. . . . I did not like it from the moment that they started to curse the woman and call her *kushit* ['blackie']. It's the most natural thing to do, defending her. It's because I'm black and I stand by the blacks."

In terms of friendships, almost all of our interviewees described having non-Ethiopian friends, many of whom they had met during their military service. Indeed, for many of our interviewees, military service was their first exposure to a wide range of Jews from diverse backgrounds. But they nevertheless described closer relationships with fellow Ethiopians. And in terms of marriage, most Israeli Ethiopians, including our interviewees, still marry predominantly within the Ethiopian community. In the few cases of inter-marriage found among our interviewees, they described ongoing difficulties with bridging the gaps between networks of friends and family. For example, an Ethiopian woman who married a Yemenite man replied in response to the interview question about who her friends are that her personal friends were solely Ethiopian but that as a couple, their friends were not Ethiopian. She nevertheless qualified her description of the latter by stating "They're just friends during trips, picnics, and holidays, not 'real' friends." For the woman, group boundaries persist at the most intimate level, which attests to her stronger sense of closeness to Ethiopians and stands out as a sign of the strength of groupness.

Mizrahi Jews. Since the 1950s, Mizrahi immigrants have been more likely than Ashkenazi immigrants to be settled by the state in the geographical periphery in development towns or on the outskirts of large cities (Swirski 1989). Mizrahi ethnicity and class often remain marked by residential loca-tion, as Liron noted earlier when referring to the stigma associated with coming from Lod, a mixed town of Jews and Palestinians known for its lower-class Mizrahi population. That Liron spoke of having moved away from Lod is also indicative of the generational aspect of segregation among Mizrahim (Steir and Shavit 2003). Indeed, Keidar (2012) found that the children of Mizrahi Jews who had immigrated to Israel in the 1950s no longer lived in neighborhoods with high concentrations of Mizrahim, al-though their parents did.

The overlap between class, generation, and ethnicity in the experience of residential segregation of Mizrahim is described by Ronnie, a Mizrahi man married to an Ethiopian woman and living in Rosh Ha'Ayin, a town resi-dentially divided by class. The older sections of town are populated mainly by working-class Yemenites, with a recent influx of Ethiopians, whereas the newer neighborhoods are populated primarily by highly educated profes-sionals, many of whom work in the high-tech sector. When asked about residential divisions with respect to ethnic groups, Ronnie noted that in his town, Yemenites (considered the darkest-skin group among Mizrahim) live in the older neighborhoods, whereas the middle class, comprising both Ashkenazim and Mizrahim, live in the newer, wealthier neighborhoods. However, he qualified his description: "But the hi-tech people are some-thing new. They aren't Mizrahim. They are Sabras [native-born Israelis] with money, nouveau riche." Ronnie's description is indicative of the way in which social class mobility and intergenerational change has erased Mizrahi identity, which attests to the lack of centrality of Mizrahi self-identification and a weak sense of groupness.

In the Mizrahi case, weak groupness also manifests itself in decisions con-cerning marriage. The rate of interethnic marriage among Mizrahim is high, especially among the middle class (Steir and Shavit 2003). Okun (2004) argues that people with mixed Mizrahi-Ashkenazi ancestry have not created a new ethnonational identity. Instead, she suggests that descendants of mixed marriages do not experience clear ethnic boundaries in Jewish society.

Although there is a high rate of intermarriage between educated Mizrahim and Ashkenazim (Okun 2004; Okun and Khait-Marelly 2008), some Mizrahi interviewees expressed the comfort found in remaining in one's cultural environment and spoke of their and their families' preferences for marriage to other Mizrahim. One interviewee explains that her mother wants her to marry an Ashkenazi, but "I told her to forget about it, it won't happen. I'm crazy about Moroccans, Yemenites, and Tripolitans. I love them—they really do it for me." Ofek, a salesclerk in his early twenties, explained his preference to marry within his ethnic group, because "You don't just marry a woman, you marry her family." And Tamar, a Mizrahi bartender, explained why marrying co-ethnics is important: "There is a natural understanding. . . . The people who understand me the most are my family and my friends who are from the same background."

In contrast to the porousness of the social boundaries between Ashkenazim and Mizrahim, and to a much lesser extent between Ethiopians and other Jewish Israelis, crossing the boundaries between Jews and Arabs with respect to marriage remains almost inconceivable. We see this from the perspective of a young Mizrahi woman who recalled that "My father would often repeat: 'I don't care who, as long as he's not an Arab or a Christian.'" While similar reactions against interracial marriage may be found in the United States, in the American context such a statement would be at odds with the normative dominance of universalism and diversity, which are among the conditions for somewhat more porous group boundaries despite strong racial self-identification among African Americans.

Identity Politics, Universalism, and Liberal Isomorphism. The social boundaries separating Ashkenazim and Mizrahim have been modified over time, as has the meaning of "Mizrahi." For years, Ashkenazi politicians and the media criticized the use of Mizrahi ethnic identity as a basis for political protest and political party creation, as they framed such a movement as separatism and a threat to the "integration of the exiles" (Bernstein 1984; Herzog 1995; Hazan 2013). Given that the inclusion of Mizrahim in Israeli society and politics was based solely on their being Jews, the only legitimate domain for expressing a separate ethnic identity was religious ritual (i.e., a distinct style of praying, religious customs and practices).

With the founding of the Mizrahi social movement and political party, Shas, in the mid-1980s, a strategic political connection was established between Mizrahi ultra-Orthodox Judaism, the broader issues of ethnic segregation, and the social distress among new Mizrahi Israelis caused by inequitable state immigrant absorption policies (Herzog 1985, 1995; Peled 1998).

This was an important moment, because for ultra-Orthodox Mizrahim who value traditionalism[28] (Leon 2008, 2009; Yadgar 2011), religious identity has typically been stronger than (secular) ethnic identification.

These trends coincided with a heightened political participation of Mizrahi intellectuals and activists in the 1990s, and with greater visibility for the group as the terms "Mizrahim" and "Mizrahiness" gained in popularity. These actors worked to legitimize Mizrahi culture as well as to have authorities acknowledge the historical stigmatization of Mizrahim in Israel (Hever, Shenhav, and Motzafi-Haller 2002). Indeed, the conception of "Mizrahiness" as a distinct ethnic identity challenged the hegemonic concept of Israeli identity as defined by the dominant Ashkenazi elite. By bringing to light that Ashkenazi is often taken to be the default Israeli identity, it became possible to make other ethnic and national identities visible, along with raising questions pertaining to the hierarchalization and stigmatization of these groups (Sasson-Levy 2013). Nevertheless, nearly all of the Mizrahi population, especially its working-class members, continued to embrace the notion of the Jewish melting pot, that is, to profess support for the Zionist state and to pursue assimilatory and participatory strategies, rather than destigmatization and the politics of recognition (Mizrachi and Herzog 2012; Bitton and Glass 2016; Mizrachi 2016). Mizrahi support for Orthodox and right-wing parties in elections goes hand in hand with Mizrahi rejection of liberal, leftish forms of identity politics (Herzog 1990a; Arian and Shamir 2011; Shamir 2015).

We use the term "liberal isomorphism" to characterize intellectuals and activists belonging to minority groups who embrace identity politics (i.e., engage in equality claims-making based on shared identity). This political stance is generally rejected by their own group as well as other disadvantaged groups (Mizrachi 2012, 2014, 2016). A parallel phenomenon can be observed in liberal social movements across the globe: These movements embrace similar forms of thinking and acting, first observed in late-twentieth-century social movements in North America and other Western liberal democracies, that is, principles that have traveled to—and been recast—in other localities. Historically, these movements focused on "difference" as the rationale for challenging the prevailing hegemonic social order and for making equality claims—commonly referred to as identity politics (Anspach 1979; Brown 1995; Kruks 2001; Bernstein 2005). Liberal isomorphism resonates with the notion of the politics of recognition as discussed by political philosophers (see Taylor 1994; Honneth 1995). It entails:

(1) demands for group recognition based on a previously stigmatized or discredited identity (e.g., women, gays, people of color, people with disabilities, and so forth); (2) use of a previously stigmatized identity as the cornerstone for authentic group and individual identity; (3) stress

on the right to equal participation as different, in contrast to inclusion despite difference; (4) debunking of hegemonic society's presumed neutrality by exposing its parochial roots (as privileging the white, male, straight, able-bodied and so forth) as the spearhead for social change; and (5) acceptance of the universal right to recognition and equality for all minority groups. (Mizrachi 2014: 139)[29]

Paradoxically, when these movements have focused on gaining legitimacy and recognition in the liberal isomorphic space (i.e., among the other social movements sharing the same morals principles, such as feminists, gay and lesbian movements, and people with disabilities), they have typically distanced themselves from their target populations outside these liberal circles at the same time as they converge with the views of critical social scientists and activists. In the Mizrahi case, our interviewees' responses attest to the gap between themselves and this type of identity politics in their lived experience.

Indeed, this form of the politics of difference, which would emphasize ethnic distinctiveness vis-à-vis Jewish identity, is by and large rejected by our Ethiopian and Mizrahi interviewees. Such a theme remains the province of intellectuals and activists, as nearly all Ethiopian and Mizrahi interviewees, especially working-class traditionalists, continue to uphold Jewish religion and cultural beliefs as their core identity.

In parallel, a new critical discourse based on identity politics and promoted by the Mizrahi Democratic Rainbow social movement has been influential in liberal circles, primarily in academia and civil society NGOs. Also third-generation Mizrahi artists, activists, and publicists have become vocal and are gaining legitimacy in liberal circles and the media.[30] At the same time, middle- and working-class Mizrahim continue to downplay their cultural distinctiveness (Mizrachi and Herzog 2012). For instance, Mizrahi students do not interpret their scant presence in the most selective educational programs as connected to ethnic discrimination (Goodman and Mizrachi 2008; Mizrachi, Goodman, and Feniger 2009).[31] This may indicate that the consolidation of Mizrahiness as a distinct ethnic identity is unlikely to provide a uniform or solid foundation for groupness. And so, despite their relatively inferior position versus the hegemonic Ashkenazi elite, and the prevalence of stigmatization and exclusion in various spheres of life, the Mizrahi sense of groupness remains weak. In contrast, the sense of groupness among Ethiopians is still relatively strong, despite their embrace of the Jewish melting pot myth and their distance from identity politics, in part because they are subject to much more severe and open forms of external categorization. They also experience much higher levels of residential and labor market segregation, and their skin color stands as an unambiguous and public sign of their distinctiveness.

CONCLUSION

Our examination of groupness has revealed striking differences between the three Israeli groups, and between the Israeli case and those of the United States and Brazil. To begin with, among all the groups studied, only the self-identity of Arab Palestinians is defined primarily through their alienation from the Israeli Jewish state. For Arab Palestinians, this is experienced in terms of a historical narrative about the 1948 war, which is referred to as "catastrophe". For the most part, they feel alienation in relation to the symbols and language of the state, as well as to its official religion, Judaism. This sense of symbolic separation is intensified by a high degree of residential and institutional segregation from Jews, which is a taken-for-granted aspect of the social landscape in Israel. It results in a strong sense of (national) groupness.

In contrast, the dissonant racial groupness of Ethiopians results from the combination of their efforts to delegitimize their categorization as outsiders and to establish their identity as Jewish Israelis, who are essentially no different from other Jewish groups in Israel. Yet their conspicuous phenotypical distinctiveness and their geographic concentration in certain towns and neighborhoods (as a result of Israeli settlement policy) feeds a strong sense of linked fate and group identity, along with a dissonant racial groupness.

Finally, Mizrahim can be characterized as having a weak sense of (ethnic) groupness, as they by and large reject narratives of group distinctiveness (i.e., identity politics) and embrace their Jewishness to claim belonging and equality. This weak sense of groupness is supported by having little exposure to residential and institutional segregation.

So we see that groupness in our three Israeli cases is shaped, at least in part, by the different positions occupied by each group vis-à-vis the dominant group, the definition of which varies with their respective positions in the social structure: each of these three groups have their own "them": undifferentiated Jewish Israelis for Arab Palestinians; a broader Jewish community, encompassing Ashkenazim and Mizrahim, for Ethiopians; and the dominant Ashkenazi elite for Mizrahim who believe they suffer from stigmatization.

As with African Americans and Black Brazilians, groupness in the three Israeli cases can be described in some respects as contradictory or strong in some respects and weak in others. For Arab Palestinians, their self-identification and drawing of group boundaries vis-à-vis Jewish Israelis is strong and unambiguous. Yet, paradoxically, their national groupness is somewhat weakened by the fact that they are denied national belonging by both Israelis, by virtue of their Arab identity, and by Palestinians, by virtue of their Israeli citizenship. In contrast, Ethiopian groupness is dissonant in that they downplay their racial and ethnic identity at the same time as they hope to be assimilated in the majority group. Finally, Mizrahi groupness is weak in terms of self-identification. While they downplay the significance of being Mizrahi in their lives, they have no trouble describing its meaning in terms of shared culture and to draw group boundaries against Ashkenazi Jews.

Our analysis points to the important role of repertoires in the formation of groupness—especially in the form of institutionalized narratives of group disadvantage and equality. Arab Palestinians are the only group that has a separate and diametric national narrative vis-à-vis the dominant group. Still, their narrative of domination parallels the narrative of slavery that contributes to the strong groupness and sense of linked fate among African Americans. In contrast, Ethiopians and Mizrahim lack institutionalized group narratives, such as the narratives of slavery, emancipation, and civil rights in the United States, which are taught in the schools and recognized by the state. In Israel, for Ethiopians and Mizrahim alike, any alternative group narratives that exist are confined to social activist milieus. Thus, these two groups mobilize elements of the Zionist repertoire regarding the Jewish melting pot as a way to claim equality. This differs considerably from African Americans, who draw on a repertoire of universalism to claim their equality or "lack of difference" with whites. Ethiopians and Mizrahim have more in common with Black Brazilians, who draw on the repertoires of racial mixture and interracial civility. However, in the Brazilian case, those repertoires contribute to a sense of national belonging and inclusiveness, rather than symbolically excluding other social groups from the polity, as is the case for narratives based on religious affiliation that are salient in the Israeli context. At their core, the repertoires that Ethiopians, Mizrahim, African Americans, and Black Brazilians draw on are premised on national belonging. As we will see, Arab Palestinian exclusion from national belonging powerfully shapes their experience and responses to stigmatization and discrimination.

SECTION 4.3: EXPERIENCES OF STIGMATIZATION AND DISCRIMINATION IN ISRAEL

In this section, we turn our attention to how our Arab Palestinian, Ethiopian, and Mizrahi interviewees describe experiences of exlusion in their daily lives. Following our standard approach, we asked them whether they had ever been treated unfairly or discriminated against at work, and we carefully coded their answers to our queries and probes, as well as their spontaneous mentions of unfair treatment mentioned during the interviews. As for the

United States and Brazilian cases, we distinguish between incidents characterized as assaults on worth and discriminatory incidents, and we find that assaults on worth are reported more frequently than discrimination incidents. Arab Palestinians report the greatest number of incidents, followed by Ethiopians and Mizrahim. Overall, 84 percent of the Arab Palestinians described at least one incident involving an assault on worth, compared to 78 percent of Ethiopians and 57 percent of Mizrahi respondents. By comparison, 58 percent of our Palestinian interviewees mentioned incidents of discrimination, compared to 48 percent of Ethiopians and 36 percent of Mizrahim. Only a small percentage of our Arab Palestinian and Ethiopian interviewees mentioned no incidents at all (14 percent and 13 percent, respectively), whereas a much larger proportion of Mizrahim (36 percent) said they never felt that they had been treated unfairly or discriminated against. (See Table A2.5 in Appendix 2 for full details.) But these numbers only begin to capture the range and texture of the respondents' experiences.

For Arab Palestinians, the deep Arab-Jewish divide and historical narratives of national dispossession and conflict that fuels a strong sense of groupness provide the primary lenses through which they experience ethnoracial exclusion. In the words of a sales clerk, "I feel as though their [Israeli Jews'] level of racism is sky-high; so it doesn't matter how close you get to them and how much you are like them, they are still racists. In the end we remain Arabs and Jews." Many of the experiences they relate are notable for their bluntness and severity, including insults and physical assaults, which are often amplified during periods of deterioration in the ongoing Israeli-Palestinian conflict. The primary basis for stigmatization and exclusion revolves around Jews' distrust of Arabs, who are viewed as potential terrorists or security risks.

Ethiopians are similar to African Americans and Black Brazilians in being marked by skin color and stigmatized on that basis, although the specific stereotypes that fuel stigmatization are somewhat different across groups: Ethiopians report feeling stereotyped as uneducated, primitive, or culturally backward instead of as low-income, violent, lazy, and the like. We will argue that these stereotypes are tied to the contrast between their status as immigrants from Africa and the Zionist ideal of the modern, Western ideal of the new Jew.

The third group, Mizrahim, tended to downplay stigma and discrimination in their personal lives. Many of the incidents they recounted pertained not to their personal experiences, but to incidents that happened to other people or to their parents being mistreated by the Ashkenazi elite—things that happened "in the past."

Comparing our three Israeli groups reveals how incidents are patterned by residential segregation, institutional separation, and homophily. Whereas

Arab Palestinians experience stigmatization primarily in public places, checkpoints, and the workplace, for Ethiopians it takes place in such institutions as schools, the army, and the workplace, as well as in public places, but more rarely in intimate settings. For Mizrahim, who are more socially integrated, more of the incidents take place in the family and close social networks. This analysis of the impact of context on experiences adds a dimension that was less present in our analysis of African Americans and Black Brazilians. Its salience is brought out by comparing groups that experience very different degrees of spatial and social segregation in the same national space.

STIGMATIZATION OR ASSAULTS ON WORTH

The narratives of the Arab Palestinian interviewees stand in sharp contrast to those of the other four groups studied, not only African Americans and Black Brazilians, but also Ethiopians and Mizrahim. It is striking that Arab Palestinians very rarely refer to being stereotyped as poor or uneducated, underestimated, misunderstood, or treated as exceptional, compared to the four other groups under consideration. For members of this group, stigmatization based on negative stereotypes associated with ethnic or racial inferiority is not salient. Instead, their experience is shaped by national belonging, distrust, and being stereotyped as potential threats, which play a similar role for this group that is played for the other groups under consideration by the experiences of feeling underestimated, misunderstood or stereotyped as poor. The legacy of the Israel-Palestinian conflict and the explicit and blatant exclusion of Arab Palestinians from crucial aspects of the polity as non-Jews (e.g., from the army) overshadow more subtle manifestations of ethnoracial exclusion.

Arab Palestinians

Being Insulted or Disrespected. Arab Palestinians experience assaults on worth similar to other groups under consideration although their experience of political stigmatization, as untrustworthy members of the polity, looms largest in their descriptions. Forty percent of our Arab Palestinian interviewees related incidents of being insulted and of disrespectful treatment that often echo the experiences of African Americans. This frequently took the form of hearing their group identity referred to in a derogatory way, as was the case when Mohi, a customer service representative who recalled that customers "throw out statements like 'this Arab' and things like that and are confident you will not hear, but you hear." In other cases the disrespect is more blatant: one of our interviewees related an incident where his class at the university discussed the ethics of testing consumer products on rabbits, and one of the Jewish students loudly suggested, only half joking, that they should be tested on Arabs.

This is a fairly extreme example. While being insulted is the most frequent type of incident that Arab Palestinians encounter, it is not necessarily representative of their day-to-day lives. As several interviewees noted, "not all Jews are like that."[32] For example, after describing a dramatic incident that occurred in a restaurant, a woman spontaneously commented about a Jewish homeopathic doctor: "He takes care of me like my brothers. You wouldn't believe how he takes care of me, my children. His clinic is in his house, and he told me 'it's is open to you and your children 24 hours a day. Just call.'" More generally, in numerous cases interviewees mentioned how supportive their Jewish managers, fellow workers, or even other customers were.

It is interesting to note that virtually all assaults on worth that took place at work involved customers rather than coworkers or bosses. This can be partly attributed to selection bias: workplaces that are hostile to Arabs will not hire them in the first place, and Arabs are less likely to apply for jobs in Jewish-dominated workplaces.[33] But it can also be viewed as an outcome of attempts by coworkers to create congenial workplace relations by separating the personal from the political (Mizrachi and Herzog 2012; Brohnstein 2015). The most widespread complaint about the workplace involved customary policies forbidding Arab workers from speaking Arabic to one another on the job.

The frequency of incidents appears to fluctuate with flare-ups in the ongoing Israeli-Palestinian conflict: incidents become more common when tensions grow. For example, one call-center worker talked about customers who recognized his accent and confronted him during Operation Cast Lead (a conflict between Gaza and Israel in 2009), stating "We are for peace, but you kill children." Also, an Arab Palestinian woman spoke of being confronted on a bus shortly after a terror attack had occurred: "This woman began to curse us: 'You Arabs! You're all alike. Barbarians!'" This behavior echoes the arguments made by Bar-Tal and Teichman (2005) regarding the tendency of Israeli Jews to lump Arab Palestinian citizens of Israel and the wider Palestinian community outside Israel into one homogeneous social category, and therefore view the former as enemies. At the time of the incident, the respondent stated, she was surprised, because she hadn't yet heard about the terror attack. Once she learned of it, she was able to contextualize the woman's reaction, even if she did not think it was appropriate or acceptable.

Physical Assaults. Although not nearly as common as being insulted or disrespected, experiences of being physically assaulted, were reported by 14 percent of our Arab Palestinian respondents, a much higher percentage than for any of the other four groups under consideration. According to the

Mossawa Center, an NGO that collects reports of violence against Arab Palestinians, the majority of incidents of violence against this group involves the police and security forces. In contrast, we find that virtually all incidents that our interviewees related were perpetrated by citizens. For instance, one Arab man recounted being hit in the stomach during a peaceful demonstration, while another respondent described her friend's harrowing experience of someone trying to run over her in a car.

Incidents were not always tied to increased tension due to the Israeli-Palestinian conflict but are part of normal, everyday life. For instance, Kabha, a young man who worked as a nurse, related the following incident: "I studied in Safed, where there's a very [ultra-Orthodox] community. . . . I was walking along one night, talking on the phone in Arabic, and when they heard me they ran after me and wanted to beat me." Another interviewee, a cable technician, described an incident of physical aggression with a customer while on the job, which was memorable for him both because of its extreme nature and because it was far beyond his usual experience interacting with Jews. His description of the scene, which began with severe verbal abuse, quickly deteriorated on both sides: "[This customer came out and yelled:] 'Get out of here, you dirty Arabs, get out of here, you ass fuckers,' . . . I just looked at him the whole time and laughed. Laughed, you understand? He grabbed a rock and threw it at [my coworker]." This experience of blunt aggression is indicative of the level of distrust that some Jews feels toward Arab Palestinians and attests to the deep social divide and animosity. Awareness of the potential for being exposed to incidents of such violence and severity set the experiences of Arab Palestinians apart from the other four groups in this study.

Stereotyped as Threatening. Across the five groups under consideration, Arab Palestinians are the only group to regularly experience mistrust in the context of national security. In line with previous studies, they reported being routinely stereotyped as threatening, regardless of changes in the intensity of the Israeli-Palestinian conflict (Bar-Tal and Teichman 2005). This stereotyping occurred mostly during security screening checks, which are conducted at the entrance to any public building or area. Passing through security (and metal detectors) is commonplace for all Israelis: security guards are typically stationed at entrances to government offices and most large public spaces, such as malls and bus terminals, as well as outside many restaurants and bars. Car trunks are checked when entering underground parking lots. While everyone is screened, Arab Palestinians are usually scrutinized more vigorously as potential security risks. Thus, after being stopped and searched at a border crossing while traveling on state business, an Arab Palestinian parliamentary assistant laments: "The security guards basically waved the Jews through. I had to undergo questioning. That gave me the feeling that no matter where I work and what my position is . . . I am and will continue to be an Arab, and will always be under suspicion."

Ethiopians and Mizrahim

In contrast to Arab Palestinians, Ethiopians and Mizrahim are symbolically included in the Israeli polity. However, as we saw, these two groups do not fit entirely with the hegemonic Ashkenazi image of Jews as modern and Western European. Originating from non-Western settings, each are stereotyped as culturally backward, but slightly differently: Ethiopians as primitive, ignorant, traditional, and technologically backward (Ben-Eliezer 2008; Zawdu Gebyanesh 2011), whereas Mizrahim are viewed as vulgar, unrefined, uneducated, and uninhibited (Mizrachi 2004). The latter stereotype applies mostly to lower-class Mizrahim, whereas stereotypes about Ethiopians tend to apply to the entire group, who as recent immigrants are also viewed as less assimilated. More Ethiopians than Mizrahim mention being underestimated or stereotyped as low status, poor, or uneducated (i.e., culturally backward).

For Ethiopians, skin color is quite salient as a basis for disrespect—for example, being called "*kooshi*" (the Hebrew equivalent of "blackie" or "nigger"). It is most often mentioned not in face-to-face encounters, but indirectly, as respondents hear it muttered "behind their backs." These blatant racist incidents often occurred at work, as when one respondent overhead a customer say to his coworker: "What? This monkey talks? This 'blackie?' Don't let him near me. God forbid, he just fell off the tree and he can already talk?" Roughly half of our Ethiopian respondents experienced incidents at work, most of which were assaults on worth rather than acts of discrimination. Not all are as blatant as this last example.

In the past, Mizrahi Jews were often derogatively referred to as "blacks," though on average their skin is only a bit darker than that of Ashkenazim, and many have a light complexion. Recent studies show that in Israeli public discourse, skin color remains a frequently used label that is still occasionally applied to the second, third, and even fourth generations of Mizrahim born in Israel (Shitrit 2004; Bitton 2012). Our Mizrahi respondents themselves often referred to skin color when self-identifying, for example, metaphorically referring to being black or dark. While some explicitly denied having a distinctive color, others (mainly Yemenites) simply used skin color as a descriptor. In contrast, none of our Arab Palestinians interviewees mentioned being stigmatized on the basis of their skin color, although they are phenotypically similar to Mizrahi Jews. In their case, national identity overshadows other markers of stigma.

Our Mizrahi interviewees also occasionally face insults or disrespect due to their presumed cultural backwardness. For instance, one woman described tensions with her Ashkenazi in-laws when she says: "My father-in-law said we came down from the trees." However, in striking contrast to both the Ethiopians and the Arab Palestinians, the Mizrahi respondents reported very few incidents in which they themselves were the object of exclusion. Instead, most describe events that happened to other people, often relatives, and usually in the past. Distancing themselves from such personal experiences is indicative of their group identity, which is characterized by its contingent detachment (Mizrachi and Herzog 2012). This detachment enables Mizrahim to acknowledge stigma—while at the same time avoiding adoption of a stigmatized group identity to protect their self worth—and to maintain their personal sense of belonging to the Jewish polity.

The one context where Mizrahi interviewees reported more incidents of stigmatization than other groups is in personal relationships. This can be explained by their greater degree of spatial and institutional integration and more frequent intermarriage, in particular between Ashkenazim and Mizrahim, in contrast to between Ashkenazim and Arab Palestinians or Ethiopians. Typically, reported incidents involve the partner or a member of his/her family making disparaging comments. For example, a working-class Mizrahi woman recounted: "My boyfriend [who is Ashkenazi] was in a cultural shock because in our family there is no kidush [sanctification of the Sabbath] without singing." She goes on explaining that her boyfriend was dismayed that her family members tell tasteless jokes. In contrast, his Ashkenazi family is more into cultural refinement and discusses the arts around dinner.

While in the early 1950s, Ashkenazi-Mizrahi intermarriages were almost unthinkable, today they are a nonissue (Sagiv 2014). However, ethnic stereotypes still exist among the children of intermarried couples. Sagiv (2014) has shown that children of these couples select their ethnic identity (Ashkenazi or Mizrahi) according to phenotype (skin tone and appearance), family name, place of residency, and the level of identification with a particular parent. Ethnic identity plays a role in shaping cultural tastes, family customs, music preferences, and so on of the children of mixed marriages.

DISCRIMINATION

Antidiscrimination legislation is a more recent development in Israel than in the United States, and it is also not as thoroughly institutionalized. While wage protection legislation goes back to 1958, only in 1988 was a law passed stipulating equality of opportunity in employment (Ben-Israel and Foubert 2004).[34] The Equal Employment Opportunity Commission established for dealing with workplace discrimination was only put in place in 2008. Antidiscrimination law is rarely enforced, and few interviewees mentioned considering or using legal means to fight discrimination or to complain to their union about unequal treatment (as shown in Appendix 2, Table A2.6). From the perspective of Abed, a working-class Arab Palestinian: "Racism and discrimination became normal in this country . . . people tolerate it, it became something acceptable. Even the Palestinians don't respond decisively against their discrimination." This is further evidence that universalist and pro-diversity repertoires are not widely institutionalized in Israel (Bitton 2008; Marantz, Kalev and Lewin-Epstein 2014). In contrast, they are quite prominent in several central institutions in the United States (Berrey 2015).

Arab Palestinians

Routine Security Profiling. Profiling and being denied opportunities are the two types of discrimination incidents most frequently mentioned by Arab Palestinians. Forty-six percent of Arab Palestinian respondents report having been profiled, typically during security screenings, while very few Mizrahim and Ethiopians mention having such an experience. A recent study of airport passengers showed that 40 percent of the Arab Palestinians and non-Israelis surveyed were asked to open their suitcases for additional searching, compared to only 9.8 percent of Israeli Jews. While the non-Israelis saw it as a legitimate requirement, the Arab Palestinians were offended and expressed less trust in the system (Hasisi, Margalioth, and Orgad 2012).[35]

Routine security checks are considered by Israeli Jews as a slightly annoying but unavoidable part of daily life, almost a taken-for-granted routine. This is generally not the case for Arab Palestinians, who, because they are more frequently singled out, view it as a context where they are unfairly marked as a potential enemy. Profiling poses a major hurdle to their integration into the polity, as it increases their alienation and mistrust of the Israeli police, army, and government. Arab Palestinian interviewees viewed as denigrating the experience of being singled out at security checks and patted down in public. Abir, the Palestinian woman whose story we told in the Introduction, described how being harassed at checkpoints felt to her like a "series of humiliations as [the soldier] 'played' with us." Civil rights organizations like the Arab Association for Human Rights, the Center Against Racism, Adalah: The Legal Center for Arab Minority Rights in Israel, and the Association for Civil Rights in Israel protest against profiling and undertake efforts to combat racism in general and toward Arab Palestinians in particular. The Israeli forms of profiling show how much the experiences of ethnoracial exclusion are shaped by the distinctive context in which the lives of the five groups under consideration evolve.

Interviewees also experienced moments of gratuitous violence in contexts where it was completely unanticipated. For example, one horrified interviewee described an incident that occurred after he was dropped off by his friend near the bus station. As he was walking with his suitcase in hand, a man ran toward him with his weapon drawn. He "shouted 'stop and lift your shirt!' and asked what was in my suitcase." The Israel-Palestinian conflict and terrorism has generated a state of pervasive violence, including the presence of suicide bombers, which has no counterpart in Brazil and the United States, where racial profiling is also common. But security profiling also has direct implications for access to resources. For example, one of our interviewees, a contractor, complained about being completely shut out of work on Israeli military bases, in contrast to Jews: "It doesn't matter what kind of Jew it is, as long as it's simply a Jew." Moreover, when profiling—either as a potential terrorist or as a criminal—results in arrest, the arrested individual becomes ineligible for jobs that require clean criminal histories.

Being Denied Opportunities. The second most common type of incident mentioned by Arab Palestinians is being denied opportunities (mentioned by 34 percent of them). This finding is in line with a recent survey conducted by the Israeli Equal Employment Opportunity Commission, in which 39 percent of the 770 respondents said they felt that their ethnicity hurts their chances of getting a job (Kupfer 2016). Such incidents include discrimination in hiring and housing. They are frequently direct, blatant, and unambiguous. For example, on losing a bid for a construction contract, a contractor explains it is "because I am Arab. [The client] told me this in public, that he prefers Jews even though they're more expensive. [He said] they deserve it because they're Jewish and they're better. And he said he prefers it over giving money to Arabs, who will turn around and support [terrorist] organizations in the territories." In a similar context, another subcontractor suspected discrimination when he was told by the construction coordinator overseeing a bid: "Listen, I trust you and have faith in you. Only, it's not me, it's the people above me. I cannot say anything, and I won't tell you the reason . . . but it didn't work out."

Similar experiences abound, as when a Palestinian nurse who graduated from nursing school in the north faced work discrimination. After being told that no jobs were available upon graduation, she told the potential employer, "'But didn't you just hire [people she had just graduated with]?' I asked them to at least bring me in for an interview, but they said no and that they had already thrown away my resume." Later, she applied for a job at a hospital in Tel Aviv and had a more positive experience. Another of our respondents dropped out of a degree program at a top science and engineering university (Technion) to attend a trade school when she learned about the difficulties experienced by a recent Arab Palestinian graduate who could not find work due to discrimination.

At the same time, one form of hiring discrimination is less blatant, if no less obvious, and is reinforced by the state's official policy of not drafting Arab Palestinians into the army: employers often make army service a prerequisite for a job, independently of its relevance to the work performed. As Remi, one of our respondents, reflects "They do not want to tell you 'we are racist.' There was a clothing store with a help wanted sign outside saying 'workers needed . . . after army.' [Does] having been in the army mean you have a more developed fashion sense?"

Housing discrimination is also pervasive. Indeed, Arab Palestinians are often told that apartments are no longer available when they show up to visit them, and unlike in the United States, rejection is often blunt, as one remembers being rejected with the comment: "Arab? Out of the question!" In the absence of housing discrimination law regulating the private housing market, one interviewee prefers to announce from the start that she is Arab: "It's absurd to even have to say that, but given the level of discrimination, it would be a waste of time not to say it." Her approach reveals by contrast the extent to which antidiscrimination laws shape interracial relationships in the United States, including by promoting a shared culture of universalism and diversity—albeit a partial and imperfect one.

Being Excluded from Public Places and Denied Service. Somewhat less common but still prevalent are experiences of being excluded from public places, which are reported by 14 percent of Arab Palestinian respondents. The low frequency of this type of experience is partly due to the high level of residential segregation and relative absence of shared public spaces, as well as to the fact that Palestinians often avoid Jewish-dominated food and entertainment services. The most frequently mentioned experience is being turned away from night clubs after showing their ID, but other respondents described being turned away from restaurants (e.g., a couple was told "there is no room" at a completely empty restaurant). This can extend to other arenas. For instance, an Arab Palestinian nurse reports that one of her colleagues, a Jewish nurse, refuses to treat Arabs "because they blow us up."

Ethiopians and Mizrahim

Ethiopian and Mizrahi interviewees mention incidents where they are denied opportunities as frequently as Arab Palestinians (see Table A2.5 in Appendix 2), but the incidents they face are, for the most part, less blatant and tend to take place in different social contexts than for Arab Palestinians, mainly due to starkly different patterns of residential and institutional segregation. For example, Arab respondents never reported being discriminated against in primary or secondary education, but that is because they study in a separate school system until university level. What also stands out when comparing these groups is that Arab Palestinian respondents were always aware that they were being discriminated against or treated unfairly due to their status as Palestinians. In contrast, some of the incidents that Ethiopians—and even more so, Mizrahim—experienced were described as more ambiguous. As a consequence, much like their Brazilian counterparts, members of both groups were more uncertain about whether a particular discriminatory incident was related to their ethnicity: "Well, I'm not sure if it was because I am Ethiopian." In some cases, the realization that an incident was due to their ethnicity occurred after the fact, sometimes years afterward. This is especially surprising in the case of Ethiopians, who are easily categorized due to their skin color. Their hesitation is enabled by their relatively low level of self-identification with their group. They also hope to belong to the Israeli polity and identify with the promise of integration tied to Zionism. This may lead them to downplay incidents. Unlike African Americans, they also do not have ready access to historical repertoires of group disadvantage on which they can readily draw to make sense of their experiences. The same holds for Mizrahim to an even greater extent. When experiencing ambiguous incidents, both Ethiopians and Mizrahim may simply view people as rude or unfriendly, and Ethiopians sometimes attribute such treatment to their recent immigrant status and believe that all new immigrants are treated in a similar manner.

For Ethiopians, discrimination at the workplace was the least ambiguous form of discrimination they faced, although it was generally not as blatant for them as it was for Arab Palestinians. Four respondents described incidents where they called about a job opening and were invited to apply, but were told that the position was no longer available when they showed up. In one case, the interviewee was hired over the phone but turned away when he arrived, which he interpreted as resulting from the employer's racism. In another case, the interviewee was told by a prospective employer that they do not "hire people with dreadlocks." Even when they did not experience it directly, incidents of this kind were considered a common experience for Ethiopians among our interviewees.

Ethiopians also experience denial of opportunities in school settings: they often complained about the de facto educational segregation that takes place due to their spatial concentration and educational tracking (as immigrants who need remedial training). One interviewee recalls a memorable moment when she qualified for a gifted student program:

> The principal directed me to the remedial class because that's where the Ethiopian students go. I told him, "No, I belong over there [in a matriculation preparatory class]. He told me, "No, you are going there." I started crying, and then my mom came and yelled at him, so I went to the class. When I entered, they had all heard the fuss and categorized me as the problematic Ethiopian. Everybody looked at me with animosity. For most of them, it was the first time in their life that they had seen an Ethiopian—like in the flesh and sitting next to them. And for the first time in my life I wondered if I should start acting like them, copying them exactly in order to be like them and be accepted, or continue [to identify] with my color.

In another case, Giora, a police officer, faced rejection when attempting to register his daughter at a local school. He interprets this experience as follows: "[T]hey're afraid. They say, okay, they're Ethiopians and they'll . . . lower the level of all sorts of things, hobby classes, for instance. . . . [They think] too many Ethiopians lower the school's level, . . . so they don't want us." For Giora, the stigmatization of Ethiopians as uneducated and culturally backward explains why he was turned away. He ascribes this experience to his status as an immigrant, which anchors his groupness.

One-fifth of Ethiopian respondents also mentioned facing social exclusion, especially in public spaces, such as buses and nightclubs. One account concerned a bus driver who skipped all the stops in an Ethiopian neighborhood. Another interviewee told about being turned away from a nightclub on the false pretense that it was full, even as "'white' patrons were let in,"[36] which left our respondent stunned with humiliation as he was left standing on the street after having gotten dressed up in excited anticipation of a night out.

In contrast, just a few of our Mizrahi interviewees spoke of discrimination as something they had themselves experienced. One attributed not obtaining a contract due to his ethnicity. Another described an instance of housing discrimination, noting that her real estate agent had advised her not to tell people she was Mizrahi. A third "went to interview at the Jewish Agency, and was told 'it's not the day for blacks.' I wasn't sure if he was joking or not. He said they were looking for people with a personal connection to the Holocaust." And as with Ethiopians, a few of our respondents mentioned being turned away from nightclubs (Bitton 2008; Carmi and Keren 2010).

But again, as with assaults on worth, for most Mizrahi respondents, descriptions of experiences of discrimination are more abstract and impersonal. For instance, when asked about experiences of discrimination, one dispassionately described having fewer educational options due to growing up outside the Tel Aviv–Jerusalem corridor. Another respondent discussed the results of an experiment she had read about, in which resumés with Ashkenazi last names were more likely to get callbacks than identical resumés with stereotypically Mizrahi last names.

Our Mizrahi respondents did not mention discrimination at school. A recent study showed that when Mizrahi students who are tracked into lower-level classes are asked to describe the group characteristics of their classmates (who are predominantly Mizrahi) and the characteristics of the students in higher tracks (who are predominantly Ashkenazi), they avoid using an ethnic signifier. Instead they use terms like "punks and geeks" or "southerners and northerners." They refer to lifestyles and individual preferences, rather than ethnicity (Mizrachi, Goodman, and Feniger 2009). This finding also attests to the gap between the critical discourse of identity politics and distributive justice (see Mizrachi 2014 on liberal isomorphism) and members of minority groups who refuse to embrace such sociological categorizations. This gap is further enabled by the lack of an institutionalized narrative about Mizrahi group disadvantage.

CONCLUSION

The most striking finding is that Arab Palestinians appear to experience the most blatant and serious incidents of stigmatization and discrimination of any of the groups discussed in this book, which is especially evident in the incidents that involved physical assaults and the interviewees who are told that they cannot rent an apartment because they are Arab. In part, these extreme experiences are enabled by the relative underdevelopment of legal tools to fight discrimination in Israel compared to those available in the United States. Employment discrimination is illegal in all three countries, but antidiscrimination and hate crime laws are relatively recent and weakly enforced in Israel, and no laws exist to curb discrimination in the private housing market. Furthermore, because Jewish-Arab relations take place against the backdrop of an armed struggle between two peoples, many Jews associate the Arab minority with the enemy. As a result, there is less normative consensus concerning the opprobrium that should accompany discrimination and racist behavior toward Arabs. This allows Israeli Jews to be relatively open and direct in their stigmatizing and discriminatory behavior toward Arab Israelis than is the case, for example, among US whites toward African Americans. Furthermore, the ongoing conflict animates an active hostility and belligerence against Arab Palestinians, which comes across in some of the more blatant and harrowing experiences. It also helps explain why Arab Palestinians are stereotyped as threatening and experience security profiling in a way that is unique among the groups in this study. At the same time, Arab Palestinians—like African Americans—have a strong sense of groupness and readily available and highly institutionalized narratives of group advantage, framed through a history of national dispossession and ongoing conflict. They are therefore apt to interpret even ambiguous incidents as related to their group identity. Arab Palestinians also very rarely report being misunderstood or stigmatized as uneducated or poor, whereas these stereotypes are more common among other groups studied here. We attribute this to the clear and unambiguous national narrative that frames their experience, which limits the range of possible interpretations. Moreover, their national belonging, which is accompanied by deep-seated mistrust and animosity, overshadows other bases of exclusion.

In comparison, Ethiopians and especially Mizrahim have less of a sense of groupness and less recourse to institutionalized narratives of group disadvantage. Even though Ethiopians have a stronger sense of linked fate than do Mizrahim, they still embrace Zionist repertories to construct a self-identity as Israelis rather than as members of a marginalized minority. This introduces somewhat more uncertainty and ambiguity into their interpretations of incidents, notwithstanding the many brazen insults they face. Mizrahim mentioned comparatively few incidents, and many of the incidents they described were experienced by other people or were events that happened in the past or to previous generations. This can be explained, we argue, by their weak sense of groupness and their contingent detachment from a stigmatized ethnic identity, as well as the relative absence of institutionalized and widely accepted narratives of Mizrahi disadvantage. Moreover, even in the legal arena, "Mizrahi" is not accepted by courts as an official category for the basis of antidiscrimination lawsuits (Bitton 2011). Like the Brazilian "racial mixture" repertoire, the narrative of the "Jewish melting pot" powerfully shapes Ethiopian and Mizrahi groupness and serves to frame many of their interactions.

Finally, we note the different array of locations and contexts where members of the three groups did—and did not—experience exclusion and discrimination. Arab Palestinians did not recount incidents involving schooling, except at the university level, nor did they point to experiences in intimate relationships. Their encounters with Jews took place mainly at the workplace or in brief, anonymous interactions. These were the sites where they experienced assaults on worth and discrimination. For their part, Ethiopians are somewhat less segregated, so they also related experiences in school, the army, and friendship networks. When Mizrahim recounted personal incidents, most of these took place among friends and extended family. Thus, the contours of their experiences were shaped by differences in their degree of residential segregation, institutional separation, and homosocial closure.

SECTION 4.4: RESPONSES TO STIGMATIZATION AND DISCRIMINATION IN ISRAEL

Sociologists and political scientists have dedicated considerable energy to studying the sociopolitical and structural conditions that engender racial, ethnic, and national inequality in Israel (Yiftachel 1997, 2006; Shafir and Peled 2002; Smooha 2002; Semyonov and Lewin-Epstein 2004). As a consequence, the literatures on the stigmatization and discrimination of Arab Palestinians, Mizrahim, and Ethiopians largely concern the political and civic domains, that is, political parties organized on the basis of ethnonational origin (Herzog 1995; Jamal 2007), protest movements (Bernstein 1984; Wolfsfeld 1988; Dahan Kalev 1999; Ben-Eliezer 2008), and civil society organizations (Jamal 2008; Ben-Porat and Turner 2011). Also, debates about how to reduce inequality and discrimination have focused on public policy and legislation—their implementation and effectiveness (Mundlak 2009). How Israelis respond to incidents and imagine alternatives has received little attention, except for a few comprehensive surveys (e.g., Smooha 2013). While the latter draw on closed questions, we use open-ended questions and a more inductive approach that can tap a wider range of responses.

As with the US case, the reaction to incidents most frequently mentioned by all three Israeli groups was confrontation, and this typically takes the form of speaking out (see Table A2.6 in Appendix 2). Among the Arab Palestinian interviewees who said they spoke out in response to an incident (28 percent), we find a variety of ways of confronting. Some felt that Jews are ignorant of Palestinian society, and so it was important to educate them about it. Notice that this differs from the Brazilian and American examples of "educating the ignorant," because in those cases it referred to educating whites about the existence of racism, whereas here it is about educating them about Arab culture. About 20 percent of our Arab Palestinian interviewees responded to incidents through management of the self, and explained their response by the need to control their anger. But another segment of our Arab Palestinian interviewees (25 percent) were quite cynical about the importance of speaking out, as they felt that it would make no difference. They chose to remain silent instead. Consistent with this cynicism is the fact that, in sharp contrast with African Americans, Arab Palestinians almost never considered recourse to the law when responding to discrimination. Ethiopians and Mizrahim were much more likely than Arab Palestinians to respond by acting against stereotypes and seeking to prove their competence through working harder.

The cynicism expressed by many Arab Palestinians in interpersonal interactions carried over to their ideal responses. They generally regarded collective action as unlikely to improve their situation, and although they did not view their incorporation into the polity as achievable, they did see a possibility of improving their social standing and economic situation. They emphasized the importance of solidarity and education as a means for group advancement, and they viewed themselves as active agents in preserving their group identity in spite of the ethnoracial exclusion they face in everyday life.

Whereas Arab Palestinians mostly viewed education as a means for collective advancement, Ethiopian and Mizrahi Jews emphasized personal responsibility and viewed education more as a means for individual advancement. Ethiopians, in particular, expressed the view that as members of their community become educated, they would be able to fully assimilate into Israeli society. Finally, when reflecting on the best way to deal with racism, this group discussed the difficulty of overcoming the personal pain and humiliation of being a target of racism.

ACTUAL RESPONSES TO INCIDENTS

Arab Palestinians

In view of their structural and political conditions, it comes as no surprise that Arab Palestinians' responses to surveys about the possibility of broad political change indicate an absence of hope for improving their deep-seated sociopolitical exclusion as citizens of Israel (e.g., Arian et al. 2010: 138–164; Smooha 2013). Nor is it surprising that this influences how they respond to stigmatization and discrimination.

Confronting. As is true for the other four groups under consideration, the most common response to stigmatization among our Arab Palestinian respondents was confrontation (38 percent of all responses, a lower percentage than in the other groups). The most common response is to speak out, which occurred in the context of heated escalations as well as in more considered exchanges. However, interviewees typically did not show the concern for civility that was often emphasized by Black Brazilians. On rare occasions confrontation turned physical, as was the case when a cable TV technician punched the aggressor who threw a rock at him in the incident mentioned in Section 4.3.

The position of Arab Palestinians vis-à-vis the Jewish polity is negotiated in a range of contexts, and their responses often reveal a mastery of the complex landscape in which they are operating. Consider the case of an Arab Palestinian woman who works in retail with Russian immigrant women. She replies to their insults by drawing on negative stereotypes about Russians to turn the tables:

> Normally they ignore me. But I feel that they're acting like they're better than us. . . . For example, sometimes as a joke [one of them] says, "Why are you dressed like an Arab?" So I answer, throwing it back at them: "Why are you dressed like a Russian prostitute?" You understand, I give it back to them, but worse.

In another case, on learning that a potential customer would not hire his services as a contractor because he is an Arab and so presumed to support terror, our interviewee responds immediately by using the language of citizenship, to demand economic inclusion and equal treatment: "we pay the same taxes and pay everything, so we deserve to work and to have a place in the labor market."

Another woman describes confronting a supermarket manager for indicating that he would only hire individuals who have served in the military. She said:

"Why did you put 'after military service' in the ad? I want to know!" He said it was because of the age.... "Why do you write 'after army' if you want [a specific] age?" He didn't know what to say to me.

She was hired by another supermarket after first lying about her name and army service. Surprisingly, the manager decided to hire her after she revealed her deception to him, as he appreciated her gumption.

Amal, a young woman who worked in retail, describes an event where a client declined a child car seat in a color she did not like, saying that it [the color] is an "Arab taste": "That really bothered me, so I told her, 'I'm sorry I'm not going to help you anymore, you'll have to find someone Jewish to help you, because I'm Arab, and I'm very proud that I'm Arab and I don't want to help you.' So I left."

Besides using their familiarity with subtle discriminatory practices to determine appropriate responses, Amar, who faced job discrimination, explained why he chose to confront this racist incident: "So when you see someone being racist, you have to stop them and not behave like in the past by turning a blind eye. It's like sweeping dirt under the carpet—you have to take care of the problem so it won't stink so much. Same with racism."

According to this view, the best way to deal with racism is to demand social recognition and respect for their culture, identity, and existence. This attitude was expressed forcefully by Mona when describing an incident where she felt unfairly profiled: "Don't put restrictions on me because you are afraid of me. If you want us to live together and do things together, give me room to breathe. As you live your life, let me live mine.... Make me feel like you believe in me as a human being ... and then I will look at you as a human being."

Our Arab Palestinian interviewees responded to specific incidents through confrontation, but in contrast to many African Americans and Black Brazilians, they are not concerned with making Jews aware of bigotry. This is due to the unambiguous and often brazen incidents they experienced. Thus, few had doubts about the intent of the aggressor or about the role played by anti-Arab prejudices in a given interaction. Many are concerned with correcting misrepresentation by the media: "Go learn the truth about the Arabs who live here in Israel.... You do not know anything besides what you hear from the media. The media is not giving it all straight, the media is not telling everything."

In stark contrast to African Americans, very few of the Arab interviewees use legal tools to respond, with only a handful of exceptions (see Table A2.6 in Appendix 2). Even in the most egregious cases—such as being told they could not rent an apartment or get a contract because they were Arab Palestinian—interviewees do not seek legal redress. This is consistent with survey results showing that Arab Palestinians have less trust in Israeli state institutions than do Jews (Arian et al. 2010; Hermann et al. 2013). Moreover, discrimination lawsuits remain rare. And, as noted earlier, the Israel Equal Employment Opportunities Commission was only established in 2008 (Mundlak 2009; Steiner 2013).

Management of the Self. The second most popular response to incidents among Arab Palestinians is the management of self, mentioned by about 20 percent of respondents. The most common form it takes is to control anger for fear of consequences. This is illustrated by a respondent who describes a situation that occurred on a university shuttle, as he was returning to his dorm with a group of Jewish students:

> Somebody looked around to see that there were no Arabs and began to curse the leftists, saying that they are worse than Arabs, and that they should be beaten up before the Arabs, and things like that. And I really felt like answering him, [yet] I thought if I did, it would lead to a confrontation that I was not interested in. . . . I didn't respond also because he was belligerent and spoke crudely.

Managing the self is imperative for Arab Palestinians at security checkpoints, much as it is for African Americans interacting with the police. Several respondents also described the need to control anger in work settings. After describing an incident at work, a postal worker explains that civil service rules forbid "talking back," which can be cause for firing. However, a significant number of respondents also stated receiving support from their employer when they stood their ground after being insulted or experiencing aggression by clients.

In several notable cases, respondents remained silent and even expressed empathy when realizing that incidents were provoked by anger or resentment over terror attacks. For example, on learning about the example cited above of a coworker who refuses to treat Arabs because "they blow us up," a Palestinian nurse states "I do not want to enter into a confrontation with this nurse. . . . She lost her brother in the war, a soldier. I understand her pain, where it comes from." Such empathic responses, albeit infrequent, stand in sharp contrast to the responses of African Americans. In Israel, both Jews and Arabs can be viewed as victims of the conflict, not merely oppressors. This may mitigate emotional injury.

Humor was also often used as a tool for managing the self. For example, on losing a bet about whether they would win a contract due to discrimination, one respondent laughed at the predictable outcome. Some made cynical jokes, which often blended management of the self and confrontation. Others used humor to maintain a sense of self-respect or to challenge authority (Hochberg 2010; Ziv 2010; Shimony 2013). For example, on being stopped by the police as he was hanging out with his Arab friend in a Jewish neighborhood at night, Abed responded in defiance, "Officer, I didn't know that speaking Arabic was against the law."

Not Responding. Many Arab Palestinian interviewees (25 percent) related incidents of stigmatization or discrimination in which they did not respond at all. Most often this took the form of ignoring the incident (19 percent). Not responding can be understood as the product of emotional detachment developed over the long term in the face of continued exposure to ethnoracial exclusion. This takes two forms: resignation and protecting self-worth.

Several of our respondents commented on how their emotional reactions had mellowed over time as their resignation increased. They did not have to actively manage themselves in response to a particular incident, because not responding came naturally. For example, a teacher in his late twenties expresses resignation by posing a rhetorical question: "If I were to respond, would it change anything?"

For most of the respondents who opted not to respond, we argue that their non-response can be understood as a way to maintain their sense of self-worth, even if they did not necessarily discuss it in those terms: they used silence to gain control over the situation, which transforms their moral experience of the incident (Mizrachi and Herzog 2012). As a postal worker explains, "the best way to stick it to someone is actually to ignore them. That's why I ignore it." A university student elaborated further on this strategy: "if somebody treats you badly and you simply ignore him, you are in fact insulting him even worse." (Such responses were coded under the Ignore/ Forgive category in Table A2.6 in Appendix 2). Still others affirm universalism (i.e., that all human beings are the same) as a way to preserve their sense of self-worth and to depoliticize daily interactions with Jews (see also Lamont, Morning, and Mooney 2002). They use universalism to explain their silence and bolster their equanimity while simultaneously using it to position themselves as superior to their stigmatizers. This is evident in the words of a working-class man as he explained why he responds to exclusion with silence: "I don't look at a person as if he is a Jew, Muslim, Christian, or Druze. I look at a person as a human being. We all were born together, we are cousins, there is no difference between us; this is what I was taught at home." Another interviewee describes this universalistic perspective in terms of his own personal transformation as he has seen "a big change in my approach. There is more tolerance, and I began to adopt the principle of 'we are all the same.'" Muhad, a middle-class man, proposes another type of universalism, one that is opposed to sectarian views and that is grounded in free market logic. Referring to some particularly close-minded Jewish coworkers, he says:

> Those people are really racist. They think that all the land here is theirs, every firm and everything belongs to them. [But], as an Arab, I have learned something—a golden rule. I separate politics, work, place of

residence, family, and everything. I do not connect to the firm where I work as Israeli, a Jew or an Arab. It is a place of work, a place whose interest it is to make a profit, and I help them in this task.

In this example, Muhad draws on a neoliberal repertoire and consciously applies free market principles to depoliticize daily encounters.

Ethiopians and Mizrahim

The most frequent response to exclusion among Arab Palestinians interviewees was confronting (with 38 percent of interviewees mentioning this response in reaction to specific incidents). Ethiopians and Mizrahim also favor this response, but in slighter larger numbers: 55 percent of our Ethiopian interviewees and 49 percent of Mizrahim (see Table A2.6 in Appendix 2). As was the case for Arab Palestinians, the majority of their confrontational responses took the form of speaking out. In their study of how Ethiopian Israelis respond to racism, Walsh and Tuval-Mashiach (2012) also find similar types of active coping responses. They find a relationship between agentic responses on the one hand, and on the other, positive feelings toward the group and strong feelings of belonging and integration.

Arab Palestinians, Ethiopians, and Mizrahim were about equally likely to respond to incidents with management of the self (20 percent, 22 percent, and 21 percent of their responses, respectively). Unlike Arab Palestinians, this management of the self sometimes took the form of acting against stereotypes for Ethiopians and Mizrahim—for example, by doing well at school to debunk stereotypes of intellectual inferiority, or by being the most assiduous employee to counter stereotypes of laziness or incompetence, and thus to demonstrate that they should not be underestimated. Ethiopian respondents also talked about managing their emotional reactions to the personal pain and humiliation they experienced by remaining silent.

An example of this type of management of the self comes from a taxi driver explaining how he reacts to someone hurling racist insults at him. He tells himself: "First of all, don't get angry. Don't put your head down. Someone curses you, you don't have to throw it back at him, you're not going to die from it. One way to deal with racism is simply to move forward. It's over." Along similar lines, a police officer states: "I am proud of [my skin color], but you get burned, okay? Later, nothing happened. You pick yourself back up and start again from the beginning. . . . If somebody hurts me, I need to be strong, not get hurt, and to get up and do what I need to do."

In addition, some Ethiopians point out that their ability to rise above the situation and not respond is a function of age and experience. As one of them puts it, "As you get older, you read a lot, you absorb a lot of knowledge;

you form your identity, you know who you are, what you are, you do not have to prove to others who you are." Nevertheless, only rarely did Ethiopians choose non-response as an option. In contrast, 21 percent of the Mizrahi mentioned not responding. This may be because, as was sometimes the case with Black Brazilians, they were unsure why they were being treated unfairly, or because the incidents they experienced were less severe. Often these took the form of offhand remarks made by people they knew, such as friends or in-laws, in which case strong confrontation might cause a rift in relationships.

IDEAL RESPONSES

We now turn to respondents' views about ideal responses to stigmatization and discrimination. We first examine their answers to the questions of how they think their group can improve its situation and what they think is the best way to deal with racism. Then we look at how they talk to their children about these issues and finally discuss their opinions about affirmative action. Their responses shed further light on the avenues for full incorporation into Israeli society available to each group. They also reveal the impact of their respective positions vis-à-vis the Jewish polity and the cultural repertoires available to each when forming these strategies and imagining their ideal reactions.

Improving Their Group Situation

ARAB PALESTINIANS

Considering the situation of Arab Palestinians, one could expect them to invest in collective action as an ideal a tool for the achievement of the political goals of this group, but this was not the case. This is striking in light of their strong groupness and the fact that nearly all Arab Palestinians vote for Arab parties as their parliamentary (Knesset) representatives. However, the agenda of Arab Palestinian political parties is primarily centered on the Israeli-Palestinian conflict. Surveys find that Arab Palestinians are dissatisfied with their political representatives, who, in their view, fail to address their constituency's daily problems (Smooha 2013: 105–110). In short, Arab Palestinians do not feel they can turn to electoral politics to improve their situation. Our interviewees also did not discuss work being done to improve Arab Palestinians' position by a proliferation of Arab Israeli NGOs (Jamal 2008). On the rare occasions they did mention political mobilization as a tool for improving their situation, it was almost always in vague terms. As one interviewee related:

The state continues to view Arabs as second- or third-class citizens, sometimes as a demographic threat, sometimes as a fifth column. . . . Even though the Arabs today are more aware of the state's discrimination against them, they've become more and more indifferent to it. . . . They are not organized. They don't struggle in an organized way for their rights.

This reaction is not surprising, in view of Arab Palestinian's estrangement from the polity. Such resignation is often coupled with the belief that racism is inexorably linked to the deep-seated animosity at the root of the Israeli-Palestinian conflict. As one woman reflected when trying to explain why she ignored an unpleasant experience: "It [racism] is all grounded [in the conflict]. I wish there were peace negotiations and all that. How many times have we tried to make peace? But the fact is, there's no chance."

In place of collective action, our interviewees emphasize Arab Palestinian solidarity as a tool for improving their collective situation. Like African Americans, Black Brazilians, and the two other Israeli groups, Arab Israelis frequently mention education as a tool for achieving mobility, but they are also fully aware of the differences in opportunity available to them and to Jewish groups in their country. But even when referring to the importance of education, they are less concerned with individual mobility than with collective improvement. As a middle-aged interviewee put it, "to improve the situation, Arabs need to unite, to 'have one hand.' Education is the most important: study and go to university." In the words of Saïd, a young casual laborer, what is needed is "education and raising awareness about everything. These are the things that will pull us out of the mud. Like I said, knowledge is power, so if we have knowledge and awareness, that will serve us as a means of improving our position in relation to others."

Similarly, Omar, a medical student who is concerned with the unequal opportunities available to Arab Palestinians, urges his co-ethnics to get serious and:

> Turn to academic education, that's the most important. To stop the internal rivalries [among Arab Palestinians], in our villages, in our families. To stop focusing on dull and unimportant customs. Young people should stop driving around with the stereo on full blast, making skid marks on the streets, paying 2,000 shekels on car accessories.

Omar's belief in education and work resonates with the findings of a survey conducted by the Israel Democracy Institute (Hermann et al. 2014). Asked to choose between two statements: "If you work hard, you'll succeed in the long run" and "Hard work does not guarantee financial success," nearly half of the Arab Palestinian surveyed (45.2 percent) supported the first statement. However, in contrast to African Americans, who put more emphasis on individual achievement, for Omar and others, individual educational success is connected to collective improvement.

Indeed, some respondents discuss the importance of education as a means to empower Arab Palestinians to demand their rights. The connection between education and social change is described by an upper-middle-class businessman: "I always say [to my parents and grandparents] that your generation is the generation that turned Palestine into a paradise. You are giving up. You lost it and we will return it, through a different education for our children, we will return Palestine."

This man is referring to a generational shift from the flourishing of Arab cultural nationalism in the early twentieth century to its collapse with the establishment of the state of Israel (Abu-Ghazaleh 1972), followed by more recent efforts by some younger, educated Arab Palestinians to create a new place for Palestinians in Israel. This new generation has been labeled the "Stand-Tall Generation" (Rabinowitz and Abu-Baker 2005). Its members, born in Israel in the last quarter of the twentieth century, are the upwardly mobile grandchildren of the generation who experienced the trauma of 1948 as young adults. This new generation spearheaded the October 2000 demonstrations by Arab Palestinian citizens of Israel in solidarity with the Palestinians in the occupied territories, which turned violent. The events were framed by the media as an expression of disloyalty toward the Israeli state, as riots, and as indicative of the radicalization of the Arab Palestinian community (Rubinstein and Institute on American Jewish–Israeli Relations 2003; Rekhess 2007). Others argue that these events indicate the new strategy of the third generation of Arab Palestinians to abandon the accommodative politics adopted by previous generations in favor of active and contentious strategies (Jamal 2007, 2009). This new generation is questioning the situation of Arab Palestinians as unwelcome "guests" in Israel and is seeking to expand the meaning of citizenship from a thin and nominal participation in elections to a fuller and more substantive participation in the polity. This means for them that the state should adopt new conditions that will meet their minority expectations of full and equal citizenship (Jamal 2007). These new political actors have developed a lively civil society of NGOs concerned with a wide range of issues, including urban planning, health services, legal rights, racism, education, and gender inequality. Notwithstanding, our interviews attest to a divorce between these developments and the outlook and experiences of average Arab Palestinians.

Smooha's (2013) survey suggests that although Arab Palestinians citizens of Israel often criticize the Israeli state, they ultimately accept it and are committed to coexisting with Jews—though in an Israel circumscribed by its pre-1967 borders. At the same time, their demands are limited to strengthening their group identity and position through increased access to sociocultural, political, and educational resources and do not include a desire to assimilate into the Jewish population (Smooha 2013: 113–116). Similarly, our Arab Palestinian interviewees made almost no reference to political activity or organized protest as a tool for gaining recognition. One cannot preclude that interviewees felt vulnerable when asked to discuss their political activities and thus were not forthcoming with their views. However, this is not likely, given that they were mostly interviewed by Arab Palestinians.

ETHIOPIANS AND MIZRAHIM

At first glance, all respondents appear to view education as an important means for advancement and change. But a closer examination reveals important differences among our three groups in their views about education. Whereas Arab Palestinians mainly viewed education as a tool for increasing group solidarity and improving their group's status vis-à-vis Jews, Ethiopians tended to view education as a tool for assimilation and integration, which would promote equality by erasing group differences. Unlike Arab Palestinians, the latter appear to be mostly concerned with education as a tool for individual mobility and to believe that it is up to individuals to take the initiative for their education, which is not unusual among immigrants, who are typically reluctant to claim group rights (Alexander 2001). For their part, Mizrahim tend to recast ethnic differences in terms of geographic contrast, opposing "center" and "periphery." And although some Mizrahim noted the need for more state investment in peripheral areas, including in education, they nevertheless stressed the role of individual initiative and hard work to enhance social and economic mobility.

Ethiopian Jews. For Ethiopians, integration into Israeli society through education is mainly about self-improvement. In the words of Erez, an Ethiopian sales clerk:

> When we arrive in Israel, what do we need to ask for? To learn more in order to be part of Israeli society, to serve Israeli society, to join every part of Israeli society just like everyone else. . . . It is best is to study, study, study, all the time study. . . . It will take time to reduce racism. First of all [Israeli society] will recognize us as educated human beings. After that it [the end of racism against Ethiopians] will come.

This view on education also appears in comments on government projects initiated to improve the educational attainment of Ethiopians as a group. As one interviewee pointed out: "We need something more personalized. Because nothing [the government] did ever worked. . . . Each of us has his or her own needs. If someone wants help with his studies you need to go with him step by step, from high school to the university."

This theme of personal responsibility was echoed by many Ethiopian respondents, when asked about the best tools to improve their group's situation. As Shlomo, a taxi driver, stated: "To initiate on your own. Not be afraid. Not be afraid to fail."

This championing of personal initiative often went hand in hand with a critical stance toward the perceived passivity of other Ethiopians. A college-educated Ethiopian woman answered the question about what tools are needed to improve her group's situation in these terms: "Personal, individual tools, that's important . . . believing in yourself and ambition. You can't sit on your butt all day and say, 'I don't have anything, they screwed me' and complain when you basically don't do anything."

But there are also areas of similarity across groups. For instance, when asked about the best way to deal with racism, like Arab Palestinians, Ethiopians favored either confrontation or ignoring the situation. Also, like Arabs, many stressed the importance of educating others about their culture. Nevertheless, Ethiopians were more likely to say that they view display of competence as the best response (17.5 percent compared to 4 percent for Arab Palestinians). Moreover, they responded to the question in personal terms, alluding to the need to manage and control their emotions. These varying responses are enabled by the different positions of Ethiopians and Arab Palestinians in the Israeli polity. Although they certainly face stigma and discrimination, Ethiopians have hope for an eventual integration and assimilation into Israeli society. Acquiring an education and demonstrating competence are means to this end and to reduce experiences of racism. Because they view themselves as members of the "imagined community" of the Jewish state, Ethiopians often express surprise when facing racism, which some appear to perceive as an act of betrayal (as if they were expecting loyalty from Israel). In contrast, the Arab Palestinians have little hope for improvement and generally understand exclusion as stemming from an interminable political conflict and exacerbated by segregation and ignorance.

Thus, the ideal responses that Ethiopians offer to ethnoracial exclusion are rooted in their assumptions about their place in the polity and their potential for integration, as clearly articulated in their views about competence, education, and silence. This is illustrated by an Ethiopian saleswoman and child counselor who remembers what a youth counselor told her about joining a planned protest: he advised her against it: "'Okay, you will demonstrate. What will come of it? After a while, new things will come up.' [Instead] he said, 'Come on, invest in yourself, study. Do a lot of things to be proud of yourself.'" She notes that "a lot of [Ethiopians] are going to university, and we are trying to get integrated and improve ourselves. . . . We also see [Ethiopian] Knesset [Israeli Parliament] members now that we are slowly, slowly getting in and integrating. . . . It's a good start." Another respondent expressed an oft-repeated sentiment about the importance of working hard to succeed and to downplay racism:

> Don't take it to heart. I think we need to ignore it, to keep moving forward and succeed. When you get to a high rank or a high position, you

don't feel like you're inferior. I think this is the best way to deal with it ... once you move ahead and study and succeed and develop ... they will not be racist to you.

Hence, Ethiopians frame education as an important avenue for individual and, thereby, group assimilation. Indeed, in their view the improvement of their individual positions should lead to more equal participation and full integration of their group into Israeli society.

Ethiopians mentioned the importance of solidarity as an ideal response more often than Arab Palestinians did (38 percent and 20 percent, respectively). Their comments reveal that they value solidarity because it provides the mutual support that facilitates individual achievement, as a female Ethiopian lawyer, explains: "The fact that we have [mutual] sympathy helps on a daily basis. It can encourage us to move forward despite the obstacles and our [otherness]. And if we maintain this part of our culture, then we can make progress."

Her statement hints at another link between group solidarity and assimilation: individual Ethiopians should gain strength and motivation through knowledge of and pride in their heritage. She is essentially describing a strategy that balances assimilation with recognition. Such a sentiment was also expressed by Shlomo, the taxi driver we heard from earlier:

We are the [Ethiopian] community. Each one should return to his roots to learn where he came from, what he was, what he was not, and move forward with what he has, with his heritage.... To study everything, to become educated. But not to forget your home, because that is what will sustain us at the end of the day.

Again, we do not interpret the emphasis that Ethiopians put on solidarity as a manifestation of identity politics, as they rarely claim group rights and emphasize individual strategies of mobility and destigmatization through education.

Mizrahi Jews. In contrast to Ethiopians, Mizrahi interviewees made almost no mention of solidarity as a tool for improving their group's situation, with only 6 percent of the interviewees ever mentioning the concept (compared to 20 percent for Arabs and 38 percent for Ethiopians). This difference speaks to the low sense of groupness found among most of our Mizrahi interviewees. In general, Mizrahim have internalized the national political ethos as well as meritocratic values. In the context of the Zionist melting pot ideology that has prevailed in Israel for decades, making claims based on ethnic political identity is seen as illegitimate for the Jewish population (Herzog 1984, 1985, 1995; Peled 1998). In the specific case of Mizrahim, Regev (2000) has shown how their demands for cultural recognition and inclusion are framed as part of the Jewish melting pot repertoire and presume to share in the goal of constructing one unique and unified Israeli culture. Since the mid-1990s, some new social movements do engage in identity politics: the Mizrahi Democratic Rainbow (a leftist liberal Mizrahi social movement), Achoti ("My Sister," a Mizrahi feminist movement), and Ars Poetica (a group of third-generation intellectual Mizrahi poets, writers, and authors challenging Ashkenazi hegemony over high culture). However, these and similar social movements attract only a small minority of highly educated Mizrahim. Thus, the mobilization of highly educated Mizrahi liberals based on group identity remains a relatively marginal phenomenon (Mizrachi 2014).

Mizrahim are politically organized mainly within ultra-Orthodox circles, where social disadvantage, religiosity, and political claims for recognition intersect (Herzog 1990b; Peled 1998). This constellation is indicative of the extent to which Mizrahi's strong sense of groupness is religiously grounded and thus compatible with the glue that cements the Israeli polity, Judaism. They express groupness by asserting their commonality with Ashkenazim and by promoting their full integration into the Jewish nation-state as equal and worthy members.

Whereas the symbolic exclusion from the polity reinforces a strong sense of groupness among Arab Palestinians, ordinary Mizrahim do not view themselves as an oppressed minority group—many do not even perceive themselves as part of a group (Lamont and Mizrachi 2012). Few have faced blatant ethnoracial exclusion, and they most strongly identify themselves as Israelis and members of the polity. Indeed, our interview question about how to improve the collective status of their group was often puzzling to them, given their low sense of groupness, and was thus frequently recast by respondents as pertaining to redistribution (the importance of giving more resources to the most disadvantaged neighborhoods), individual responsibility (help those who help themselves), or class (low income populations need more support).

A good example comes from Rachel, a woman who rejected the premise of the question by asking: "Does it have to be the group? Because I would invest in education generally." She went on to reframe the question in geographic terms: "Actually, [we could improve] by investing in developing towns and marginalized areas, distressed neighborhoods. It's very important that the next generation kid doesn't grow up like [his] father, does not degenerate into crime . . . that he [has access to] better tools than his parents had."

As this quote suggests, the low socioeconomic status of Mizrahim is reframed as spatial disparities (rich versus low-income neighborhoods or towns). Such geographic terms as "center" and "periphery" serve as euphemisms to describe the high incidence of social disadvantage among Mizrahim and to downplay ethnicity as the organizing principle of disadvantage.

In line with their strong identification with the state, Mizrahi framing of disadvantage in geographic terms often goes hand in hand with the promotion of state policies to alleviate poverty and redistribute resources, with no mention of the potential benefits to the Mizrahim per se. As one respondent puts it, the state should "change the flow of resources in society ... more schools, education, employment. Listen, you go to areas in the south and you have no jobs, there's nothing."

Mizrahi interviewees also consistently answered our question concerning group tools to improve the group's situation by pointing to the need for individuals to take the initiative to improve their situation. In this, they resemble African Americans and Ethiopian Jews. This is illustrated by a teacher who declares that "progress needs to begin with education, because I often say that there is a culture of poverty. Many times, when you give too much, it creates a mindset of dependency: 'I deserve benefits.' And so they don't develop their own strengths and abilities and achieve things on their own."

A manager in an advertising company expresses a similar sentiment: "I got where I am because I'm a hard worker.... I believed in myself. I believed that I wanted to leave my position and get to another one." This emphasis on individual achievement and responsibility accords with neoliberal discourse and is in line with studies of the Israeli school system (Mizrachi, Goodman, and Feniger 2009), which find that even Mizrahi students, who are typically tracked into low-achievement classes, perceive the structure of educational opportunity through a neoliberal cultural repertoire: it is a fair contest where the individual student's motivation and, to a lesser extent, intelligence, are the prime determinants of success (independent of ethnicity, which provides unequal access to resources). This belief appears to hold despite the unmistakable and widely documented persistence of ethnic inequality in educational resources (Cohen, Haberfeld, and Kristal 2007).

Mizrahi responses to the question about the best way to deal with racism stand in stark contrast to the responses of Arab Palestinians and Ethiopians. Whereas Palestinians and Ethiopians immediately understood the question to refer to racism against *them*, many of the Mizrahi interviewees understood the question in abstract terms. For example, when first asked this question, Galit, a 32-year-old Mizrahi professional with a law degree, generalizes the problem to all groups: "Yeah there's a lot of racism, I think. Toward Russians, Ethiopians, Mizrahim, Ashkenazim, you know, though Ashkenazim the least." This statement demonstrates a higher degree of awareness of discrimination than most of our Mizrahi respondents displayed, but this does not translate in her embracing identity politics by, for example, emphasizing her distinctive identity as Mizrahi by joining a pro-Mizrahi advocacy movement. Indeed, we learn later that she gives her time to universalist causes, when she states "Now I am really in a period when I am more about contributing to society. I am already contributing to the Noga Legal Center for Victims of Crime.[37] ... I volunteer not for things that are specifically related to Mizrahim but rather for more general things."

That many Mizrahi respondents have a low sense of groupness and had not experienced ethnoracial exclusion directly contributes to their interpretation of our question as not pertaining to their ethnic group. And some qualified further by pointing to declining discrimination, as illustrated by one individual who noted "I don't feel it [racism] as much as 20 to 30 years ago; also my kids feel it less." For the same reason, others' answers were couched in a hypothetical "what if." At the same time, the narrative of the progressive integration of Mizrahim may enable them to feel more empowered to fight back, as when one respondent, whose family had immigrated from Iraq, declared with much conviction: "If somebody tells me I'm a stinking Iraqi, I would tell them they're stupid."

Lessons for Children

Our questions about what is learned from parents and taught to children about ethnoracial exclusion also inform our understanding of ideal responses. Interestingly, many Arab Palestinians say they were not explicitly taught by their parents about the political situation in Israel. However, they wish their children to be more informed. They also want to instill in their children the importance of treating everyone with respect and equality.

Ethiopians anticipated that their children would be targets of racism and prepared their kids to cope with this by fostering self-esteem. As with the question about the best way to fight racism, Mizrahim did not think about themselves or their children as targets of racism. They answered the question, "What do you teach your children about racism?" by emphasizing the importance of teaching their children not to be racist.

ARAB PALESTINIANS

The Israel-Palestinian conflict and the Arab Palestinian experience of discrimination are deeply intertwined, including through what is taught at school. Unlike the curricula on race relations taught in the United States and Brazil, the history of Arab Palestinians—including the 1948 war of independence—taught in both Jewish and Arab schools reflects the Jewish narrative exclusively (Makkawi 2002).[38] This narrative is in profound tension with the oral history concerning Arab-Jewish relations that Arab Palestinian children learn through community and kinship networks. This oral history offers alternative lenses through which to make sense of family history and how it has been affected by political events. It is also a means for transmitting personal and collective memories, as they are intertwined with national identity (Sa'di 2002; Nusair 2010).

The one-sided official history curriculum can be explained not only by the official ideology of the Zionist state, but also by the fact that until the 1990s,

Arab Palestinian scholarship was almost completely silent concerning the *Nakba* "catastrophe." Moreover, little was written about the harsh conditions and institutional discrimination experienced by this group (Hanafi 2009). The absence of scholarship and the inability of the "1948 generation"[39] to openly discuss their experiences with their children and grandchildren is the result of the intersection of at least two forces: the trauma and shame of losing the war, on the one hand, and the Israeli control and censorship imposed on the Arab Palestinians who were under military regime until late 1966, on the other (Hanafi 2009; Rabinowitz and Abu-Baker 2002). Our interviewees told of the reluctance of their parents and grandparents to discuss discrimination, both past and present. Politics in particular was excised from any of their accounts.

Hennie, a cashier in a supermarket, referred indirectly to her parents' silence about the traumatic events that have marked their lives, and to her decision to follow a different path when she said: "I don't want to be like my parents." She is teaching her children about Arab Palestinian history and inequality:

My parents did not teach me anything about the Jews, neither good nor bad. After I married and went to work and met Jews, I began forming my opinions about them, and I concluded how to behave based on experience. I teach my children that this is the people the state belongs to, to treat them with respect as long as they respect us. When they do not respect us, we need to know how to protect ourselves and how to preserve our honor. I will find a way to explain that they conquered us and took our land and houses. I'll try to teach them the truth, the whole picture, and when they grow up, they will already have figured out on their own how to behave. But it is important that they know that we live in this country and we should be friends with them [the Jews] and work with them.

Against a background of generalized silence, it is not surprising that most of our Palestinian respondents ignored our question about what they learned from their parents about racism. When they addressed it, most underscored how they teach their children what they were taught by their parents. A middle-class woman hinted to past and present situations by describing how her father learned to be distrustful due to past experiences:

My father was always telling us to be careful and not too naive. Pay attention. Be good with everyone, but do not be too close to anyone.... Now I have children and tell them the same thing. If someone wrongs them, avoid them. But without violence, without cursing ... without fighting. Just do not go back there, it's very simple.

The responses of Arab Palestinians' concerning lessons about exclusion fell into four categories, which range from more conciliatory, to pragmatic, to more oppositional. The first can be described as a discourse that invokes universalist maxims, such as "we are all human." For instance, a homemaker said that she instructs her children "not to be racist and not to judge others on the basis of religion or race, [I] raise them with the values of love and respect for others and [tell them] to treat others like themselves." In a similar vein, a vice-principal from a large Arab Palestinian town reflects on passing his values to his children:

> My mother used to always say that we are all human beings, no matter if Arab or Jewish, we are all human, brothers and sons of Enosh.... We never talked about discrimination or racism, we didn't have it in our lexicon at all. And as a role model and father to a family, I teach my girls and instruct them to deal with all situations and treat all people with respect and equality.

The second category includes more pragmatic responses having to do with management of the self as a member of a minority group. It includes, for example, the importance of maintaining good relations with Jews, who are the more powerful group in society. This type of response often includes advice such as "stay away from racism," "don't hate anyone," and "occupy yourself with good things only," which are framed as elements of a survival strategy.

Such pragmatic responses also include treating others with honor or respect, which can be described as a means to an end. Speaking of her child-rearing strategy, one interviewee says:

> Since [my children] were little I taught them how to respect themselves and whoever is in front of them, and this is how to earn the respect of others. I taught them to speak softly, quietly, to express what they want without getting upset, without anger, quietly and wisely. And everything they want they get in a pleasant and relaxing manner, and this is how they will get respect from others.

Here, self-management is viewed as essential for maintaining self-worth and well-being and for managing the situation. By restraining temper, the stigmatized person can remain rational, secure self-worth, and further other goals. The reinforced objective of respecting others is in line with a universalist approach that emphasizes living with differences. The latter was not often central in the responses described in this chapter (in contrast to the responses of African Americans, which are more centered on the obligation of living with diversity; Berrey 2015).

The third category emphasizes pride in belonging, and the need to confront and to be an active agent for social change. Rebecca, a local political female activist who is fighting against the expropriation of Arab Palestinian families in an old Jaffa neighborhood, teaches her children to follow in her footsteps:

> I have the ability to teach Jamila and Elias, 10 and 6 years old ... the basics. I teach them they are Arabs and their language is Arabic, and our presence here is essential, our staying here in Jaffa.... You know, today when the police came to evacuate a house [against which I was protesting], someone said to me: "What are you doing here? Go take care of your children." I sometimes take my kids to these protest activities, [so that they can] see what happens; it is very important.

Abed, a middle-class man, talked about how he wants his sons to respond to stigma and discrimination:

> I want them to talk, to defend themselves. Withdrawal is not a solution. You need to speak up and bring knowledge and change people's minds. We need to show who we are, what our society is, what our religion means—to explain, not be silent.

The fourth category involves treating children as free agents, trusting their judgment, and respecting their choices for how to react to racism. Thus, a middle-class man explains:

> I do not prepare my children in advance [concerning] how to react in case of discrimination because I cannot know how I would react. [If this occurs], they are responsible enough to use good judgment and respond to the situation. In a roundabout way I give them things to read and [get them] to draw conclusions from.

He gives the example of a book that describes continuity in the Islamic tradition as a source of information for stigma management. He uses such reading about historical events to help his children develop a positive identity and emotional and moral strength.

ETHIOPIANS AND MIZRAHIM

Ethiopians emphasize self-respect when discussing teaching their children about racism. This is important, given the high likelihood that they will experience stigmatization. One Ethiopian respondent reflects on the importance of teaching self-respect:

> First of all, I learned at home that I should respect myself, love myself, not to lie to myself, that I should be proud of what I am, that I can be super successful at everything I want. . . . That gives you confidence. And that's something I will pass on to my kids.

In contrast, again Mizrahim often did not interpret the question as refer-ring to racism directed at them, instead viewing it as a question about how they teach their children to not be racist, as illustrated by this man's state-ment: "I teach [my son] that there are good people and bad people.... And it's not because they are Arab that they are bad or good. There are good Arabs, and most people just want to live.... I don't agree with generaliza-tions. Every person is an individual. I try to teach him not to generalize with such things."

That most of our Mizrahi interviewees did not interpret this question as pertaining to exclusion against Mizrahim attests to their weak groupness and strong sense of belonging. From their point of view, racism is directed at outsiders. This is illustrated by one of our interviewees who downplays group identity in favor of Israeli identity. She rejects the notion that her children experienced exclusion and should be taught anything about it: "My kids didn't grow up with that, don't even know what it is. My kids are Israeli in every sense."

Is Affirmative Action an Option?

Contrary to the situation in Brazil and the United States, one does not find a wide range of assumptions concerning the need to provide affirmation action for disadvantaged groups in Israel. Instead, because the Israeli State is built on immigration, it prioritized policies of preferential treatment in housing and education for new immigrants as part of a broader set of inte-gration policies described in Section 4.1. Other programs of assistance were created to help lower-class Jews who immigrated from Arab countries (Miz-rahim). However, these were perceived as addressing not discrimination but failure of absorption (Dagan-Buzaglo 2008).

The legal term used for "affirmative action" in Hebrew translates as "re-storative preference," but the colloquial and widely used term for it trans-lates roughly as "restorative discrimination" or "reparative discrimination." Thus, compared to "affirmative action," the Israeli term has a more negative connotation, as it directly implies unfair and undeserved preference at the expense of others. This form of "reparative discrimination" was first intro-duced in 1993, when the Israeli Knesset passed an amendment to the Gov-ernment Companies' Act (passed in 1975) to secure women's representation on corporate boards of directors (Izraeli 2000). Only in the mid-2000s did the government (not the legislature) adopt a form of affirmative action poli-cies for Arab Palestinians and Ethiopians, and these mostly apply to public sector personnel (these policies also included ultra-Orthodox Jews seeking to enter the labor market). These policies are not broadly applied or widely known. When we asked our respondents about their opinions on affirma-tive action, several of them had not heard the term, and the interviewer had to explain it. And when they understood it, most were critical of it.

This is one of the strongest contrasts between all Israeli interviewees on the one hand, and American and Brazilian interviewees on the other. This non-salience of affirmation action in Israel is indicative of the relative absence of a culture of universalism and diversity in the country.

ARAB PALESTINIANS

Among our Arab Palestinians interviewees, 24 percent supported affirmative action. Most justified their position by pointing to the need for justice and reparation for past oppression, as expressed by one of our interviewees:

> I'm for [it], if it compensates the Arabs and gives them a chance to advance, it's good. Is anyone opposed to that? Many people have studied and have invested in diplomas [but] have no place to work. Why not let them prove themselves? Compensation for years of oppression. At least that.

A few respondents supported in principle the need for affirmative action but commented that it is insufficient or unlikely to remedy the situation. A few were supportive of it as a means to increase contact between groups and improve mutual understanding:

> It's preferable to have more groups [in the workplace or school]. Because when I know your customs, it creates more love between people. Like, there will be no love between people if I make a school for me and you make a school for you and he makes a school for him, then we move away from each other and are afraid of each other.

Palestinian criticisms of affirmative action were somewhat varied, with many respondents (28 percent) raising several objections, portraying it as unfair or as reverse discrimination. One expressed concern for anticipated consequences: "If you start 'restorative discrimination,' pretty soon we'll need to fix that!"—while another feared that it would encourage Arabs to be less ambitious. Yet others described it as stigmatizing, either because it presumes incompetence or because it is inspired by pity: "Choose me for my abilities, not because you feel sorry for me." In general, these responses imply more concern that affirmative action is an affront to honor than a stigma working against inclusion (the concern more frequently expressed in the United States).

Finally, some viewed affirmative action as counterproductive, because it cannot solve the fundamental problem. As one person states, "[Affirmative action] is very good, but here it's a trap. The state of Israel didn't create it; it just uses it as cover: 'Look here, there are Arabs in the Knesset, etc.' We know that the state is racist, this is only pretense." Others urge: "Deal with the cause and don't bother with the symptoms!" The most forceful example of this is someone who compared affirmative action to reparation: "There is no such thing as 'restorative discrimination.' . . . The only thing that counts as 'restorative discrimination' are full reparations." Arab Palestinian responses to affirmative action are tainted by their deep sense of injustice and exclusion.

ETHIOPIANS AND MIZRAHIM

For their part, Ethiopians express mixed support for affirmative action as the only possible means of gaining equality in the face of persistent discrimination. Moreover, not being familiar with the term or the policy, some seemed to conflate affirmative action with laws against discrimination. On the whole, 15 percent of Ethiopians and 13 percent of Mizrahim expressed support for affirmative action, while 40 percent of Ethiopians and nearly 30 percent of Mizrahim criticized it. Also instructive were the critiques of affirmative action, which were stronger and more frequent than those of African Americans and Black Brazilians. For instance, some remarked that it was not fair and would not solve the problem: "The problem is discrimination, that's what we need to get rid of. 'Restorative discrimination' is the same thing" or "just because I'm hurt is no reason to bring me a treat. You shouldn't hurt me in the first place." Such cross-national differences are indicative of the greater prominence of legal tools for addressing the protection of rights in the United States compared to Israel, where even members of the most excluded group do not seem attuned to the possibility of mobilizing the law for fighting exclusion, as evidenced by the very few Israeli interviewees who mentioned seeking legal redress in comparison to the US interviewees.

For Ethiopians, the more significant and more frequently discussed problem with affirmative action was its potential for strengthening group boundaries and the stigma of being a member of this group. This generated skepticism concerning its usefulness: "If you reserve me a spot because I'm Ethiopian, then you're just reminding me that I'm Ethiopian." As a stigma, "it means you cannot succeed on your own." Other interviewees expressed the idea that affirmative action would do more harm than good by stigmatizing Ethiopians, who can become integrated without it: "It's a matter of time, I told you. Give it time. You'll see that everything will be fine."

Among our Mizrahi respondents, very few expressed support for affirmative action, though those who did mostly stressed how it helps Arabs gain more equality. But most objected to affirmative action as antithetical to equality. In these and other cases, as with the question about the best way to deal with racism, only rarely did members of this group spontaneously think of themselves or other Mizrahim as possible beneficiaries of affirmative action. Typically, they objected to affirmative action because they value individual determination and merit as leading to success. In some cases, they also offered themselves as examples of upward mobility and success (despite being Mizrahi). As one stockbroker puts it as he reflects on his trajectory as an employee in the largest law firm in the country:

> When I started working there three years ago, I was sure that there wouldn't be any Mizrahim working in these big companies. Suddenly, I see all these Yemenites, Ethiopians, Russians, and everyone in all kinds of these big companies. So I've got nothing to say to you. I mean, who wants to get there gets there. . . . Restorative discrimination is something you have to make for yourself.

CONCLUSION

The normative responses of our three Israeli groups reveal important differences in their respective sense of groupness, their positioning in the polity, and their narratives of incorporation, which carry over to how they deal with stigmatization and discrimination more generally. Arab Palestinians recognize their location as outside the Israeli polity and see their continued exclusion as rooted in the Israeli-Palestinian conflict. This leads to resignation, as they understand the problem to be political and structural and, hence, outside their control and unlikely to be resolved. They recognize that their interactions with Jews are overdetermined by the chasm between the two groups. In face-to-face interactions, they are thus more likely than the other groups to ignore incidents. They also do not act against stereotypes or seek to work against stereotypes because of an overall sense of futility and because the stereotypes they face are not related to incompetence but rather to mistrust. At the strategic level, they believe change in their social position will only come from a resolution of this conflict, which most view as beyond their influence. They stress the importance of education and hard work, together with accepting "the other," as ideal tools for dealing with exclusion. Their embrace of the meritocratic ideal resembles that of Mizrahim and Ethiopians, although for Arabs education is framed more as a tool for collective improvement rather than assimilation.

For their part, as full members of the polity, Mizrahim and Ethiopians adopt less reactive or defiant strategies to respond to exclusion, and fewer make claims on the basis of their identity that would position them as separate from the majority in the polity. They want to mobilize public resources to improve education, welfare, and opportunities to enable assimilation of their groups. Mizrahim's weak sense of groupness and their tendency to detach themselves from the stigmatized Mizrahi identity is indicated by their tendency to substitute ethnic self-labeling by referring to geographic labels (i.e., "the periphery"). In both groups, nearly all interviewees emphasize individual choices and responsibilities, and they view assimilation as a product of individual agency, which reinforces their sense of worth. But this also makes the experience of stigmatization and discrimination more personal. Especially for Ethiopians, who experience exclusion more frequently and bluntly than do Mizrahim, being the target of mistreatment may have a stronger effect on self-worth than it does for Arab Palestinians, who are more likely to view such acts through the prism of intergroup conflict than through that of personal failure.

We also learned a great deal from the reasons our three groups offered to explain their objection to affirmative action: Arab Palestinians criticize this policy as a counterproductive panacea that provides the appearance of equality or fairness, whereas Ethiopians believe it impedes their incorporation into society by both stigmatizing them as inferior and reinforcing group boundaries. For their part, Mizrahi interviewees did not perceive themselves as the potential beneficiaries of affirmative action; they mostly objected to it in the name of individualist and meritocratic success. In the next section, we turn to a broader discussion of our results and offer some comparisons to the findings in the United States and Brazil.

SECTION 4.5: MAKING SENSE OF THE ISRAELI CASE

In this chapter, we examined the ethnoracial exclusion of three groups in Israel: Arab Palestinians, Ethiopians, and Mizrahim. In this concluding section, we seek to situate our findings in the broader international context of the study. Before turning to these more general conclusions, we consider the ways that members of these three groups experience and cope with stigma and discrimination in light of their groups' varied historical backgrounds, segregation and inequality, groupness, and available cultural repertoires.

Again, Arab Palestinians have served as the key comparison group with African Americans and Black Brazilians. We have argued that unlike the two latter cases, race and skin color do not serve as the primary basis for the exclusion of Arab Palestinians, nor is the legacy of slavery relevant. Instead, the history of the Israeli-Palestinian conflict serves as a basis for ethnoracial exclusion and groupness. The creation of the state of Israel opened a fracture between Arab Palestinians who are citizens of Israel and those who are not. Although Arab Palestinians are citizens, they are symbolically excluded from the Jewish polity and the national "imagined community" (Anderson 1983; Mizrachi, Drori, and Anspach 2007; Guetzkow and Fast 2016).

Furthermore, they are generally distrusted as potential "enemies within." Indeed, distrust is a recurrent theme in many of the incidents of stigmatization our Arab respondents described, where they frequently felt suspected of being terrorists when, for example, they were singled out or subject to heightened scrutiny during routine security checks (e.g., at entrances to shopping centers). But this background does more than help explain why Arab Palestinians reported being profiled with such frequency: across a broad range of contexts, such as in the workplace or public spaces, their experiences of stigmatization were intensified during flare-ups in the Israeli-Palestinian conflict. These incidents speak not just to distrust but also to animosity or anger that Jewish Israelis sometimes directed at them, evident in the harshness and bluntness of many of the incidents described by our interviewees. In our comparison, Arab Palestinians stand out, because they typically did not express doubt about whether an incident had occurred. Their accounts of ethnoracial exclusion typically left little room for alternative interpretations concerning the basis for stigma (nationality versus class, education, gender, or personal behavior, which are salient for our other four groups). No nuanced social reading was needed to decipher the character of the interaction due to the often explicit, direct, or blatant intent of the stigmatizer. In other cases, the incidents themselves may have been more ambiguous, but the range of possible interpretations remained restricted. In these less blatant incidents, stigmatization or discrimination are often unambiguously connected to the individual being an Arab. Alternative interpretations are constrained by the high level of groupness they experience, bolstered by widely available, institutionalized repertoires of group disadvantage, intergroup conflict, and straightforward exclusion.

Accounts of stigmatizing incidents are also shaped by the high level of residential segregation, institutional separation, and homosocial closure separating Arab Palestinian citizens of Israel from Jewish Israelis, all of which work to limit the range of settings in which Arab Palestinians encounter Jewish Israelis. In contexts where they do interact, their interactions are, for the most part, brief and anonymous—as strangers who are unlikely to meet again (with the exception of coworkers and employers). These interactions likewise occur in such contexts as security checkpoints, public transportation, shops, and restaurants. And it is in such settings that Arab Palestinians tend to experience discrimination and assaults on worth, as well as confront the pervasive Jewish ignorance about their lives and that of their co-ethnics. Because Jews and Arab Palestinians attend separate primary and secondary education systems, extended contacts and ongoing relationships develop primarily at the university and in the workplace. This structuring of physical encounters helps explain why Arab Palestinian interviewees, when describing incidents that occurred in the workplace, frequently refer to brief encounters with customers rather than relationships with coworkers or employers, from whom they typically (though not always) describe receiving support and comfort when facing exclusion.

Groupness based on a separate national identity that is reinforced by symbolic exclusion from the polity looms large in explaining Arab Palestinian responses to exclusion that differs from the other groups. Their exclusion stems from a deep political divide that many interviewees viewed as likely to be bridged only with the resolution of the Israeli-Palestinian conflict. They have little hope or expectations of full incorporation, and they tend to interpret their experiences in light of their position as perennial outsiders. As a result, even though they do confront incidents of stigmatization and discrimination, they often do so with little hope of creating social change. They generally do not respond in ways that seek to call attention to the stigmatizing behavior, nor do they attempt to "educate the ignorant" about the reality of the bigotry and discrimination they face. Both types of responses were evident in the case of African Americans and Black Brazilians, who were enabled by inclusion in the polity and the expectation that it should come together with equality and full incorporation. Arab Palestinians, in contrast, tended to be more cynical and resigned, even though they do confront. Being excluded from the polity, their responses, both actual and ideal, are not directed at improving assimilation or incorporation. Their use of humor is indicative of their cynicism. Their framing of incidents through the lens of the Israeli-Palestinian conflict thus enables them to detach their sense of worth from stigmatizing and discriminatory treatment to some extent. This detachment enables not responding to incidents, which can also be interpreted as indicating a kind of resignation or hopelessness, nurtured by their awareness that incorporation is not on the horizon. Their framing of incidents through the lens of the Israeli-Palestinian conflict also enables empathy when responding to incidents, especially toward Jewish stigmatizers whose friends or family members had died in the conflict. Notably, none of the other groups in this study ever suggested that they understood why their stigmatizers acted as they did.

The strong groupness of Arab Palestinians also helps us understand their ideal responses, if they define this ideal as a political resolution of the conflict. Given that they believe the solution is in the hands of international and national state actors, they do not view their own collective political action as an effective means of advancement, favoring instead group solidarity and a pragmatic improvement of their collective situation through education. They teach their children that "we are all human" and also instruct them to ignore racism in a country where they are a dominated minority. Their views on affirmative action similarly reflect this understanding, as they believe policies cannot overcome the massive institutional and symbolic barriers to their full incorporation into the Israeli nation-state.

In contrast, Ethiopian and Mizrahi Jews are awarded full symbolic membership in the Israeli polity based on the Zionist narrative of the "ingathering of the exiles," institutionalized in the Law of Return and the Jewish melting pot cultural repertoire. Ethiopians, who began immigrating to Israel in the 1980s, make up a small minority of the population, only about 2 percent. Their dissonant groupness is shaped by the tension between their self-categorization as Jewish and Israeli and the stigmatization they experience due to their skin color, which distinguishes them starkly from other Jewish groups, as well as marked social and structural boundaries. They contest their exclusion by drawing on the repertoire of the Israeli melting pot and historical narratives about incorporation of successive waves of Jewish immigrants to substantiate their belief that they will inevitably become assimilated as equal members of the Jewish state. The many insults and acts of disrespect members of this group say they encounter left no doubt as to their stigmatization on the basis of skin color. But in other cases, our Ethiopian interviewees felt they were underestimated or stereotyped as poor, uneducated, or culturally backward. They appear to take such incidents very personally, more so than Palestinians do, and they talk quite openly about dealing with the emotional pain of such incidents. This reaction to exclusion, we argue, is enabled by their symbolic incorporation in the polity and their use of the Jewish melting pot repertoire. Because of their self-identification as Jewish Israelis, it could be said that such incidents can be likened to rejection by family or friends.

Like blacks in the United States and Brazil, Ethiopians say that they believe responding to incidents by displaying competence and acting against stereotypes is an appropriate strategy: they want to show that stereotypes about their groups are unjustified and, ultimately, to prove their personal self-worth. This is especially evident in their normative discussion of the best ways to fight racism. Because they expect to eventually be fully incorporated, Ethiopian interviewees believe their collective situation will improve and that racism is best dealt with through assimilation achieved through individual success and education. Concordantly, most reject affirmative action, because it would stigmatize them as different and therefore stymie their assimilation. However, a wave of protests in the spring of 2015 announced the emergence of a newly energized, grass-roots Ethiopian social movement that sought to promote the equality of Ethiopians after two decades of stagnation in the face of continued racism and discrimination. Still, the rhetoric of this protest was by-and-large one of demanding equality based not on recognition of cultural differences but on full assimilation into the Jewish polity. This strategy attests to the consistent gap between intellectuals and social activists, who embrace the politics of difference—the right to equal participation as different and based on demands for recognition as being different—and the majority of Ethiopian Jews who seek full integration into the Jewish Israeli society (on the phenomenon of liberal isomorphism, see Mizrachi and Zawdu 2012; Mizrachi 2014). This participatory strategy (Mizrachi and Zawdu 2012) is enabled by their adoption of the Zionist repertoire of the Jewish melting pot and their self-identification as Jews who should, as such, have full cultural membership and equality in Israel.

Mizrahim display the weakest sense of groupness of all the groups in this study: they generally downplay their ethnicity and lack a highly institutionalized narrative of group disadvantage.[40] They make up a majority of the Jewish population in Israel; marriage between Ashkenazim and Mizrahim is now relatively frequent, with variations across classes and levels of education. Over a third of our Mizrahi respondents could not recall any incidents where they were treated unfairly or discriminated against—by far the highest proportion of any of the groups studied. Yet existing research shows unambiguously that Mizrahim face continued discrimination in the labor market and experience greater inequality of resources than do Ashkenazim. We argue that they do not perceive themselves as experiencing incidents of ethnoracial exclusion on account of their weak sense of groupness. Whereas such incidents are interpreted unambiguously for Arab Palestinians as cases of racism or exclusion, our Mizrahi interviewees were more likely to downplay or not to perceive unfair treatment, or to attribute it to other factors, such as ordinary unfriendliness or rudeness. When interviewees did recognize instances of unfair treatment, they often described these incidents as having occurred not to themselves but to others, while dismissing mistreatment of Mizrahim as a thing of the past.

Ironically, because of high levels of Mizrahi integration and intermarriage, stigmatizers of this group are often friends or extended family, which sometimes made responding more difficult than if the stigmatizers had been strangers. Not being exposed to the most egregious forms of stigmatization that marked the experiences of Palestinians and Ethiopians (such as being called a dirty Arab or a "blackie"), Mizrahim were stunned on the rare occasions they encountered such treatment. The rarity of such incidents undoubtedly contributed to their perception that ethnoracial exclusion against Mizrahim is largely a thing of the past. They did not interpret our questions about the best ways to deal with racism as concerning their group, and they often pointed to the structural disadvantages faced by people living in the "periphery" or talked about the racism directed at other groups. They were more likely to talk to their children about the importance of not being racist themselves rather than about how to cope with the racism directed at them. As for affirmative action, they generally believed that it would not help other groups advance and was, in any case, unnecessary for themselves, because they could succeed on the basis of merit and hard work.

Our comparison of three groups in the same national space highlights the different contexts in which incidents tend to occur—a topic that was less central in Chapters 2 and 3 on the United States and Brazil, respectively. Given the varying levels and degrees of residential segregation, institutional separation, and homosocial closure, members of the three groups in Israel tend to experience exclusion in different contexts. Arab Palestinians do not encounter incidents in primary and secondary education, and their limited social networks mean limited exposure to stigmatization in friendship and family relations. Most incidents occur in the workplace; in brief, anonymous public encounters; or at security checkpoints and other sites salient to the Israel-Palestinian conflict. Ethiopians are more likely to encounter stigmatization from an early age in schools, as well as in the army and the workplace. Yet due to relatively limited close interpersonal networks, they do not experience much stigmatization in such contexts. Mizrahim, in contrast, did experience stigmatization in close personal networks of friends and (extended) family.

Israeli antidiscrimination law also plays a role in limiting the range of responses. Antidiscrimination law is comparatively recent and poorly enforced. There are no laws against discrimination in the private housing market, and affirmative action policies are very limited, unlike in the United States. Furthermore, the category of "Mizrahi" is not even recognized by the courts, meaning that Mizrahi Jews cannot sue for discrimination should they wish to (Bitton 2008, 2011). The legal framework related to antidiscrimination in Israel thus stands in strong contrast to that of the United States and limits the likelihood that Mizrahim and others can employ the law to respond to ethnoracial exclusion.

Overall, the Israeli case enables us to revisit the place of race or skin color in relation to nationality and ethnicity as bases of exclusion. Whereas the research on these issues has been balkanized (Brubaker 2009), here we have reexamined the relationships among these categories in one political space: Israel. The contrast with Arab Palestinians demonstrates what can happen when exclusion and reactive strategies are contingent on national belonging rather than on race or ethnicity. In the Israeli case, when national belonging and race are juxtaposed as bases for groupness, the central importance of race recedes into the background. Many of the findings garnered through the analysis of African Americans, Black Brazilians, and Ethiopians can thus be understood as resting implicitly on a sense of national belonging among blacks in those countries, which holds out the possibility of full incorporation and equality. For example, like African Americans and Black Brazilians, Ethiopians respond to stigmatization by acting against stereotypes, persevering, and working harder to prove their self-worth, which Mizrachi and Herzog (2012) call "participatory destigmatization" in the Israeli case. These groups emphasize the importance of education for individual advancement, and they embrace narratives of racial integration and incorporation. Given the emphasis in contemporary research on race and ethnicity as the primary organizing principles of minority groups' marginalization, the Israeli case broadens our theoretical and empirical horizons by casting new light on the role of national belonging in shaping experiences of and reactions to stigmatization and exclusion. It also shows how experiences and responses are profoundly shaped by background factors, groupness, and available cultural repertoires.

CONCLUSION

ZOOMING OUT

In contemporary societies, questions pertaining to diversity and cultural membership continue to excite passions: the quality of societies is measured not only by questions of distribution (who gets what and how much) but also by questions of recognition, inclusion, and voice. In an age of globalization and greater spatial mobility, groups come in contact at an accelerated pace, and opportunities for competition and the creation of status orders abound. Intergroup conflicts remain a constant of the human experience, even as social scientists attempt to refine our understanding of what drives them and how to attenuate them. This is the conversation in which we want to partake.

In our effort to contribute to the collective inquiry, we did not examine the opinion of leaders, geopolitical dynamics, or the spread of social movements. Instead, we focused on ordinary people who are members of variously stigmatized ethnoracial groups living in differently structured contexts with access to different cultural tools. By trying to illuminate how they make sense of their predicaments and mold their situations, we aimed to enrich our fundamental understandings of how specific groups experience ethnoracial exclusion and respond to it. In doing so, we wanted to nudge the literature to deploy new tools of analysis (especially groupness and cultural repertoires) to explore how these enable and constrain—and thus explain—patterned responses to stigmatization and discrimination. "Exit, voice, and loyalty" (Hirschman 1970) take different forms across contexts, and this is what we aimed to document and account for by combining specific analytical tools.

It has not been an easy task, as the literature concerning questions of race and ethnicity tends to be organized around a few canonical approaches and questions (e.g., is racial inequality more determinant than class inequality in the last instance?). It proves to be quite a challenge to move lines of inquiry beyond institutionalized paths of analysis. To shed new light on familiar phenomena, we took the gamble of juxtaposing an unusual set of cases that represent different configurations of ways of being a group. The devil is in the details, and readers will be the judges of whether our gamble paid off.

How should one make sense of what we have accomplished? The linear progression of the book is such that the reader moves from a general framework about how the five groups coalesce differently to specific cases. In the Introduction and Chapter 1, the framework presented highlights cross-group variations on the bases of similarity within groups (phenotype, nationality, ethnicity) as well as the strengths of groupness. While reading Chapter 2 on the United States, the reader comes to understand how this framework animates our empirical analysis, as well as how we mobilize different explanatory elements to account for the patterns we identify (for instance, the high salience of confrontation and of individualized responses in the United States). Our inductive approach will have paid off if it leads the reader to think differently about the challenges African Americans meet—the literature on race in the United States being so well developed, we are well aware that it is a tall order to say anything new on the topic.

Chapter 3 on Brazil, while largely paralleling the US chapter, plays a very different role in our analysis: here we add a layer of complexity by deploying the same analytical tools and revisiting the same set of questions as those explored in Chapter 2. But we do so in a very different context, one where group boundaries are not as sharp despite a clear sense of racial identification among Black Brazilians and the acknowledgement of white privilege. We argue that this different type of groupness influences how Black Brazilians identify ethnoracial exclusion (largely through the conflation of race and class) and how they respond to it (avoiding aggressive confrontation and more commonly defending colorblind strategies of redistribution). Thus, we offer a demonstration of the usefulness of our analytical framework by shedding new light on a well-developed comparative topic, that of race relations and racial identity in the United States and Brazil.

In Chapter 4 on Israel, we continue to add new levels of complexity to the argument by introducing three groups who are stigmatized differently than African Americans and Black Brazilians. It is in this chapter that the fruitfulness of our comparative framework becomes fully realized, as we mobilize our analytical approach to capture and explain the configurations of groupness, experiences, and responses that are characteristic of Arab Palestinians (our primary concern), but also of Ethiopian and Mizrahi Jews. The juxtaposition of these three cases shows how one national context shapes ethnoracial exclusion differently for each group, depending on how their stigmatized characteristics fit in national history and in the Zionist political project. The inclusion of Ethiopian Jews, a phenotypically black group that has not experienced slavery in Israel, sheds new light on the African American and Black Brazilian cases. It shows how these three groups also fit differently in the national myths of their country as well and in their current landscapes. Thus we detail how and why blackness functions differently as a driver of exclusion across national contexts. Finally, the cases of Arab Palestinians and Mizrahim (respectively the least and one of the most socially integrated groups in Israel) add complexity to our analysis by focusing on how the understandings of their place in the present and future of their society by our three groups enables different responses to stigmatization.

Thus, through our three country chapters, the book evolves in several directions as we add elements of complexity and analysis in transversal (inter-chapter) comparisons as well as within each country case study. Although each chapter could have been developed as a self-standing book, we believe the analytical payoff of the comparison justifies the project.

Readers interested in a summary of the findings of each country chapter can refer to the conclusion section in each of them. In this final chapter, we step back to reflect on some of the big themes developed in this book. We highlight some of the analytical gains made by the study as well as the challenges ahead. We also take stock of unrealized objectives and the potential for future development.

ANALYTICAL GAINS AND FOOD FOR THOUGHT

Comparing Ethnoracial Exclusions as Cultural Phenomena: Macro Lenses and Micro Experiences

The main contribution of our book is to provide an original and systematic analysis of micro-experiences of ethnoracial exclusion and responses to those experiences, and to account for them through a macro comparison of three distinct national contexts, with a particular focus on the meso-level elements within these contexts—cultural repertoires in particular, but also historical and institutional elements.

Traditional cross-national comparisons of ethnoracial relations used to privilege macro-comparisons, focusing on how different racial orders have been constructed (e.g., Freyre 1933; Tannenbaum 1946). Such comparisons of national contexts have largely understood these differences as stable "political cultures" that would not allow change or transformation. Such explanations have been rejected due to both their essentialist characterizations of political cultures and their naturalization of national boundaries—the so-called methodological nationalism.

More recently, some authors have emphasized the historical transnational character of ethnoracial boundaries—see the literature on Afro-diaspora (Gilroy 1993) and paths of convergence (Winant 2001, Daniel 2006). Although these explanations are essential for understanding that ethnoracial categories neither begin nor end within nation-state borders, social scientists tend to underplay how national institutions and cultural dimensions largely shape ethnoracial experiences. Our focus on repertoires allows for a more nuanced explanation that takes into consideration variations in the supply side of cultural tool-kits across contexts without falling into cultural essentialism.

By considering such repertoires as neoliberalism (especially in the United States) or national myths (e.g., racial democracy in Brazil or Zionism in Israel), we capture how these repertoires shape the phenomenology of ethnoracial exclusion (i.e., individual interpretations of incidents). By locating responses in the context of class cultures and considering class differences in responses, we also take into consideration some intra-national variations. Previous studies of individual understandings and responses to stigmatization have been largely dominated by psychological studies that focus on individual resilience and coping. Similarly, studies of ethnoracial mobilization have often treated reactions to stigmatization as universal choices based on resource mobilization (e.g., McAdam 1988) and political opportunity (e.g., Tarrow 1994). More culturally oriented studies influenced by the framing approach (e.g., Snow, Cress, and Anderson 1994) view ethnoracial mobilization as a natural consequence of collective identity—at times describing alternative paths as demonstrating a lack of racial consciousness (e.g., Hanchard 1994). In contrast, our inductive approach puts meaning-making front and center. In our focus on narratives and meaning-making, our approach converges with that of more culturally oriented social movements scholars who have written about stigmatization and the transformation of collective identity (e.g., Polletta 2009; Jasper 2014).

Like Wimmer (2013), we understand responses to stigmatization as ethnoracial boundary making that is shaped by historical processes. However, while Wimmer's analytical approach privileges specific mechanisms (e.g., institutional closure, path-dependency, homophily in social networks), we consider how processes unfold through thick meaning-making and boundary work. By parsing out how individuals identify stigmatization and discrimination across different national contexts, we focus on how actors both actively make sense of the world and rely on institutionalized scripts that are products of, but also reproduce, national patterns.[1] We also insist on the importance of cultural repertoires in enabling and constraining responses.

As discussed in the Brazilian chapter (Chapter 3), previous comparisons of the United States and Brazil have either tended to consider the latter as a country where racism is weaker or where blacks are somehow alienated, suffer from false consciousness, or cannot identify stigmatization (e.g., Hanchard 1994; Marx 1998; Twine 1998). More recently, studies have focused on how Brazil can be more racist than the United States on certain dimensions while being less so on others (as suggested by Telles's 2004 distinction between vertical and horizontal racial inequalities). Nevertheless, the literature has not yet offered a systematic comparison of how such inequalities are experienced. This is one of our signal contributions, as we bridge a phenomenological approach to both class inequality and ethnoracial exclusion with an explanatory effort to account for cross-national differences.

Black Brazilian and African American respondents alike often report experiences of stigmatization and discrimination. Nevertheless, when describing incidents of stigmatization, African Americans tend to be much more certain that stigmatization occurred than are Black Brazilians. For instance, while receiving services in restaurant or while shopping, they are more likely to interpret poor service as a form of racism, but Brazilians may understand such experiences as a way of marking class boundaries. Whereas previous literature has tended to interpret such a cross-national difference as revealing a lack of racial awareness (or a form of racial blindness) in Brazil, we argued that our Black Brazilian respondents usually interpret such incidents as indicative of both racial and class exclusion—even as they believe that class discrimination is more central than race as a driver of their exclusion as a group. We argued that this interpretation is less dependent on the continuing influence of the myth of racial democracy in denying racial stigmatization than on the widespread view that the steep class inequality characteristic of Brazilian society creates strong barriers to access to resources. This interpretation is supported by the finding that Black Brazilian middle-class respondents, who were able to get to upper socioeconomic positions, tend to identify racial stigmatization more often than working-class respondents do.

We argued that cross-national differences in responses are also enabled by available cultural repertoires: while confrontation is highly legitimized in the United States by civil rights narratives and by more frequently enforced antidiscrimination laws, in Brazil respondents are less readily exposed to repertoires of black disadvantage and often state that they run the risk of being viewed as paranoid if they point to the racial character of an incident and confront it as such—except when incidents are blatantly racist. Moreover, beyond the Brazilian national myth of racial democracy, commitment to the ideal of racial mixture serves to discourage social mobilization along racial lines; the latter comes to be largely perceived as a form of reverse racism (*racismo as avessas*). The recent implementation of affirmative action policies that target class more than race exemplifies a tendency to resist race-centered policies and shows the pervasive influence of racially inclusive repertoires. By including poor whites as beneficiaries of such policies alongside poor blacks, current affirmative action policies in Brazil have gained widespread support and are now largely uncontested. Nevertheless, although Brazilian national myths tend to value racial mixture, such ideal commitments are compatible with a collective normative commitment to address racial inequality. This might help explain recent findings that Latin Americans tend to value redistribution and racial equality policies more than North

Americans do (e.g., Telles and Bailey 2013). In short, as we have stressed, Brazilians see class and race as deeply intertwined, because they recognize that a larger proportion of blacks than whites are very poor. The steep inequality prevailing in the country fuels the conflation of race and class as well as the normative preference for policy initiatives that target both dimensions of inequality.

The contrast between Arab Palestinians and African Americans represents an opportunity to consider groups that vary in the degree of institutional and legal exclusion and the subordination they face in their respective countries. We have argued that Arab Palestinians are largely symbolically excluded from the "imagined community" of the Israeli polity and from dominant national institutions—for example, by being prevented from serving in the army and generally being relegated to a separate and unequal educational system. They also experience intense geographical (and often voluntary) residential segregation. Their historical conditions shape their patterns of response to stigmatization and discrimination—the fact that, more than African Americans, many of them choose to remain silent or believe there is little they can do, as they have little hope of improving their situation. Moreover, the extent to which US blacks use legal means as a resource for responding to ethnoracial exclusion comes in full view when compared with how rarely Arab Palestinians in Israel use such tools to respond to incidents. This is hardly surprising, given the latter group's non-identification with the state and the fact that antidiscrimination laws are relatively recent in Israel and are not widely activated.

The case of the Ethiopian Jews allows us to consider the stigma of blackness through a broad framework that highlights the importance of national myths in shaping how phenotype is interpreted, even in a period when transnational diasporic identities of blackness are gaining in salience (Seigel 2005). This case also sheds new light on the canonical comparison between Black Brazilians and African Americans by bringing into the analysis such dimensions as the place of the group in the history of the country, its relative size and status in relation to other stigmatized groups, the extent of the multiracial character of the society, and much more. The fact that Ethiopian Jews embrace Zionism and demand respect based on their Jewishness, instead of multiculturalism or universalist orientations, offers a strong contrast with the other two phenotypically black groups we have studied.

Finally, by comparing Mizrahim and Black Brazilians, we come to realize how relatively weak group boundedness (although weak for different reasons) may generate hesitations in identifying incidents of stigmatization and discrimination, particularly if the groups are also stereotyped as poor, which adds ambiguity to views concerning what motivates an incident—race or class. But the fact that most of our Mizrahi respondents embrace Zionism seems to lead them to underplay ethnic stigmatization (and see it more exclusively as class or place exclusion). In contrast, Black Brazilians challenge the idea of their country as a racial democracy and see a convergence between racial and class stigmatization. This difference may be explained by the stronger awareness of class inequalities as well as the strength of multicultural and transnational repertoires of the black diaspora in Brazil compared to Israel.[2]

Thus, this multivalent cross-national comparison allows a better understanding of the key role cultural repertoires play in the interpretation of stigmatization as well as in choosing strategies of response. Equally central in our explanation is groupness, to which we now turn.

Groupness and Boundaries

Many sociologists have written on forms of groupness, going back to Georg Simmel and Emile Durkheim (with a focus on *gemeinshaft,* incorporation, social capital, collective identity, homophily, and more). Recent and influential contributions to this debate stress how groupness should be understood as a process, not through essentialized and stable notions of identity (in Brubaker 2009 in particular). Our contribution is an important complement to the earlier literature on symbolic boundaries, which, inspired by the work of Barth (1969), Jenkins (1996), and Bourdieu (1979), concentrated on moral boundary work in the construction of group identity (e.g., Lamont 1992, 2000). According to this framework, groups should be conceptualized not as having a unified shared culture but as "in the making."

One of this book's innovations has been to operationalize groupness as a mix of identification and group boundaries. In our conceptualization, these aspects include boundaries drawn toward out-groups, the spatial segregation experienced by the group, perceived patterns of sociability and homophily, meaning associated with the group, and closure or universalistic orientation. This conceptualization of groupness adds a spatial and network dimension to the social psychological dimension of groupness that consists of self-identification and group categorization (Jenkins 1996).

We showed how this operationalization captures the multidimensionality of groupness. While previous approaches tend to think about groupness as either weak or strong (as in Mary Douglas's *Purity and Danger* 1966 or Bailey 2009), in our view, groupness can be simultaneously strong in some dimensions (e.g., identification) but weak in others (e.g., homophily or normative universalism). These differences create different types of groupness across our five cases, which we have described.

We believe this operationalization is a significant contribution that could be extended to explore varying dimensions of groupness for a wide range of social entities (e.g., LGBT, the poor, the obese, African Americans—e.g., Clair, Daniel, and Lamont 2015). Specifically, scholars could examine how the various dimensions of their groupness emerge, are institutionalized, and are sustained historically; their respective strengths; the role of various actors (e.g., social movements, legal and medical experts, ordinary people) in providing the categories through which groupness (stigmatized or not) becomes institutionalized; and so forth. More generally, complementing Brubaker (2009), we consider groupness to be an essential and novel lens through which to view the processes of stigmatization and destigmatization, which have not been fully conceptualized to date.

As discussed in the Introduction, our five cases illustrate how groupness is shaped by the variable dynamics between symbolic boundaries (of self-identification and boundary work toward out-groups) and social boundaries (manifested in patterns of socioeconomic inequality and social segregation). While the case of African Americans can be described as combining both strong symbolic boundaries (i.e., strong self-identification and boundary work toward whites) with strong social boundaries (spatial segregation and socioeconomic deprivation), we find different patterns in the cases of other groups. In contrast, mixed social boundaries (in particular, strong socioeconomic inequalities between in-group and out-group, but weaker spatial segregation) coexist with weak (even if differently defined) symbolic boundaries toward out-groups for Black Brazilians and Mizrahim, and, to a lesser extent, Ethiopians (these three groups do not draw strong boundaries toward out-groups). Corresponding with these various cases are the different patterns of groupness described in Chapters 2–4. For their part, Arab Palestinians experience strong symbolic and social boundaries, as they are strongly identified, generally draw strong boundaries toward dominant out-groups, and are strongly segregated (in the labor market, residential patterns, and access to resources).

These different boundary dynamics, combined with other background factors, also have important consequences for the preferred strategies of responses to stigmatization, which in turn have consequences for how those boundaries are reproduced and transformed. For African Americans, strong groupness has gone hand in hand with confrontation to achieve racial equality—a strategy successfully mobilized by civil rights activists and their many successors. Mizrahim downplay their ethnoracial exclusion, because they largely view themselves as fully incorporated into the Zionist nation. Ethiopians also downplay their racial exclusion (as Jews), but they also confront racism, even if often perceiving it as temporary. Because several factors coalesce to limit the full inclusion of Arab Palestinians in the Jewish polity, this strongly bounded group has little hope of achieving full social, cultural, and political participation in the Jewish state. Experiencing simultaneously strong symbolic and social boundaries, their responses are often limited and strongly tinged with a sense of inevitability and cynicism. They can avoid confrontation, not out of a desire to deflect stereotypes and gain acceptance (as with other groups in Israel) but from a sense that there is nothing they can do to improve the situation. As for Black Brazilians, this group experiences the paradoxical position of having their racial identification gaining in strength as the black movement gains visibility (a reinforcement of symbolic boundaries) even as they experience strong national identification as Brazilians. In their responses to ethnoracial exclusion, this translates into a mix of acknowledging racism while wanting to maintain interracial conviviality.

We saw that groupness is sustained not only by individual orientations but also by meso-level cultural repertoires that may or may not encourage groupness (e.g., in the form of identity salience and closure). For instance, contrary to the US case, where the heightened awareness of white privilege and racism sustain strong self-identification and high groupness among African American, the Black Brazilian and Ethiopian Israeli cases exemplify how perceptions of stigmatization and discrimination may not lead to strong in-group identification. In the Brazilian case, the valorization of mixture as an element of shared national identity leads to porous group boundaries, while in the Ethiopian case, weak group boundaries result in part from a persistent belief in the integration of Ethiopian Jews in the Israeli Jewish melting pot. However, these boundaries are reinforced by racist experiences. Again Mizrahim and Ethiopian Jews downplay symbolic boundary work to achieve greater socioeconomic integration (and thus, weaker socioeconomic boundaries).

Finally, groupness is also sustained by meso-level institutional tools that governments and polities may mobilize to make groups coalesce or to achieve greater equity (Hall and Lamont 2013). This leads us to the topic of recognition, that is, to how institutions contribute to defining various segments of the population as valuable and worthy.

Redistribution and Recognition

What Hannah Arendt has called "the right to have rights" (Arendt 1949; Michelman 1996; Somers 2008), or "membership," is one of the most important goods that political societies distribute (Walzer 1983). Inspired by T. H. Marshall (1950), scholars writing on membership have tended to focus on citizenship, including civil, political, and social rights. In recent decades, the growing awareness of the importance of difference has also brought attention to the related questions of broadening cultural membership and recognition, both of which entail a weakening of external group boundaries as well as a strengthening of boundaries internal to the group. We contribute to the sociological analysis of recognition, thus offering an essential sociological complement to more philosophical writings on this topic (Fraser and Honneth 2003; see also Hall and Lamont 2013).

Cultural membership is given to those who meet the standards of shared definitions of who is worthy in a symbolic community (Ong 1996). Such individuals are viewed as "like us" and worthy of being protected and fought for, which generally depends on shared definitions of moral worth (Alexander 1992; Lamont 2000). Although the term "recognition" has many definitions, for Charles Taylor (1992) it concerns the acknowledgment of equality and worthiness across groups that are considered different. It is the opposite of exclusion. Both Taylor (1992) and Honneth (1995) mention the relational character of recognition: it is a status provided by others in the community.[3] As Nancy Fraser (2000: 114) puts it: "whatever the differences in form, the core of the injustice remains the same: in each case, an institutionalized pattern of cultural value constitutes some social actors as less than full members of society and prevents them from participating as peers."

Literature on these topics is concerned with the boundaries of symbolic communities, largely as they manifest themselves at the macro institutional and political levels. Relevant here are studies of macro processes, such as citizenship and immigration (Joppke 2010), political incorporation (Hochschild, Weaver, and Burch 2012), multiculturalism and diversity (Kymlicka 1995), as well as postnational citizenship (Soysal 1994) and cosmopolitanism proper (Brock and Brighouse 2005). Certainly, gaining legal rights is an important step for membership, but as we know from the US example, this focus fails to address all dimensions of the experiences of stigmatization and discrimination. Similarly, gaining political power is an important step for gaining recognition (Paschel 2016), but it is far from a guarantee of social inclusion. It is against the backdrop of this literature that we have aimed to make a contribution to current understandings of recognition. So while most of the literature focuses on historical and institutional processes, we propose a different, and in some ways, more encompassing understanding that focuses on the daily actions of ordinary people as they experience and respond to ethnoracial exclusion. Of course, when responding to incidents, people do not always aim to get recognition or to create social change. They may be more focused on keeping their jobs or maintaining their reputation as competent professionals. Nevertheless, we claim that micro struggles for gaining respect and recognition add up and are likely to have substantial impact on both destigmatization and how groups coexist.

A particularly striking finding was how often incidents of stigmatization (what we termed "assault on worth") were mentioned across our five groups, compared to mentions of incidents of discrimination (when access to resources was the key issue). The high frequency of assaults on worth reveals that issues of recognition are at least as central, if not more so, to the experience of ethnoracially excluded groups than being deprived of resources, which has been the focus of the bulk of the US literature on racism. At the same time, we acknowledge that discrimination often goes hand in hand with stigmatization; hence the need for examining closely, but also separately, manifestation of these two sociocultural processes.

A second striking finding has to do with degrees of similarities and differences between middle- and working-class members of stigmatized groups, or how class heterogeneity in ethnoracial groups influences responses: among the ethnoracially stigmatized, we compared those who are also stigmatized on the basis of class and those who are not. In general, we found different degrees of similarity in ethnoracial groups and across classes (broadly related to the socioeconomic distance between class groups and strength of repertoires of racial stigmatization). We found that overall, class made less of a difference for experiences of ethnoracial exclusion and responses than we had originally expected.

Third, through our comparative framework, we were able to see how the issues of redistribution and recognition are dealt with very differently across our sites. In the United States, issues of recognition are usually understood as separate from those of redistribution. This is particularly the case with the African American middle class: members of this group are far more concerned with racism than with class inequality, as indicated by the strong boundaries that some draw toward lower-class African Americans and their strong investment in individual upward mobility and the myths of meritocracy and the American Dream. In Brazil, redistribution and recognition appear to be more intertwined, as many respondents seem unable to think about one without thinking of the other (even at the risk of subordinating recognition to redistribution). Indeed, as documented in Chapter 3, our Brazilian interviewees were often unable or unwilling to separate race from class stigmatization and, when probed, often attributed greater importance to socioeconomic inequality over ethnoracial exclusion. This is also manifested in Brazilian affirmative action policies that target the poor, including the large number of whites concentrated in this group. In Israel, issues of recognition and redistribution are largely viewed as futile by Arab Palestinians, given their taken-for-granted exclusion (as national "others") from the economy and the polity. For many Ethiopian Jews and Mizrahim, recognition of being different is antithetical to their espousal of the national Zionist narrative as well as their strong sense of belonging to the Jewish state. In 2015, Ethiopians demonstrated against discrimination and police brutality in the streets of Jerusalem, Haifa, and Tel Aviv, suggesting perhaps an important shift in this regard, particularly in light of transnational influence from the United States concerning protests against police brutality. This is not incompatible with their wishing for the Zionist dream to deliver on its promise of integration. Indeed, the predominant message emerging from these protests was the demand not for recognition as a distinct ethnic group but instead for assimilation and equality based on sameness. All in all, most Israelis, including members of ethnoracial minorities, may be more concerned with security than with either distribution or recognition. Moreover, as compared to their working class counterpart, highly educated middle-class Ethiopian and Mizrahi Jews (primarily activists and academics) embrace the politics of difference within the framework of "liberal isomorphism" (Mizrachi 2014). These findings may speak to the need to further the conversation between political philosophy and cultural sociology.

As a consequence of such cross-national variation in understandings of redistribution and recognition, the solutions to reconciling redistribution and recognition in these societies are also very different. Even if ethnoracial projects are also subject to the simultaneous influence of human rights and other postnational forces transmitted by international organizations and transnational social movements (Soysal 1994; Kymlicka 2007), their national outcomes largely diverge. To assume that institutional solutions (e.g., civil rights laws, affirmative action policies, or other legal instruments) can be transposed from one national context to another, or to envision a multicultural turn across societies as having a homogeneous impact, would require ignoring the distinctive cultural context at work in each case, as manifested in the construction of the polity, available cultural repertoires, and more. In spite of transnational forces, ethnoracial projects are highly context dependent and are unlikely to converge, given the various forces at work. This is implied in the multidimensional explanatory framework presented in the Introduction.

From a sociological perspective, it is worth underscoring the role of cultural repertoires in enabling recognition. Instead of attributing resilience to individual grit, which is often eulogized by psychologists (e.g., Duckworth et al. 2007), we emphasize the extent to which the various societies provide their members with cultural repertoires that may sustain collective resilience (i.e., cultural narratives or frames on which they can base their actions while claiming membership). Such frames are generated, sustained, and diffused by the law, social movements, and medical and other experts, as suggested above (Clair, Daniel, and Lamont 2016). While it is not our objective to provide here an analysis of destigmatization processes, it is important to underscore that cultural repertoires act as crucial resources—as scaffolding, buffers, and protection—favoring the development of social resilience, which is a property of groups, not of individuals (Hall and Lamont 2013). This is exemplified by the ready availability of a repertoire of confrontation for African Americans. Such repertoires are historical products that enable distinctive types of actions directed toward social change, which potentially feeds social resilience. More work needs to be conducted on how such repertoires can enable social change and societal well-being by providing empowering messages, mobilizing social movements, and creating greater social cohesion and mutuality.[4]

Despite our awareness of the importance of normative issues for the improvement of ethnoracially excluded groups, we are not comfortable with drawing conclusions (or making predictions) concerning which of the three societies under consideration offers the most favorable conditions from the perspective of stigmatized groups. We hope to have demonstrated that each presents different challenges from the perspective of distribution and recognition, as each of our five groups evolves within a configuration of conditions that are largely incommensurable and that result in highly variegated constructions of groupness. Aiming for a simple answer would not do justice to the complexity of the cases we have analyzed.

Racial Formations, Reproductions, and Transformations

These national contexts are not static. In fact, important changes have occurred in the three countries under consideration even during the research and writing of this book: the United States saw the election of its first black president in 2008, leading many to argue that the country was experiencing a postracial era (Bobo 2011; Bonilla-Silva and Dietrich 2011; Welburn and Pittman 2012). There have also been massive African American street protests following several highly visible incidents of police violence against blacks. In Brazil, the implementation of affirmative action and the state's institutionalization of the black movement agenda have radically changed official discourses on race (Paschel 2016). In Israel, issues of ethnic and economic inequality as well as the political participation of Arab Palestinians continue to reverberate in the media, even as groups press for resolutions to the continuous deep-seated national animosity and ongoing Palestinian-Israeli conflict, as seen in the 2015 national elections.

Because we do not have longitudinal data, we cannot discuss how our interviewees' understandings have been changed by such political events. Nevertheless, from the interviewees' responses to ethnoracial exclusion, we can speculate concerning how their responses, actual and ideal, might be related to these changes as well as to the reproduction, legitimation, or transformation of historical racial formations.

In the United States, the persistence of confrontational responses coupled with liberal repertoires seems to have contributed to the decline of social movement organizations and organized responses. If civil rights and religion still appear prominent among normative responses, respondents more often point to individual strategies of educational and occupational mobility, which may make racialized experiences less visible. Nevertheless, the continuing importance of confrontation in responses to incidents still makes racialization more visible in the United States compared to other sites. For example, social movements such as Black Lives Matter show new paths for mobilization and the persistent consequences of race for life and death in the United States. It is too early to evaluate the short- and long-term impacts of this movement, but it may be entirely compatible with the pursuit of individual projects of mobility that heighten class boundaries among African Americans.

In Brazil, hesitation about labeling incidents as racial as well as continuous reliance on universal policies to address racial inequalities seem to make race and racism less visible than in the United States. Nevertheless, growing awareness of black transnational movements and the social mobility of a black middle class—a group that clearly identified and denounced racial stigmatization among our Brazilian interviewees—serve to challenge the historical hegemonic myth of racial democracy. It is unclear what the alternative project is, but such an effort seems to combine a continuous defense of porous symbolic boundaries between racial groups with a demand for less inequality and weaker socioeconomic boundaries between blacks and whites in the country.

In Israel, we found a less promising and more challenging situation, given the continuous institutional exclusion of Arab Palestinian citizens from the polity and the scarcely visible opportunities of symbolic inclusion. Our Palestinian interviewees' actual and ideal responses to incidents expressed this sense of resignation. At the same time, Arab Palestinians have experienced large gains in their economic standing over the past few decades and for the first time ever in the 2015 elections, they elected a united block of representatives to the Israeli legislature. For their part, Mizrahim and Ethiopians still largely embrace the Zionist project, even if they are to varying degrees aware of their lower status in the ethnoracial pecking order.

NEW VENUES OF RESEARCH

A project with a scope as large as this one is bound to raise as many, or more, questions as it answers. We are aware that we made analytical choices that shed light on certain issues while leaving others unexplored. Without aiming to be exhaustive, we conclude by pointing to a few questions that we hoped to address but in the end chose not to because of the obvious complexity of our project. We list them not only to acknowledge our study's limitations but also with the hope that others will take them on.

1. *Variations within stigmatized groups.* The focus of our book was variations across countries and classes. Although we consider gender and age differences in the United States and Brazil, we were not able to fully explore these topics. For instance, we have only pointed to a few instances in which gender plays a role in shaping stigmatization and responses. We were surprised to find only small differences across gender groups, which may be due to our focus on ethnora-

cial experiences. We also barely approached the question of intersectionality, because a careful operationalization of the concept would require an analysis beyond a sum of class, race, gender, and age disadvantages (McCall 2005).

2. *Subnational experiences.* Our interviews were conducted in three major metropolitan areas. It is possible that stigmatized groups in less developed and less urbanized regions in the three countries may have access to fewer and less transnational narratives of responses to ethnoracial exclusion. Recent studies have focused, for example, on the differences between the racialized experiences of African Americans in the North and South of the United States (Pendergrass 2013). The subnational experiences of other ethnoracial minorities, such as Asian Americans in the United States, could also be the focus of study (e.g., Lee and Zhou 2015).

3. *Perceptions of dominant groups.* By relying on the narratives of stigmatized groups, we studied only half of the stigmatization relationship, excluding the dominant groups from our inquiry. The dominant groups were captured only through the stigmatized groups' perceptions of them. Many unexamined questions remain. For instance, do whites in Brazil and Ashkenazim in Israel value mixture as much Mizrahim, Ethiopians, and Black Brazilians do? Qualitative studies about how dominant groups perceive stigmatization and how they feel it should be dealt with would provide a more complete picture of the degree to which the cultural repertoires we documented are shared or contested. Nevertheless, we consider the study of the stigmatized group's perspective a crucial step in the development of a more theoretically informed approach to a phenomenology of everyday antiracism.

4. *Transnational ties and international law.* In our study we have briefly discussed how transnational ties and international laws and treaties might influence the responses of Brazilian and Ethiopian interviewees, but we did not dwelve on this question in detail (e.g., Koser 2003). This topic is essential but would have required a different analytical frame from the one we adopted, which privileges experiences of groupness and everyday negotiation of boundaries in national settings.

5. *Ethnographies of everyday stigmatization.* While we see our comparative analysis as deeply connected to the work of such ethnographers as Anderson (2011), Carter (2012), Lacy (2007), Pattillo (1999), and Young (2004), among others, we could not closely compare our interview-based findings with their detailed results. A complementary effort to our study would be to observe how the narratives of stigmatization we have documented play out in environments like

the corporate world and public spaces. Moreover, because our study is not based on the observation of interactions, we did not give much attention to the role of emotions in the formation of responses to incidents or to how responses evolve in time (e.g., Rivera 2015). These are important complementary issues that we hope will be taken up by ethnographers, who may consider interactions in the context of broader narratives.

6. *Broadening the generativity of our analysis.* Our analysis opens the door to other potentially generative comparative analysis of configurations of groupness across societies. For instance, one could consider how various stigmatized groups in Canada (Inuit, First Nation, and Metis, Caribbean immigrants and French Canadians), experience and respond to exclusion in light of their different histories, degrees of groupness, and relationships with the polity. In the European context, a similar framework could be applied to the experience of the Roma, and West Africans and Maghreb immigrants in France, as well as Turkish immigrants and refugees in Germany—especially as Islam is becoming a more salient basis for boundary work (Witte 2015; Mijs, Bakhtiari, and Lamont 2016). We have yet to explore the full potential of our study for theoretical development based on such comparisons, as well as a future expansion into a broader research agenda.

Despite the limitations of and gaps in our study, we have brought to light new aspects of the experience of stigmatized groups that had been left unexamined to date. We also have reinforced the importance of recognition as both a cultural process and a demand of those who are misrecognized. Most importantly, we have endeavored to capture the complexity and urgency of the narratives of those we spoke to, as our effort is, above all, motivated by their quest for respect.

APPENDIX 1
METHODOLOGY

UNITED STATES

Research Design

We conducted interviews with a relatively large number of respondents (by the standards of qualitative methods), with the goals of reaching saturation and systematically comparing responses across class groups, gender, and age cohorts.[1] The data collection consisted of open-ended two-hour interviews with working- and middle-class men and women. We conducted interviews in the New York metropolitan area, which presents a full spectrum of social classes for both majority and minority groups. Like the metropolitan areas of Rio de Janeiro and Tel Aviv, the New York metropolitan area is mixed—relationships among members of various ethnoracial groups are frequent and highly routinized, without the clear predominance of one particular group (on mixed cities, see Monterescu and Rabinowitz 2007). These metropolises should not be viewed as representative of the national population, because there are large regional variations in the spatial distribution of ethnoracial groups in each of the three countries under consideration.

Selection of Respondents

Respondents were limited to individuals who self-identified as US native born and black. The samples comprise men and women in roughly comparable numbers (see Table A1.1 for details). Middle-class respondents have a four-year college degree or some college and are typically professionals or managers (although some individuals with semi-professional occupations are included in the sample). The working-class respondents have a high school degree (or equivalent) but no college degree.[2] The age range is between 20 and 70 years old, with a mean of 46.8 and a median of 49. Only individuals who had worked at least 30 hours per week in paid employment for the previous 6 months were selected, with the goal of ensuring relatively stable class identification among our respondents. To qualify, interviewees had to have resided in the New York area for at least 3 years. The respondents were found in New Jersey counties, such as Bergen, Essex, Hudson, Middlesex, Passaic, Monmouth, and Westchester counties. They were sampled from towns with relatively high proportions of middle- or working-class African Americans (identified using census data). These ranged from 20 percent of the population that is African American (Elizabeth, New Jersey) to 90 percent (East Orange, New Jersey).

Sampling

Methods for sampling respondents varied slightly cross-nationally in response to the specific challenges associated with locating respondents from various class and racial groups, given the local patterns of social and spatial segregation and concentration, and cultural factors.

In the United States, middle- and working-class respondents were recruited using two primary techniques. First, we employed a survey research company to recruit participants. The company used census tracking and marketing data to identify potential participants who met the criteria described above. Then we mailed letters announcing the study to these randomly sampled African Americans living in northern New Jersey and the company called potential participants to invite them to be interviewed and confirm their eligibility for the study. Interviewers then followed up to set up the interview. Second, to increase our sample size, we employed snowball sampling techniques, with no more than three referrals per participant. This method was particularly fruitful for recruiting working-class respondents and men, who were less likely to respond to requests from our survey research company. Respondents were paid $20 for their participation. Table A1.1 provides details concerning the distribution of middle- and working-class respondents across occupational categories and gender.

Interviewing

The interviews were confidential and were conducted in a location of the respondent's choosing. Respondents were questioned on a range of issues concerning what it means to be African American, similarities and differences between them and other ethnoracial groups, their views on social mobility and inequality, what they have learned in their family and at school about how to deal with exclusion, and so on. Discourse was elicited by asking respondents to describe past experiences with being treated unfairly and the strategies they used for handling these situations.

TABLE A1.1. AFRICAN AMERICAN RESPONDENTS BY CLASS, OCCUPATIONAL CATEGORY, AND GENDER

MIDDLE CLASS	MALE		FEMALE		TOTAL	
	N	%	N	%	N	%
Executive, administrative, and managerial	9	12	8	11	17	11
Professional and technical	18	24	30	41	48	32
Sales	4	5	1	1	5	3
Other	2	3	2	3	4	3
Subtotal	33	43	41	55	74	49
WORKING CLASS						
Administrative support (including clerical)	6	8	11	15	17	11
Sales	0	0	3	4	3	3
Precision production, craft, and repair	9	12	1	1	10	7
Service occupations	18	24	16	22	34	23
Laborers	6	8	0	0	6	6
Other	4	5	2	3	6	4
Subtotal	43	57	33	45	76	51
Total	76		74		150	

Note: % Columns may not sum to 100 due to rounding.

We documented responses to stigmatization by asking interviewees about ideal or best approaches for dealing with racism, independently of context, their responses to specific racist incidents, the lessons they teach their children about how to deal with racism, their views on the best tools their group has at its disposal to improve their situation, and their reactions to a list of specific strategies. We also considered how these responses vary with a number of social and cultural indicators (including gender, class, age, and whether individuals live in integrated or segregated environments and whether racist incidents occurred in public or private spaces).

The interview schedule, first developed for the US case, was carefully adapted to the Brazilian and Israeli cultural contexts. The questions were revised after some pilot interviews were conducted in the three countries. Most importantly in the Brazilian case, instead of explicitly asking questions about racial identity, we waited for the topic to emerge spontaneously in the context of the interview. If it did not, we asked questions about it at the end of the interview—the salience of racial identity being one of the key foci of the project. We initially postponed mentioning the centrality of race in our project in the interviews with African Americans, but this created awkward situations, as most respondents expected the study to be concerned with this topic. The interview schedule is available on request.

We tried to increase consistency across interviews by training interviewers and having them do team interviews before venturing out solo. Interviewers aimed to create a conversational tone during the interview. They first obtained informed consent from respondents, according to the standards defined by the Institutional Review Board of Harvard University. They concluded the interview by administering questionnaires pertaining to past experiences with racism and to subjective well-being. They also invited respondents to contact them if the respondents had questions. Most interviewees covered the full range of questions included in our interview schedule. However, there were variations in the order of questions and occasionally in the wording of questions. Also, at times, some questions were omitted. Interviewers would isolate themselves shortly after the interview to write fieldnotes. These were uploaded onto the website of the project and shared among coders (although they were not the object of analysis).

Respondents were interviewed by an ethnoracial (but not necessarily a class) in-group member. Alford Young (2004) has argued persuasively that there are advantages and disadvantages to interviews being conducted by in-group members. Because of shared experiences, in-group members can often elicit more candid responses from research participants. However, because respondents may assume that such interviewers share a similar set of experiences, it can be more challenging for them to get detailed responses to interview questions. In our case, respondents and interviewers shared a set of assumptions, such as a general understanding of the African American experience in the United States (e.g., ideas about racial identity and experiences with racism and discrimination). This made respondents more forthcoming about their views. However, interviewers faced the challenge of ensuring that respondents fully explained their answers and did not assume that the interviewer understood abbreviated descriptions of their experiences.

Michèle Lamont, the principal investigator, is a white francophone Québecoise. She worked closely with a team composed largely of African American graduate students. While the students took responsibility for interviewing and coding, and the principal investigator provided guidance and feedback through regular meetings, the writing was her responsibility and that of Jessica Welburn, an African American who has been a pivotal member of the project from the start. The relationship between the principal investigator and research assistants was one of reciprocal learning. While Lamont mentored and provided opportunities for developing research skills and publishing, she gained knowledge from the junior social scientists involved in the project—particularly in the interpretation of the data on experiences of stigmatization and through their feedback on the book and articles that have come out of the project.

Coding and Data Analysis

The interviews were fully transcribed and systematically coded by a team of research assistants with the help of the qualitative data analysis software Atlas.ti. The coding scheme was developed iteratively by the three national teams of coders, with the US coders generally taking the lead. Regular meetings were held for several months (often weekly) to discuss the interpretation of the data, harmonize coding keys across the three cases, and determine the appropriate way to categorize incidents and responses. Experienced coders and novices were paired for greater reliability when needed. A more experienced researcher played the role of coordinator at various times during the lengthy coding process. Documentation for aspects of this process is available on request, as is the coding key. This American coding scheme includes more than 1,500 entries. Fifteen percent of the interviews were double-coded to ensure consistency. Discrepancies were discussed and adjusted after consultation with a third person when appropriate. An anonymized list of interviewees (described by age and occupation) is available on request.

Some of the differences we identified across country sites are undoubtedly due to the skills of interviewers and their level of experience, as well as to differences in coding procedures. Although we cannot guarantee that the consistency is optimal, extensive efforts were made to enhance the comparability of the data.

BRAZIL

Research Design

The research design in Brazil largely followed that of the United States. We conducted interviews with a slightly larger sample than in the United States (160 interviewees) with similar goals of reaching saturation and systematically comparing responses across class groups, gender, and age cohorts. As in the United States, the data collection consisted of open-ended two-hour interviews with working- and middle-class men and women. We conducted interviews in the Rio de Janeiro metropolitan area, which presents a full spectrum of social classes for both majority and minority groups. As mentioned earlier, this sample should not be viewed as representative of the national population, because there are large regional variations in the spatial distribution and experiences of ethnoracial groups in Brazil.

Selection of Respondents

The Brazilian sample includes people who were born in Brazil, have been living for at least 3 years in the Rio de Janeiro metropolitan area, were aged between 25 and 65 years old (mean, 38), and identified themselves as pretos (blacks) and pardos (browns) according to the official census categories. We decided to include in our definition of Black Brazilian those who identify as pardos, because they make up nearly 80 percent of the population of African descent in Brazil. Not including pardos would make the black population a minority in Brazil (about 10 percent of the population). Moreover, although the boundaries between whites and non-whites are perceived as clear, those between pretos and pardos are much more contested, especially because they share much lower socioeconomic status in comparison with whites, and both are considered discriminated racial groups (Silva 1979; Telles 2004). A few authors have argued, correctly, that not all pardos have African or black ancestry but rather have an indigenous ancestry (Véran 2010); this is especially the case in Northern Brazil. In the Southeast, and among our interviewees, however, pardo is commonly understood as a mixture of black and white (IBGE 2011).

However, the official classification system has its shortcomings, and interviewees largely criticized it. To overcome some of these limitations, each interviewee was asked two racial questions: (1) the interviewee's open-ended self-classification (i.e., what is your color/race?) and (2) the interviewee's classification according to official precodified census categories (preto, pardo, branco, amarelo, and indigena). Table A1.2 shows the distribution of our interviewees according to these two types of racial classification.

Our sample was intentionally split between male and female respondents and by what we termed working and middle class. Brazilian working-class respondents (1) had a high school diploma and (2) had held their current job for at least 1 year. We opted to include only people who belong to the formal sector and excluded those in the informal labor sector, which offers neither job stability nor access to legally established rights, and includes people who do not have a specific profession or formal training. This selection allowed for better comparability to the United States and Israel but created a sample that could be perceived as low-middle class according to Brazilian standards. Middle-class interviewees (1) had a university degree and (2) were employed in professional occupations. Table A1.3 summarizes the occupational distribution of our sample.

TABLE A1.2. DISTRIBUTION OF THE BRAZILIAN SAMPLE BY SPONTANEOUS IDENTIFICATION, CENSUS CATEGORIES, AND CLASS

	CENSUS CATEGORIES						
	MIDDLE CLASS			WORKING CLASS			
Spontaneous racial ID	Pardo	Preto	No ID[a]	Pardo	Preto	No ID[a]	Total
Moreno		1		2			3
Mulato	2	1					3
Negro	24	33	3	13	32	3	108
Pardo	5			24	1		30
Preto		11			2		13
No identification						3	3
Total	31	46	3	39	35	6	160

Notes: [a] Six respondents preferred not to identify according to census categories, and three were not directly asked about their racial identification.

TABLE A1.3. BRAZILIAN RESPONDENTS BY CLASS, OCCUPATIONAL CATEGORY, AND GENDER

MIDDLE CLASS	MALE		FEMALE		TOTAL	
	N	%	N	%	N	%
Executive, administrative, and managerial	8	10	12	15	20	13
Professional and technical	29	37	27	33	56	35
Sales	0	0	0	0	0	0
Other	0	0	4	5	4	3
Total	37	47	43	53	80	50
WORKING CLASS						
Adminitrative support (including clerical)	13	16	17	21	30	19
Precision occupations, crafts, and repair	8	10	3	4	11	7
Sales	4	5	7	9	11	7
Service occupations	13	16	11	14	24	15
Laborers	1	1	0	0	1	1
Other	3	4	0	0	3	2
Total	42	53	38	47	80	50
Total	79		81		160	

Note: % Columns may not sum to 100 due to rounding.

Sampling

For the working-class respondents, we hired a firm to sample according to residence in working-class neighborhoods in the northern and western suburbs of Rio (e.g., Madureira, Cascadura, Campo Grande, and Queimados). The firm relied on street recruitment to select 80 interviewees by approaching people in public spaces. Brazilian interviewees were not paid, but they were given money for transportation and snacks. Participants had no previous experience in academic and marketing research.

Middle-class Black Brazilians are not concentrated in specific neighborhoods, therefore we could not rely on residential sampling, as done in the US. Because there are no datasets on Black Brazilian professionals, we had to rely on snowball sampling. The initial sample criteria included people identified by referrals as blacks and working in senior positions in key economic sectors (oil, telecommunication, health, and banking) and mainstream occupations (engineers, lawyers, doctors). When asking for referrals, we established a maximum of two referrals from each interviewee.

Interviewing and Coding

Interviewing and coding procedures in Brazil largely followed those for the US. The main difference, was that Brazilian interviewees were not told beforehand that the interview was about ethnoracial experiences. They were told the project was about trajectories of social mobility. This strategy was approved by the Harvard Institutional Review Board, and required that interviewees were briefed after the interview about the "real" goals of the research and agreed with them. This strategy was chosen to identify how and when racial identification would emerge in a context in which the centrality of ethnoracial identities have been historically largely challenged.

In Brazil, all but one of the interviewers identified as black. The only white interviewer was Graziella Moraes Silva, one of the book authors, who limited her interviews to the middle-class interviewees. When analyzing the interviews and comparing the patterns of response to the white interviewer and the black interviewers, we did not find any significant difference in type or frequency of incidents or responses reported.

Coding procedures were similar to those used by the US team and followed the same coding scheme, adding new codes when necessary to address issues that were particular to the Brazilian context (e.g., experiences of being treated as exceptional, analyzed in Section 3.2 of the Brazilian chapter).

ISRAEL

Research Design

The Israeli sample consisted of 140 interviewees: 50 interviews were conducted with Arab Palestinians, 50 with Mizrahim, and 40 with Ethiopians (see Table A1.4 for a breakdown by class, occupation, and gender). Three of the Mizrahi interviews were ultimately not included due to corruption of the transcripts; hence, the final sample size was 137. The data collection consisted of open-ended interviews with working- and middle-class men and women lasting between 1 and 2 hours (with an average of 1.5 hours). Most of the interviews were conducted in Hebrew;[3] only ten were conducted in Arabic. One Ethiopian interviewer was fluent in Amharic and used it when needed. For the Arab Palestinians, for whom Hebrew is their second language, we employed various interviewers. About two-thirds of the Arab Palestinian interviewees were interviewed by Arab interviewers.

Selection of Respondents

As discussed in Section 4.1 of Chapter 4, interviews were conducted with people who lived or worked in the Tel Aviv metropolitan area. Although this area should not be viewed as representative of the national population, it offers the widest range of class- and group-level diversity of any area in Israel. The majority of Arab Palestinian interviewees resided in Jaffa. However, for the sake of diversity, we added some Arab Palestinians from neighboring Arab towns who nevertheless worked in Tel Aviv. Our Ethiopian interviewees were, for the most part, second-generation residents, born in Israel; some had immigrated at a very young age. The Mizrahi interviewees generally resided in suburban towns around Tel Aviv (Petach Tiqva, Holon, and Bat Yam), populated by middle- and working-class Mizrahim.

We are fully aware of the potential biases introduced by selecting this specific area, which is far more secular in character than the rest of Israel, which may significantly impact the contours of the issues at stake. For example, the porousness of the ethnic boundaries between the Mizrahim and Ashkenazim, which depend primarily on class, would not have appeared in the manner described had ultra-Orthodox Jews been included in the sample. Among ultra-Orthodox Jews, the social and symbolic boundaries between these groups are impermeable, with the groups also divided by rigid institutional arrangements, such as those found in schools and synagogues (Bitton and Glass 2016).[4]

TABLE A1.4. ARAB PALESTINIAN, ETHIOPIAN, AND MIZRAHI
RESPONDENTS BY CLASS, GENDER, AND OCCUPATIONAL CATEGORY

MIDDLE CLASS	ARAB PALESTINIAN CITIZENS		ETHIOPIANS		MIZRAHIM		TOTAL	
	N	%	N	%	N	%	N	%
Executive, administrative, and managerial	0	0	0	0	5	11	5	4
Professional and technical	15	30	8	20	8	17	31	23
Administrative support/clerical	0	0	0	0	2	4	2	1
Sales	0	0	0	0	0	0	0	0
Other	9	18	7	18	10	21	26	19
Total	24	48	15	38	25	53	64	47
WORKING CLASS								
Executive, administrative, and managerial	0	0	0	0	1	2	1	1
Professional and technical	1	2	1	3	0	0	2	1
Administrative support/clerical	1	2	3	8	1	2	5	4
Sales	3	6	3	8	4	9	10	7
Service occupations	4	8	6	15	8	17	18	13
Laborers	4	8	4	10	0	0	8	6
Other	13	26	8	20	8	17	29	21
Total	26	52	25	63	22	47	73	53
GENDER								
Male	24	48	21	53	22	47	67	49
Female	26	52	19	48	25	53	70	51
Total	50		40		47		137	

Note: % Columns may not sum to 100 due to rounding.

Sampling

The interviewees were equally divided between working-class and middle-class and between male and female. We used snowball sampling for all three groups, starting with between three to five original interviewees, who were dissimilar from one another, for each group; we then added their referrals to our sample. The majority of our interviewees lived in the greater Tel Aviv metropolitan area. Special care was taken to ensure diversity and check that additional interviewees were different from the referring interviewees on important dimensions (neighborhood, family, gender, class). Due to limitations of sample size, and the fact that we were sampling three different groups, the number of interviewees was insufficient to make comparisons within groups across lines of class, gender, and age cohorts.

Interviewing and Coding

The coding scheme was developed in coordination with the US and Brazilian researchers, and coding procedures followed were similar to those in the US and Brazilian cases. The interviews were fully transcribed and systematically coded by three research assistants with the help of the qualitative data analysis software Atlas.ti. One of the senior researchers who coauthored the study trained the assistants and coordinated their work. Discrepancies were discussed and adjusted after consultation with a third person when appropriate.

APPENDIX 2
TABLES OF FREQUENCY OF EXPERIENCES WITH AND RESPONSES TO STIGMATIZATION AND DISCRIMINATION BY RESPONDENTS

TABLE A2.1. UNITED STATES: TYPES OF INCIDENTS BY INTERVIEWEES

Metatype	Subtype	MIDDLE CLASS		WORKING CLASS		TOTAL	
		N	%	N	%	N	%
I. Assault on worth							
	Stereotyped as low status, poor, uneducated	22	30	14	18	36	24
	Insulted/disrespected	51	69	49	64	100	67
	Poor service	26	35	22	29	48	32
	Jokes	10	14	9	12	19	13
	Stereotyped as threatening	16	22	9	12	25	17
	Underestimated	22	30	12	16	34	23
	Double standards	20	27	26	34	46	31
	Stereotyped—other	21	28	15	20	36	24
	Networks	5	7	3	4	8	5
	Ignored	13	18	7	9	20	13
	Stereotyped as exceptional (Brazil sample only)	n.a.	n.a.	n.a.	n.a.	n.a.	n.a.
	Misunderstood	37	50	40	53	77	51
	Physical assault	15	20	12	16	27	18
	Threat	7	9	4	5	11	7
	Vandalism	8	11	4	5	12	8
	Total	72	97	72	95	144	96
II. Discrimination							
	Denied opportunities	35	47	36	47	71	47
	Profiling	29	39	28	37	57	38
	Exclusion (segregation, exclusion from public space, exclusion from service)	13	18	14	18	27	18
	Credit	6	8	5	7	11	7
	Total	55	74	53	70	108	72
III. Other types							
	Total	3	4	2	3	5	3
Total		74	100	76	100	150	100

Notes: n.a.: not applicable. The columns do not sum to the total, because the number of incidents for each type refers to the total number of interviewees who mentioned each type. Percentages are calculated from the number of interviewees, which is given at the bottom of the table as the total N. Interviewees who mentioned the same type multiple times were counted only once. Thirty-two percent (80/252) of incidents were coded as both assault on worth and discrimination. Sixty-three percent (90/144) were double-coded as belonging to two categories in the assault on worth group. Only seven percent (8/108) of the discrimination incidents were double-coded as belonging to two categories in the discrimination group.

TABLE A2.2. UNITED STATES: TYPES OF RESPONSES BY INTERVIEWEES

Metatype	Subtype	MIDDLE CLASS		WORKING CLASS		TOTAL	
		N	%	N	%	N	%
I. Confronting							
	Speaking out	56	76	43	57	99	67
	Formal complaint/sue	24	32	28	37	52	35
	Physical threat/intimidation	10	14	11	14	21	15
	Screaming and insulting	8	11	5	7	13	7
	Total	64	86	54	71	118	81
II. Management of self							
	Acting against stereotypes	5	7	1	1	6	3
	Preservation of self/energy	20	27	25	33	45	30
	Humor	4	5	5	7	9	6
	Manage anger/pick battle	19	26	21	28	40	26
	Strategic silence	8	11	2	3	10	7
	Total	35	47	38	50	73	49
III. Not responding							
	Ignore	12	16	11	14	23	15
	None/circumstantial reasons, shock, passivity	30	41	27	36	57	37
	Avoid	1	1	2	3	3	1
	Total	36	49	34	45	70	45

TABLE A2.2. (*continued*)

Metatype	Subtype	MIDDLE CLASS		WORKING CLASS		TOTAL	
		N	%	N	%	N	%
IV. Competence/work							
	Persevere	10	14	8	11	18	11
	Work harder	9	12	4	5	13	9
	Total	18	24	12	16	30	19
V. Isolation/autonomy							
	Refuse to assimilate/self-segregation	3	4	7	9	10	7
	Boycott	8	11	4	5	12	8
	Total	11	15	10	13	21	14
VI. Miscellaneous responses							
	Other	25	34	23	30	48	32
	Maturity	7	9	4	5	11	7
	Protect children	8	11	6	8	14	9
	Assimilation	8	11	2	3	10	7
	Total	40	54	27	36	67	45
Total		74	100	76	100	150	100

Notes: The columns do not sum to the total, because the number of responses for each type refers to the total number of interviewees who mentioned each type. Percentages are calculated from the number of interviewees, which is given at the bottom of the table as the total *N*. Interviewees who mentioned the same type multiple times were counted only once. Twenty-two percent of all incidents were described without any reference to response (*N* = 158/874). Eighteen percent of the incidents were double-coded across response categories (125/874), and 42 percent were double-coded within categories. The tables present data that concern the first code assigned only, though including all codes does not substantively change the results.

TABLE A2.3. BRAZIL: TYPES OF INCIDENTS BY INTERVIEWEES

		MIDDLE CLASS		WORKING CLASS		TOTAL	
		N	%	N	%	N	%
I. Assault on worth							
	Stereotyped as low status, poor, uneducated	46	58	24	30	70	44
	Insulted/disrespected	20	25	22	28	42	26
	Poor service	25	31	25	31	50	31
	Jokes	16	20	22	28	38	24
	Stereotyped as threatening	14	18	13	16	27	17
	Underestimated	26	33	11	14	37	23
	Double standards	19	24	5	6	24	15
	Stereotyped—other	17	21	7	9	24	15
	Networks	11	14	11	14	22	14
	Ignored	13	16	12	15	25	16
	Stereotyped as exceptional (Brazil sample only)	25	31	8	10	33	21
	Misunderstood	12	15	6	8	18	11
	Physical assault	2	3	0	0	2	1
	Threat	1	1	1	1	2	1
	Vandalism	1	1	0	0	1	1
	Total	67	84	60	75	127	79
II. Discrimination							
	Denied opportunities	28	35	29	36	57	36
	Profiling	29	36	18	23	47	29
	Exclusion	18	23	10	13	28	18
	Credit	1	1	0	0	1	1
	Total	53	66	43	54	96	60
III. Other types		2	3	0	0	2	1
Total		80	100	80	100	160	100

Notes: The columns do not sum to the total, because the number of incidents for each type refers to the total number of interviewees who mentioned each type. Percentages are calculated from the number of interviewees, which is given at the bottom of the table as the total *N*. Interviewees who mentioned the same type multiple times were counted only once. Of the 543 narratives of incidents, thirty-eight percent (205/543) were double coded. Of those, twenty-seven percent (56/205) were double coded as assault on worth and discrimination, sixty-seven percent (132/205) within assault on worth, and eight percent (17/205) within discrimination incidents.

TABLE A2.4. BRAZIL: TYPES OF RESPONSES BY INTERVIEWEES

Metatype	Subtype	MIDDLE CLASS		WORKING CLASS		TOTAL	
		N	%	N	%	N	%
I. Confronting	Speaking out	45	56	30	38	75	47
	Formal complaint/sue	11	14	9	11	20	13
	Physical threat/intimidate	8	10	7	9	15	9
	Screaming and insulting	6	8	3	4	9	6
	Total	46	58	37	46	83	52
II. Management of self	Acting against stereotypes	26	33	15	19	41	26
	Preservation of self/energy	18	23	28	35	46	29
	Humor	15	19	13	16	28	18
	Manage anger/pick battle	9	11	8	10	17	11
	Strategic silence	4	5	6	8	10	6
	Total	45	56	43	54	88	55
III. Not responding	Ignore/forgive	37	46	33	41	70	44
	None/circumstantial reasons, shock, passivity	39	49	26	33	65	41
	Avoid	0	0		0		0
	Total	45	56	39	49	84	53
IV. Competence/work	Persevere	11	14	8	10	19	12
	Work harder	5	6	1	1	6	4
	Total	14	18	8	10	22	14
V. Isolation/autonomy	Refuse to assimilate/ self-segregation	9	11	4	5	13	8
	Boycott	5	6	3	4	8	5
	Total	15	19	8	10	23	14
VI. Miscellaneous responses	Other	0	0	1	1	1	1
	Maturity	12	15	2	3	14	9
	Protect children	1	1	1	1	2	1
	Assimilation	1	1	0	0	1	1
	Total	14	18	4	5	18	11
Total		80		80		160	

Notes: The columns do not sum to the total, because the number of incidents for each type refers to the total number of interviewees who mentioned each type. Percentages are calculated from the number of interviewees, which is given at the bottom of the table as the total N. Interviewees who mentioned the same type multiple times were counted only once. Twenty-three percent of all incidents were described without any reference to response ($N = 127$). Forty-five percent of the recorded responses were double-coded (185/416). Of those, fifty-seven percent (105/185) were double-coded across response meta-categories (i.e., confront, management of the self, no response, etc.), and the remaining forty-three percent (80/185) were double-coded within meta-categories.

TABLE A2.5. ISRAEL: TYPES OF INCIDENTS BY INTERVIEWEES

Metatype	Subtype	ARAB PALESTINIAN CITIZENS		ETHIOPIANS		MIZRAHIM	
		N	%	N	%	N	%
I. Assault on worth	Stereotyped as low status, poor, uneducated	3	6	5	13	5	11
	Insulted/disrespected	20	40	12	30	8	17
	Poor service	1	2	3	8	0	0
	Jokes	0	0	5	13	5	11
	Stereotyped as threatening	8	16	3	8	3	6
	Underestimated	2	4	14	35	2	4
	Double standards	3	6	2	5	1	2
	Stereotyped—other	5	10	11	28	7	15
	Networks	2	4	4	10	10	21
	Ignored	1	2	3	8	2	4
	Stereotyped as exceptional (Brazil sample only)	n.a.	n.a.	n.a.	n.a.	n.a.	n.a.
	Misunderstood	0	0	2	5	0	0
	Being stared at	5	10	2	5	0	0

TABLE A2.5. (*continued*)

Metatype	Subtype	ARAB PALESTINIAN CITIZENS		ETHIOPIANS		MIZRAHIM	
		N	%	N	%	N	%
	Physical assault	7	14	2	5	1	2
	Threat	1	2	0	0	1	2
	Vandalism	n.a.	n.a.	n.a.	n.a.	n.a.	n.a.
	Total	42	84	31	78	27	57
II. Discrimination							
	Denied opportunities	17	34	12	30	14	30
	Profiling	23	46	4	10	0	0
	Exclusion (segregation, exclusion from public space and from service)	7	14	7	18	4	9
	Denied credit	2	4	0	0	1	2
	Total	29	58	19	48	17	36
III. Other types		15	30	5	13	7	15
Total		50	100	40	100	47	100

Notes: n.a., not applicable. The columns do not sum to the total, because the number of incidents for each type refers to the total number of interviewees who mentioned each type. Percentages are calculated from the number of interviewees, which is given at the bottom of the table as the total *N*. Interviewees who mentioned the same type multiple times were counted only once. Frequencies are based on the number of interviewees whose answers about incidents were coded with that particular subtype. Interviewees who mentioned the same incident subtype multiple times were only counted once. Percentages are thus calculated from the number of interviewees that mentioned the subtype at least once divided by the total number of interviewees in that group.

TABLE A2.6. ISRAEL: TYPES OF RESPONSES BY INTERVIEWEES

Metatype	Subtype	ARAB PALESTINIAN CITIZENS		ETHIOPIANS		MIZRAHIM	
		N	%	N	%	N	%
I. Confront							
	Speaking out	14	28	14	35	21	44
	Formal complaint/sue	2	5	4	10	0	0
	Physical threat/intimidate	1	2	1	3	0	0
	Screaming and insulting	2	4	3	7	2	4
	Total	19	38	22	55	23	49
II. Management of self							
	Acting against stereotypes	0	0	5	13	5	10
	Preservation of self/energy	3	6	2	5	2	4
	Humor	3	6	2	5	1	2
	Manage anger/pick battle	4	8	2	5	1	2
	Strategic silence	n.a.	n.a.	n.a.	n.a.	n.a.	n.a.
	Total	10	20	9	22	10	21
III. Not responding							
	Ignore/forgive	9	18	1	3	2	4
	None/circumstantial reasons, shock, passivity	3	6	1	3	8	17
	Avoid	n.a.	n.a.	n.a.	n.a.	n.a.	n.a.
	Total	12	24	2	5	10	21

TABLE A2.6. (*continued*)

Metatype	Subtype	ARAB PALESTINIAN CITIZENS		ETHIOPIANS		MIZRAHIM	
		N	%	N	%	N	%
IV. Competence/work							
	Persevere	2	4	6	15	0	0
	Work harder	0	0	8	20	2	4
	Total	2	4	5	13	2	4
V. Isolation/autonomy							
	Refuse to assimilate/self-segregation	2	4	2	5	0	0
	Boycott	2	4	2	5	1	2
	Total	4	8	4	10	1	2
VI. Miscellaneous responses							
	Other	3	6	5	13	2	4
	Maturity	n.a.	n.a.	n.a.	n.a.	n.a.	n.a.
	Protect children	n.a.	n.a.	n.a.	n.a.	n.a.	n.a.
	Assimilation	0	0	3	8	1	2
	Total	3	6	8	20	3	6
Total		50	100	40	100	47	100

Notes: n.a., not applicable. The columns do not sum to the total, because the number of responses for each type refers to the total number of interviewees who mentioned each type. Percentages are calculated from the number of interviewees, which is given at the bottom of the table as the total N. Interviewees who mentioned the same type multiple times were counted only once. Frequencies are based on the number of interviewees whose answers about responses were coded with that particular subtype. Interviewees who mentioned the same response subtype multiple times were only counted once. Percentages are thus calculated from the number of interviewees that mentioned the subtype at least once divided by the total number of interviewees in that group.

NOTES

NOTES TO PREFACE

1. In addition to most of the coauthors, participants include Maria Kefalas (St-Joseph University), Jane Mansbridge (Harvard University), Mica Pollock (University of California at San Diego), Sally Merry (New York University), Richard Jenkins (Lancaster University), Andreas Wimmer (Princeton University), Jennifer Todd and Alice Feldman (University College Dublin), and Yehouda Shenhav (Tel Aviv University).

NOTES TO INTRODUCTION

1. When probed on categorical self-labeling, the majority of African Americans we interviewed indicated a preference for the category "black," and almost a third expressed a preference for "African American," while some chose both options. We alternate between these labels to reflect this diversity of opinion.

2. By "Black Brazilians," we refer to individuals who identify as pardo (brown) or preto (black) according to the Brazilian census categories.

3. For years, Israel's Palestinian citizens were referred to as "Israeli Arabs," a term that ignores their national identity and affinity with the territory on which the Israeli state was established. Indeed, this terminology is still widely used by the public and in academic writings. Any decision about which term to use to refer to this group entails taking a stand in the politics of representation (see Rabinowitz 1993; Rabinowitz and Abu-Baker 2002). Since many of the interviewees call themselves "Arabs" and almost no one used the term "Palestinian Israeli," we decided to employ the dual terminology: Arab Palestinian. But we occasionally use the terms "Arabs" or "Palestinians" for simplicity. Note that our study is not concerned with Palestinians living in the West Bank or Gaza who are not Israeli citizens.

4. We build on an important literature on stigma and stigmatization that focuses on the perspective of the victim (Link and Phelan 2013; Pescosolido and Martin 2015). Our approach differs in its emphasis on the role of cultural repertoires in enabling responses (Clair, Daniel, and Lamont 2016). For a psychological perspective, see Branscombe and Ellemers (1998). Experts on racial disparities in health have also focused on the victim's perspective (Krieger 2014).

5. This approach is in line with a recent turn toward micro-interaction processes of racial identification. See, for example, Hughey (2015).

6. See Lamont and Bail (2005) for an analysis of the contrasted symbolic and social boundary patterns of stigmatized groups in Brazil, Ireland, Israel, and Québec. Whereas

symbolic boundaries concern representations and categorizations of types of people, social boundaries concern their access to resources and separation in time and space. Symbolic boundaries concern perceptions of similarities and differences, likes and dislikes, inferiority and superiority between groups.

7. This hypothesis is inspired by the sociology of Mary Douglas (1966) and Basil Bernstein (1971) on elaborate and restricted codes.

8. For a classical discussion of types of stigma, see Jones, Scott, and Markus (1984).

9. The classics include the works of Frantz Fanon, Albert Memmi, W. E. B. Dubois, Zora Neale Hurston, and many more. Contemporary contributions include the important work of black feminists and intersectionality theorists, such as Patricia Hill Collins, who have focused on the experience of stigmatized populations.

10. A popular definition of racism is provided by Omi and Winant (1994: 69–76): racism is a racial project that combines essentialist representations of race (stereotyping, xenophobia, aversion, etc.) with patterns of domination (violence, hierarchy, super-exploitation, etc.). For his part, Wilson (1999: 14) writes: "At root, racism is an ideology of racial domination in which the presumed biological and cultural superiority of one or more racial groups is used to justify or prescribe the inferior treatment or social position(s) of other racial groups." See Berman and Paradies (2010) for a recent review. Social psychologists and sociologists have proposed various terms to capture types of racism, for example, blatant, symbolic, aversive, laissez-faire, biological, and cultural. See Sears, Sidanius, and Bobo (2000) for a summary and Clair and Denis (2015) for a broader discussion of this literature. In our analysis, we build explicitly on the literature on everyday racism (Essed 1991; Feagin and Sikes 1994) and antiracism (Warren 2010). Like many scholars, we view the term "racism" as an essentially contested concept (Sartori 1984) that is polysemic, abstract, and evaluative and cannot be settled by cumulative evidence alone.

11. This last question was included to tap a wider range of types of interactions with whites than is generally included in surveys on racism (see Krysan 2012 for a review). Although some of our questions prime for responses having to do with a specific ethno-racial groups, most of our prompts are open ended and can be answered in reference to race, class, and gender.

12. According to Somers (1994: 614), "People are guided to act in certain ways and not others on the basis of the projections, expectations, and memories derived from a multiplicity but ultimately limited repertoire of available social, public, and cultural narratives." For instance, Moon's (2012) study of stigmatized groups—Jews and Lesbian, Gay, Bisexual, and Transgender—shows that their collective selfhood contains assumptions about the boundaries between self and other, and the sources of personal change, and that these differences lead to preferences for group action.

13. In their influential review of the literature on discrimination, Pager and Shepherd (2008: 182) define racial discrimination as the "unequal treatment of persons or groups on the basis of their race or ethnicity." After specifying that discrimination concerns behavior, they add, "Discrimination is distinct from racial prejudice (attitudes), racial stereotypes (beliefs), and racism (ideologies) that may also be associated with racial disadvantage." They view racial stereotypes, prejudice, and racism as motivation on the part of the perpetrator. They are concerned with the perpetrator's action and not with the experiential dimension of stigmas from the victim's perspective. This is where our effort expands theirs. While these authors defend field experiments as a way to get around the problem of misperception of reality, as cultural sociologists, we treat narratives as data to better understand when and how people perceive, interpret, and react to stigmatization.

14. We draw inspiration from Goffman. In his foundational work, Goffman (1963) distinguished between three types of stigma: (1) stigma on the basis of physical or ex-

ternal attributes/marks (e.g., obesity); (2) stigma on the basis of internal or personal attributes and character (e.g., mental illness or deviant behavior); and (3) tribal stigma on the basis of racial, ethnic, or religious attributes. Phelan, Link, and Dovidio (2008) also differentiate among three types of stigma, but differently. They argue that stigmatized groups are best differentiated not by the location of their discredited attribute, but by the processes that allow for stigmatization. They identify stigma among groups of people who are (1) exploited and dominated (e.g., ethnic minorities, women, and the poor); (2) victims of norm enforcement (e.g., sexual "deviants" and the overweight); and (3) stigmatized as having perceived diseases (e.g., those with HIV/AIDs and the mentally ill).

15. Note that the term "racism" is both highly contested in the narratives of some of our interviewees and in the national literatures (e.g., Herzog, Sharon, and Leykin 2008; Bailey 2009a). Of course, we do not deny the centrality of race, racialism, and racism in the construction of national projects in the three national contexts (Omi and Winant 1994).

16. Sue et al. (2007: 273) describe micro-aggressions as "brief and commonplace daily verbal, behavioral, or environmental indignities, whether intentional or unintentional, that communicate hostile, derogatory, or negative racial slights and insults toward people of color." The range of experiences we document go beyond insults and racial slights.

17. But see Loury (2003) for a seminal contribution. See also Feagin and Sikes (1994). It should be noted that in public health, widely used questionnaires such as the "experience of discrimination" instrument, asks "Have you ever experienced discrimination, been prevented from doing something, or been hassled or made to feel inferior in any of the following situations because of your race, ethnicity, or color?" (Krieger et al. 2005: 1590). Thus, this instrument can be interpreted as covering both discrimination and stigmatization.

18. Note that French hate speech law protects against racist insult, defamation, provocation to violence, hatred, or discrimination. Thus, in France one can be convicted for a television show that describes Muslims as thieves, as it can be considered provocation to hatred. We thank Erik Bleich for his comments.

19. Lamont, Beljean, and Clair (2014) provide a description, with a focus on the cultural processes of identification (through racialization and stigmatization) and rationalization (through standardization and evaluation).

20. Lamont and Fosse (2015) found that in the workplace, compared to confrontational responses, nonconfrontational responses (e.g., working harder, being more competitive) were associated with lower risk of depression and anxiety, as measured by the short-form of the Mental Health Inventory (MHI-5).

21. Hirschman (1970) framed his model as responses to decline (in firms, organizations, and states), but his reasoning perfectly applies to any challenging situation and not just to "declining" situations that logically presuppose some sort of a reduction of existing resources of any sort.

22. We are not particularly concerned with desirability effects (Randall and Fernandes 1991), as we do not know what is desired by the actors. Moreover, if such effects exist, we consider them as a finding, because they inform us of what our respondents consider to be normatively optimal.

23. This finding could be dismissed as a recall bias, which is a prominent concern in the literature on the retrospective reporting of events. One could object that violent events would be more readily recallable by respondents than quotidian experiences, and that this bias operates consistently. Here again, we consider significant that we find cross-national differences.

24. Anderson (2015) does discuss the challenges of navigating "white spaces" for middle-class African Americans.

25. Hall and Lamont (2013) and their collaborators regard neoliberalism as a syncretic phenomenon that opens and closes possibilities for action in various environments: the impact of neoliberal policies, accounting practices, and ideology/values are not homogeneously negative. See the chapter by Evans and Sewell (2013) for more details.

26. The issue of class differences within stigmatized groups has been much more extensively studied in the United States than in the other countries studied here. In Brazil, although the class/race debate is central, very little has been written about the black middle class. This is partly because it is much smaller than in the United States. For an overview, see Moraes Silva (2010) and Moraes Silva and Reis (2011).

27. Recently they have been viewed as having converging paths (e.g., Daniel 2006).

28. That we consider only one group in the US and Brazil is a well-considered choice based on the constraints of an already ambitious comparative research design. The inclusion of other groups in Israel is also justified by the contrast between the most radical exclusion of Palestinians in Israel and the partial inclusion of Ethiopian Jews and Mizrahi, whose position can be considered as more similar to that of African Americans and Black Brazilians.

29. Mizrahi Jews constitute a slim majority of the Jewish population of Israel. The extent to which they are marked by accent and habitus will be discussed in Chapter 4.

30. According to national household survey data from the Brazilian Census Bureau (IBGE), the Gini coefficient in Brazil has dropped from more than 0.6 in the late 1980s to 0.53 in 2012—the lowest level ever recorded since the survey was first conducted in the late 1960s.

31. For an overview of recent trends in immigration in Brazil, see Vilela (2011).

32. The "one-drop rule" is a principle of racial classification asserting that any person with a black ancestor is black. This rule was historically prominent in the United States and was turned into law in the US South after the Civil War. It served as the basis for Jim Crow segregation. For example, Omi and Winant (1994: 53) mention "a Louisiana 1970 state law that declared anyone with at least 1/32 'Negro blood' to be black."

33. For the debate on Latin Americanization of American race relations, see, for example, Bonilla-Silva (2010), Goldberg (2008), and Roth (2012).

34. A few pilot interviews were conducted in the United States in 2006, and a few interviews were conducted in Brazil in 2009.

35. To take only the US case, of course, varied patterns would have emerged had we included immigrant groups (e.g., Asian Americans, Latinos), each of which experience different types of symbolic and social boundaries as they make their place in American society. We already know that black immigrants from the West Indies experience racism differently than African Americans do and draw boundaries toward this group (Waters 2000) and that Chinese and Vietnamese immigrants use their ethnicity as a resource to construct a strict "success frame" (Lee and Zhou 2014).

36. See, for example, Lamont (2000); Brubaker (2004), Morning (2011: 31), and Roth (2012: 22).

NOTES TO CHAPTER 1

1. On the distinction between explanation and causality, see Cartwright (2004).

2. See Thelen and Mahoney (2015). See Patterson (2014) for a parallel effort.

3. Note that this literature is often concerned with high-profile events, whereas we focus on the micro-level everyday interactions. We thank Christopher Bail for his insights on this question.

4. For Swidler (1986: 273), repertoires are "'tool kit(s)' of habits, skills, and styles from which people construct their 'strategies of action.'"

5. There is a literature that deals with the selective appropriation of narratives (Somers 1994; Ewick and Silbey 2003). It is concerned with microdynamics around cases that are more fine-grained than what we study here. See Lamont and Thévenot (2000) on national cultural repertoires, or the relative availability of cultural repertoires across national contexts.

6. See the 2013 symposium on "Rethinking Racial Formation" in *Ethnic and Racial Studies*, featuring a debate between these two approaches (Feagin and Elias 2013; Omi and Winant 2013).

7. Note, however, that our methodological approach cannot account for why individuals draw on some cultural repertoires rather than on others. Addressing this question would require centering the analysis on individuals and their behavior instead of considering patterns across groups.

8. This operationalization of groupness can be contrasted with that offered by Bailey (2009a), which focuses more on self-identification and cultural tastes than on how people perceive similarities and differences across groups. In addition, our inductive approach captures nuances that cannot be captured by predefined questionnaire surveys. Despite such differences, there are considerable affinities between our approach and Bailey's, as we build on his work on considering variations in groupness as a crucial part of the puzzle explaining perceptions of racism. Like Bailey, we also consider groupness as a phenomenon to be studied empirically.

9. By using this term, these authors point out the "widely varying ways in which actors ... attribute meaning and significance to" commonalities and connectedness, with the goal of distinguishing "instances of strongly binding vehemently felt groupness from more loosely structured, weakly constraining forms of affinities and affiliations" (Brubaker and Cooper 2000: 21).

10. Most studies that concern feelings of closeness among blacks import questions from the Survey of Black Americans to ask respondents how close they feel to specific group (Demo and Hughes 1990; Smith and Moore 2000).

11. Tönnies's (1887) writings on *Gemeinschaft* (community), Simmel's (1908) on sociation, and Granovetter's (1973) classic paper "The Strength of Weak Ties" have addressed what makes a group a group. As a concept, groupness can be assimilated to the notion of "linked fate," which refers to the degree to which members of a group perceive themselves as bound together (Dawson 1995). Inspired by Barth (1969), as well as Jenkins, some scholars have adopted compatible approaches (e.g., Lamont and Bail 2005; Todd 2005; Edgell, Gerteis, and Hartmann 2006; Cornell and Hartmann 1998; Wimmer 2008, 2013; Brubaker 2009; Morning 2011; Roth 2012). See Pachucki, Pendergrass, and Lamont (2007) for a review.

12. Building on Tilly (1995) and his students, and on Blumer's (1958) theory of group positioning, we also consider the extent to which the group is a group, as manifested in its network structure, interactions, and competition for power and resources (for a review, see Pachucki and Breiger 2010; see also Nagel 1995).

13. One difference between our approach and Wimmer's is that he tends to put more weight on the control of material resources (institutional, economic, networks, and others) to account for boundary patterns. Also, although he has offered alternative interpretation at times, his overall framework presents similarities with interest-driven microsociology.

14. As described in Appendix 1, for the United States and Israel, we interviewed individuals who self-identified as members of the groups that concern us in a prescreening interview. In Brazil, respondents were identified through various means, but mostly through snowball sampling. Individuals were asked about their racial identification

toward the end of the interview, with the goal of capturing the relative salience of the latter. Mizrahim were recruited through snowball sampling: interviewers asked interviewees for the names of other Mizrahi men and women that they know.

15. This is also a central argument of the literature on whiteness.

16. To further clarify differences between positions: Lamont and Molnár (2002) define boundaries as evaluative distinctions between groups, such as social classes or race, which are anchored in social institutions and enacted in daily practices and interactions. Brubaker (2009) conceptualizes groupness as a process of micro-interactions. His analysis of national identity formation emphasizes the importance of cultural leaders and other determinants. For his part, Wimmer (2008) considers the formation of ethnic groups as it is affected by macro-level institutional factors. In particular, he focuses on social closure and cultural maintenance as key processes connecting macro-level constraints to the making and unmaking of group boundaries.

17. Psychologists do not use the concept of groupness but that of cohesion to designate the phenomenon that concerns us here (Forsyth 2006). Although some consider broader community factors in the production of social cohesion (e.g., Postmes and Branscombe 2002), the dominant psychological approach, Social Identity Theory, remains largely cognitive.

18. A growing literature connects symbolic, social, and spatial boundaries, notably through classification and segregation practices. See, for instance, Hwang (2016) and Tissot (2015). See also Logan (2012).

19. Sellers et al. (2003) have proposed an influential multidimensional model for approaching racial identity (with a focus on identity salience and centrality, public regard, and ideology), which remains largely ideational. For them, racial identity refers to the attitudes and beliefs a person maintains with regard to the meaning and importance of race and racial group membership for their self-concept. Salience refers to the extent to which an identity (e.g., a person's race) is a relevant part of a person's self-concept at a particular moment (i.e., it refers to specific events). Centrality refers to the extent to which an identity (e.g., race) is a core part of an individual's self-concept (see Sellers et al. 2003: 306). Ideology refers to an individual's beliefs, opinions, and attitudes about how their group should act. In contrast to Sellers et al. (2003), our approach puts more weight on properly sociospatial dimensions (i.e., patterns of social and spatial boundaries, which exist outside the minds of individuals). We are also more attentive to meaning-making.

20. This focus on a priori constructs is also exemplified by influential psychological research on gender stereotypes pertaining to "warmth versus competence" (Fiske et al. 2002).

21. Caren, Ghoshal, and Ribas (2011: 142–43) show that "individuals without a high school degree are the least likely to have protested (7.4 percent), and those with a college degree (23.5) are two times more likely to have protested than those with a high school degree and no college experience (11.8)." They draw on a dataset on individuals having attended protests between 1973 and 2008. See Mizrachi's (2014) notion of liberal isomorphism.

22. We differentiate ourselves from the macrohistorical approaches of comparative ethnic and racial studies by taking seriously the dynamic nature of groupness and group boundaries. By analyzing narratives about micro-interactions, we can observe how distinctions are expressed through daily assertions and contestations of identity, for instance, in how individuals contest stereotypes assigned to themselves and to their group—group categorization (i.e., how outsiders define them), as well as how they assert who they are—self-identification. This follows the Jenkins (1996) theory of social identity (see also Cornell and Hartmann 1998). This microboundary work includes responses to stigma, and it results in the construction of symbolic boundaries.

While Gieryn (1983) applied the metaphor of boundary work to the case of competition among scientists, the theorization of boundary work between racialized and class groups has required discussion of the properties and mechanisms of boundary work (included in Molnár and Lamont 2002). These topics were not salient in Barth's (1969) original contributions on the topic of ethnic boundaries. Other social scientists have adopted the language of boundaries to study race and ethnicity, without always making the effort of theoretical integration, which is needed for cumulative theorizing.

NOTES TO CHAPTER 2

1. One of the pull factors was the recruitment of Southern black labor by Northern industrialists due to the labor shortage cause by immigration restrictions following the outbreak of World War I and the labor demands of the war economy. See Wilson (2012: 65–70).

2. Hochschild and Weaver (2015: 1252) write: "In 1970, African Americans in metropolitan areas lived in neighborhoods with the least income segregation; by 2009, they lived in neighborhoods with the most income segregation. Their level of separation by income was 65 percent greater than that among whites."

3. According to Kasinitz et al. (2008: 2, 3), immigrants now form the majority of the population of the New York metropolitan area. Thirty-five percent "are foreign born, and their native born children constitute another 17 percent [of the population]." In addition, "about 45 percent of the city's black population are immigrants or the children of immigrants, as are 40 percent of the white population."

4. The historical legacy of the antagonism between whites and blacks shapes representations and intergroup conflicts even in the face of demographic changes across many American industrial cities (e.g., Sugrue 2005). This is particularly the case in the New York metropolitan area, compared to southern California (Keogan 2002). Even at the historical level, social scientists have been documenting the growing polarization between blacks and non-blacks (Gans 1999; Lee and Bean 2010).

5. These statistics are not seasonally adjusted.

6. Alford Young (2004) has argued persuasively that there are advantages and disadvantages to interviews being conducted by in-group members. Note, however, that interviewers and interviewees were not necessarily matched by gender. Moreover, interviewers were Harvard graduate students, who may have been perceived by interviewees as dissimilar to themselves in socioeconomic status. Appendix 1 discusses further how the conditions under which the research was conducted may have affected our results.

7. The letter to potential Brazilian respondents did not mention race, while the letter to American interviewees did. We determined that the latter approach was called for in the United States after sending some letters without such a mention, which led to respondents' curiosity about the target population and puzzlement about why they were being contacted. Based on the literature on racial identification among African Americans (e.g., Bobo and Simmons 2009; Bobo 2011), we also determined that race is so central to internal and external categorization for this group that it made no sense to conceal our criteria for sample eligibility. That we had to make this adjustment while our Brazilian collaborators did not is itself evidence of differences in self-identification between blacks in the two countries. Given our stated focus on blacks, it is possible that individuals with weak ethnoracial identity selected out of the study at a higher rate than did other potential participants.

8. We acknowledge the contribution of Crystal Fleming to writing an early draft of this section.

9. Here we borrow the Sellers et al. (1998: 25) definition of racial centrality as "the extent to which a person normatively defines himself or herself in respect to race. Unlike salience, centrality is, by definition, relatively stable across situations. The unit of analysis is . . . the individual's normative perception of self with respect to race across a number of different situations."

10. This contrasts with patterns documented by the National Survey of Black Workers (conducted in 1998–2000), in which respondents were asked, "Do you prefer the term "black" or "African- American" to describe your racial identity?" This survey revealed roughly equal preference for both terms, with the latter being slightly more popular among middle-class people (Sigelman, Tuch, and Martin 2005).

11. Nearly a quarter of our respondents (33 mentions) spontaneously drew boundaries against or bridges toward Africans when explaining their ethnoracial identification, indicating the high salience of Africa and its population as a point of reference. Although some respondents liked the term "African American" because of their ancestral ties to Africa, others rejected the label, because they do not see themselves as African. For instance, a writer explains that he does not describe himself as African American because "I'm not African, even though I'm from African descent, no doubt, but I'm just not African. I don't feel a connection to that. I really feel American, to be honest with you."

12. Multiracials were not screened out from the sample. But self-identifying as black was a criterion for inclusion, which may have led some multiracials to self-exclude.

13. Note that we did not probe respondents explicitly on their feelings of national pride and identity. Here we rely on the interviewees who spontaneously broached the topic.

14. Cohen (2010: 136) finds that black youth who have experienced discrimination are "34 percent less likely to feel like full and equal citizens, compared to black youth who score the lowest on the personal discrimination scale." While feelings of cultural citizenship and national identity are not the same, they are likely to be correlated.

15. These categories were identified inductively.

16. On racial differences in collective memory and the meanings of place, see also Glassberg (2001).

17. Note that the percentage may be somewhat inflated, as some respondents were queried about the meaning they give to slavery at the very end of the interview.

18. As argued by Rosenzweig and Thelen (1998), Americans use narratives of past events to make sense of their current situation and draw lessons for the future. These authors found important differences when whites and blacks are asked about "an event or period in the past that most affected you." Among the public events mentioned in their study, civil rights are mentioned by 22.4 percent of blacks and 5.4 percent of whites; slavery is mentioned by 11.2 percent of blacks and 1.2 percent of whites; and World War II is mentioned by 6.7 percent of blacks and 12.5 percent of whites (Rosenzweig and Thelen 1998: 151).

19. This racialized view pertains to the effect of race on "what one is likely to achieve as an individual, that blacks have arrived at rough economic parity with whites, and that full racial equality is a near term or already accomplished fact" (Bobo 2012: 60).

20. See http://www.gallup.com/poll/4435/public-overestimates-us-black-hispanic -populations.aspx.

21. See Emirbayer and Desmond (2015). See also Lamont, Welburn, and Fleming (2013) on connections with the sustenance of collective resilience.

22. Sociologists are only starting to tackle the dynamics of this relationship. See especially Massey (2007); Anderson (2010); Peterson and Krivo (2012); Harding and Hepburn (2014); Tissot (2015). See also Brubaker (2012), who however is moving away from the study of boundaries (Brubaker 2014).

23. The racial composition of the current neighborhood cannot be determined for 24 respondents, and 5 respondents live in majority-Latino neighborhoods.

24. The remaining respondents work in a mix of settings, or the racial composition of their workplace cannot be determined. Three work in a majority-Latino setting.

25. Respondents were assigned a score of 1 to 3 to indicate the level of racial integration they experienced. A score of 1 or 3 reflects segregated environments, with 1 being predominantly black and 3 being predominantly white; a score of 2 indicates mixed or multiracial. The overall average score is 1.788 for the middle class, compared to 1.667 for the working class. These scores are to be regarded as purely indicative, as they are based on narrative data.

26. With a score of 2.165 for the middle class and 1.825 for the working class.

27. With a score of 2.033 for the working class compared to 2.189 for the middle class.

28. Herzfeld's (1997) concept of cultural intimacy points to referents about shared identity that are hidden to outsiders (their "dirty secrets"). In contrast, we use the concept to point to the shared and valued identity taken for granted, or a sense of familiarity that gives individuals a collective identity, feeling of belonging, or shared experiences and points of references.

29. A minority of interviewees responded that they do not have many non-black friends or they have very few friends in general.

30. Greater pessimism about race relations grew following incidents of police violence in the summer and fall 2014, as documented by surveys by the Pew Foundation http://www.nytimes.com/2015/05/05/us/negative-view-of-us-race-relations-grows-poll-finds.html.

31. We asked: "When you think about what's the distinctiveness of African Americans, do you have any thoughts about what differentiates black from other racial groups?" and "What are the most positive things about being black? What do you value? Why? Do you feel that the distinctiveness of African Americans should be preserved?" But one question also asked interviewees to describe cases where they interacted with whites and felt misunderstood.

32. This last question was included to tap a wider range of types of interactions with whites than is generally included in surveys on racism. See Krysan (2012) for a review.

33. Thirty-seven African American respondents narrated between one and three incidents. Seventy-eight reported between four and six incidents. Twenty-nine reported between seven and ten incidents.

34. The tables in Appendix 2 show the number of interviewees who mentioned each type of experience or response at least once. Interviewees who mentioned the same type multiple times were counted only once. Counting instead the total number of types mentioned overall does not substantively alter the findings or comparisons between countries. See the notes to the tables in Appendix 2 for more details.

35. In these 80 cases, respondents explicitly referred to both the stigmatizing and discriminating aspects of their experience in their narratives. Ninety incidents were double-coded as belonging to two categories in the assault-on-worth group. Only eight of the discrimination incidents were double-coded as belonging to two categories in the incident group.

36. In contrast, European countries, such as Germany and France, have lagged in antidiscrimination regulations but have better developed hate speech laws prohibiting racist language and symbols (Bleich 2011: chapter 2).

37. See the types of discrimination established by the Equal Employment Opportunity Commission: http://www.eeoc.gov/laws/types/.

38. Note that 125 responses were double-coded across response categories. There were 42 responses double-coded within a response category. No response were recorded for 158 incidents.

39. Contact theory is still puzzling over how to explain continued racism in the face of daily encounters (Denis 2015).

40. There were 133 mentions of the word "nigger" in our descriptions of incidents, as well as 24 mentions of the "N-word." In some cases, the description of one incident included several mentions.

41. "In 2010, the violent victimization rate for black non-Hispanics was 25.9 per 1,000, which was higher than the rates for white non-Hispanics (18.3) and Hispanics (16.8). By 2011, no statistically significant differences were detected in the rate of violent victimization among white non-Hispanics (21.5 violent victimizations per 1,000 persons), black non-Hispanics (26.4 per 1,000), and Hispanics (23.8 per 1,000)." Quoted from the US Department of Justice: Bureau of Justice Statistics (Truman and Planty 2012: 5).

42. This perception of phoniness can also be a measure of the cultural distance between respondents and their coworkers. On the concept of "phoniness" and its meaning in the American middle class, see Lamont (1992).

43. We classified receiving poor service as "assault on worth," because, while it may often deprive people of resources, it always marks a status differential.

44. See Rieder (1987) for an analysis of a diverse working-class neighborhood's dynamics. See also (Kefalas 2003).

45. As documented by Lichter and Waldinger (1998: 20) in a study based on in-depth interviews conducted with managers and owners of 230 multiethnic establishments in Los Angeles in the mid-1990s, blacks are often excluded "because employers often share workers' prejudices against black workers, and because black workers have difficulty functioning in a predominantly Spanish-speaking environment. Further, African Americans are unable to expand or maintain their footholds as well as immigrants, because they have smaller families and their personal networks, as far as we can tell, are not as large or as strong as those forged by immigrants in the migration process."

46. See Hunt (2007) for a detailed analysis of the prevalence of structural and individualist explanations of racial inequality across racial groups in the United States. Also see Welburn and Pittman (2012) for such explanations among middle-class African American respondents.

47. In addition, we have a rich literature on discrimination and the law in the United States. Light, Roscigno, and Kalev (2011) studied the content of claims brought before the Ohio Civil Rights Commission between 1988 and 2003 and found that they most often concerned differential treatment in promotion or firing (56 percent), followed by incidents having to do with overt racism (27 percent) and isolation in majority-white workplaces (8 percent).

48. In particular, Feagin and Sikes (1994) analyze the various contexts in which discrimination takes place.

49. Compared with the United States, work is less central as a context for incidents in Brazil, perhaps because interracial relationships are not concentrated in the workplace in the way that they are in the United States due to lower overall racial segregation. In Israel, we will see that security barriers are particularly salient as contexts for incidents.

50. It is the case for 41 percent of middle-class respondents versus 21 percent of the working-class respondents.

51. There exists a sizable literature on the context of racist incidents in the United States. Anderson (2011) compares the types of intergroup exchanges that are enabled by workplace contexts and cosmopolitan contexts where diverse individuals can engage in a more open way about their differences. Feagin and Sikes (1994) compare experiences with discrimination and racism in public accommodations (streets, restaurants,

hotels, etc.); white institutions of learning (elementary, secondary, and college level); the middle-class workplace; and neighborhood/home/renting. For her part, Bickerstaff (2012: 114) differentiates between contexts where incidents involve impersonal or personal relationships, while Kasinitz et al. (2008: 326) compare responses to various types of experiences across contexts among children of immigrants.

52.   Responses were coded for all categories spontaneously mentioned.

53.   While C. B. Macpherson (1962) defined possessive individualism as a political liberal ideology that construes the individual as owning himself and not having obligations toward others, we use the term to describe an ontological construction of the individual that defines him/her by the ability to consume and to engage in social relationships through the market.

54.   As documented in food culture (Johnston and Baumann 2010) and in audience research (Butsch 2005).

55.   Starker differences could have appeared had we had an upper-middle class sample (e.g., Lacy 2007). Note however that throughout the data analysis, we examined differences between an upper middle class narrowly defined as including only college-educated professionals and managers and other respondents to assess whether stronger differentiation manifested itself (see p. 75 for an illustration).

56.   However, one cannot rule out that starker class differences would have appeared had we compared upper-middle-class with working-class people who are closer to the poverty line. The latter group is likely to be excluded: individuals had to have been employed regularly for 3 years to qualify for our sample.

57.   Also noteworthy are various case studies that concern specific occupational groups or other segments of the population (Higginbotham and Weber 1992; Higginbotham 1994).

58.   Lareau (2003) stresses similarities in child-rearing practices across races and within classes, suggesting a high degree of similarity among her blacks and white middle-class samples. In contrast, Hochschild (1996) argues for greater class differentiation: because middle-class blacks spend more time with whites than do working-class and poor blacks, they are more likely to have heightened awareness of racism, which leads them to experience more of the American Dream but to enjoy it less. Note, however, that Hochschild does not provide a detailed systematic comparison of experiences of and responses to racism across classes.

59.   For this survey, see http://kff.org/disparities-policy/poll-finding/washington-postkaiser-family-foundationharvard-survey-of-african/.

60.   Quillian and Pager (2001) also cite several studies demonstrating that African American males are perceived as criminal, aggressive, and violent, and that the percentage of young black men in a neighborhood is positively associated with perceptions of neighborhood crime level.

61.   However, again, being interviewed by co-ethnics may have made racial identity salient for our interviewees.

62.   Although the examples above suggest that disadvantage may be cumulative, other research emphasizes how context determines the effects of various identities on experiences. O'Connor (2001) offers a useful framework for explaining such an overlap in a study where she draws on 46 in-depth interviews to explore how low-income African American youth perceive the opportunity structure in the United States. She examines whether respondents believe a particular social identity has a significant or minimal impact on their ability to get ahead, and whether they contextualize the role of a particular identity by emphasizing that it has an impact on their opportunities in certain situations only. She suggests that African Americans employ co-narratives; that is, narratives that point to how race and gender may combine to affect opportunities.

Her work is particularly useful in making sense of the gendered character of how our respondents understand their experiences across contexts. Further, it helps explain why black women perceive more disadvantage than do black men in some contexts, while the reverse occurs in other contexts.

63. More specifically, we compared respondents who self-identified as 57 years old or older, between 45 and 56 years old, or 44 years old or younger in 2008.

64. See Mansbridge and Flaster (2007) on everyday feminism as a condition and aspect of the feminist social movement. On how social movements around stigmatized identity may lead to further stigmatization, see also Jasper (2010).

65. There are only 11 such responses, which include references to the impact of gaining maturity in responses.

66. Whereas Black Brazilians were asked about "the best tools that Brazil has at its disposal to deal with racial inequality," for African Americans the question was worded without reference to racial inequality. Thus, the two sets of responses are not fully comparable.

67. Social scientists studying responses to mental illness stigma have focused on resistance (Thoits 2011), which includes deflecting and challenging (see also Link et al. 2002), as well as concealing, educating, and withdrawing (Link et al. 1989). Although important parallel comparison could be drawn with the case of racial stigma, this is beyond the scope of our study.

68. In the review by Clair (2016) of the literature on stigma, the following responses have been identified as salient in the literature (in roughly decreasing order of frequency of treatment, with selected references): confrontation/challenging, legal action, avoidance/withdrawal (Anderson 2011); collective level strategies (Denis 2012; Dhingra 2012; Fleming 2012); social support (Brondolo et al. 2009; Mellor 2004); educating (Fleming 2012; Fleming, Lamont, and Welburn 2012; Mellor 2004; Moraes Silva 2012); identity change/concealment, management of the self (Fleming, Lamont, and Welburn 2012; Steele 2011); socialization of children (Feagin and Sikes 1994; Mellor 2004); integration/making ties with stigmatizers (Dhingra 2012; Moraes Silva 2012); conflict deflating (Bickerstaff 2012; Fleming, Lamont, and Welburn 2012); work/competence (Kasinitz et al. 2008; Lamont and Fleming 2005); distancing from others (Kasinitz et al. 2008); racial identity development (Brondolo et al. 2009); resigned acceptance (Feagin and Sikes 1994); political action (Denis 2012); anger suppression (Brondolo et al. 2009); and defense/preparation (Anderson 2011).

69. Others have made similar efforts. For instance, in a study of 34 aboriginals from Australia, Mellor (2004) provides a particularly exhaustive typology of modes of coping with racism centered on protecting the self, self-control, and confronting racism. These categories overlap with ours in several respects—most significantly, protecting the self and self-control overlap partly with management of the self, with a focus on ignoring and avoiding. However, our meta-categories also include a range of responses not included in Mellor (2004), such as the use of humor; avoiding behaving in stereotypical ways; and picking battles, which is salient in the American context. Similarly, our "confronting" category includes several important aspects that are not salient in Mellor's research, such as physical threat. These differences underscore the importance of looking at responses in the context of the broader institutional and cultural environments, which enable and constrain what tools are available to individuals for dealing with stigmatization and discrimination. In another review of the literature—in a social psychological vein this time—Brondolo et al. (2009) review coping strategies among various groups (whites, blacks, Black Canadians, Asians, etc.) for incidents that took place in interpersonal relationships and other contexts. They consider three groups of responses and their impact on stress: anger expression, social support, and racial identity develop-

ment. Although racial identity development is an important category in our analysis of ideal responses, it was not salient among responses to actual events. As for seeking social support, it is not very salient in our data.

70. From the control of "governmentality," to put it in Foucaultian terms (Rose 1999).

71. We explored the associations between the following code combinations reported among respondents: (1) incidents and responses, (2) incidents and contexts, and (3) contexts and responses. To examine the above code combinations, we ran pairwise Pearson R correlations of each set of codes (i.e., incidents, contexts, and responses). To adjust for false detection of statistically significant associations (i.e., Type II errors), we used Bonferroni adjustments of the p-values. We also assessed the effect size of the correlations, to interpret the substantive significance of each pairwise correlation. In addition to running these analyses for the full sample of respondents, we also ran analyses stratified along gender (i.e., separately for male and female respondents) and social class (i.e., separately for working- and middle-class respondents). Although the analyses were inductive, we were motivated to assess a number of deductive hypotheses (e.g., that incidents of blatant assaults on worth were associated with more confrontational responses; that the context of public spaces was correlated with confrontation to violent incidents). The pairwise correlation analyses failed to yield systematic patterns in the data, which we leave as a task for future studies. There are at least two reasons for the results. First, it is possible that the sample size did not yield enough statistical power to detect social patterns that exist among the theoretical population of inquiry. Future research would benefit from larger-N analyses of these associations, particularly among important subgroups, such as between male and female respondents, where samples may lack power. Second, we examined pairwise correlations without adjusting for the correlation of observations (i.e., incidents) within participants. This decision, however, would only have increased the probability of false positive correlations; that we failed to find such associations in light of this relaxed assumption suggests that more conservative estimates adjusting for clustering would yield less insight. Notwithstanding, examining the multilevel nature of the incident-context-response nexus (i.e., with incidents nested within individuals, and potentially contexts and responses nested within incidents) may provide additional insight (Gelman and Hill 2006). We thank Charlotte Lloyd and Nathan Fosse for their leading role in this aspect of our analysis.

72. Feagin and Sikes (1994) analyze the various contexts in which discrimination takes place (public places, educational settings, and workplaces). They suggest that responses depend on the situation/context, but they do not systematically connect responses to their various contexts. They document at least four kinds of responses: avoidance, confrontation, court system, and social support. Our close reading of their book suggests that they find: (1) more limited responses in the street context, especially if it involves dealing with strangers or the police; (2) in the workplace, responses tended to be more aggressive, but the responses still only came after periods of "careful assessment" (Feagin and Sikes 1994: 275) to be sure that it was a racially motivated assault on dignity (also, in the workplace, some respondents take legal action); (3) in college contexts, responses tended to be more aggressive (verbal confrontation), particularly if the assault was student-to-student, but if a student felt discrimination from a professor, the response would often be to be resigned to the assault or to respond by overachievement in class/work; and (4) in housing, lending, and neighborhood contexts, the responses were to move out or to find another agent or landlord.

73. Confronting is most frequent in retail and commerce (a quarter of responses), workplaces (20 percent), and least frequent in schools (14 percent), public spaces (13 percent), and family relationships (12 percent). In contrast, management of the self is most frequent in family relations and retail and commerce (23 percent each), followed by work

(18 percent) and public spaces (11 percent). For its part, not responding is most popular in workplaces (20 percent), public spaces (17 percent), retail/commerce (16 percent), and least frequent in family relations (15 percent).

74. This passage was double coded as management of the self and confronting.

75. Again, in contrast, most European countries are more concerned with controlling hate speech and less with adopting and enforcing antidiscrimination laws. Great Britain's policy falls between that of the United States and other European countries. See Bleich (2003).

76. This relates to managing "front stage" presentation of the self in a way one considers satisfactory (Goffman 1963). There is a growing literature on stigma management in the workplace (e.g., Tilcsik, Anteby, and Knight 2015).

77. See the *Washington Post*/Kaiser Family Foundation/Harvard survey of African American Men: http://kff.org/disparities-policy/poll-finding/washington-postkaiser -family-foundationharvard-survey-of-african.

78. This study is based on aggregated cross-sectional survey data on political involvement from 34,241 respondents. The authors find that blacks were 1.4 times more likely than whites to report attending a protest, while more whites signed petitions.

79. Generally we asked, "How do you feel about affirmative action policy?" Sometimes the question was also worded as "What do you think about affirmative action?" or "What is your opinion about affirmative action?" As a follow-up question, respondents were often asked what they thought about others' claims that blacks are taking their spots.

80. Some of our interviewees were born or grew up in the South (30 of them), and 112 of them have at least one parent who was born in the South (out of 135 respondents for whom we have information on this topic). Because less blatant discrimination may be experienced in the North than in the South, Northern parents may have been less concerned about preparing their children for it.

81. Class differences in parental teaching about racism are even greater if we compare our narrower definition of the middle class to our broader working class (which includes semi-professionals): in this case, 76 percent of the middle-class respondents declare having received lessons, compared to 56 percent of the working class.

82. This subsection on lessons taught about racism was cowritten with Crystal Fleming.

NOTES TO CHAPTER 3

1. Most studies, however, make implicit comparisons to the United States without clearly specifying the basis of comparison.

2. There are a few exceptions, cited when relevant. One study was published in 1983 by a psychologist who interviewed ten upwardly mobile blacks. Its focus, however, was the psychological consequences of black upward mobility (Souza 1983). Another is Twine's (1998) ethnography, conducted in a small town in the state of Rio de Janeiro that also relied on in-depth interviews with black and brown respondents. For her part Figueiredo (2002) conducted 25 in-depth interviews with black middle-class respondents in Salvador, Bahia. Finally, there are the books "Fala Crioulo" of narratives of black people from different social backgrounds, collected by the artist Haroldo Campo in 1982 (Costa 1982).

3. Even if black movements have become stronger since democratization in the late 1980s (Paschel 2016), they are small, under-resourced, unpopular with the masses, and, until recently, had little political support.

4. More recent studies estimate even larger differences, with 5,848,265 slaves coming to Brazil and Portugal and 305,326 to the United States, a ratio of nearly 20 to 1. See http://www.slavevoyages.org/tast/assessment/estimates.face.

5. Although it is plausible that lighter-skinned individuals were more often categorized as brown and were more often free, it is important to note that slaves were probably darkened by census takers. For a discussion of Brazilian (and Latin American) nineteenth-century censuses, see Loveman (2014).

6. Even before Freyre proposed his ideas, the image of Brazil as a country with harmonious race relations (especially compared to the United States) was present, at least internationally. In the nineteenth century, the North American abolitionist Frederick Douglass praised Brazilian race relations (Guimarães 2001), and some African American intellectuals wrote articles reflecting the widespread belief that prejudice and discrimination were not problems in Brazil (Hellwig 1992).

7. The idea of *mestizaje* was central not only in Brazil but also in other Latin American countries. There are important similarities between Freyre's ideas and those of José Vasconcelos, the Mexican philosopher, for example. Although Freyre encouraged exchange among Latin American intellectuals, he rarely mentioned or cited their work or ideas himself (Crespo 2003).

8. In the First Congress of Brazilian Blacks (I Congresso do Negro Brasileiro) in 1950, black intellectuals praised the Brazilian trajectory toward a racial democracy as an example for other countries (Guimarães 2001).

9. UNESCO commissioned Brazilian and foreign scholars to develop a series of research projects on race relations in different regions of the country. Authors such as Roger Bastide, Florestan Fernandes, Costa Pinto, and Oracy Nogueira showed the persistence of racial prejudice and inequalities in studies ranging from ethnographies to descriptive statistical analysis. As discussed by Telles (2004), other authors, such as Marvin Harris and Thales de Azevedo, were closer to the racial democracy paradigm. Because of space limitations, we focus here on studies conducted by Brazilian scholars, which enjoy a wider reception nowadays. Most relied on the 1940 census data (the first to have information about race since 1890, right after abolition) to show that inequalities between blacks and whites were still quite strong and racial democracy more a myth than a reality (Costa Pinto 1952; Fernandes 1969).

10. Overall, the UNESCO studies were much more influential in academic than in policy-making circles. In September 1952, a report in the *UNESCO Courier* (UNESCO's internationally circulated magazine) still presented Brazil as a model for race relations. Domestic and foreign understandings about race relations in Brazil remained dominated by the imagery of racial democracy until at least the 1980s. This may explain why, until recently, Brazil was regarded internationally as the counterexample of racist societies such as South Africa during the apartheid regime (Telles 2004; Paschel 2016).

11. As pointed out by Guimarães (2001), the irony of the idea of racial democracy was that it allowed no right of racial representation, as race organizations did not have a voice.

12. Brazil was one of the few Latin American countries to collect statistics on racial identification through most of the twentieth century. These statistics made it possible for scholars and militants to denounce the persistence of racial inequalities after democratization (Nobles 2000; Loveman 2014; Paschel 2016).

13. The 1990 census was also the first one to include the question "What is your race or color?" Before that the census question was "What is your color?" The 2010 census was the first census since 1950 in which the percentage of whites was larger than the sum of percentages of pretos and pardos (brown). Demographers have argued that the changes in race classification in Brazil are largely due to reclassification rather than structural demographic changes (Carvalho, Wood, and Andrade 2004).

14. We do not discuss perceptions about indigenous and Asian in Brazil, because they were not salient in our interviews. Nevertheless, ethnoracial exclusion against indigenous groups should not be underestimated. See Oliveira (1999).

15. Our tabulations are from "Mortes Violentas no Brasil: uma análise do fluxo de informação." This 2012 report is available at http://www.lav.uerj.br/relat2012.html.

16. See http://atualidadesdodireito.com.br/lfg/2013/08/14/perfil-dos-presos-no-brasil-em-2012/.

17. Other studies, however, show that marriage between brancos and pretos is much less frequent than that between brancos and pardos or pardos and pretos, and this is not simply a product of demographics. This points to a pigmentocracy of the marriage market, which has been confirmed in other recent studies, which parallels the United States (Monk 2014).

18. Nevertheless, other recent studies have found a "penalty for darkness," measured by a negative association between higher education and marrying a darker spouse (Gullickson and Torche 2014). Other recent and more qualitative studies also show that these high interracial marriages rates do not mean that incidents of stigmatization are uncommon (Osuji 2013). We discuss this evidence later in the chapter.

19. The rise of a middle class in Brazil is largely contested, because even though a few authors note the increased access to goods and education, others argue that the rise is assessed not on the acquirement of skills or property but on consumption, usually accompanied by debt.

20. Nevertheless, according to the 2010 census, only 13 percent of those between 18 and 24 years old were enrolled in (or had completed) higher education.

21. The same report shows that in the United States, one of the most unequal countries among the OECD countries, the college educated earn 2.8 times the average salary of those without secondary education and 1.7 times more than those with upper secondary education. For more, see http://www.oecd.org/edu/Education-at-a-Glance-2014.pdf.

22. Today São Paulo's racial distribution is 63.9 percent whites (brancos), 29.1 percent pardos, and 5.5 percent pretos, according to the 2010 national census.

23. For comparison, the US human development index was 0.937 in 2012, according to http://hdr.undp.org/sites/default/files/Country-Profiles/USA.pdf.

24. Again, unlike American respondents, Brazilian interviewees were not told beforehand that our study targeted Black Brazilians in particular to avoid priming, as one of our goals was to explore when and how ethnoracial identity was salient in narratives about stigmatization and disadvantage. Instead, they were told that the study concerned social mobility and professional trajectories. Questions about racial identification were mentioned in the second half of the interview only. A similar approach was tried in the United States, but generated probing questions, as African American respondents were eager to ascertain whether interviews concerned racial issues from the start (unlike their Brazilian counterparts).

25. The exact question was "In your opinion, in Brazil, are people's lives influenced by their race or color?" (Em sua opinião, no Brasil, a vida das pessoas é influenciada por sua cor ou raça?). Respondents could answer yes or no. In 2008, IBGE (the Brazilian census bureau) conducted a survey called PCERP (Pesquisa das Características Étnico-Raciais da População) in six metropolitan areas in the five regions of the country (plus Brasília, the political capital) to "broaden the understanding of official statistics in relation to ethnoracial issues" (IBGE 2011: 17). It interviewed a total of 15,000 Brazilians from a range of racial groups.

26. There are not many studies comparing self- and hetero-classification in the United States. Relying on the National Longitudinal Study of Adolescent Health, Harris

and Sim (2002) found 99.9 percent consistency among whites and 99.8 percent consistency among blacks.

27. In his analysis of a survey conducted in 2000 sampling the population of the state of Rio de Janeiro, Bailey (2009a: 51) found 77 percent consistency in the white category, 60 percent in the pardo category, and 56 percent in the preto category. From these numbers, not so distinct of those from Telles and Lim, he reaches very different conclusions "The external and internal definitions are divergent enough, therefore, to suggest significant relative ambiguity between color categories in Brazil, in turn suggesting lower levels of groupness in populations named by the census."

28. The remaining respondents chose preta (1.4 percent), yellow/Asian (1.5 percent), and indigenous (0.4 percent).

29. Pretos choose the negro identification more often than pardos (40 percent versus 3 percent, respectively). In 2000, relying on a survey in the state of Rio de Janeiro, Bailey (2009a) found 42 percent of those who identified as pretos and 3 percent of those who identified as pardos according to the IBGE category identified as negro in open-ended questions.

30. The remaining 53 identified as pardo (30), preto (13) and other less-common categories, like moreno and mulatto. This information is summarized in Table A1.2 in Appendix 1.

31. For example, in a recent study relying on national surveys (PERLA and the Latin American Public Opinion Project, or LAPOP), Telles and Paschel (2014) found that in comparison to other Latin American countries, in Brazil having higher education was more strongly associated with identifying as negro, when the authors were comparing respondents who were classified by interviewer as having the same skin color. They also found that wealth was associated with whitening, but because our operationalization of middle class is largely based on higher education, we believe the first finding better explain our results.

32. In fact, those who identified as negros commonly relied on the black movement slogan, which states that preto is a color but negro is a race, rejecting the color category as merely descriptive and affirming the political importance of race. As voiced by a 28-year-old female hairdresser: "People still say they are preto, but when I read in a book that preto was a color, but negro was my race, it made sense, it made sense. Now I say, I am not a preta, I am a negra."

33. As discussed in Appendix 1 on methodology, we recruited interviewees who would identify as either black or brown, following the IBGE census categories.

34. In the few cases where mixed identification was very salient in the interviews, respondents were also asked what did it mean to identify as pardo or moreno.

35. This question was multiple choice, and they could pick as many as three options. The list included culture and tradition (mentioned by 28.1 percent), phenotype (57.7 percent), family origin and ancestry (47.6 percent), skin color (82.3 percent), political or ideological position (4 percent), socioeconomic origin or class (27 percent), and other (0.7 percent).

36. That the black middle-class interviewees in Brazil were not selected by neighborhood as in the United States may also contribute to such a striking difference. See Appendix 1 for details on sampling.

37. In addition, 89 percent of Brazilians agree completely (76 percent) or partially (13 percent) that "a good thing about the Brazilian people is racial mixture." Racial mixture is usually understood in Brazil as a reference to interracial relationships.

38. Osuji (2014) argues that in-laws racism against dark partners in Rio de Janeiro is much more blatant than in Los Angeles. As discussed later, the use of jokes to mask discomfort is also common.

39. Note that in contrast to the United States, "working class" and "poor" are largely perceived as synonymous, perhaps because of the great inequality that makes both groups so distant from the middle class.

40. Also according to the Datafolha (2008), respondents with higher education tend to oppose racial quotas, also regardless of race (although most respondents in this group are white).

41. Here conflation means the common reference to race and class as interchangeable as well as the inability to disentangle them. We do not imply that our interviewees are wrong or confused, but that they are unable or unwilling to separate the two concepts.

42. The exact phrasing is "According to census data, blacks are poorer than whites in Brazil. According to this scale (from agree completely/5 to disagree completely/1), what is your opinion about the following statements." The statement about unfair treatment reads "Blacks are poorer because they are treated unfairly."

43. The statement about culture reads: "Blacks are poorer because they do not want to change their culture." The statement about morality reads: "Blacks are poorer because they do not work enough."

44. A 1995 Datafolha national survey also analyzed by Bailey (2009a) produced similar results and no racial differential, with 72 percent of whites and blacks attributing inequality to racial prejudice and discrimination.

45. Sometimes, especially for working-class respondents, we had to explain the concept of racial democracy. We defined it as "a country in which racism was not very strong."

46. In all surveys, those who identify as preto/dark black tend to say they experience discrimination more often that those who identify as pardo/brown. See Moraes Silva and Souza Leão (2012).

47. See http://abcnews.go.com/images/PollingUnit/1085a2RaceRelations.pdf (accessed October 5, 2015). Another 2010 survey conducted in 26 countries in the Americas, the American Barometer, found that Brazil was the country with the lowest rate of self-reported discrimination (Rennó et al. 2012).

48. Nearly all those who do not mention incidents identify as pardo, not preto. A few interviewees (19) self-identified consistently as pardos (browns) or morenos and explicitly reject the negro identification altogether. Those who do situate themselves between whites and blacks. They justify doing so by referring to their skin color: they claim to be less dark than blacks. They also claim that pretos, not pardos, are the prime victims of the stigmatization. And indeed, recent studies of skin color in Latin America (including Brazil) have demonstrated its centrality in explaining inequality—skin color is an even better indicator than racial identification (Telles and PERLA team 2014). These studies, however, do not justify reifying skin color as the absolute determinant of racial identification, because the latter is somewhat contextual. Indeed, as noted by Joseph (2015), while some self-identified White Brazilians would easily be considered black in the United States, some African Americans would be considered white in Brazil. Also, consistent with our findings, Telles and Paschel (2014) show that in Brazil, middle-class respondents with lighter skin tend to identify as black. Similarly, some of our upwardly mobile interviewees claimed that when growing up in low-income neighborhoods, they considered themselves brown, but after experiencing being the darkest person in their elite environments, they started to identify as negros. Some interviewees also insisted on separating their identification as negros from their perceptions of skin color: they may spontaneously identify as negros but be classified as pardos according to the census. A more detailed analysis of the respondents who identified as pardos can be found in Moraes Silva and Souza Leão (2012).

49.   Nearly half (74) of the interviewees mentioned between two and four incidents. The remaining interviewees (52) reported more than five (up to 22) incidents.

50.   Table A2.3 in Appendix 2 summarizes the frequencies of those incidents by class and gender. Of the 543 incidents, 205 were double coded. Fifty-six were double coded as assault on worth and discrimination, 132 as only assault on worth, and 17 as only discrimination incidents.

51.   Again, African Americans were invited to participate in our study as members of their group, whereas racial identity was not mentioned when recruiting Black Brazilians. This may account for some of the differences.

52.   Stigmatization of blacks by blacks is also mentioned (by 52 out of 180 respondents). On the one hand, middle-class respondents often mentioned that working-class blacks were resentful of the the former group's upward mobility and refused to treat them as equal to middle-class whites—as in the case of a black domestic worker who refused to work for a black social worker. On the other hand, working-class respondents mentioned that blacks from higher status are more arrogant—for instance, a bank security guard stating that white managers greet him but black managers do not. Ironically, in both class groups, black racism was identified in the patterns of choosing spouses. This is consistent with the findings of Osuji (2013), who discusses in detail these preferences as accusations of whitening.

53.   In Brazil, people who have manual jobs are routinely asked to use a separate, service elevator. Because blacks are often assumed to be manual workers, they are commonly sent to service elevators. Under the 1988 democratic Brazilian constitution, this practice is considered illegal. Nevertheless, it is still common in the country.

54.   These gender differences in stigmatization have been an important issue in the creation of an autonomous female black movement. Black female activists have commonly claimed that their experiences were invisible to the black movement and to the women's movement. In the 1980s, several black female organizations were created, relying on the more successful experience of female organization in the country (compared to black organizations). They focused on the racialized interfaces of the gendered experience and the gendered dimensions of the racial experiences. For a more detailed discussion of these issues, see Caldwell (2007) and Paschel (2016: chapter 3).

55.   Being stereotyped as threatening was reported by 26 percent of men and 8 percent of women. This code includes incidents in which men were mistaken for potential criminals: being followed by security in stores, having women fear them in public spaces, or being avoided when using public transportation.

56.   In 2014 there were at least two highly publicized racial insult incidents involving soccer players. Daniel Alves, a Brazilian player at Barcelona Spain, was thrown a banana in the soccer field. A large campaign was launched encouraging people to post on Facebook "we are all monkeys" in solidarity to the player. In the second incident, the goal-keeper of the Santos team was called a monkey by supporters of a rival tam. Cameras captured a few images of supporters calling him monkey, and they were identified and brought to court.

57.   An analysis of 90 legal complaints (*queixas*) presented over 11 months in São Paulo revealed that 82 percent (or 74) were about racial insults (Guimarães 2000).

58.   Silva (2002) reviews studies that identified instances of discrimination among children at school and usually emphasized the lack of reaction from teachers.

59.   According to the UNDP (2005), 11.1 percent of the population identifies as preto using the census categories, but 32.4 percent of those killed by the police are identified as pretos. In contrast, 54.5 percent of the population identifies as branco, but only 19.7 percent of those killed by the police are identified as white. Those who identify as pardos are 34 percent of the state's population, but make up to 21.8 percent of those

killed by police. As mentioned earlier, the differences between pretos and pardos can largely be attributed to the inconsistencies between self- and hetero-classifications between those groups. In this case inconsistencies are probably even higher, since the classification was done by doctors when assessing the cause of death.

60.   These two unarmed African Americans were killed by police in 2012 and 2014, triggering a series of demonstrations both peaceful and violent.

61.   Interviewers were also instructed to probe interviewees on how they responded after each narrative of incident of ethnoracial exclusion. We do not have information for responses in 127 cases out of 543 narratives of incidents. Table 2.4 in Appendix 2 shows the types of responses made by interviewees.

62.   The Portuguese word "branco" means both blank and white. So by asking people not to answer in white (or blank), the campaign hoped to encourage people to reply to the race/color question in the census and not to whiten themselves. In addition, the words "sense" and "census" in Portuguese are also similar, so by asking people to reply with good sense to the race/color question, the campaign was also asking them to help make a "good" (i.e., accurate) census (Piza and Rosemberg 1999).

63.   This information is from http://www.seppir.gov.br/ouvidoria, retrieved February 23, 2016.

64.   For a more recent study about the low rate of conviction in the state of Rio de Janeiro, see Soares Silva, Gonçalves Costa, and Caldeira Lopes (2013).

65.   Almost an illustration of Claude Steele's book *Whistling Vivaldi* (2011).

66.   This attitude may be related to the strength of forgiving as a repertoire in Catholicism, historically the official religion of Brazil. According to the 2010 census, 64.6 percent of the population identifies as Catholic. Although this number has been declining, Catholicism is still by far the most common religious faith in the country.

67.   We interpreted it as their rejection to the idea that racial inequality should be dealt with through the collective initiatives restricted to their group. We present evidence of this later in the chapter, when discussing their opinions of the black movement.

68.   Brazilian racial statistics gained prominence during and after the Durban I conference in 2001. For the impact of the conference on bringing about greater awareness of racial inequalities, see Guimarães (2006), Htun (2004), Paschel (2016), and Telles and PERLA team (2014).

69.   Not wanting to change their culture (13 percent), not wanting to work (12 percent), and not being smart (7 percent) were mentioned by small minorities.

70.   As discussed in Section 3.1, since 2003 some public universities—the most prestigious and selective in Brazil—use racial quotas to guarantee a representative number of black students (based on regional demographics). More recently, racial quotas have also been approved for civil service positions.

71.   In fact, Brazilian racial quotas have increasingly adopted socioeconomic criteria in a first round of evaluation. Among those who qualify based on economic criteria, those selected should have racial distribution similar to that of the region.

72.   Relying on more recent data, from 2010 and 2012, Bailey, Fialho, and Peria (2015) found great differences in Brazil depending on how the question is framed. In particular, if affirmative action is presented as a zero-sum game, approval tends to drop substantially, especially among whites.

73.   Because the black middle class in Brazil is so small, national survey results usually do not have a large sample of this group. Therefore it is very difficult to find significant differences in attitudes between middle- and working-class blacks. In her dissertation, Moraes Silva (2010) relied on surveys and in-depth interviews, but she found little difference in perceptions of the black middle class compared to both the white middle

class and the working class. Similarly, other studies comparing attitudes toward inequality in the middle class and working class in Brazil found little difference between these groups (e.g., Reis 2004; Scalon 2004).

74. There are multiple organizations and much diversity among those involved in fighting for black rights in Brazil. For historical narratives of these multiple black movements, see Alberti and Pereira (2007). Although we acknowledge this multiplicity, we refer to the ensemble of these organizations and movements that denounce racial discrimination and demand recognition as the "black movement" (in the singular), as it is described as such by our interviewees.

75. Paschel (2016) discusses in detail the complex relationship between an increasingly institutionalized black movement and the state, including issues of co-optation and autonomy.

76. This finding is consistent with the PERLA 2010 survey, which found that more than 50 percent of respondents across racial groups supported black organizations in their fight for black rights (Moraes Silva and Paixão 2014).

NOTES TO CHAPTER 4

1. While the Palestinians call this war and its results the *Nakba* (catastrophe), Israeli Jews call it the War of Independence. The history of the 1948 war, in particular the question of "who started it" and what caused the flight of as many as 800,000 Arab refugees from Israeli-controlled territory, is a hotly debated issue framed by competing ideological narratives. Here we seek to sidestep those debates by simply noting that a war was fought.

2. The Law of Return is considered a major tool for implementing Zionist aspirations to bring back the Jews to their historic homeland. The law stipulates the four major criteria on which citizenship is predicated, the most significant one being Jewish as defined in Jewish religious law, according to which a person is considered Jewish if their biological mother is Jewish or if they undergo a formal process of conversion to Judaism. The other three avenues to citizenship stipulated in the Law of Return are being born to Israeli parents, residence, and naturalization. Arab Palestinians in Israel are citizens only by virtue of the fact that they resided within Israel's postwar boundaries. Palestinian refugees from the 1948 war who resided outside Israel were not permitted to return, whereas those Palestinians who remained within Israel's borders were granted formal citizenship.

3. Our sample includes only Muslims and Christians. We did not include any members of the Druze minority, who are also classified as Arab but who have a different symbolic and institutional relation with the state and generally do not live in the Tel Aviv metropolitan area. The Druze minority comprises about 9 percent of the Arab population of Israel. We also did not include any Bedouins in our sample, mainly because so few of them live in central areas. Bedouins make up about 1 percent of the Arab population in Israel.

4. Note that the term "Arab Palestinian" may be understood by some as implying a close political affinity with the broader Palestinian people who are involved in a political struggle with Israel. Many Arab speakers, such as the Muslim Druze, who serve in the Israeli army, would reject this label.

5. Druze and Circassian Arabs are conscripted into the army, and many Bedouins enlist. Muslim and Christian Arabs can enlist in the army, but very few do so. They are also generally kept out of elite units because of security concerns.

6. The law was passed in a modified form that only requires the oath to be taken by non-Jews applying for citizenship. In practice, this law affects mainly noncitizen Palestinians who married Arab Palestinian citizens of Israel and applied for citizenship.

7. The First (late 1987 until the early 1990s) and Second (2000–2005) Intifadas were civilian uprisings begun by Arab Palestinians in the Gaza Strip and West Bank (who are not Israeli citizens) in protest against continued Israeli occupation of these territories.

8. All settlements with more than 2,000 residents (i.e., insufficiently large to qualify as cities) are governed by local councils.

9. Jaffa, Acre, Lod, Haifa, and Ramla, specifically.

10. See http://www.jewishagency.org/aliyah/program/456.

11. According to the Knesset Research and Information Center (2011), the average value of apartments owned or occupied by Ethiopians is about a third lower than the Israeli average (NIS 687,000 and NIS 1,061,000, respectively).

12. There are two major Jewish geographically linked cultural traditions: Ashkenazi and Sephardi. The term "Ashkenazi" refers to the halachic and other traditions associated with Jews originally from or still residing in Europe (a territory known as "Ashkenaz") and North America. The term "Sephardi" refers primarily to the liturgical tradition originally followed by the Jews expelled from the Iberian Peninsula in 1492. The term "Mizrahi" refers to the Jewish ethnic groups who formerly lived in Middle Eastern Muslim countries. The Mizrahim share the Sephardic liturgical and halachic traditions (Westreich 2012). In the context of contemporary Israel, the term "Mizrahi" is applied to both groups. Its sociopolitical connotations are discussed in the Introduction. Colloquially, the term "Sephardi" carries fewer stigmatized connotations than does "Mizrahi" in the contemporary context.

13. Historically, "black" or "schwartze" (in Yiddish) was often used as a derogatory term to refer to Mizrahi Jews, having strong Orientalist connotations (Shohat 1988, 1999). Now these terms are generally reserved for Ethiopian Jews.

14. Official statistics on Mizrahim are compiled by grouping together individuals who immigrated from, or whose parents immigrated from, Arab and North African countries. However, the category "Mizrahim" does not exist in the official legal discourse despite its de facto presence. Bitton (2011) points out that this lacuna has enabled the legal system to deny compensation to Mizrahi victims of ethnic discrimination (e.g., exclusion from night clubs), despite legal prohibitions of such acts. Bitton further argues that the legal system does more than maintain discrimination against Mizrahim; by rejecting use of the category "Mizrahim" in court, discrimination against Mizrahim outside the court is reinforced.

15. These categories are based on the convention of defining Ashkenazim as born in Europe, America, or Oceania or born in Israel to at least one parent born in Europe/America/Oceania and no parent born in Asia or Africa. Mizrahi Jews are defined as born in Africa/Asia or in Israel to at least one parent born in Asia/Africa and no parent born in Europe/America/Oceania. The category of third-generation Jewish and mixed Israelis is defined as born in Israel to Israeli-born parents or one parent born in Asia/Africa and the other in Europe/America. New immigrants are defined as foreign-born persons who arrived in Israel after 1989.

16. The wave of immigration from the former Soviet Union has had far-reaching effects on the ethnic division of Israel's population, the consequences of which are still being felt. Between 1989 and 2006, about 979,000 Jews from the former Soviet Union migrated to Israel. The majority of these immigrants came from the same regions as did the early Zionist pioneers and so, on the face of it, they strengthened the Ashkenazi population. Yet this same wave consisted of a diversified population in terms of ideological affiliation with Zionism and the emerging state of Israel, as well as in terms

of geographic and ethnic origins. In addition, the timing of their arrival was crucial for understanding the ensuing change in ethnic dynamics with respect to social structure. By the late 1980s, Mizrahim had begun to achieve political clout on the municipal level and the national political arena, resulting from the growth of a Mizrahi middle class. From a formal, statistical perspective, Russian immigrants are relegated to the category of new immigrants rather than Ashkenazim.

17.   Current Ashkenazi average income equals NIS 11,879, whereas Mizrahi average income amounts to NIS 10,033 (Swirski, Connor-Attias, and Ophir 2014).

18.   In the present context, by second-generation Ashkenazim we mean Ashkenazi immigrants who arrived after 1950, a group that includes Holocaust survivors and communities formerly living in Poland, among others.

19.   The data are limited, because the Israeli census does not allow for easy follow-up of ethnicity, given that third-generation Ashkenazim and Mizrahim are automatically categorized as Israelis. A study by Cohen, Haberfeld, and Kristal (2007) indicated almost unbridgeable gaps in education between second- and third-generation Israeli Jews aged 25–34 in 1995. Importantly, the latter study focused on the first years of the Mizrahi socio-economic upswing.

20.   Numerous studies on the ultra-Orthodox (*Haredim* in Hebrew) community are available. See, for example, Stadler (2002) and Shilhav (1989).

21.   This remark reflects the suspicion with which Palestinian citizens of Israel are often viewed by Palestinians and Arabs outside Israel (Herzog 1999).

22.   Smooha's findings about attitudes among the general Palestinian population are in contrast to the main body of literature on Arab Palestinians, which focuses on political, social, and academic elites, including social and political activists.

23.   In principle, both Hebrew and Arabic are official languages as a legacy of the British Mandatory government regime, and Jewish schoolchildren in secular schools learn Arabic from a young age. In practice, most affairs of state are conducted in Hebrew, although legislation and legal rulings have secured a guarantee that some information must also be disseminated in Arabic.

24.   In the Israeli context, the term "periphery" refers to distance not just from the geographic center but also the social center. Nonetheless, the term's meaning as a geographic periphery does not exhaust its social and cultural import. In its broadest sense, the term is equated with Mizrahim and other minority groups. Hence, the geographic periphery need not equate with the social periphery; that is, middle-class communities can be found in the geographic periphery, whereas working-class Mizrahi and other minority neighborhoods located in the center belong to the social periphery. In the public discourse, the term is often used as a euphemism for Mizrahim.

25.   For Jews, choosing to live in an Arab town or neighborhood is almost inconceivable. One prominent exception is the traditionally Arab-dominated neighborhoods in south Tel Aviv that have been undergoing a process of gentrification, with Jews moving into the area since the early 2000s. Another exception includes the phenomenon of Jewish settlers moving into neighborhoods in East Jerusalem and Hebron.

26.   It is worth noting that the social boundaries dividing subgroups in the broader Arab Palestinian community (e.g., Christians, Muslims, Druze, and Bedouins) also present a high barrier to intermarriage between these subgroups.

27.   This parallels Eliasoph's (1998) analysis of sociability and politics in the United States.

28.   "Traditionalist" Jews are characterized by substantial observance of Jewish religious tradition, yet the degree of their observance is much more flexible than that of Orthodox Jews. The favored image of traditionalism is that of going to synagogue or making Kiddush on the Sabbath and then driving to the beach or to a football game.

For many years, traditionalism was treated as a transitional or residual category. It was assumed that Jews from "pre-modern" (or developing) Middle Eastern or North African countries arriving in the modern secular state of Israel would first adopt flexible 'traditionalist' behaviors before abandoning religion altogether (Fischer 2010: 315–339). Contemporary social scientists studying religion in Israel often reject the assumptions made by sociologists of modernization, who view the traditionalist mindset as insufficient in terms of either secular modernism or Orthodox religiosity. Instead, the traditionalist attitude associated primarily with Mizrahi Jews, is viewed as a valid position in itself, as an alternative to the polar division among Ashkenazi Jews between secularism and Orthodoxy (Fischer 2010; Yadgar 2011).

29. The term "isomorphism" is borrowed from Powell and DiMaggio (1991) and applied to the context of liberal movements in their promotion of identity politics. Liberal isomorphism refers to mimetic behavior. It alludes to the link between a group's mirroring of forms and practices and its acquisition of social legitimacy.

30. See Margolin (2015) and Smith (2014).

31. During the 2000s, Mizrahi intellectuals criticized the binary division between Jew and non-Jew that ordered both the national discourse and the ethnic discourse associated with Mizrahim and Ashkenazim. They claimed that a division of this nature de-Arabizes the Jews originating from the Arab countries, obliterating their culture and its relevance for the Zionist effort (Shenhav 2006). They argued that this de-Arabization serves to marginalize intermediary cultural and political spaces, such as that occupied by Arab Palestinians. They further claimed that creating boundaries between Jews and Arabs during the initial consolidation of a collective Jewish national identity was a rupture in the history of the Jews from Arab countries and obliged them to embrace the Zionist notion of the Jewish melting pot.

32. We did not detect any differences regardless of whether the person conducting the interview was Arab or Jewish. Approximately two-thirds of the interviews were conducted with Arab interviewers (see Appendix 1).

33. Because the labor market and residence are highly segregated along Jewish/Arab lines, for Arab Palestinian high school teachers, for instance, applying for a job in a school located in an Arab community seems natural, whereas applying for a job in a school in a Jewish city is not. In some cases, it is even a political statement. We should note, however, that not every occupation is equally affected by this trend, as we can see, for example, in the number of Arab Palestinian mechanics and pharmacists employed in Jewish towns and cities.

34. Israel also has several laws prohibiting discrimination on the basis of race, religion, and political beliefs (Navot 2007: 190–250).

35. A report of the Arab Association for Human Rights and the Center Against Racism documented the way Arab Palestinians are treated in security checks for international and local flights (Arab Association for Human Rights and Center Against Racism 2007), and the Arab Association for Human Rights and the Center Against Racism appealed to the Israel High Court in 2011.

36. Ethiopians occasionally use the word "white" in reference to non-Ethiopians, whether Ashkenazim or Mizrahim.

37. This organization gives legal advice and representation to victims of serious crimes and raises awareness in Israel of the needs of the victims.

38. The official narrative of the war is that after the Arab states rejected the 1947 UN Partition Plan to divide Palestine into independent Arab and Jewish states, they invaded Israel with the goal of expelling or murdering the Jewish residents. This invasion sparked the War of Independence.

39.   The term is used to describe the Palestinians who remained within the Green Line of the state of Israel, as opposed to the Palestinian refugees and those living in the West Bank.

40.   See Herzog's early work on the inability of Mizrahim to self-organize politically solely on the foundations of ethnicity (Herzog 1990a, 1995) and Mizrachi's recent work on Mizrahi identification with the Jewish state (Mizrachi 2011; 2016).

NOTES TO CONCLUSION

1.   In this sense, our approach is similar to what Goldberg (2008) has termed "racial regionalism," but while he focuses on the philosophical debate, we adopt a more inductive and empirical approach.

2.   This finding seems to be consistent at least among the working- and middle-class Mizrahim and Ethiopians we interviewed in Israel. Critical voices among Mizrahi activists and intellectuals employ the language of identity politics and stress recognition of Mizrahi exclusion and stigmatization based on class and ethnic differences (Mizrachi 2011, 2014).

3.   Honneth (1995) distinguishes between recognition given in three domains: the domain of intimacy, through love; the domain of collectivity, through solidarity (expressed in contribution to a group through work, for instance); and the domain of rights, through equality. These three types of recognition provided by others feed self-respect and self-confidence. Human beings have moral expectations of one another that concern the fulfillment of these types of recognition—in a moral social contract of sorts.

4.   This is the topic of a special issue of *Social Science and Medicine* on "Cultures of Health," edited by Mabel Berezin, Michele Lamont, Alonzo Plough, and Matthew Trujillo (forthcoming). This issue aims to inform the research agenda of the Robert Wood Johnson Foundation on "Cultures of Health."

NOTES TO APPENDIX 1

1.   On the advantages and limitations of interviewing compared to ethnographic research and other methods, see Lamont and Swidler (2014).

2.   We used Bureau of Labor Statistics' (BSL) standard occupational classification (http://www.bls.gov/soc/) to determine how to classify each occupation. We combined the BSL classification and the level of education to make a final decision about which group they should be placed in. Categories A and B are generally managerial and are considered middle class. Categories D–K were generally working class. An individual with an associate degree who is in a low-status white collar occupation (e.g., bank clerk, salesperson) would be classified as middle class. But an individual without a two-year college diploma would be classified as working class. In ambiguous situations (e.g., a teacher's assistant), level of education trumped occupation.

3.   On the benefit of using Hebrew in interviewing subjects when Hebrew is their second language, see Lomsky-Feder and Rapoport (2004).

4.   For more research on ultra-Orthodox Jews in Israel, see Friedman (1991) and Leon (2014).

REFERENCES

Abu-Ghazaleh, Adnan. 1972. "Arab Cultural Nationalism in Palestine during the British Mandate." *Journal of Palestine Studies* 1(3): 37–63.

Abu-Rabia-Queder, Sarab. 2007. "The Activism of Bedouin Women: Social and Political Resistance." *Hagar: International Social Science Review* 7(2): 67–84.

Abu-Rabia-Queder, Sarab, and Naomi Weiner-Levy. 2013. "Between Local and Foreign Structures: Exploring the Agency of Palestinian Women in Israel." *Social Politics: International Studies in Gender, State & Society* 20(1): 88–108.

Ainsworth-Darnell, James W., and Douglas B. Downey. 1998. "Assessing the Oppositional Culture Explanation for Racial/Ethnic Differences in School Performance." *American Sociological Review* 63(4): 536–53.

Alba, Richard D. 2005. "Bright vs. Blurred Boundaries: Second-Generation Assimilation and Exclusion in France, Germany and the United States." *Ethnic and Racial Studies* 28(1): 20–49.

———. 2009. *Blurring the Color Line: The New Chance for a More Integrated America*. Cambridge, MA: Harvard University Press.

Alba, Richard D., and Victor Nee. 2005. *Remaking the American Mainstream: Assimilation and Contemporary Immigration*. Cambridge, MA: Harvard University Press.

Alberti, Verena, and Amilcar Araujo Pereira. 2007. *Histórias do movimento negro no Brasil: depoimento ao CPDOC*. Rio de Janeiro: Fundação Getúlio Vargas.

Alexander, Jeffrey C. 1992. "Citizen and Enemy as Symbolic Classification: On the Polarizing Discourse of Civil Society." Pp. 289–308 in *Where Culture Talks: Exclusion and the Making of Society*, edited by M. Lamont and M. Fournier. Chicago: University of Chicago Press.

———. 2001. "Theorizing the 'Modes of Incorporation': Assimilation, Hyphenation, and Multiculturalism as Varieties of Civil Participation." *Sociological Theory* 19(3): 237–49.

Alexander, Michelle. 2012. *The New Jim Crow: Mass Incarceration in the Age of Colorblindness*. New York: New Press.

Almeida, Alberto Carlos. 2007. *A cabeça do brasileiro*. Rio de Janeiro: Record.

Alonso-Villar, Olga, Coral Del Rio, and Carlos Gradin. 2012. "The Extent of Occupational Segregation in the United States: Differences by Race, Ethnicity, and Gender." *Industrial Relations: A Journal of Economy and Society* 51(2): 179–212.

Alves, Jaime Amparo. 2014. "From Necropolis to Blackpolis: Necropolitical Governance and Black Spatial Praxis in São Paulo, Brazil." *Antipode* 46(2): 323–39.

Amara, Muhammad, and Izhak Schnell. 2004. "Identity Repertoires among Arabs in Israel." *Journal of Ethnic and Migration Studies* 30(1): 175–93.

Anderson, Benedict R. O'G. 1983. *Imagined Communities: Reflections on the Origin and Spread of Nationalism*. London: Verso.

Anderson, Elijah. 2011. *The Cosmopolitan Canopy: Race and Civility in Everyday Life*. New York: W. W. Norton & Company.

———. 2015. "'The White Space.'" *Sociology of Race and Ethnicity* 1(1): 10–21.

Anderson, Elizabeth. 2010. *The Imperative of Integration*. Reprint edition. Princeton, NJ: Princeton University Press.

Andrews, George Reid. 2004. *Afro-Latin America, 1800–2000*. New York: Oxford University Press.

Anspach, Renee R. 1979. "From Stigma to Identity Politics: Political Activism among the Physically Disabled and Former Mental Patients." *Social Science & Medicine. Part A: Medical Psychology & Medical Sociology* 13: 765–73.

Anthias, Floya. 1995. "Cultural Racism or Racist Culture? Rethinking Racist Exclusions." *Economy and Society* 24(2): 279–301.

Arab Association for Human Rights and Center Against Racism. 2007. *Suspected Citizens: Racial Profiling against Arab Passengers by Israeli Airports and Airlines*. Retrieved June 3, 2015 (http://electronicintifada.net/content/suspected-citizens-racial-profiling-against-arab-passengers-israeli-airports-and-airlines).

Arar, Khalid. 2012. "Israeli Education Policy since 1948 and the State of Arab Education in Israel." *Italian Journal of Sociology of Education* 1: 113–45.

Arendt, Hannah. 1949. "The Rights of Man: What Are They?" *Modern Review* 3(1): 24–36.

Arian, Asher, Tamar Hermann, Yuval Lebel, Anna Knafelman, Michael Philippov, and Hila Zaban. 2010. *The 2010 Israeli Democracy Index: Democratic Principles in Practice*. Jerusalem: Israel Democracy Institute.

Arian, Asher, and Michal Shamir, eds. 2011. *The Elections in Israel 2009*. New Brunswick, NJ: Transaction Publishers.

Bail, Christopher A. 2008. "The Configuration of Symbolic Boundaries against Immigrants in Europe." *American Sociological Review* 73(1): 37–59.

Bailey, Stanley R. 2008. "Unmixing for Race Making in Brazil." *American Journal of Sociology* 114(3): 577–614.

———. 2009a. *Legacies of Race: Identities, Attitudes, and Politics in Brazil*. Stanford, CA: Stanford University Press.

———. 2009b. "Public Opinion on Nonwhite Underrepresentation and Racial Identity Politics in Brazil." *Latin American Politics and Society* 51(4): 69–99.

Bailey, Stanley R., Fabrício Fialho, and Michelle Peria. 2015. "Support for Race-Targeted Affirmative Action in Brazil." *Ethnicities*. Retrieved September 28, 2015 (http://etn.sagepub.com/cgi/doi/10.1177/1468796814567787).

Banks, Patricia A. 2009. *Represent: Art and Identity among the Black Upper-Middle Class*. New York: Routledge.

Banting, Keith, and Will Kymlicka, eds. Forthcoming. *The Strains of Commitment: The Political Sources of Solidarity in Diverse Societies*. New York: Oxford University Press.

Banton, Michael. 2012. "The Colour Line and the Colour Scale in the Twentieth Century." *Ethnic and Racial Studies* 35(7): 1109–31.

Barbosa, Márcio. 1998. *Frente Negra Brasileira: depoimentos*. São Paulo: Quilombhoje.

Bar-Tal, Daniel, and Yona Teichman. 2005. *Stereotypes and Prejudice in Conflict: Representations of Arabs in Israeli Jewish Society*. New York: Cambridge University Press.

Bartels, Larry M. 2009. "Economic Inequality and Political Representation." In *The Unsustainable American State*, edited by L. Jacobs and D. King. Oxford: Oxford University Press.

Barth, Fredrik. 1969. *Ethnic Groups and Boundaries: The Social Organization of Culture Difference*. Bergen; London: Universitetsforlaget and Allen & Unwin.

Beller, Emily, and Michael Hout. 2006. "Intergenerational Social Mobility: The United States in Comparative Perspective." *Future of Children* 16(2): 19–36.

Ben-Eliezer, Uri. 2004. "Becoming a Black Jew: Cultural Racism and Anti-racism in Contemporary Israel." *Social Identities: Journal for the Study of Race, Nation and Culture* 10(2): 245–66.

———. 2008. "Multicultural Society and Everyday Cultural Racism: Second Generation of Ethiopian Jews in Israel's 'Crisis of Modernization.'" *Ethnic and Racial Studies* 31(5): 935–61.

Ben-Israel, Ruth, and P.M.V. Foubert. 2004. "Equality and Prohibition of Discrimination in Employment." Pp. 321–58 in *Comparative Labour Law and Industrial Relations in Industrialised Countries*, edited by R. Blanpain. The Netherlands: Kluwer Law International.

Ben-Porat, Guy, and Bryan S. Turner. 2011. *The Contradictions of Israeli Citizenship: Land, Religion and State*. New York: Taylor & Francis.

Berezin, Mabel, Michèle Lamont, Alonzo Plough, and Matthew Trujillo, eds. Forthcoming. Special Issue: "Solidarity and Health Cultures." *Social Science and Medicine*.

Berger, Peter L., and Thomas Luckmann. 1967. *The Social Construction of Reality: A Treatise in the Sociology of Knowledge*. Garden City, NY: Anchor Books.

Berkman, Lisa F., and Thomas Glass. 2000. "Social Integration, Social Networks, Social Support, and Health." Pp. 137–73 in *Social Epidemiology*, edited by L. F. Berkman and I. Kawachi. New York: Oxford University Press.

Berman, Gabrielle, and Yin Paradies. 2010. "Racism, Disadvantage, and Multiculturalism: Towards Effective Anti-Racist Praxis." *Ethnic and Racial Studies* 33(2): 214–32.

Bernardino, Joaze, and Daniela Galdino, eds. 2004. *Levando a raça a sério: ação afirmativa e universidade*. Rio de Janeiro: DP&A.

Bernstein, Basil. 1971. *Class, Codes and Control. Volume 1: Theoretical Studies Towards a Sociology of Language*. Boston: Routledge and Kegan Paul.

Bernstein, Deborah. 2007. "Contested Contact: Proximity and Social Control in Pre-1948 Jaffa and Tel-Aviv." Pp. 215–41 in *Mixed Towns, Trapped Communities: Historical Narratives, Spatial Dynamics, Gender Relations and Cultural Encounters in Ethnically Mixed Towns in Israel/Palestine*, edited by D. Monterescu and D. Rabinowitz. Hampshire, England and Burlington: Ashgate.

Bernstein, Deborah S. 1984. "Conflict and Protest in Israeli Society: The Case of the Black Panthers in Israel." *Youth and Society* 16(2): 129–52.

Bernstein, Mary. 2005. "Identity Politics." *Annual Review of Sociology* 31(1): 47–74.

Berrey, Ellen. 2015. *The Enigma of Diversity: The Language of Race and the Limits of Racial Justice*. Chicago: University of Chicago Press.

Bethell, Leslie. 1970. *The Abolition of the Brazilian Slave Trade: Britain, Brazil and the Slave Trade Question, 1807–1869*. New York: Cambridge University Press.

Bickerstaff, Jovonne J. 2012. "All Responses Are Not Created Equal." *Du Bois Review: Social Science Research on Race* 9(1): 107–31.

Bishara, Azmi. 2000. "The Arab Israeli: Considerations of a Conflicted Political Discourse." Pp. 35–70 (Hebrew) in *The Jewish-Ar: A Reader*, edited by R. Gavison and D. Hacker. Jerusalem: Israel Democracy Institute.

Bitton, Yifat. 2008. "Wishing for Discrimination? A Comparative Gaze on Categorization, Racism and the Law." *Sortuz: Oñati Journal of Emergent Socio-legal Studies* 2(1): 39–92.

———. 2011. "Mizrahis and the Law: Absence as Existence." *Mishpatim (Hebrew University Law Review)* 41(315): 455–516 (Hebrew).

———. 2012. "Finally, Our Own Brown! (?)." *Israel Law Review* 45(2): 267–89.

Bitton, Yifat, and Ella Glass. 2016. "A Woman of Valor Goes to Court: Tort Law as an Instrument of Social Change under Multiculturalist Conditions." Unpublished paper, Sha'arei Mishpatim Law College, Hod HaSharon, Israel.

Blair, Barbara. 2005. "Though Justice Sleeps: 1880–1900." Pp. 3–66 in *To Make Our World Anew: A History of African Americans from 1880*, vol. 2, edited by R. D. G. Kelley and E. Lewis. New York: Oxford University Press.

Bleich, Erik. 2003. *Race Politics in Britain and France: Ideas and Policymaking Since the 1960s*. Cambridge: Cambridge University Press.

———. 2011. *The Freedom to Be Racist? How the United States and Europe Struggle to Preserve Freedom and Combat Racism*. New York: Oxford University Press.

Bligh, Alexander. 2003. *The Israeli Palestinians: An Arab Minority in the Jewish State*. London; Portland, OR: Frank Cass.

Block, Fred, and Margaret R. Somers. 2014. *The Power of Market Fundamentalism: Karl Polanyi's Critique*. Cambridge, MA: Harvard University Press.

Blumer, Herbert. 1958. "Race Prejudice as a Sense of Group Position." *Pacific Sociological Review* 1(1): 3–7.

Bobo, Lawrence. 1991. "Social Responsibility, Individualism, and Redistributive Policies." *Sociological Forum* 6(1): 71–92.

———. 2011. "Somewhere between Jim Crow and Post-Racialism: Reflections on the Racial Divide in America Today." *Daedalus* 140(2): 11–36.

———. 2012. "An American Conundrum: Race, Sociology and the African-American Road to Citizenship." Pp. 20–70 in *The Oxford Handbook of African American Citizenship, 1865–Present*, edited by H. L. Gates Jr., C. Steele, L. D. Bobo, M. C. Dawson, G. Jaynes, L. Crooms-Robinson, and L. Darling-Hammond. New York: Oxford University Press.

Bobo, Lawrence D., and Camille Z. Charles. 2009. "Race in the American Mind: From the Moynihan Report to the Obama Candidacy." *Annals of the American Academy of Political and Social Science* 621: 243–59.

Bobo, Lawrence, Camille Z. Charles, Maria Krysan, and Alicia D. Simmons. 2012. "The Real Record on Racial Attitudes." Pp. 38–83 in *Social Trends in the United States 1972–2008: Evidence from the General Social Survey*, edited by P. V. Marsden. Princeton, NJ: Princeton University Press.

Bobo, Lawrence D., and Michael C. Dawson. 2009. "A Change Has Come: Race, Politics, and the Path to the Obama Presidency." *Du Bois Review: Social Science Research on Race* 6(1): 1–14.

Bobo, Lawrence D., and Alicia Simmons. 2009. "The Race Cues, Attitudes, and Punitiveness Survey." Unpublished manuscript, Department of Sociology, Harvard University, Cambridge, MA.

Bobo, Lawrence D., and Ryan A. Smith. 1998. "From Jim Crow Racism to Laissez-Faire Racism: The Transformation of Racial Attitudes." Pp. 182–220 in *Beyond Pluralism: The Conception of Groups and Group Identities in America*, edited by W. F. Katkin, N. Landsman, and A. Tyree. Urbana: University of Illinois Press.

Boltanski, Luc. 2008. "Domination Revisited: From the French Critical Sociology of the 1970s to Present-Day Pragmatic Sociology." *Graduate Faculty Philosophy Journal* 29(1): 27–70.

———. 2011. *On Critique: A Sociology of Emancipation*. Malden, MA: Polity.

Boltanski, Luc, and Laurent Thévenot. 1991. *De la justification. Les économies de la grandeur*. Paris: Gallimard.

Bonilla-Silva, Eduardo. 2010. *Racism without Racists: Color-Blind Racism and the Persistence of Racial Inequality in the United States*. Third edition. Lanham, MD: Rowman & Littlefield.

Bonilla-Silva, Eduardo, and David Dietrich. 2011. "The Sweet Enchantment of Color-Blind Racism in Obamerica." *Annals of the American Academy of Political and Social Science* 634(1): 190–206.

Bonnet, François, and Clément Théry. 2014. "Ferguson and the New Black Condition in the United States." *Books&Ideas.net*, November 24. Retrieved January 7, 2015 (http://www.booksandideas.net/Ferguson-and-the-New-Black.html).

Bouchard, Gérard. 2013. *National Myths: Constructed Pasts, Contested Presents*. New York: Routledge.

Bourdieu, Pierre. 1972. *Esquisse d'une théorie de la pratique*. Geneva: Droz.

———. 1977. *Outline of a Theory of Practice*. New York: Cambridge University Press.

———. 1979. *La distinction: critique sociale du jugement*. Paris: Les Editions de Minuit.

―――. 1984. *Distinction: A Social Critique of the Judgment of Taste*. Translated by Richard Nice. Cambridge, MA: Harvard University Press.

Bourdieu, Pierre, and Loïc Wacquant. 1999. "On the Cunning of Imperialist Reason." *Theory, Culture & Society* 16(1): 41–58.

―――. 2001a. "Neoliberal Speak: Notes on the New Planetary Vulgate." *Radical Philosophy* 105: 2–5.

―――. 2001b. "Symbolic Capital and Social Classes." *Journal of Classical Sociology* 13(2): 292–302.

Branscombe, Nyla R., and Naomi Ellemers. 1998. "Coping with Group-Based Discrimination: Individualist versus Group-Level Strategies." Pp. 244–67 in *Prejudice: The Target's Perspective*, edited by J. K. Swim and C. Stangor. San Diego, CA: Academic Press.

BRASIL. 1989. "Lei 7716, 1989. Artigos 1 a 22." Retrieved December 3, 2015 (http://www.planalto.gov.br/ccivil_03/LEIS/L7716.htm).

―――. 2011. *Censo Demográfico—Características da População e dos domicílios: resultados do universo*. Rio de Janeiro: IBGE. Retrieved December 3, 2015 (http://www.sidra.ibge.gov.br/cd/defaultcd2010.asp?o=4&i=P).

Bresser-Pereira, Luiz Carlos. 2009. *From Old to New Developmentalism in Latin America*. Escola de Economia de São Paulo, Getulio Vargas Foundation (Brazil). Retrieved March 18, 2015 (https://ideas.repec.org/p/fgv/eesptd/193.html).

Bresser-Pereira, Luiz Carlos, and Daniela Theuer. 2012. "Um Estado novo-desenvolvimentista na América Latina?" *Economia e Sociedade* 21(Número especial): 811–29.

Brint, Steven, and Kristopher Proctor. 2011. "Middle-Class Respectability in Twenty-First-Century America: Work and Lifestyle in the Professional-Managerial Stratum." Pp. 462–90 in *Thrift and Thriving in America: Capitalism and Moral Order from the Puritans to the Present*, edited by J. J. Yates and J. D. Hunter. New York: Oxford University Press.

Brock, Gillian, and Harry Brighouse, eds. 2005. *The Political Philosophy of Cosmopolitanism*. Cambridge; New York: Cambridge University Press.

Bröer, Christian, and Jan Willem Duyvendak. 2009. "Discursive Opportunities, Feeling Rules, and the Rise of Protests against Aircraft Noise." *Mobilization: An International Quarterly* 14(3): 337–56.

Brondolo, Elizabeth, Nisha Brady ver Halen, Melissa Pencille, Danielle Beatty, and Richard J. Contrada. 2009. "Coping with Racism: A Selective Review of the Literature and a Theoretical and Methodological Critique." *Journal of Behavioral Medicine* 32(1): 64–88.

Bronshtein, Viki. 2015. "The Auto Repair Center as a Protected Space? The Relations between Jewish and Arab Workers at the Auto Repair Center and Their Worlds of Meanings." MA Thesis, Department of Sociology and Anthropology, Tel Aviv University, Tel Aviv.

Brooks, Roy L. 2009. *Racial Justice in the Age of Obama*. Princeton, NJ: Princeton University Press.

Brown, Eric S. 2013. *The Black Professional Middle Class: Race, Class, and Community in the Post-Civil Rights Era*. New York: Routledge.

Brown, Wendy. 1995. *States of Injury: Power and Freedom in Late Modernity*. Princeton, NJ: Princeton University Press.

Brubaker, Rogers. 1996. *Nationalism Reframed: Nationhood and the National Question in the New Europe*. Cambridge: Cambridge University Press.

―――. 2004. *Ethnicity without Groups*. Cambridge, MA: Harvard University Press.

―――. 2009. "Ethnicity, Race, and Nationalism." *Annual Review of Sociology* 35(1): 21–42.

―――. 2012. "Principles of Vision and Division and Cohort Succession: Macro-Cognitive and Demographic Perspectives on Social Change." Paper presented to the Successful Societies Research Program, Canadian Institute for Advanced Research, Toronto, Canada, May 12, 2012.

―――. 2014. "Beyond Ethnicity." *Ethnic and Racial Studies* 37(5): 804–8.

Brubaker, Rogers, and Frederick Cooper. 2000. "Beyond 'Identity.'" *Theory and Society* 29: 1–47.

Brubaker, Rogers, Margit Feischmidt, Jon Fox, and Liana Grancea. 2006. *Nationalist Politics and Everyday Ethnicity in a Transylvanian Town*. Princeton, NJ: Princeton University Press.

Bueno, Natália Salgado, and Fabrício Mendes Fialho. 2009. "Race, Resources, and Political Participation in a Brazilian City." *Latin American Research Review* 44(2): 59–83.

Bullock, Heather E. 2008. "Justifying Inequality: A Social Psychological Analysis of Beliefs about Poverty and the Poor." Pp. 52–75 in *The Colors of Poverty: Why Racial and Ethnic Disparities Persist*, edited by A. C. Lin and D. R. Harris. New York: Russell Sage Foundation.

Burdick, John. 1998. *Blessed Anastácia: Women, Race, and Popular Christianity in Brazil*. New York: Routledge.

Butsch, Richard. 2005. "Five Decades and Three Hundred Sitcoms about Class and Gender." Pp. 111–35 in *Thinking Outside the Box: A Contemporary Television Genre Reader*, edited by G. R. Edgerton and B. G. Rose. Lexington: University Press of Kentucky.

Caldwell, Kia Lilly. 2007. *Negras in Brazil: Re-envisioning Black Women, Citizenship, and the Politics of Identity*. New Brunswick, NJ: Rutgers University Press.

Campos, Luiz Augusto, and Carlos Machado. 2015. "A cor dos eleitos: determinantes da sub-representação política dos não brancos no Brasil." *Revista Brasileira de Ciência Política* (16): 121–51.

Cano, Ignacio. 1997. *The Use of Lethal Force by Police in Rio de Janeiro*. Rio de Janeiro: ISER.

———. 2000. *Racial Bias in Lethal Police Action in Brazil*. Rio de Janeiro: ISER.

Caren, Neal, Raj Andrew Ghoshal, and Vanesa Ribas. 2011. "A Social Movement Generation: Cohort and Period Trends in Protest Attendance and Petition Signing." *American Sociological Review* 76(1): 125–51.

Carmi, Tomer, and Elad Keren. 2010. "Club Selectivity in the Courts." Retrieved March 15, 2015 (http://www.academics.co.il/Articles/Article16042.aspx).

Carter, Prudence L. 2005. *Keepin' It Real: School Success beyond Black and White*. Oxford; New York: Oxford University Press.

———. 2012. *Stubborn Roots: Race, Culture and Inequality in US and South African Schools*. Oxford: Oxford University Press.

Cartwright, Nancy. 2004. "From Causation to Explanation and Back." Pp. 230–45 in *The Future for Philosophy*, edited by B. Leiter. New York: Oxford University Press.

Carvalho, Bruno. 2013. *Porous City: A Cultural History of Rio de Janeiro (from the 1810s Onward)*. Liverpool: Liverpool University Press.

Carvalho, José Alberto Magno de, Charles H. Wood, and Flávia Cristina Drumond Andrade. 2004. "Estimating the Stability of Census-Based Racial/Ethnic Classifications: The Case of Brazil." *Population Studies* 58(3): 331–43.

Castoriadis, Cornelius. 1987. *The Imaginary Institution of Society*. London: Polity Press.

Central Bureau of Statistics. 2014. *Statistical Abstract of Israel 2014-No.65*. Jerusalem: Central Bureau of Statistics (Israel).

Chandler, Michael J., and Christopher Lalonde. 1998. "Cultural Continuity as a Hedge against Suicide in Canada's First Nations." *Transcultural Psychiatry* 35(2): 191–219.

Charles, Camille Zubrinsky. 2000. "Neighborhood Racial-Composition Preferences: Evidence from a Multiethnic Metropolis." *Social Problems* 47(3): 379–407.

Cherlin, Andrew J. 2014. *Labor's Love Lost: The Rise and Fall of the Working-Class Family in America*. New York: Russell Sage Foundation.

Choo, Hae Yeon, and Myra Marx Ferree. 2010. "Practicing Intersectionality in Sociological Research: A Critical Analysis of Inclusions, Interactions, and Institutions in the Study of Inequalities." *Sociological Theory* 28(2): 129–49.

Cicalo, André. 2012. *Urban Encounters: Affirmative Action and Black Identities in Brazil*. New York: Palgrave Macmillan.

Clair, Matthew. 2016. "The Social Dimensions of Stigma." Unpublished paper, Department of Sociology, Harvard University, Cambridge, MA.

Clair, Matthew, Caitlin Daniel, and Michèle Lamont. 2015. "Destigmatization and Health: The Role of Culture." Plenary paper presented at the Workshop on Consumption and Social Change, Tellus Institute, Boston, October 8, 2015.

———. 2016. "Destigmatization and Health: Cultural Constructions and the Long-Term Reduction of Stigma." *Social Science & Medicine* (forthcoming).

Clair, Matthew, and Jeffrey S. Denis. 2015. "Sociology of Racism." Pp. 857–863 in *International Encyclopedia of the Social and Behavioral Sciences*, edited by J. D. Wright. New York: Elsevier.

Cobb, Jelani. 2014. "Talking Openly about Obama and Race." *New Yorker*, July 15. Retrieved December 15, 2014 (http://www.newyorker.com/news/daily-comment/talking-openly-about -obama-and-race).

Cohen, Cathy J. 2010. *Democracy Remixed: Black Youth and the Future of American Politics*. New York: Oxford University Press.

Cohen, Lizabeth. 2003. *A Consumers' Republic: The Politics of Mass Consumption in Postwar America*. New York: Vintage Books.

Cohen, Yinon. 2015. "The Politics of Spatial Inequalities in Israel." *Israeli Sociology (Hebrew)* 17(1): 7–31.

Cohen, Yinon, Yitchak Haberfeld, and Tali Kristal. 2007. "Ethnicity and Mixed Ethnicity: Educational Gaps among Israeli-Born Jews." *Ethnic and Racial Studies* 30(5): 896–917.

Collins, Patricia Hill. 1990. *Black Feminist Thought: Knowledge, Consciousness, and the Politics of Employment*. New York and London: Routledge.

———. 2005. *Black Sexual Politics: African Americans, Gender, and the New Racism*. New York: Routledge.

Connor, Walker. 1993. *Ethnonationalism*. Princeton, NJ: Princeton University Press.

Conrad, Robert. 1972. *The Destruction of Brazilian Slavery, 1850–1888*. Berkeley: University of California Press.

Cooper, Frederick. 1996. "Race, Ideology, and the Perils of Comparative History." *American Historical Review* 101(4): 1122–38.

Cornell, Stephen Ellicott, and Douglas Hartmann. 1998. *Ethnicity and Race: Making Identities in a Changing World*. First edition. Thousand Oaks, CA: Pine Forge Press.

Costa, Haroldo. 1982. *Fala, Crioulo: depoimentos*. Rio de Janeiro: Editora Record.

Costa, Sérgio. 2001. "A mestiçagem e seus contrários: etnicidade e nacionalidade no Brasil contemporâneo." *Tempo Social* 13(1): 143–58.

Costa Pinto, Luís Aguiar da. 1952. *O Negro no Rio de Janeiro: relações de raça numa sociedade em mudança*. Rio de Janeiro: UFRJ.

Covin, David. 2006. *The Unified Black Movement in Brazil, 1978–2002*. Jefferson, NC: McFarland.

Crespo, Regina Aída. 2003. "Gilberto Freyre e suas relações com o universo cultural hispânico." Pp. 181–204 in *Gilberto Freyre em quatro tempos*, edited by E. Kosminsky, C. Lépine, and F. Peixoto. São Paulo: UNESP.

Curtin, Philip D. 1969. *The Atlantic Slave Trade: A Census*. Madison: University of Wisconsin Press.

da Costa Neves, Paulo Sérgio. 2009. "Les discriminations positives dans une perspective comparée. Les cas brésilien et français." *Hommes et migrations. Revue française de référence sur les dynamiques migratoires* (1281): 92–101.

Dagan-Buzaglo, Noga. 2008. *Non-Discriminatory Hiring Practices in Israel towards Arab Citizens, Ethiopian Israelis and New Immigrants from Bukhara and the Caucasus*. Tel Aviv: Adva Center.

Dahan Kalev, Henriette. 1999. "Patterns of Oppression in Israel: The Case of the Wadi Salib Rebels." *Theory and Criticism* 12–13: 31–44.

Dahan, Momi. 2013. "Has the Melting Pot Succeeded in the Economics Field?" *Economic Quarterly* 60: 107–52.

Daniel, Caitlin. 2015. "Changing Childrearing Beliefs among Indigenous Rural-to-Urban Migrants in El Alto, Bolivia." *Sociological Forum* 30(4): 949–70.

Daniel, G. Reginald. 2006. *Race and Multiraciality in Brazil and the United States: Converging Paths?* University Park: Pennsylvania State University Press.

Datafolha. 1995. "Dataset: Racismo Cordial." Retrieved at Consorcio de Informações Sociais da Universidade de São Paulo (USP).

———. 2008. "Dataset: Racismo Confrontado." Retrieved at Consorcio de Informações Sociais da Universidade de São Paulo (USP).

David, M. B. 2014. "Study Finds White Americans Believe They Experience More Racism Than African Americans." *Political Blind Spot*. Retrieved January 3, 2015 (http://politicalblind spot.com/study-finds-white-americans-believe-they-experience-more-racism-than-african -americans/).

Davis, F. James. 1991. *Who Is Black? One Nation's Definition*. University Park: Pennsylvania State University Press.

Dawson, Michael C. 1995. *Behind the Mule: Race and Class in African-American Politics*. Princeton, NJ: Princeton University Press.

———. 2001. *Black Visions: The Roots of Contemporary African-American Political Ideologies*. Chicago: University of Chicago Press.

———. 2009. "Black and Blue: Black Identity and Black Solidarity in an Era of Conservative Triumph." Pp. 175–202 in *Measuring Identity: A Guide for Social Scientists*, edited by R. Abdelal, Y. M. Herrera, A. I. Johnston, and R. McDermott. New York: Cambridge University Press.

———. 2011. *Not in Our Lifetimes: The Future of Black Politics*. Chicago: University of Chicago Press.

Degler, Carl N. 1971. *Neither Black nor White: Slavery and Race Relations in Brazil and the United States*. New York: Macmillan.

DellaPergola, Sergio. 2007. *"Sephardic and Oriental" Jews in Israel and Western Countries: Migration, Social Changes, and Identification*. Jerusalem: Avraham Harman Institute of Contemporary Jewry.

Demo, David H., and Michael Hughes. 1990. "Socialization and Racial Identity among Black Americans." *Social Psychology Quarterly* 53(4): 364–74.

DeNavas-Walt, Carmen, and Bernadette D. Proctor. 2014. *Income and Poverty in the United States: 2013*. US Census Bureau. (http://www.census.gov/content/dam/Census/library/publications /2014/demo/p60-249.pdf).

DeNavas-Walt, Carmen, Bernadette D. Proctor, and Jessica C. Smith. 2013. *Income, Poverty, and Health Insurance Coverage in the United States: 2012*. US Census Bureau. (https://www.census .gov/prod/2013pubs/p60-245.pdf).

Denis, Jeffrey S. 2012. "Transforming Meanings and Group Positions: Tactics and Framing in Anishinaabe-White Relations in Northwestern Ontario, Canada." *Ethnic and Racial Studies* 35(3): 453–70.

———. 2015. "Contact Theory in a Small-Town Settler-Colonial Context: The Reproduction of Prejudice in Indigenous-White Canadian Relations." *American Sociological Review* 80(1): 218–42.

Desmond, Matthew, and Mustafa Emirbayer. 2009. "What Is Racial Domination?" *Du Bois Review: Social Science Research on Race* 6(2): 335–55.

de Souza, Amaury. 1971. "Raça e política no Brasil Urbano." *RAE-Revista de Administração de Empresas* 11(4): 61–70.

de Tocqueville, Alexis. 2004. *Democracy in America*. New York: Library of America.

Dhingra, Pawan. 2012. *Life behind the Lobby: Indian American Motel Owners and the American Dream*. Stanford, CA: Stanford University Press.

Diniz, Eli, ed. 2007. *Globalização, estado e desenvolvimento: dilemas do Brasil no novo milênio*. Rio de Janeiro: FGV Editora.

Diniz, Eli, and Renato Boschi. 2007. *A difícil rota do desenvolvimento: empresários e a agenda pós-neoliberal*. Belo Horizonte: Editora UFMG.

DiTomasso, Nancy. 2013. *The American Non-dilemma: Racial Inequality without Racism*. New York: Russell Sage Foundation.

Dobbin, Frank. 2009. *Inventing Equal Opportunity*. Princeton, NJ: Princeton University Press.

Domingues, Petrônio. 2007. "Movimento Negro Brasileiro: alguns apontamentos históricos." *Revista Tempo* 12(23): 100–122.

Douglas, Mary. 1966. *Purity and Danger: An Analysis of Concepts of Pollution and Taboo*. London: Routledge and Kegan Paul.

Drake, St. Clair, and Horace R. Cayton. 1945. *Black Metropolis: A Study of Negro Life in a Northern City*. Chicago: University of Chicago Press.

Du Bois, W. E. B. 1899. *The Philadelphia Negro: A Social Study*. Philadelphia, PA: University of Pennsylvania Press.

———. 1935. *Black Reconstruction: An Essay toward a History of the Part Which Black Folk Played in the Attempt to Reconstruct Democracy in America, 1860–1880*. New York: Russell & Russell.

Duckworth, Angela L., Christopher Peterson, Michael D. Matthews, and Dennis R. Kelly. 2007. "Grit: Perseverance and Passion for Long-Term Goals." *Journal of Personality and Social Psychology* 92(6): 1087–1101.

Duvoux, Nicolas. 2014. "La philanthropie contre la pauvreté urbaine. Étude de cas à Boston." *Revue française des affaires sociales* 1(1): 144–68.

Edgell, Penny, Joseph Gerteis, and Douglas Hartmann. 2006. "Atheists As 'Other': Moral Boundaries and Cultural Membership in American Society." *American Sociological Review* 71(2): 211–34.

Edin, Kathryn, and Maria J. Kefalas. 2005. *Promises I Can Keep: Why Poor Women Put Motherhood before Marriage*. Berkeley: University of California Press.

Eliasoph, Nina. 1998. *Avoiding Politics: How Americans Produce Apathy in Everyday Life*. Cambridge: Cambridge University Press.

Ellison, Ralph. 1952. *Invisible Man*. New York: Vintage International.

Emirbayer, Mustafa, and Matthew Desmond. 2015. *The Racial Order*. Chicago: University of Chicago Press.

Entman, Robert M., and Andrew Rojecki. 2000. *The Black Image in the White Mind: Media and Race in America*. Chicago: University of Chicago Press.

Essed, Philomena. 1991. *Understanding Everyday Racism: An Interdisciplinary Theory*. Newbury Park: Sage Publications.

Evans, Peter, and William H. Sewell. 2013. "Neoliberalism: Policy Regimes, International Regimes, and Social Effects." Pp. 35–68 in *Social Resilience in the Neoliberal Era*, edited by P. A. Hall and M. Lamont. New York: Cambridge University Press.

Ewick, Patricia, and Susan Silbey. 2003. "Narrating Social Structure: Stories of Resistance to Legal Authority." *American Journal of Sociology* 108(6): 1328–72.

Eyal, Gil. 2006. *The Disenchantment of the Orient: Expertise in Arab Affairs and the Israeli State*. Stanford, CA: Stanford University Press.

Falah, Ghazi. 1996. "Living Together Apart: Residential Segregation in Mixed Arab-Jewish Cities in Israel." *Urban Studies* 33(6): 823–57.

Falleti, Tulia G., and Julia F. Lynch. 2009. "Context and Causal Mechanisms in Political Analysis." *Comparative Political Studies* 42(9): 1143–66.

Favell, Adrian. 1998. *Philosophies of Integration: Immigration and the Idea of Citizenship in France and Britain*. Basingstoke: Palgrave Macmillan.

Feagin, Joe R. 2006. *Systemic Racism: A Theory of Oppression*. Kindle Edition: Routledge.

Feagin, Joe R., and Sean Elias. 2013. "Rethinking Racial Formation Theory: A Systemic Racism Critique." *Ethnic and Racial Studies* 36(6): 931–60.

Feagin, Joe R., and Melvin P. Sikes. 1994. *Living with Racism: The Black Middle-Class Experience*. Boston: Beacon Press.

Fernandes, Florestan. 1969. *The Negro in Brazilian Society*. New York: Columbia University Press.

Figueiredo, Angela. 2002. *Novas elites de cor: estudo sobre os profissionais liberais negros de Salvador*. São Paulo: Annablume.

Fischer, Mary J. 2011. "Interracial Contact and Changes in the Racial Attitudes of White College Students." *Social Psychology of Education* 14(4): 547–74.

Fischer, Shlomo. 2010. "Judaism and Global Trends: Some Contemporary Developments." Pp. 315–50 in *World Religions and Multiculturalism: A Dialectic Relation*, edited by E. Ben-Raphael and Y. Sternberg. Boston: Brill Academic Press.

Fiske, Susan T., Amy J. C. Cuddy, Peter Glick, and Jun Xu. 2002. "A Model of (Often Mixed) Stereotype Content: Competence and Warmth Respectively Follow from Perceived Status and Competition." *Journal of Personality and Social Psychology* 82(6): 878–902.

Fleming, Crystal M. 2012. "White Cruelty or Republican Sins? Competing Frames of Stigma Reversal in French Commemorations of Slavery." *Ethnic and Racial Studies* 35(3): 488–505.

Fleming, Crystal M., Michèle Lamont, and Jessica Welburn. 2012. "Responding to Stigmatization and Gaining Recognition: Evidence from Middle Class and Working Class African Americans." *Ethnic and Racial Studies* 35: 400–417.

Foot-Hardmann, Francisco, and Victor Leonardi. 1988. *História da indústria e do trabalho no Brasil*. São Paulo: Ática.

Forsyth, Donelson R. 2006. *Group Dynamics*. Fourth edition. Belmont, CA: Thomson/Wadsworth.

Fraser, Nancy. 2000. "Rethinking Recognition." *New Left Review* (3): 107–20.

Fraser, Nancy, and Axel Honneth. 2003. *Redistribution or Recognition? A Political-Philosophical Exchange*. London: Verso.

Fredrickson, George M. 1988. *The Arrogance of Race: Historical Perspectives on Slavery, Racism, and Social Inequity*. Middletown, CT: Wesleyan.

Frey, William H. 2011. *The New Metropolitan Minority Map: Regional Shifts in Hispanics, Asians, and Blacks from Census 2010*. Washington, DC: Brookings Institution. Retrieved December 15, 2014 (http://www.brookings.edu/research/papers/2011/08/31-census-race-frey).

Freyre, Gilberto. 1933. *The Masters and the Slaves (Casa-Grande & Senzala): A Study in the Development of Brazilian Civilization*. Second English language edition. New York: Knopf.

Friedman, Menachem. 1991. *The Haredi (Ultra-Orthodox) Society: Sources, Trends and Processes*. Jerusalem: Jerusalem Institute for Israel Studies (Hebrew).

Fry, Peter, Yvonne Maggie, Marcos Chor Maio, Simone Monteiro, and Ricardo Ventura dos Santos. 2007. *Divisões perigosas: políticas raciais no Brasil contemporâneo*. Rio de Janeiro: Civilização Brasileira.

Gans, H. 1999. "The Possibility of a New Racial Hierarchy in the Twenty-First Century United States." Pp. 371–90 in *The Cultural Territories of Race: Black and White Boundaries*; edited by M. Lamont. Chicago and New York: University of Chicago Press and Russell Sage Foundation.

Garces, Liliana M. 2012. "Racial Diversity, Legitimacy, and the Citizenry: The Impact of Affirmative Action Bans on Graduate School Enrollment." *Review of Higher Education* 36(1): 93–132.

Garcia Lopes, Felix, and Fábio de Sá e Silva. 2014. *Valores e Estrutura Social no Brasil*. Brasilia: IPEA. Retrieved October 5, 2015 (http://www.ipea.gov.br/portal/images/stories/pdfs/tds/td_1946.pdf).

Gelman, Andrew, and Jennifer Hill. 2006. *Data Analysis Using Regression and Multilevel/Hierarchical Models*. Cambridge: Cambridge University Press.

Ghanem, As'ad. 2001. *The Palestinian-Arab Minority in Israel, 1948–2000: A Political Study*. Albany: State University of New York Press.

Ghanim, Honaida. 2009. *Reinventing the Nation: Palestinian Intellectuals in Israel*. Jerusalem: Hebrew University Magnes Press and Eshkolot Library, Levi Eshkol Institute (Hebrew).

Gharrah, Ramsees, ed. 2013. *Arab Society in Israel: Population, Society, Economy*. Jerusalem: Van Leer Institute (Hebrew).

Gieryn, Thomas F. 1983. "Boundary-Work and the Demarcation of Science from Non-science: Strains and Interests in Professional Ideologies of Scientists." *American Sociological Review* 48(6): 781–95.

Gilens, Martin. 1996. "Race and Poverty in America: Public Misperceptions and the American News Media." *Public Opinion Quarterly* 60(4): 515–41.

———. 1999. *Why Americans Hate Welfare: Race, Media, and the Politics of Antipoverty Policy*. Chicago: University of Chicago Press.

Gilroy, Paul. 1993. *The Black Atlantic: Modernity and Double Consciousness*. Cambridge, MA: Harvard University Press.

Glassberg, David. 2001. *Sense of History: The Place of the Past in American Life*. Boston: University of Massachusetts Press.

Goffman, Erving. 1963. *Stigma: Notes on the Management of Spoiled Identity*. Englewood Cliffs, NJ: Prentice Hall.

Goldberg, David Theo. 2008. *The Threat of Race: Reflections on Racial Neoliberalism*. Malden, MA: Wiley-Blackwell.

Goodman, Yehuda C. 2008. "Citizenship, Modernity and Faith in the Nation-State: Racialization and De-racialization in the Conversion of Russians and Ethiopians in Israel." Pp. 381–415 in *Racism in Israel*, edited by Y. Shenhav and Y. Yonah. Jerusalem and Tel Aviv: Van Leer Jerusalem Institute and Hakibbutz Hameuchad Publishing House (Hebrew).

Goodman, Yehuda C., and Nissim Mizrachi. 2008. "'The Holocaust Does Not Belong to European Jews Alone': The Differential Use of Memory Techniques in Israeli High Schools." *American Ethnologist* 35: 95–114.

Graham, Richard. 1970. "Brazilian Slavery Re-examined: A Review Article." *Journal of Social History* 3(4): 431–53.

Granovetter, Mark S. 1973. "The Strength of Weak Ties." *American Journal of Sociology* 78(6): 1360–80.

Greenwald, Anthony G., Debbie E. McGhee, and Jordan L. K. Schwartz. 1998. "Measuring Individual Differences in Implicit Cognition: The Implicit Association Test." *Journal of Personality and Social Psychology* 74(6): 1464–80.

Grinberg, Lev Luis. 1989. *Public Activists of Histadrut and Local Authorities: The Ethnic Dimension*. Research Report 33. Jerusalem: Jerusalem Institute for Israel Studies (Hebrew).

Grossman, James R. 2005. "A Chance to Make Good: 1900–1929." Pp. 67–130 in *To Make Our World Anew: A History of African Americans from 1880*, edited by R. D. G. Kelley and E. Lewis. New York: Oxford University Press.

Guetzkow, Joshua, and Idit Fast. 2016. "How Symbolic Boundaries Shape the Experience of Social Exclusion: A Case Comparison of Arab Palestinian Citizens and Ethiopian Jews in Israel." *American Behavioral Scientist* 59(15): 1–22.

Guimarães, Antônio Sérgio Alfredo. 1998. *Preconceito e Discriminação: queixas de ofensas e tratamento desigual dos negros no brasil*. Salvador: Novos Toques.

———. 2000. "O insulto racial: as ofensas verbais registradas em queixas de discriminação." *Estudos Afro-Asiáticos* (38): 31–48.

———. 2001. "Democracia Racial: o ideal, o pacto, e o mito." *Novos Estudos do CEBRAP* 61: 147–62.

———. 2006. "Depois da democracia racial." *Tempo Social* 18(2): 269–87.

Gullickson, Aaron, and Florencia Torche. 2014. "Patterns of Racial and Educational Assortative Mating in Brazil." *Demography* 51(3): 835–56.

Haberfeld, Yitchak, and Yinon Cohen. 2007. "Gender, Ethnic, and National Earnings Gaps in Israel: The Role of Rising Inequality." *Social Science Research* 36(2): 654–72.

Habib, Jack, Hani Halaban-Eilat, Adar Shatz, and Yehonatan Almog. 2010. *Follow-Up on Key Indicators of the Nationwide Situation of the Ethiopian-Israeli Population.* Jerusalem: Myers-Joint-Brookdale.

Hall, Peter A., and Michèle Lamont, eds. 2013. *Social Resilience in the Neoliberal Era.* New York: Cambridge University Press.

Hamilton, Darrick, Algernon Austin, and William Darity Jr. 2011. *Whiter Jobs, Higher Wages: Occupational Segregation and the Lower Wages of Black Men.* Washington, DC: Economic Policy Institute. Retrieved December 15, 2014 (http://www.epi.org/publication/whiter_jobs_higher_wages/).

Hanafi, Sari. 2009. "Haifa and Its Refugees: The Remembered, the Forgotten and the Repressed." *Kyoto Bulletin of Islamic Area Studies* (3–1): 176–91.

Hanchard, Michael. 1994. *Orpheus and Power: The Movimento Negro of Rio de Janeiro and São Paulo, Brazil, 1945–1988.* Princeton, NJ: Princeton University Press.

———. 1999. *Racial Politics in Contemporary Brazil.* Durham, NC: Duke University Press.

Harding, David, and Peter Hepburn. 2014. "Cultural Mechanisms in Neighborhood Effects Research in the United States." *Sociologia urbana e rurale* (103): 37–73.

Harding, David, Michèle Lamont, and Mario Small, eds. 2010. "Reconsidering Culture and Poverty: Special Issue." *Annals of the American Academy of Political and Social Science.* 629: 6–27.

Harris, David R., and Jeremiah Joseph Sim. 2002. "Who Is Multiracial? Assessing the Complexity of Lived Race." *American Sociological Review* 67(4): 614.

Harris, Frederick C. 2014. "The Rise of Respectability Politics." *Dissent Magazine.* Retrieved January 3, 2015 (http://www.dissentmagazine.org/article/the-rise-of-respectability-politics).

Harris, Marvin. 1964. *Patterns of Race in the Americas.* Westport, CT: Greenwood Press.

Hasan, Manar. 2002. "The Politics of Honor: Patriarchy, the State and the Murder of Women in the Name of the Family Honor." *Journal of Israeli History* 21(2): 1–37.

Hasenbalg, Carlos Alfredo. 1979. *Discriminação e desigualdades raciais no Brasil.* Rio de Janeiro: Graal.

Hasenbalg, Carlos Alfredo, and Nelson Valle e Silva. 1988. *Estrutura social, mobilidade e raça.* São Paulo: Vértice.

———. 1999. "Notes on Racial and Political Inequality in Brazil." Pp. 154–78 in *Racial Politics in Contemporary Brazil,* edited by M. Hanchard. Durham, NC: Duke University Press.

Hasisi, Badi, Yoram Margalioth, and Liav Orgad. 2012. "Ethnic Profiling in Airport Screening: Lessons from Israel, 1968–2010." *American Law and Economics Review* 14(2): 517–60.

Hays, Sharon. 1998. *The Cultural Contradictions of Motherhood.* New Haven, CT: Yale University Press.

Hazan, Noa. 2013. "The Elasticity of the Color Line." *Cultural Dynamics* 25(1): 49–73.

Hellerstein, Judith, David Neumark, and Melissa McInerney. 2008. "Changes in Workplace Segregation in the United States between 1990 and 2000: Evidence from Matched Employer-Employee Data." Pp. 163–95 in *The Analysis of Firms and Employees: Quantitative and Qualitative Approaches,* edited by S. Bender, J. Lane, K. Shaw, F. Andersson, and T. von Wachter. Chicago: University of Chicago Press.

Hellwig, David J. 1992. *African-American Reflections on Brazil's Racial Paradise.* Philadelphia, PA: Temple University Press.

Hendels, Shuki. 2013. "The Feeling of Discrimination among Workers and Employment Seekers, and What the Public Thinks about This." Jerusalem: Ministry of Industry, Trade and Labor. Planning, Research & Economics Administration.

Heringer, Rosana, and Sonia Aguiar Lopes. 2003. "Sonhar o futuro, mudar o presente: diálogos pela inclusão racial no Brasil." Rio de Janeiro: IBASE.

Hermann, Tamar, Ella Heller, Nir Atmor, and Yuval Lebel. 2013. *The Israeli Democracy Index 2013*. Jerusalem: Israel Democracy Institute (Hebrew).

Hermann, Tamar, Ella Heller, Chanan Cohen, Gilad Be'ery, and Yuval Lebel. 2014. *The Israeli Democracy Index 2014*. Jerusalem: Israel Democracy Institute.

Hertzog, Esther. 1998. *Bureaucracy and Ethiopian Immigrants in the Absorption Centers*. Tel Aviv: Tcherikover Press.

Herzfeld, Michael. 1997. *Cultural Intimacy: Social Poetics in the Nation-State*. New York: Routledge.

Herzog, Hanna. 1984. "Ethnicity as a Product of Political Negotiation: The Case of Israel." *Ethnic and Racial Studies* 7(4): 517–33.

———. 1985. "Social Construction of Reality in Ethnic Terms: The Case of Political Ethnicity in Israel." *International Review of Modern Sociology* 15(1/2): 45–61.

———. 1990a. "Midway between Political and Cultural Ethnicity: An Analysis of the Ethnic Lists in the 1984 Elections." Pp. 87–118 in *Israel's Odd Couple: The 1984 Elections and National Unity Government*, edited by E. Daneil, H. Penniman, and S. Shmuel. Detroit, MI: Wayne State University Press.

———. 1990b. "Was It on the Agenda? The Hidden Agenda of the 1988 Campaign." Pp. 37–62 in *The Elections in Israel—1988*, edited by A. Arian and M. Shamir. Boulder: Westview Press.

———. 1995. "Penetrating the System: The Politics of Collective Identities." Pp. 81–102 in *The Elections in Israel—1992*, edited by A. Arian and M. Shamir. Albany: State University of New York Press.

———. 1999. "A Space of Their Own: Social-Civil Discourses among Palestinian Israeli Women in Peace Organizations." *Social Politics: International Studies of Gender, State and Society* 6: 344–69.

———. 2004. "'Both an Arab and a Woman': Gendered, Racialised Experiences of Female Palestinian Citizens of Israel." *Social Identities* 10(1): 53–82.

———. 2007. "Mixed Cities as a Place of Choice: The Palestinian Women's Perspective." Pp. 243–57 in *Mixed Towns, Trapped Communities: Historical Narratives, Spatial Dynamics, Gender Relations and Cultural Encounters in Ethnically Mixed Towns in Israel/Palestine*, edited by D. Montcrescu and D. Rabinowitz. Hampshire, England and Burlington, VT: Ashgate.

Herzog, Hanna, Smadar Sharon, and Inna Leykin. 2008. "Racism and the Politics of Signification: Israeli Public Discourse on Racism towards Palestinian Citizens." *Ethnic and Racial Studies* 31(6): 1091–1109.

Herzog, Hanna, and Taghreed Yahia-Younis. 2007. "Men's Bargaining with Patriarchy: The Case of Primaries within Hamula in Palestinian-Arab Communities in Israel." *Gender & Society* 21(4): 579–602.

Hever, Hannan, Yehouda Shenhav, and Pnina Motzafi-Haller, eds. 2002. *Mizrahim in Israel: A Critical Observation into Israel's Ethnicity*. Tel Aviv: Van Leer Jerusalem Institute and Hakibbutz Hameuchad Publishing House.

Higginbotham, Elizabeth, and Lynn Weber. 1992. "Moving Up with Kin and Community: Upward Social Mobility for Black and White Women." *Gender and Society* 6(3): 416–40.

Higginbotham, Evelyn Brooks. 1994. *Righteous Discontent: The Women's Movement in the Black Baptist Church, 1880–1920*. Cambridge, MA: Harvard University Press.

Hill, Nancy F. 2006. "Disentangling Ethnicity, Socioeconomic Status and Parenting: Interactions, Influences and Meaning." *Vulnerable Children and Youth Studies* 1(1): 114–24.

Hirsch, Nicole Arlette. 2014. "When Black Jokes Cross the Line: An Intersectional Analysis of Everyday African-American Humor about Race." Paper presented at the Second Annual Black Doctoral Network Conference, Philadelphia, PA, October 23–25, 2014. Retrieved January 7, 2015 (http://citation.allacademic.com/meta/p_mla_apa_research_citation/7/2/5/2/6/p725265_index.html).

Hirsch, Nicole Arlette, and Anthony Abraham Jack. 2012. "What We Face: Framing Problems in the Black Community." *Du Bois Review: Social Science Research on Race* 9(1): 133–48.

Hirschman, Albert. 1970. *Exit, Voice and Loyalty*. Cambridge, MA: Harvard University Press.

Hochberg, Gil. 2010. "To Be or Not to Be an Israeli Arab: Sayed Kashua and the Prospect of Minority Speech-Acts." *Comparative Literature* 62(1): 68–88.

Hochschild, Arlie Russell. 1983. *The Managed Heart: Commercialization of Human Feeling*. Berkeley: University of California Press.

Hochschild, Jennifer L. 1996. *Facing Up to the American Dream: Race, Class, and the Soul of the Nation*. Princeton, NJ: Princeton University Press.

Hochschild, Jennifer L., and Vesla Weaver. 2015. "Is the Significance of Race Declining in the Political Arena? Yes, and No." *Ethnic and Racial Studies* 38(8): 1250–57.

Hochschild, Jennifer L., Vesla Weaver, and Traci Burch. 2012. *Creating a New Racial Order: How Immigration, Multiracialism, Genomics, and the Young Can Remake Race in America*. Princeton, NJ: Princeton University Press.

Hodson, Randy. 2001. *Dignity at Work*. New York: Cambridge University Press.

Homel, Katrina. 2012. "Law and the Production of Ethiopian Jews as Other: Locating Alternative Discourses of Judaism in Israel's Racial-Ethnic Hierarchy." *Georgetown Journal of Law and Modern Critical Race Perspectives* 4: 51–74.

Honneth, Axel. 1995. *The Struggle for Recognition: The Moral Grammar of Social Conflicts*. London: Polity Press.

———. 2012. *The I in We: Studies in the Theory of Recognition*. Malden, MA: Polity Press.

Htun, Mala. 2004. "From 'Racial Democracy' to Affirmative Action: Changing State Policy on Race in Brazil." *Latin American Research Review* 39(1): 60–89.

Huddy, Leonie, and Nadia Khatib. 2007. "American Patriotism, National Identity, and Political Involvement." *American Journal of Political Science* 51(1): 63–77.

Hughes, Diane, James Rodriguez, Emilie P. Smith, Deborah J. Johnson, Howard C. Stevenson, and Paul Spicer. 2006. "Parents' Ethnic-Racial Socialization Practices: A Review of Research and Directions for Future Study." *Developmental Psychology* 42(5): 747–70.

Hughey, Matthew W. 2015. "We've Been Framed! A Focus on Identity and Interaction for a Better Vision of Racialized Social Movements." *Sociology of Race and Ethnicity* 1(1): 137–52.

Hunt, Matthew O. 1996. "The Individual, Society, or Both? A Comparison of Black, Latino, and White Beliefs about the Causes of Poverty." *Social Forces* 75(1): 293–322.

———. 2004. "Race/Ethnicity and Beliefs about Wealth and Poverty." *Social Science Quarterly* 85(3): 827–53.

———. 2007. "African American, Hispanic, and White Beliefs about Black/White Inequality, 1977–2004." *American Sociological Review* 72(3): 390–415.

Hwang, Jackelyn. 2016. "The Social Construction of a Gentrifying Neighborhood: Reifying and Redefining Identity and Boundaries in Inequality." *Urban Affairs Review* 52(1): 98–128.

IBGE (Instituto Brasileiro de Geografia e Estatística). 2011. *Características étnico-raciais da população*. Rio de Janeiro: IBGE.

Illouz, Eva. 2008. *Saving the Modern Soul: Therapy, Emotions, and the Culture of Self-Help*. Berkeley: University of California Press.

Illuz-Eilon, Haim. 2011. *Summary of Activity 2010*. Jerusalem: Prisoners' Rehabilitation Authority.

Israel Central Bureau of Statistics. 2013. "Localities, Population and Density per Km, by Metropolitan Area and Selected Localities." *Statistical Abstract of Israel* 64: 161–63. Retrieved June 3, 2015 (http://www1.cbs.gov.il/reader/shnaton/templ_shnaton_e.html?num_tab=st02_25&CYear=2013).

Israel State Comptroller's Report. 2013. Retrieved June 3, 2015 (https://www.friendsofethiopianjews.org/comptroller.html).

Izraeli, Dafna. 2000. "The Paradox of Affirmative Action for Women Directors in Israel." Pp. 75–96 in *Women on Corporate Boards of Directors: International Challenges and Opportunities*, edited by R. J. Burke and M. C. Mattis. Boston: Kluwer Academic.

Jackall, Robert. 2010. *Moral Mazes: The World of Corporate Managers*. New York: Oxford University Press.

Jackson, Brandon A., and Adia Harvey Wingfield. 2013. "Getting Angry to Get Ahead: Black College Men, Emotional Performance, and Encouraging Respectable Masculinity." *Symbolic Interaction* 36(3): 275–92.

Jamal, Amal. 2007. "Strategies of Minority Struggle for Equality in Ethnic States: Arab Politics in Israel." *Citizenship Studies* 11(3): 263–82.

———. 2008. "The Political Ethos of Palestinian Citizens of Israel: Critical Reading in the Future Vision Documents." *Israel Studies Forum* 23(2): 3–28.

———. 2009. *The Arab Public Sphere in Israel: Media Space and Cultural Resistance*. Bloomington: Indiana University Press.

Jasper, James M. 2010. "Strategic Marginalizations, Emotional Marginalities: The Dilemma of Stigmatized Identities." Pp. 29–37 in *Surviving against Odds: The Marginalized in a Globalizing World*, edited by D. K. SinghaRoy. New Delhi: Manohar Publishers. Retrieved March 23, 2015 (http://www.jamesmjasper.org/files/uncorrected_proofs.pdf).

———. 2014. *Protest: A Cultural Introduction to Social Movements*. Hoboken, NJ: John Wiley & Sons.

Jenkins, R. 1996. *Social Identity*. London: Routledge.

Jenson, Jane, and Ron Levi. 2013. "Narratives and Regimes of Social and Human Rights: The Jack Pines of the Neoliberal Era." Pp. 69–98 in *Social Resilience in the Age of Neoliberalism*, edited by P. A. Hall and M. Lamont. New York: Cambridge University Press.

Johnston, Josee, and Shyon Baumann. 2010. *Foodies: Democracy and Distinction in the Gourmet Foodscape*. New York: Routledge.

Jones, Edward E., Robert A. Scott, and Hazel Markus. 1984. *Social Stigma: The Psychology of Marked Relationships*. New York: W. H. Freeman & Company.

Jones, Nicholas A., and Jungmiwha Bullock. 2012. *The Two or More Races Population: 2010*. Washington, DC: United States Census Bureau.

Joppke, Christian. 2010. *Citizenship and Immigration*. Cambridge: Polity.

Joseph, Tiffany D. 2013. "How Does Racial Democracy Exist in Brazil? Perceptions from Brazilians in Governador Valadares, Minas Gerais." *Ethnic and Racial Studies* 36(10): 1524–43.

———. 2015. *Race on the Move: Brazilian Migrants and the Global Reconstruction of Race*. Stanford, CA: Stanford University Press.

Kanaaneh, Rhoda Ann. 2002. *Birthing the Nation: Strategies of Palestinian Women in Israel*. Berkeley: University of California Press.

Kanaaneh, Rhoda Ann, and Isis Nusair, eds. 2010. *Displaced at Home: Ethnicity and Gender among Palestinians in Israel*. Albany: State University of New York Press.

Kanter, Rosabeth Moss. 1977a. *Men and Women of the Corporation*. New York: Basic Books.

———. 1977b. "Some Effects of Proportions on Group Life: Skewed Sex Ratios and Responses to Token Women." *American Journal of Sociology* 82(5): 965–90.

Kaplan, Steven. 1988. "The Beta Israel and the Rabbanate: Law, Ritual and Politics." *Social Science Information* 27(3): 357–70.

———. 1997. "Everyday Resistance and the Study of Ethiopian Jews." *Theory and Criticism: An Israeli Forum* 10: 163–67 (Hebrew).

Kaplan, Steven, and Chaim Rosen. 1993. "Ethiopian Immigrants in Israel: Between Preservation of Culture and Invention of Tradition." *Jewish Journal of Sociology* 35(1): 35–48.

Kaplan, Steven, and Hagar Salamon. 2004. "Ethiopian Jews in Israel: A Part of the People or Apart from the People?" Pp. 118–48 in *Jews in Israel: Contemporary Social and Cultural Patterns*, edited by U. Rebhun and C. I. Waxman. Hanover: Brandeis University Press.

Kasinitz, Philip, John H. Mollenkopf, Mary C. Waters, and Jennifer Holdaway. 2008. *Inheriting the City: The Children of Immigrants Come of Age*. New York and Cambridge, MA: Russell Sage Foundation and Harvard University Press.

Katz-Gerro, Tally, Sharon Raz, and Meir Yaish. 2007. "Class, Status and the Intergenerational Transmission of Musical Tastes in Israel." *Poetics* 35(2): 152–67.

Kefalas, Maria J. 2003. *Working-Class Heroes: Protecting Home, Community, and Nation in a Chicago Neighborhood*. Berkeley: University of California Press.

Keidar, Noga. 2012. "Ethnic Boundary Creation in an Ethno-national Social Based Context: Examination of Residential Segregation Processes in Israel, 1961–2008." MA Thesis, Hebrew University of Jerusalem, Jerusalem.

Keogan, Kevin. 2002. "A Sense of Place: The Politics of Immigration and the Symbolic Construction of Identity in Southern California and the New York Metropolitan Area." *Sociological Forum* 17(2): 223–53.

Khamaysi, Rassem. 2011. *Arab Society in Israel (4): Population, Society, Economy*. Tel Aviv: Van Leer Jerusalem Institute and Hakibbutz Hameuchad Publishing House.

Khazzom, Aziza. 2003. "The Great Chain of Orientalism: Jewish Identity, Stigma Management, and Ethnic Exclusion in Israel." *American Sociological Review* 68(4): 481–510.

Kimmerling, Baruch. 2001. *The End of Ashkenazi Hegemony*. Jerusalem: Keter.

———. 2004. *Immigrants, Settlers, Natives: The Israeli State and Society between Cultural Pluralism and Cultural Wars*. Tel Aviv: Am Oved (Hebrew).

Kinder, Donald R., and David O. Sears. 1981. "Prejudice and Politics: Symbolic Racism versus Racial Threats to the Good Life." *Journal of Personality and Social Psychology* 40(3): 414–31.

Kitwana, Bakari. 2002. *The Hip Hop Generation: Young Blacks and the Crisis in African American Culture*. New York: Basic Civitas Books.

Kluegel, James R. 1990. "Trends in Whites' Explanations of the Black-White Gap in Socioeconomic Status, 1977–1989." *American Sociological Review* 55(4): 512–25.

Knesset Research and Information Center. 2011. "Housing Grants to Ethiopian Families Are Conditional upon Purchasing Apartments in Specific Places Only: A Situation Report." Jerusalem: Knesset Research and Information Center.

Kochhar, Rakesh, Richard Fry, and Paul Taylor. 2011. *Wealth Gaps Rise to Record Highs between Whites, Blacks, Hispanics*. Washington, DC: Pew Research Center. Retrieved July 31, 2014 (http://www.pewsocialtrends.org/files/2011/07/SDT-Wealth-Report_7-26-11_FINAL.pdf).

Komarraju, Meera, Steven J. Karau, and Ronald R. Schmeck. 2009. "Role of the Big Five Personality Traits in Predicting College Students' Academic Motivation and Achievement." *Learning and Individual Differences* 19(1): 47–52.

Koopmans, Ruud, and Paul Statham. 2000. "Migration and Ethnic Relations as a Field of Political Contention: An Opportunity Structure Approach." Pp. 13–56 in *Challenging Immigration and Ethnic Relations Politics: Comparative European Perspectives*, edited by R. Koopmans and P. Statham. New York: Oxford University Press.

Korn, Alina. 2003. "Rates of Incarceration and Main Trends in Israeli Prisons." *Criminology and Criminal Justice* 3(1): 29–55.

Koser, Khalid. 2003. *New African Diasporas*. London: Routledge.

Krieger, Nancy. 2014. "Discrimination and Health Inequities." Pp. 66–125 in *Social Epidemiology*, edited by L. F. Berkman, I. Kawachi, and M. Glymour. New York: Oxford University Press.

Krieger, Nancy, Kevin Smith, Deepa Naishadham, Cathy Hartman, and Elizabeth M. Barbeau. 2005. "Experiences of Discrimination: Validity and Reliability of a Self-Report Measure for Population Health Research on Racism and Health." *Social Science & Medicine* 61(7): 1576–96.

Krogstad, Jens Manuel, and Richard Fry. 2014. *Public School Enrollment Disparities Exist 60 Years after Historic Desegregation Ruling*. Washington, DC: Pew Research Center. Retrieved December 15, 2014 (http://www.pewresearch.org/fact-tank/2014/05/16/public-school-enrollment-disparities-exist-60-years-after-historic-desegregation-ruling/).

Kruks, Sonia. 2001. *Retrieving Experience: Subjectivity and Recognition in Feminist Politics*. Ithaca, NY: Cornell University Press.

Krysan, Maria. 2012. "From Color Caste to Color Blind, Part III: Contemporary Era Racial Attitudes, 1976–2004." Pp. 235–78 in *The Oxford Handbook of African American Citizenship, 1865–Present*, edited by H. L. Gates Jr., C. Steele, L. D. Bobo, M. C. Dawson, G. Jaynes, L. Crooms-Robinson, and L. Darling-Hammond. New York: Oxford University Press.

Kupfer, Hanna. 2016. *Feelings and Experiences of Discrimination of Arab Israeli Workers*. Report of the Ministry of the Economy and Industry, Jerusalem.

Kymlicka, Will. 1995. *Multicultural Citizenship: A Liberal Theory of Minority Rights*. Oxford: Oxford University Press.

———. 2007. *Multicultural Odysseys: Navigating the New International Politics of Diversity*. Oxford: Oxford University Press.

Lacy, Karyn R. 2004. "Black Spaces, Black Places: Strategic Assimilation and Identity Construction in Middle-Class Suburbia." *Ethnic and Racial Studies* 27(6): 908–30.

———. 2007. *Blue-Chip Black: Race, Class, and Status in the New Black Middle Class*. Berkeley: University of California Press.

Lamont, Michèle. 1992. *Money, Morals, and Manners: The Culture of the French and the American Upper-Middle Class*. Chicago: University of Chicago Press.

———. 2000. *The Dignity of Working Men: Morality and the Boundaries of Race, Class, and Immigration*. Cambridge, MA: Harvard University Press.

Lamont, Michèle, and Christopher Bail. 2005. "Sur les frontières de la reconnaissance. Les catégories internes et externes de l'identité collective." *Revue européenne des migrations internationales* 21(Special Issue): 61–90.

Lamont, Michèle, Stefan Beljean, and Matthew Clair. 2014. "What Is Missing? Cultural Processes and Causal Pathways to Inequality." *Socio-Economic Review* 12(3): 573–608.

Lamont, Michèle, and Crystal Fleming. 2005. "Everyday Anti-racism: Competence and Religion in the Cultural Repertoire of the African-American Elite and Working Class." *Du Bois Review: Social Science Research on Race* 2: 29–43.

Lamont, Michèle, and Nathan Fosse. 2015. "Confrontational and Non-confrontational Responses to Workplace Discrimination and the Mental Health of African Americans." Unpublished manuscript, Department of Sociology, Harvard University, Cambridge, MA.

Lamont, Michèle, and Nissim Mizrachi. 2012. "Ordinary People Doing Extraordinary Things: Responses to Stigmatization in Comparative Perspective." *Ethnic and Racial Studies* 35(3): 365–81.

Lamont, Michèle, and Viràg Molnár. 2001. "How Blacks Use Consumption to Shape Their Collective Identity: Evidence from African-American Marketing Specialists." *Journal of Consumer Culture* 1: 31–45.

———. 2002. "The Study of Boundaries in the Social Sciences." *Annual Review of Sociology* 28: 167–95.

Lamont, Michèle, Ann Morning, and Margarita Mooney. 2002. "Particular Universalisms: North African Immigrants Respond to French Racism." *Ethnic and Racial Studies* 25(3): 390–414.

Lamont, Michèle, and Mario Luis Small. 2008. "How Culture Matters: Enriching Our Understanding of Poverty." Pp. 76–102 in *The Colors of Poverty: Why Racial and Ethnic Disparities Persist*, edited by D. R. Harris and A. C. Lin. New York: Russell Sage Foundation.

Lamont, Michèle, and Ann Swidler. 2014. "Methodological Pluralism and the Possibilities and Limits of Interviewing." *Qualitative Sociology* 37(2): 153–71.

Lamont, Michèle, and Laurent Thévenot. 2000. *Rethinking Comparative Cultural Sociology: Repertoires of Evaluation in France and the United States*. New York: Cambridge University Press.

Lamont, Michèle, Jessica S. Welburn, and Crystal M. Fleming. 2013. "Responses to Discrimination and Social Resilience under Neoliberalism: The United States Compared." Pp. 129–57 in *Social Resilience in the Neoliberal Age*, edited by P. A. Hall and M. Lamont. New York: Cambridge University Press.

Landry, Bart, and Kris Marsh. 2011. "The Evolution of the New Black Middle Class." *Annual Review of Sociology* 37: 373–94.

Lara, Fernandez Luiz. 2013. "Converging Income Inequality in Brazil and the United States: Some Uncomfortable Realities." *Inequalities*. Retrieved January 3, 2015 (https://inequalities blog.wordpress.com/2013/02/23/converging-income-inequality-in-brazil-and-the-united -states-some-uncomfortable-realities/).

Lareau, Annette. 2003. *Unequal Childhoods: Class, Race, and Family Life*. Berkeley: University of California Press.

Lareau, Annette, and Kimberly A. Goyette. 2014. *Choosing Homes, Choosing Schools*. New York: Russell Sage Foundation.

Lee, Jennifer, and Frank D. Bean. 2010. *The Diversity Paradox: Immigration and the Color Line in Twenty-First Century America*. New York: Russell Sage Foundation.

Lee, Jennifer, and Min Zhou. 2014. "The Success Frame and Achievement Paradox: The Costs and Consequences for Asian Americans." *Race and Social Problems* 6(1): 38–55.

———. 2015. *The Asian American Achievement Paradox*. New York: Russell Sage Foundation.

Leidner, Robin. 1993. *Fast Food, Fast Talk: Service Work and the Routinization of Everyday Life*. Berkeley: University of California Press.

Leon, Nissim. 2008. "The Secular Origins of Mizrahi Traditionalism." *Israel Studies* 13(3): 22–42.

———. 2009. *Gentle Ultra-Ortodoxy (Soft Haredi)—Religious Renewal in Oriental Jewry in Israel*. Jerusalem: Yad Ben Tzvi (Hebrew).

———. 2014. "Ethno-religious Fundamentalism and Theo-ethnocratic Politics in Israel." *Studies in Ethnicity and Nationalism* 14(1): 20–35.

Leu, Lorraine. 2014. "Deviant Geographies: Black Spaces of Cultural Expression in Early 20th-Century Rio de Janeiro." *Latin American and Caribbean Ethnic Studies* 9(2): 177–94.

Lewin-Epstein, Noah, and Moshe Semyonov. 1993. *The Arab Minority in Israel's Economy—Patterns of Ethnic Inequality*. Boulder: Westview Press.

Lichter, Michael, and Roger Waldinger. 1998. "'It Isn't All White Americans. . . .' Intergroup Conflict in the Multi-ethnic Workplace." Retrieved August 8, 2013 (http://www.sscnet.ucla .edu/soc/faculty/waldinger/articles/five.pdf).

Lieberson, Stanley. 1992. "Small *N*'s and Big Conclusions." Pp. 105–18 in *What is a Case?*, edited by C. C. Ragin and H. S. Becker. New York: Cambridge University Press.

Light, Ivan Hubert, and Carolyn Nancy Rosenstein. 1995. *Race, Ethnicity, and Entrepreneurship in Urban America*. New York: Aldine de Gruyter.

Light, Ryan, Vincent J. Roscigno, and Alexandra Kalev. 2011. "Racial Discrimination, Interpretation, and Legitimation at Work." *Annals of the American Academy of Political and Social Science* 634(1): 39–59.

Link, Bruce G., Francis T. Cullen, Elmer Struening, Patrick E. Shrout, and Bruce P. Dohrenwend. 1989. "A Modified Labeling Theory Approach to Mental Disorders: An Empirical Assessment." *American Sociological Review* 54(3): 400–423.

Link, Bruce G., and Jo C. Phelan. 2013. "Labeling and Stigma." Pp. 525–42 in *Handbook of the Sociology of Mental Health*, edited by C. S. Aneshensel, J. C. Phelan, and A. Bierman. New York: Springer.

Link, Bruce G., Elmer L. Struening, Sheree Neese-Todd, Sara Asmussen, and Jo C. Phelan. 2002. "On Describing and Seeking to Change the Experience of Stigma." *Psychiatric Rehabilitation Skills* 6(2): 201–31.

Lipset, Seymour Martin. 1979. *The First New Nation: The United States in Historical and Comparative Perspective*. New York: W. W. Norton & Company.

———. 1997. *American Exceptionalism: A Double-Edged Sword*. New York: W. W. Norton & Company.

Lipsitz, George. 2011. *How Racism Takes Place*. Philadelphia: Temple University Press.

Logan, John R. 2012. "Making a Place for Space: Spatial Thinking in Social Science." *Annual Review of Sociology* 38: 507–24.

Logan, John R., and Brian Stults. 2011. *The Persistence of Segregation in the Metropolis: New Findings from the 2010 Census*. Providence, RI: Project US2010.

Lomsky-Feder, Edna, and Tamar Rapoport. 2004. "Speaking Their Language? Identity, Home and Power Relations in Interviews with Immigrants." Pp. 329–53 in *The Autobiographic Adventure—Theory and Practice*, edited by M. H. Menna and B. Abrahao. Porto Alegre, Brazil: Edipucrs.

López-Calva, Luis Felipe, and Nora Lustig. 2010. *Declining Inequality in Latin America: A Decade of Progress?* New York: Brookings Institution Press.

Loury, Glenn C. 2003. *The Anatomy of Racial Inequality*. Cambridge, MA: Harvard University Press.

Loveman, Mara. 1999. "Comment: Is 'Race' Essential?" *American Sociological Review* 64(6): 891–98.

———. 2014. *National Colors: Racial Classification and the State in Latin America*. New York: Oxford University Press.

Loveman, Mara, Jeronimo Muniz, and Stanley Bailey. 2012. "Brazil in Black and White? Race Categories, the Census, and the Study of Inequality." *Ethnic and Racial Studies* 35(8): 1466–83.

Lustick, Ian. 1980. *Arabs in the Jewish State*. Austin: University of Texas Press.

Machado, Marta, Natália Santos, and Carolina Ferreira. 2014. "Legislação antirracista punitiva no Brasil: uma aproximação à aplicação do Direito pelos tribunais brasileiros." Presentation at Associação Nacional de Pós-Graduação e Pesquisa em Ciências Sociais (ANPOCS), Caxambú, Brazil, October 2014.

MacLeod, Jay. 1987. *Ain't No Makin' It: Leveled Aspirations in a Low-Income Neighborhood*. Boulder: Westview Press.

Macpherson, Crawford Brough. 1962. *The Political Theory of Possessive Individualism: Hobbes to Locke*. Oxford: Clarendon Press.

Maggie, Yvonne. 1992. *Medo do feitiço: relações entre magia e poder no Brasil*. Rio de Janeiro: Imprensa Nacional.

Maio, Marcos Chor. 1999. "O projeto Unesco e a agenda das relações raciais no Brasil nos anos 40 E 50." *Revista Brasileira de Ciências Sociais* 14(41): 141–58.

Major, Brenda. 1993. "From Social Inequality to Personal Entitlement: The Role of Social Comparisons, Legitimacy Appraisals, and Group Membership." Pp. 293–355 in *Advances in Experimental Social Psychology*, edited by M. P. Zanna. Waltham, MA: Elsevier.

Makkawi, Ibrahim. 2002. "Role Conflict and the Dilemma of Palestinian Teachers in Israel." *Comparative Education* 38(1): 39–52.

Mansbridge, Jane, and Katherine Flaster. 2007. "The Cultural Politics of Everyday Discourse: The Case of 'Male Chauvinist.'" *Critical Sociology* 33(4): 627–60.

Marantz, Erez Aharon, Alexandra Kalev, and Noah Lewin-Epstein. 2014. "Globally Themed Organizations as Labor Market Intermediaries: The Rise of Israeli-Palestinian Women's Employment in Retail." *Social Forces* 93(2): 595–622.

Margolin, Madison. 2015. "The Mizrahi Thorn in the Side of Israeli Left." *Forward*, September 3. Retrieved September 3, 2015 (http://forward.com/culture/320255/the-mizrahi-thorn-in-israels-leftist-side).

Markus, Hazel Rose. 2010. "Who Am I? Race, Ethnicity and Identity." Pp. 359–89 in *Doing Race: 21 Essays for the 21st Century*, edited by H. R. Markus and P. M. L. Moya. New York: W. W. Norton & Company.

Marshall, T. H. 1950. "Class, Citizenship, and Social Development." Pp. 10–14 in *Citizenship and Social Class and Other Essays*, edited by T. H. Marshall. Cambridge, MA: Harvard University Press.

Marteleto, Leticia. 2012. "Educational Inequality by Race in Brazil, 1982–2007: Structural Changes and Shifts in Racial Classification." *Demography* 49: 337–58.

Marx, Anthony. 1998. *Making Race and Nation: A Comparison of South Africa, the United States, and Brazil*. New York: Cambridge University Press.

Massey, Douglas S. 2007. *Categorically Unequal: The American Stratification System*. New York: Russell Sage Foundation.

Massey, Douglas S., Camille Z. Charles, Garvey F. Lundy, and Mary J. Fischer. 2003. *The Source of the River: The Social Origins of Freshmen at America's Selective Colleges and Universities*. Princeton, NJ: Princeton University Press.

Massey, Douglas S., and Nancy A. Denton. 1993. *American Apartheid: Segregation and the Making of the Underclass*. Cambridge, MA: Harvard University Press.

McAdam, Doug. 1988. *Freedom Summer*. New York: Oxford University Press.

McCall, Leslie. 2005. "The Complexity of Intersectionality." *Signs* 30(3): 1771–1800.

———. 2013. *The Undeserving Rich: American Beliefs about Inequality, Opportunity, and Redistribution*. Cambridge: Cambridge University Press.

McConahay, John B. 1986. "Modern Racism, Ambivalence, and the Modern Racism Scale." Pp. 91–125 in *Prejudice, Discrimination, and Racism*, edited by J. F. Dovidio and S. L. Gaertner. Orlando: Academic Press.

McIntosh, Peggy. 2007. "White Privilege: Unpacking the Invisible Knapsack." Pp. 177–82 in *Race, Class, and Gender in the United States*, edited by P. S. Rothenberg. New York: Worth Publishers.

McLafferty, Sarah, and Valerie Preston. 1992. "Spatial Mismatch and Labor Market Segmentation for African-American and Latina Women." *Economic Geography* 68: 406–31.

McLanahan, Sara S., and Irwin Garfinkel. 2012. "Fragile Families: Debates, Facts, and Solutions." Pp. 142–69 in *Marriage at the Crossroads: Law, Policy, and the Brave New World of Twenty-First-Century Families*, edited by M. Garrison and E. S. Scott. New York: Cambridge University Press.

McPherson, Miller, Lynn Smith-Lovin, and James M. Cook. 2001. "Birds of a Feather: Homophily in Social Networks." *Annual Review of Sociology* 27: 415–44.

Mellor, David. 2004. "Responses to Racism: A Taxonomy of Coping Styles Used by Aboriginal Australians." *American Journal of Orthopsychiatry* 74(1): 56–71.

Meyer, John W., John Boli, and George M. Thomas. 1987. "Ontology and Rationalization in the Western Cultural Account." Pp. 12–37 in *Institutional Structure: Constituting State, Society, and the Individual*, edited by G. M. Thomas, J. W. Meyer, F. O. Ramirez, and J. Boli. Newbury Park: Sage.

Mi'ari, Mahmoud. 1987. "Traditionalism and Political Identity of Arabs in Israel." *Journal of Asian and African Studies* 22(1–2): 33–44.

Michelman, Frank I. 1996. "Parsing 'a Right to Have Rights.'" *Constellations* 3(2): 200–208.

Mijs, Jonathan J. B., Elyas Bakhtiari, and Michèle Lamont. 2016. "Neoliberalism and Symbolic Boundaries in Europe: Global Diffusion, Local Context, Regional Variation." *Socius: Sociological Research for a Dynamic World* 2: 1–8.

Misztal, Barbara. 2013. *Trust in Modern Societies: The Search for the Bases of Social Order*. Malden, MA: John Wiley & Sons.

Mitchell, Gladys L. 2009. "Politicizing Blackness: Afro-Brazilian Color Identification and Candidate Preference." Pp. 35–48 in *Brazil's New Racial Politics*, edited by B. Reiter and G. L. Mitchell. Boulder: Lynne Rienner.

Mizrachi, Nissim. 2004. "'From Badness to Sickness': The Role of Ethnopsychology in Shaping Ethnic Hierarchies in Israel." *Social Identities* 10(2): 219–43.

———. 2011. "Beyond the Garden and the Jungle: On the Social Limits of Human Rights Discourse in Israel." *Ma'asei Mishpat* 4: 51–74 (Hebrew).

———. 2012. "On the Mismatch between Multicultural Education and Its Subjects in the Field." *British Journal of Sociology of Education* 33(2): 185–201.

————. 2014. "Translating Disability in a Muslim Community: A Case of Modular Translation." *Culture, Medicine, and Psychiatry* 38(1): 133–59.

————. 2016. "Sociology in the Garden: Beyond the Liberal Grammar of Contemporary Sociology." *Israel Studies Review* 31(1): 36–65.

Mizrachi, Nissim, Israel Drori, and Renee R. Anspach. 2007. "Repertoires of Trust: The Practice of Trust in a Multinational Organization amid Political Conflict." *American Sociological Review* 72(1): 143–65.

Mizrachi, Nissim, Yehuda C. Goodman, and Yariv Feniger. 2009. "'I Don't Want to See It': Decoupling Ethnicity and Class from Social Structure in Jewish Israeli High Schools." *Ethnic and Racial Studies* 32(7): 1203–25.

Mizrachi, Nissim, and Hanna Herzog. 2012. "Participatory Destigmatization Strategies among Palestinian Citizens, Ethiopian Jews and Mizrahi Jews in Israel." *Ethnic and Racial Studies* 35(3): 418–35.

Mizrachi, Nissim, and Adane Zawdu. 2012. "Between Global Racial and Bounded Identity: Choice of Destigmatization Strategies among Ethiopian Jews in Israel." *Ethnic and Racial Studies* 35(3): 436–52.

Molnár, Virág, and Michèle Lamont. 2002. "Social Categorization and Group Identification: How African Americans Shape Their Collective Identity through Consumption." Pp. 88–111 in *Innovation by Demand: An Interdisciplinary Approach to the Study of Demand and Its Role in Innovation*, edited by A. McMeekin, K. Green, M. Tomlinson, and V. Walsh. New York: Manchester University Press.

Monk Jr., Ellis P. 2014. "Skin Tone Stratification among Black Americans, 2001–2003." *Social Forces* 92(4): 1313–37.

Monterescu, Daniel. 2006. "Stranger Masculinities: Gender and Politics in a Palestinian-Israeli 'Third Space.'" Pp. 123–43 in *Islamic Masculinities*, edited by L. Ouzgane. London: Zed Press.

————. 2007. "Heteronomy: The Cultural Logic of Urban Space and Sociality in Jaffa." Pp. 157–79 in *Mixed Towns, Trapped Communities: Historical Narratives, Spatial Dynamics, Gender Relations and Cultural Encounters in Palestinian-Israeli Towns*, edited by D. Monterescu and D. Rabinowitz. London: Ashgate.

Monterescu, Daniel, and Dan Rabinowitz. 2007. *Mixed Towns, Trapped Communities: Historical Narratives, Spatial Dynamics, Gender Relations and Cultural Encounters in Palestinian-Israeli Towns*. London: Ashgate.

Moody, Mia. 2012. "From Jezebel to Ho: An Analysis of Creative and Imaginative Shared Representations of African-American Women." *Journal of Research on Women and Gender* 4: 74–94. Retrieved January 7, 2015 (https://digital.library.txstate.edu/handle/10877/4478).

Moon, Dawne. 2012. "Who Am I and Who Are We? Conflicting Narratives of Collective Selfhood in Stigmatized Groups." *American Journal of Sociology* 117(5): 1336–79.

Mora, G. Cristina. 2014. *Making Hispanics: How Activists, Bureaucrats, and Media Constructed a New American*. Chicago: University of Chicago Press.

Moraes Silva, Graziella. 2007. "Recent Debates on Affirmative Action." *ReVista: Harvard Review of Latin American Studies* 6(3): 56–60.

————. 2010. "Re-making Race and Nation: Black Professionals in Brazil and South Africa." Harvard University, Cambridge, MA.

————. 2012. "Folk Conceptualizations of Racism and Antiracism in Brazil and South Africa." *Ethnic and Racial Studies* 35(3): 506–22.

————. 2013. "The Interface of Race and National Identity in Brazil and South Africa." *Revista Estudos Políticos* 6: 61–76.

Moraes Silva, Graziella, and Marcelo Paixão. 2014. "Mixed and Unequal: New Perspectives on Brazilian Ethnoracial Relations." Pp. 172–217 in *Pigmentocracies: Ethnicity, Race, and Color in Latin America*, edited by E. E. Telles. Chapell Hill: North Carolina University Press.

Moraes Silva, Graziella, and Elisa P. Reis. 2011. "Perceptions of Social Mobility, Inequality and Racial Discrimination among Black Professionals in Rio de Janeiro." *Latin American Research Review* 46(2): 55–78.

———. 2012. "Multiple Meanings of Racial Mixture." *Ethnic and Racial Studies* 35(3): 382–99.

Moraes Silva, Graziella, and Luciana Souza Leão. 2012. "O paradoxo da mistura: identidades, desigualdades e percepção de discriminação entre brasileiros pardos." *Revista Brasileira de Ciências Sociais* 27(80): 117–33.

Morning, Ann J. 2011. *The Nature of Race: How Scientists Think and Teach about Human Difference*. Berkeley: University of California Press.

Morrill, Calvin. 1995. *The Executive Way: Conflict Management in Corporations*. Chicago: University of Chicago Press.

Moura, Roberto. 1988. *Tia Ciata e a pequena África no Rio de Janeiro*. Rio de Janeiro: Funarte.

Mouw, Ted, and Barbara Entwisle. 2006. "Residential Segregation and Interracial Friendship in Schools." *American Journal of Sociology* 112(2): 394–441.

Munanga, Kabengele. 2008. *Rediscutindo a Mestiçagem no Brasil: identidade nacional versus identidade negra*. Belo Horizonte: Autêntica.

Mundlak, Guy. 2009. "The Law of Equal Opportunities in Employment: Between Equality and Polarization." *Comparative Labor Law & Policy Journal* 30(2): 213–43.

Myrdal, Gunnar. 1944. *An American Dilemma: The Negro Problem and Modern Democracy*. New York: Harper.

Nagel, Joane. 1995. "Resource Competition Theories." *American Behavioral Scientist* 38(3): 442–58.

Navot, Suzie. 2007. *The Constitutional Law of Israel*. Alphen aan den Rijn, The Netherlands: Kluwer Law International.

Nederhof, Anton J. 1985. "Methods of Coping with Social Desirability Bias: A Review." *European Journal of Social Psychology* 15(3): 263–80.

Nielsen, Laura Beth, and Robert L. Nelson. 2005. "Rights Realized? An Empirical Analysis of Employment Discrimination Litigation as a Claiming System." *Wisconsin Law Review* 2005(2): 663–711.

Nixon, Darren. 2009. "'I Can't Put a Smiley Face On': Working-Class Masculinity, Emotional Labour and Service Work in the 'New Economy.'" *Gender, Work & Organization* 16(3): 300–322.

Nobles, Melissa. 2000. *Shades of Citizenship: Race and the Census in Modern Politics*. Stanford, CA: Stanford University Press.

Nogueira, Oracy. 1985. *Tanto preto quanto branco: estudos de relações raciais*. São Paulo: T. A. Queiroz.

Norton, Michael I., and Samuel R. Sommers. 2011. "Whites See Racism as a Zero-Sum Game That They Are Now Losing." *Perspectives on Psychological Science* 6(3): 215–18.

Nusair, Isis. 2010. "Displaced at Home: Ethnicity and Gender among Palestinians in Israel." Pp. 75–92 in *Gendering the Narratives of Three Generations of Palestinian Women in Israel*, edited by R. A. Kanaaneh and I. Nusair. Albany: State University of New York Press.

O'Connor, Alice. 2001. *Poverty Knowledge: Social Science, Social Policy, and the Poor in Twentieth-Century U.S. History*. Princeton, NJ: Princeton University Press.

OECD (Organisation for Economic Co-operation and Development). 2012. "OECD Stat-Extracts." Retrieved August 6, 2014 (http://stats.oecd.org/Index.aspx?DataSetCode=IDD).

Offer, Shira. 2004. "The Socio-economic Integration of the Ethiopian Community in Israel." *International Migration* 42(3): 29–55.

Okun, Barbara S. 2004. "Insight into Ethnic Flux: Marriage Patterns among Jews of Mixed Ancestry in Israel." *Demography* 41(1): 173–87.

Okun, Barbara S., and Orna Khait-Marelly. 2008. "Demographic Behaviour of Adults of Mixed Ethnic Ancestry: Jews in Israel." *Ethnic and Racial Studies* 31(8): 1357–80.

Oliveira, João Pacheco de. 1999. "Entrando e saindo da 'mistura': os indígenas nos censos nacionais." Pp. 124–54 in *Ensaios em antropologia histórica*, edited by J. P. de Oliveira. Rio de Janeiro: Editora UFRJ.

Oliver, Melvin, and Thomas M. Shapiro, eds. 2006. *Black Wealth/White Wealth: A New Perspective on Racial Inequality*. Second edition. New York: Routledge.

Omi, Michael, and Howard Winant. 1986. *Racial Formation in the United States: From the 1960s to the 1980s*. New York: Routledge & Kegan Paul.

———. 1994. *Racial Formation in the United States: From the 1960s to the 1990s*. New York: Routledge.

———. 2013. "Resistance Is Futile? A Response to Feagin and Elias." *Ethnic and Racial Studies* 36(6): 961–73.

Ong, Aihwa. 1996. "Cultural Citizenship as Subject-Making: Immigrants Negotiate Racial and Culture Boundaries in the United States." *Current Anthropology* 37: 737–62.

Opportunity Agenda. 2011. *Social Science Literature Review: Media Representations and Impact on the Lives of Black Men and Boys*. Retrieved January 6, 2015 (http://www.racialequitytools.org /resourcefiles/Media-Impact-onLives-of-Black-Men-and-Boys-OppAgenda.pdf).

Orfield, Gary, and Michal Kurlaender, eds. 2001. *Diversity Challenged: Evidence on the Impact of Affirmative Action*. Cambridge, MA: Harvard Educational Publishing Group.

Osuji, Chinyere. 2013. "Confronting Whitening in an Era of Black Consciousness: Racial Ideology and Black-White Interracial Marriages in Rio de Janeiro." *Ethnic and Racial Studies* 36(10): 1490–1506.

———. 2014. "Divergence or Convergence in the U.S. and Brazil: Understanding Race Relations through White Family Reactions to Black-White Interracial Couples." *Qualitative Sociology* 37(1): 93–115.

Oyserman, Daphna, Deborah Bybee, and Kathy Terry. 2006. "Possible Selves and Academic Outcomes: How and When Possible Selves Impel Action." *Journal of Personality and Social Psychology* 91(1): 188–204.

Pachucki, Mark A., and Ronald L. Breiger. 2010. "Cultural Holes: Beyond Relationality in Social Networks and Culture." *Annual Review of Sociology* 36: 205–24.

Pachucki, Mark A., Sabrina Pendergrass, and Michèle Lamont. 2007. "Boundary Processes: Recent Theoretical Developments and New Contributions." *Poetics* 35(6): 331–51.

Pager, Devah, and Hana Shepherd. 2008. "The Sociology of Discrimination: Racial Discrimination in Employment, Housing, Credit, and Consumer Markets." *Annual Review of Sociology* 34: 181–209.

Paiva, Angela, ed. 2010. *Entre Dados E Fatos: Ação Afirmativa Nas Universidades Públicas Brasileiras*. Rio de Janeiro: Pallas.

Paixão, Marcelo, and Luiz M. Carvano, eds. 2008. *Relatório anual das desigualdades raciais no Brasil; 2007–2008*. Rio de Janeiro: Editora Garamond Ltda.

Paixão, Marcelo, Irene Rossetto, Fabiana Montovanele, and Luiz M. Carvano. 2011. *Relatório anual das desigualdades raciais no Brasil; 2009–2010*. Rio de Janeiro: Editora Garamond Ltda.

Park, Ji Hoon, Nadine G. Gabbadon, and Ariel R. Chernin. 2006. "Naturalizing Racial Differences through Comedy: Asian, Black, and White Views on Racial Stereotypes in 'Rush Hour 2.'" *Journal of Communication* 56(1): 157–77.

Paschel, Tianna. 2016. *Becoming Black Political Subjects: Movements, Alignments and Ethno-Racial Rights in Brazil and Colombia*. Princeton, NJ: Princeton University Press.

Passel, Jeffrey S., Wendy Wang, and Paul Taylor. 2010. *One-in-Seven New U.S. Marriages Is Interracial or Interethnic*. Retrieved January 14, 2015 (http://www.pewsocialtrends.org/2010/06/04 /marrying-out/).

Patterson, Orlando. 2014. "Making Sense of Culture." *Annual Review of Sociology* 40: 1–30.

Patterson, Orlando, and Ethan Fosse, eds. 2015. *The Cultural Matrix: Understanding Black Youth*. Cambridge, MA: Harvard University Press.

Pattillo, Mary. 2005. "Black Middle-Class Neighborhoods." *Annual Review of Sociology* 31: 305–29.

Pattillo-McCoy, Mary. 1999. *Black Picket Fences: Privilege and Peril among the Black Middle Class*. Chicago: University of Chicago Press.

Payne, Charles M. 1995. *I've Got the Light of Freedom: The Organizing Tradition and the Mississippi Freedom Struggle*. Berkeley: University of California Press.

Pearson, Adam R., John F. Dovidio, and Samuel L. Gaertner. 2009. "The Nature of Contemporary Prejudice: Insights from Aversive Racism." *Social and Personality Psychology Compass* 3(3): 314–38.

Peled, Yoav. 1992. "Ethnic Democracy and the Legal Construction of Citizenship: Arab Citizens of the Jewish State." *American Political Science Review* 86(2): 432–43.

———. 1998. "Towards a Redefinition of Jewish Nationalism in Israel? The Enigma of Shas." *Ethnic and Racial Studies* 21(4): 703–27.

Pendergrass, Sabrina. 2013. "Perceptions of Race and Region in the Black Reverse Migration to the South." *Du Bois Review: Social Science Research on Race* 10(1): 155–78.

Pescosolido, Bernice A., and Jack K. Martin. 2015. "The Stigma Complex." *Annual Review of Sociology* 41: 87–116.

Peterson, Ruth D., and Lauren J. Krivo. 2012. *Divergent Social Worlds: Neighborhood Crime and the Racial-Spatial Divide*. Reprint edition. New York: Russell Sage Foundation.

Pew Forum on Religion & Public Life. 2008. *U.S. Religious Landscape Survey—Religious Affiliation: Diverse and Dynamic*. Washington, DC.

Pew Research Center and NPR. 2010. "A Year after Obama's Election: Blacks Upbeat about Black Progress, Prospects." Retrieved August 8, 2013 (http://www.pewsocialtrends.org/2010/01/12/blacks-upbeat-about-black-progress-prospects/).

Phelan, Jo C., Bruce G. Link, and John F. Dovidio. 2008. "Stigma and Prejudice: One Animal or Two?" *Social Science & Medicine* 67(3): 358–67.

Phillips-Fein, Kim. 2009. *Invisible Hands: The Making of the Conservative Movement from the New Deal to Reagan*. New York: W. W. Norton & Company.

Phinney, Jean S., and Anthony D. Ong. 2007. "Conceptualization and Measurement of Ethnic Identity: Current Status and Future Directions." *Journal of Counseling Psychology* 54(3): 271–81.

Phinney, Jean S., and Mukosolu Onwughalu. 1996. "Racial Identity and Perception of American Ideals among African American and African Students in the United States." *International Journal of Intercultural Relations* 20(2): 127–40.

Pierson, Donald. 1942. "Negroes in Brazil: A Study of Race Contact at Bahia." PhD thesis, University of Chicago.

Piketty, Thomas, and Emmanuel Saez. 2003. "Income Inequality in the United States, 1913–1998." *Quarterly Journal of Economics* 118(1): 1–39.

Pittman, Cassi. 2011. "Ethnicity/Race." Pp. 545–52 in *Encyclopedia of Consumer Culture*. London: SAGE Publications.

Piza, Edith, and Fúlvia Rosemberg. 1999. "Cor Nos Censos Brasileiros." *Revista USP* (40): 122–37.

Pochmann, Marcio. 2012. *Nova classe média? O trabalho na base da pirâmide social brasileira*. São Paulo: Boitempo Editorial.

Poli, Alexandra. 2005. "Faire face au racisme en France et au Brésil: de la condamnation morale à l'aide aux victimes." *Cultures et conflits* 59: 11–45.

Polletta, Francesca. 2002. *Freedom Is an Endless Meeting: Democracy in American Social Movements*. Chicago: University of Chicago Press.

————. 2009. *It Was Like a Fever: Storytelling in Protest and Politics*. Chicago: University of Chicago Press.

Polletta, Francesca, Pang Ching Bobby Chen, Beth Gharrity Gardner, and Alice Motes. 2011. "The Sociology of Storytelling." *Annual Review of Sociology* 37: 109–30.

Portes, Alejandro, and Rubén G. Rumbaut. 2001. *Legacies: The Story of the Immigrant Second Generation*. Berkeley: University of California Press.

Portes, Alejandro, and Jozsef Borocz. 1989. "Contemporary Immigration: Theoretical Perspectives on Its Determinants and Modes of Incorporation." *International Migration Review* 23(3): 606–30.

Postmes, Tom, and Nyla R. Branscombe. 2002. "Influence of Long-Term Racial Environmental Composition on Subjective Well-Being in African Americans." *Journal of Personality and Social Psychology* 83(3): 735–51.

Powell, Walter W., and Paul J. DiMaggio, eds. 1991. *The New Institutionalism in Organizational Analysis*. Chicago: University of Chicago Press.

Praxedes, Rosângela Rosa. 2006. "Negros de classe média na cidade de Maringá." Pontifícia Universidade Católica de São Paulo, São Paulo.

Purdie-Vaughns, Valerie, Claude M. Steele, Paul G. Davies, Ruth Ditlmann, and Jennifer Randall Crosby. 2008. "Social Identity Contingencies: How Diversity Cues Signal Threat or Safety for African-Americans in Mainstream Institutions." *Journal of Personality and Social Psychology* 94(4): 615–30.

Quillian, Lincoln. 2006. "New Approaches to Understanding Racial Prejudice and Discrimination." *Annual Review of Sociology* 32: 299–328.

Quillian, Lincoln, and Mary E. Campbell. 2003. "Beyond Black and White: The Present and Future of Multiracial Friendship Segregation." *American Sociological Review* 68(4): 540–66.

Quillian, Lincoln, and Devah Pager. 2001. "Black Neighbors, Higher Crime? The Role of Racial Stereotypes in Evaluations of Neighborhood Crime." *American Journal of Sociology* 107(3): 717–67.

Rabinowitz, Dan. 1993. "Oriental Nostalgia: How the Palestinians Became 'Israel's Arabs.'" *Teorya Uvikoret* (4): 141–52 (Hebrew).

————. 2001. "The Palestinian Citizens of Israel, the Concept of Trapped Minority and the Discourse of Transnationalism in Anthropology." *Ethnic and Racial Studies* 24(1): 64–85.

Rabinowitz, Dan, and Khawla Abu-Baker. 2002. *The Stand Tall Generation: The Palestinian Citizens of Israel Today*. Jerusalem: Keter Publication (Hebrew).

————. 2005. *Coffins on Our Shoulders: The Experience of the Palestinian Citizens in Israel*. Berkeley: University of California Press.

Racusen, Seth. 2002. "'A Mulato Cannot Be Prejudiced': The Legal Construction of Racial Discrimination in Contemporary Brazil." PhD thesis, Massachusetts Institute of Technology, Cambridge, MA. Retrieved March 5, 2015 (http://dspace.mit.edu/handle/1721.1/31104).

————. 2004. "The Ideology of the Brazilian Nation and the Brazilian Legal Theory of Racial Discrimination." *Social Identities* 10(6): 775–809.

Rahat, Gideon, and Reut Itzkovitch Malka. 2012. "Political Representation in Israel: Minority Sectors vs. Women." *Representation* 48(3): 307–19.

Ramseyer, J. Mark, and Eric B. Rasmusen. 2010. "Comparative Litigation Rates." Retrieved October 28, 2013 (http://www.law.harvard.edu/programs/olin_center/papers/pdf/Ramseyer_681.pdf).

Randall, Donna M., and Maria F. Fernandes. 1991. "The Social Desirability Response Bias in Ethics Research." *Journal of Business Ethics* 10(11): 805–17.

Rebhun, Uzi, and Gilad Malach. 2009. *Demographic Trends in Israel*. Jerusalem: Metzilah Center.

Regev, Motti. 2000. "To Have a Culture of Our Own: On Israeliness and Its Variants." *Ethnic and Racial Studies* 23(2): 223–47.

Reich, John W., Alex J. Zautra, and John Stuart Hall. 2012. *Handbook of Adult Resilience*. New York: Guilford Press.

Reis, Elisa P. 1999. "Elite Perceptions of Poverty: Brazil." *IDS Bulletin* 30(2): 127–38.

———. 2004. "A desigualdade na visão das elites e do povo brasileiro." Pp. 37–73 in *Imagens da desigualdade*, edited by M. C. Scalon. Belo Horizonte: Editora UFMG.

Reis, Elisa P., and Mick Moore. 2005. *Elite Perceptions of Poverty & Inequality*. London: Zed Books.

Reis, Eustáquio, and Elisa P. Reis. 1988. "As elites agrárias e a abolição da escravidão no Brasil." *Dados* 31(3): 309–41.

Reis, Fabio Wanderley. 1996. "Mito e valor da democracia racial." Pp. 221–31 in *Multiculturalismo e racismo: o papel da ação afirmativa nos estados democráticos contemporâneos*, edited by J. Souza. Brasília: Ministério da Justiça.

Reis, João José. 1988. *Escravidão e invenção da liberdade: estudos sobre o negro no Brasil*. São Paulo: Editora Brasiliense em co-edição com o Conselho Nacional de Desenvolvimento Científico e Tecnológico.

Rekhess, Eli. 2007. "The Evolvement of an Arab–Palestinian National Minority in Israel." *Israel Studies* 12(3): 1–28.

Rennó, Lucio, Amy Smith, Matthew Layton, and Frederico Batista. 2012. *Legitimidade E Qualidade Da Democracia No Brasil: Uma Visão Da Cidadania*. São Paulo: Intermeios/LAPOP.

Ribeiro, Carlos Antonio Costa, and Nelson do Valle Silva. 2009. "Cor, educação e casamento: tendências da seletividade marital no Brasil, 1960 a 2000." *Dados* 52(1): 7–51.

Ribeiro, Luiz César Queiroz. 2000. "Cidade desigual ou cidade partida? Tendências da metrópole do Rio de Janeiro." Pp. 63–97 in *O futuro das metrópoles: desigualdades e governabilidade*, edited by L. C. Q. Ribeiro. Rio de Janeiro: Editora Revan.

———. 2007. "Status, cor e desigualdades sócio-espaciais na metrópole do Rio de Janeiro." *Anais: Encontros Nacionais da ANPUR* 12: 1–22. Retrieved July 1, 2014 (http://www.anpur.org.br/revista/rbeur/index.php/anais/article/view/2997).

Ridgeway, Cecilia. 2013. "Why Status Matters for Inequality." *American Sociological Review* 79(1): 1–16.

Rieder, Jonathan. 1987. *Canarsie: The Jews and Italians of Brooklyn against Liberalism*. Cambridge, MA: Harvard University Press.

Rivera, Lauren A. 2015. "Go with Your Gut: Emotion and Evaluation in Job Interviews." *American Journal of Sociology* 120(5): 1339–89.

Rocha, Luciane de Oliveira. 2012. "Black Mothers' Experiences of Violence in Rio de Janeiro." *Cultural Dynamics* 24(1): 59–73.

Rodgers, Daniel T. 2011. *Age of Fracture*. Cambridge, MA: Belknap Press of Harvard University Press.

Roscigno, Vincent J. 2007. *The Face of Discrimination: How Race and Gender Impact Work and Home Lives*. New York: Rowman & Littlefield.

Rose, Nikolas. 1999. *Powers of Freedom: Reframing Political Thought*. Cambridge: Cambridge University Press.

Rosenfeld, Henry. 1964. "From Peasantry to Wage Labour and Residual Peasantry: The Transformation of an Arab Village." Pp. 211–34 in *Process and Patterns in Culture*, edited by R. A. Manners. Chicago: Aldine.

Rosenzweig, Roy, and David P. Thelen. 1998. *The Presence of the Past: Popular Uses of History in American Life*. New York: Columbia University Press.

Roth, Wendy. 2012. *Race Migrations: Latinos and the Cultural Transformation of Race*. Stanford, CA: Stanford University Press.

Rouhana, Nadim. 1989. "The Political Transformation of the Palestinians in Israel: From Acquiescence to Challenge." *Journal of Palestinian Studies* 18(3): 38–59.

————. 1997. *Palestinian Citizens in an Ethnic Jewish State: Identities in Conflict*. New Haven, CT: Yale University Press.

Rubinstein, Amnon, and Institute on American Jewish-Israeli Relations. 2003. *Israeli Arabs and Jews: Dispelling the Myths, Narrowing the Gaps*. New York: American Jewish Committee, Dorothy and Julius Koppelman Institute on American Jewish-Israeli Relations.

Rumbaut, Rubén G. 2009. "Pigments of Our Imagination: On the Racialization and Racial Identities of 'Hispanics' and 'Latinos.'" Pp. 15–36 in *How the U.S. Racializes Latinos: White Hegemony and Its Consequences*, edited by José A. Cobas, Jorge Duany, and Joe R. Feagin. Boulder: Paradigm Publishers. Retrieved June 10, 2015 (http://papers.ssrn.com/abstract =1878732).

Sa'di, Ahmad H. 2002. "Catastrophe, Memory and Identity: Al-Nakbah as a Component of Palestinian Identity." *Israel Studies* 7(2): 175–98.

Sa'di, Ahmad H., and Lila Abu-Lughod. 2007. *Nakba: Palestine, 1948, and the Claims of Memory*. New York: Columbia University Press.

Sagiv, Talia. 2014. *On the Fault Line: Israelis of Mixed Ethnicity*. Tel Aviv: Hakibbutz Hameuchad.

Saguy, Abigail C. 2003. *What Is Sexual Harassment? From Capitol Hill to the Sorbonne*. Berkeley: University of California Press.

Said, Edward. 1978. *Orientalism*. New York: Vintage Books.

Samon, Hagar. 2003. "Blackness in Transition: Decoding Racial Constructs through Stories of Ethiopian Jews." *Journal of Folklore Research* 40(1): 3–32.

Sandelson, Jasmin. 2014. "Relational Resources: Collaboration and Culture among Impoverished Adolescents." Department of Sociology, Harvard University, Cambridge, MA.

Sansone, Livio. 1997. "The New Politics of Black Culture in Bahia, Brazil." Pp. 277–309 in *The Politics of Ethnic Consciousness*, edited by C. Govers and H. Vermeulen. New York: St. Martin's Press.

————. 2003. *Blackness without Ethnicity: Constructing Race in Brazil*. New York: Palgrave Macmillan.

Santos, Gevanilda Gomes, and Maria Palmira da Silva. 2005. *Racismo no Brasil: percepções da discriminação e do preconceito racial no século XXI*. São Paulo: Editora Fundação Perseu Abramo/ Fundação Rosa Luxemburg.

Santos, Sales Augusto dos. 2000. *A ausência de uma bancada suprapartidária afro-brasileira no Congresso Nacional (legislatura 1995–1998)*. Brasília: Centro de Estudos Afro-Asiáticos.

Santos, Wanderley Guilherme. 1979. *Cidadania e justiça: a política social na ordem brasileira*. Rio de Janeiro: Editora Campus Ltda.

Saperstein, Aliya, and Andrew M. Penner. 2012. "Racial Fluidity and Inequality in the United States." *American Journal of Sociology* 118(3): 676–727.

Sartori, Giovanni. 1984. *Social Science Concepts: A Systematic Analysis*. London: Sage Publications.

Sasson-Levy, Orna. 2013. "A Different Kind of Whiteness: Marking and Unmarking of Social Boundaries in the Construction of Hegemonic Ethnicity." *Sociological Forum* 28(1): 27–50.

Sasson-Levy, Orna, and Avi Shoshana. 2013. "'Passing' as (Non) Ethnic: The Israeli Version of Acting White." *Sociological Inquiry* 83(3): 448–72.

Sauder, Michael. 2006. "Third Parties and Status Position: How the Characteristics of Status Systems Matter." *Theory and Society* 35(3): 299–321.

Scalon, Maria Celi. 2004. *Imagens da desigualdade*. Belo Horizonte: Editora UFMG.

Scalon, Maria Celi, and André Salata. 2012. "Uma nova classe média no Brasil da última década? O debate a partir da perspectiva sociológica." *Sociedade e Estado* 27(2): 387–407.

Schnittker, Jason, Michael Massoglia, and Christopher Uggen. 2011. "Incarceration and the Health of the African American Community." *Du Bois Review: Social Science Research on Race* 8(1): 133–41.

Schuman, Howard, Charlotte Steeh, Lawrence Bobo, and Maria Krysan. 1997. *Racial Attitudes in America: Trends and Interpretations*. Revised edition Cambridge, MA: Harvard University Press.

Schwartzman, Luisa Farah. 2007. "Does Money Whiten? Intergenerational Changes in Racial Classification in Brazil." *American Sociological Review* 72(6): 940–64.

Schwartzman, Luisa Farah, and Graziella Moraes Silva. 2012. "Unexpected Narratives from Multicultural Policies: Translations of Affirmative Action in Brazil." *Latin American and Caribbean Ethnic Studies* 7(1): 31–48.

Schwartzman, Simon. 1999. "Fora de foco: diversidade e identidades étnicas no Brasil." *Novos Estudos CEBRAP* 55: 83–96.

Schwarz, Ori. 2015. "The Sound of Stigmatization: Sonic Habitus, Sonic Styles, and Boundary Work in an Urban Slum." *American Journal of Sociology* 121(1): 205–42.

Sears, David O., James Sidanius, and Lawrence Bobo, eds. 2000. *Racialized Politics: The Debate about Racism in America*. Chicago: University of Chicago Press.

Seigel, Micol. 2005. "Beyond Compare: Comparative Method after the Transnational Turn." *Radical History Review* 91(1): 62–90.

Sellers, Robert M., Cleopatra H. Caldwell, Karen H. Schmeelk-Cone, and Marc A. Zimmerman. 2003. "Racial Identity, Racial Discrimination, Perceived Stress, and Psychological Distress among African American Young Adults." *Journal of Health and Social Behavior* 44(3): 302–17.

Sellers, Robert M., Mia A. Smith, J. Nicole Shelton, Stephanie A. J. Rowley, and Tabbye M. Chavous. 1998. "Multidimensional Model of Racial Identity: A Reconceptualization of African American Racial Identity." *Personality and Social Psychology Review* 2(1): 18–39.

Semyonov, Moshe, and Noah Lewin-Epstein. 2004. *Stratification in Israel: Class, Ethnicity, and Gender*. New Brunswick, NJ: Transaction Publishers.

Shabtai, Malka. 1999. *Best Brothers: The Identity Journey of Ethiopian Immigrant Soldiers*. Tel Aviv: Tcherikover (Hebrew).

———. 2001. *Between Reggae and Rap, the Integration Challenge of Ethiopian Youth in Israel*. Tel Aviv: Tcherikover Press (Hebrew).

Shabtai, Malka, and Lea Kagen, eds. 2005. *Ethiopian Women and Girls in Spaces, Worlds and Journeys between Cultures*. Tel Aviv: Lashon Tzaha Publication (Hebrew).

Shafir, Gershon, and Yoav Peled. 2002. *Being Israeli: The Dynamics of Multiple Citizenship*. Cambridge: Cambridge University Press.

Shamir, Michal, ed. 2015. *The Elections in Israel 2013*. Jerusalem: Israel Democracy Institute.

Sharone, Ofer. 2014. *Flawed System/Flawed Self: Job Searching and Unemployment Experiences*. Chicago: University of Chicago Press.

Shavit, Yossi. 1984. "Tracking and Ethnicity in Israeli Secondary Education." *American Sociological Review* 49(2): 210–20.

Shelby, Tommie. 2007. *We Who Are Dark: The Philosophical Foundations of Black Solidarity*. Cambridge, MA: Belknap Press of Harvard University Press.

———. 2014. "Racism, Moralism, and Social Criticism." *Du Bois Review: Social Science Research on Race* 11(1): 57–74.

Shenhav, Yehouda A. 2006. *The Arab Jews: A Postcolonial Reading of Nationalism, Religion, and Ethnicity*. Stanford, CA: Stanford University Press.

Sheriff, Robin E. 2001. *Dreaming Equality: Color, Race, and Racism in Urban Brazil*. New Brunswick, NJ: Rutgers University Press.

Sherman, Rachel. 2005. "Producing the Superior Self: Strategic Comparison and Symbolic Boundaries among Luxury Hotel Workers." *Ethnography* 6(2): 131–58.

Shields, Alexandra Elizabeth, Mehdi Najafzadeh, and Anna Boonin Schachter. 2013. "Bumps along the Translational Pathway: Anticipating Uptake of Tailored Smoking Cessation Treatment." *Personalized Medicine* 10(8). Retrieved January 7, 2015 (http://www.ncbi.nlm.nih.gov/pmc/articles/PMC3882128/).

Shilhav, Yosseph. 1989. "The Haredi Ghetto: The Theology behind the Geography." *Contemporary Jewry* 10(2): 51–65.

Shiloah, Amnon, and Erik Cohen. 1983. "The Dynamics of Change in Jewish Oriental Ethnic Music in Israel." *Ethnomusicology* 27(2): 227–52.

Shimony, Batya. 2013. "Shaping Israeli-Arab Identity in Hebrew Words—The Case of Sayed Kashua." *Israel Studies* 18(1): 146–69.

Shitrit, Sammy Shalom. 2004. *The Mizrahi Struggle in Israel*. Tel Aviv: Am Oved–Sifriyat Afikim (Hebrew).

Shohat, Ella. 1988. "Sephardim in Israel: Zionism from the Standpoint of Its Jewish Victims." *Social Text* 19–20: 1–34.

———. 1999. "The Invention of the Mizrahim." *Journal of Palestine Studies* 29(1): 5–20.

Shonkoff, Jack P., Andrew S. Garner, Benjamin S. Siegel, Mary I. Dobbins, Marian F. Earls, and Andrew S. Garner. 2012. "The Lifelong Effects of Early Childhood Adversity and Toxic Stress." *Pediatrics* 129(1): 232–46.

Shwed, Uri, Yossi Shavit, Maisalon Dellashi, and Moran Ofek. 2014. "Integration of Arab Israelis and Jews in Schools in Israel." Pp. 323–46 in *State of the Nation Report: Society, Economy and Policy in Israel*, edited by D. Ben-David. Tel Aviv: Taub Center for Social Policy Studies in Israel.

Sidanius, Jim, Seymour Feshbach, Shana Levin, and Felicia Pratto. 1997. "The Interface between Ethnic and National Attachment: Ethnic Pluralism or Ethnic Dominance?" *Public Opinion Quarterly* 61(1): 102–33.

Sigelman, Lee, Steven Tuch, and Jack Martin. 2005. "What's in a Name? Preference for 'Black' versus 'African-American' among Americans of African Descent." *Public Opinion Quarterly* 69(3): 429–38.

Silva, Jennifer M. 2013. *Coming Up Short: Working-Class Adulthood in an Age of Uncertainty*. New York: Oxford University Press.

Silva, Hédio, Jr. 2002. *Discriminação racial nas escolas: entre a lei e as práticas sociais*. Brasília: UNESCO.

Silva, Nelson do Valle. 1979. "White-Non-White Income Differentials: Brazil." PhD thesis, University of Michigan, Ann Arbor.

Simmel, Georg. 1908. *Sociology: Investigations on the Forms of Sociation*. Berlin: Duncker & Humblot.

Skeggs, Beverley. 2004. *Class, Self, Culture*. London: Routledge.

Skidmore, Thomas E. 1972. "Toward a Comparative Analysis of Race Relations since Abolition in Brazil and the United States." *Journal of Latin American Studies* 4(1): 1–28.

———. 1993. *Black into White: Race and Nationality in Brazilian Thought*. Durham, NC: Duke University Press.

Skrentny, John David. 2009. *The Minority Rights Revolution*. Cambridge, MA: Harvard University Press.

Small, Mario Luis. 2009. "'How Many Cases Do I Need?' On Science and the Logic of Case Selection in Field-Based Research." *Ethnography* 10(1): 5–38.

Smith, Sandra S., and Mignon R. Moore. 2000. "Intraracial Diversity and Relations among African-Americans: Closeness among Black Students at a Predominantly White University." *American Journal of Sociology* 106(1): 1–39.

Smith, Zachary. 2014. "On the Mizrahi Margins: Rethinking Israel." MA thesis, School of Oriental and African Studies, University of London, (https://arabjews.files.wordpress.com/2014/10/smith-zachary-on-the-mizrahi-margins.pdf).

Smooha, Sammy. 1990. "Minority Status in an Ethnic Democracy: The Status of the Arab Minority in Israel." *Ethnic and Racial Studies* 13: 389–413.

———. 1999. *Autonomy for Arabs in Israel*. Ra'anana: Institute for Israeli Arab Studies.

———. 2002. "The Model of Ethnic Democracy: Israel as a Jewish and Democratic State." *Nations and Nationalism* 8(4): 475–503.

———. 2013. *Still Playing by the Rules: Index of Arab-Jewish Relations in Israel 2012*. Jerusalem: Haifa University and Israel Democracy Institute (Hebrew).

———. 2016. *Still Playing by the Rules: Index of Arab-Jewish Relations in Israel 2015*. Haifa: University of Haifa (Hebrew).

Snow, David A., Daniel Cress, and Anderson. 1994. "Negotiating the Public Realm: Stigma Management and Collective Action among the Homeless." Pp. 121–43 in *Research in Community Sociology*, vol. 1, edited by D. A. Chekki. Greenwich, CT.: JAI Press.

Soares, Glaucio Ary Dillon, and Nelson do Valle Silva. 1987. "Urbanization, Race, and Class in Brazilian Politics." *Latin American Research Review* 22(2): 155–76.

Soares, Reinaldo da Silva. 2004. "Negros de classe média em São Paulo: estilo de vida e identidade negra." Universidad de São Paulo, São Paulo.

Soares Silva, Luciana, Lygia Gonçalves Costa, and Aline Caldeira Lopes. 2013. "Detalhes de crime, racismo e campo jurídico: uma cartografia das decisões de segunda instância do tribunal de justiça do Rio de Janeiro." Retrieved November 12, 2015 (http://www.anpocs .org/portal/index.php?option=com_docman&task=doc_details&gid=8561&Itemid=459).

Somers, Margaret R. 1994. "The Narrative Constitution of Identity: A Relational and Network Approach." *Theory and Society* 23(5): 605–49.

———. 2008. *Genealogies of Citizenship: Markets, Statelessness, and the Right to Have Rights*. Cambridge: Cambridge University Press.

Souza, Neusa Santos. 1983. *Tornar-se Negro, ou, as vicissitudes da identidade do negro brasileiro em ascensão social*. Rio de Janeiro: Graal.

Sovik, Liv. 2004. "We Are Family: Whiteness in the Brazilian Media." *Journal of Latin American Cultural Studies* 13(3): 315–25.

Soysal, Yasemin Nuhoglu. 1994. *Limits of Citizenship: Migrants and Postnational Membership in Europe*. Chicago: University of Chicago Press.

Stadler, Nurit. 2002. "Is Profane Work an Obstacle to Salvation? The Case of Ultra Orthodox (Haredi) Jews in Contemporary Israel." *Sociology of Religion* 63(4): 455–74.

Stainback, Kevin, and Donald Tomaskovic-Devey. 2012. *Documenting Desegregation: Racial and Gender Segregation in Private-Sector Employment since the Civil Rights Act*. New York: Russell Sage Foundation.

Stampp, Kenneth. 1956. *The Peculiar Institution: Slavery in the Ante-Bellum South*. New York: Knopf.

Steele, Claude M. 2011. *Whistling Vivaldi: How Stereotypes Affect Us and What We Can Do*. Reprint edition. New York: W. W. Norton & Company.

Steele, Claude M., and Joshua Aronson. 1995. "Stereotype Threat and the Intellectual Test Performance of African Americans." *Journal of Personality and Social Psychology* 69(5): 797–811.

Steiner, Talya. 2013. *Combating Discrimination against Arabs in the Israeli Workforce*. Jerusalem: Israel Democracy Institute (Hebrew).

Steir, Haya, and Yossi Shavit. 2003. "Two Decades of Educational Intermarriage in Israel." Pp. 315–30 in *Who Marries Whom?*, edited by H. Blossfeld and A. Timm. Dordrecht, The Netherlands: Springer.

Sue, Christina A., and Tanya Golash-Boza. 2013. "'It Was Only a Joke': How Racial Humour Fuels Colour-Blind Ideologies in Mexico and Peru." *Ethnic and Racial Studies* 36(10): 1582–98.

Sue, Derald Wing, Christina M. Capodilupo, Gina C. Torino, Jennifer M. Bucceri, Aisha M. B. Holder, Kevin L. Nadal, and Marta Esquilin. 2007. "Racial Microaggressions in Everyday Life: Implications for Clinical Practice." *American Psychologist* 62(4): 271–86.

Sugrue, Thomas J. 2005. *The Origins of the Urban Crisis: Race and Inequality in Postwar Detroit*. Revised edition. Princeton, NJ: Princeton University Press.

Swidler, Ann. 1986. "Culture in Action: Symbols and Strategies." *American Sociological Review* 51: 273–86.

Swirski, Shlomo. 1989. *Israel: The Oriental Majority*. London: Zed Books.

Swirski, Shlomo, Etty Connor-Attias, and Ariane Ophir. 2014. *Israel: A Social Report—2013*. Tel Aviv: Adva Center.

Swirski, Shlomo, and Barbara Swirski. 2002. *Ethiopian Jews in Israel: Housing, Employment and Education*. Tel Aviv: Adva Center (Hebrew).

Tannenbaum, Frank. 1946. *Slave and Citizen: The Negro in the Americas*. New York: A. A. Knopf.

Tarman, Christopher, and David O. Sears. 2005. "The Conceptualization and Measurement of Symbolic Racism." *Journal of Politics* 67(3): 731–61. Retrieved January 13, 2015 (http://onlinelibrary.wiley.com/doi/10.1111/j.1468-2508.2005.00337.x/abstract).

Tarrow, Sidney. 1994. *Power in Movement: Social Movements, Collective Action and Politics*. Cambridge: Cambridge University Press.

Taylor, Charles. 1992. *Multiculturalism and the Politics of Recognition*. Princeton, NJ: Princeton University Press.

———. 1994. "The Politics of Recognition." Pp. 25–73 in *Multiculturalism: Examining the Politics of Recognition*, edited by A. Gutmann. Princeton, NJ: Princeton University Press.

Taylor, Paul, Wendy Wang, Kim Parker, Jeffrey S. Passel, Eileen Patten, and Seth Motel. 2012. *The Rise of Intermarriage: Rates, Characteristics Vary by Race and Gender*. Washington, DC: Pew Research Center. Retrieved December 15, 2014 (http://www.pewsocialtrends.org/files/2012/02/SDT-Intermarriage-II.pdf).

Teixeira, Moema de Poli. 2003. *Negros na universidade: identidade e trajetorias de ascensão social no Rio de Janeiro*. Rio de Janeiro: Pallas.

Telles, Edward E. 1992. "Residential Segregation by Skin Color in Brazil." *American Sociological Review* 57(2): 186–97.

———. 1999. "Ethnic Boundaries and Political Mobilization among African Brazilians: Comparisons with the U.S. Case." Pp. 154–78 in *Racial Politics in Contemporary Brazil*, edited by M. Hanchard. Durham, NC: Duke University Press.

———. 2003. "US Foundations and Racial Reasoning in Brazil." *Theory, Culture, and Society* 20(4): 31–47.

———. 2004. *Race in Another America: The Significance of Skin Color in Brazil*. Princeton, NJ: Princeton University Press.

Telles, Edward E., and Stanley Bailey. 2013. "Understanding Latin American Beliefs about Racial Inequality." *American Journal of Sociology* 118(6): 1559–95.

Telles, Edward E., and Denia Garcia. 2013. "Mestizaje and Public Opinion." *Latin American Research Review* 48(3): 130–52.

Telles, Edward E., and Nelson Lim. 1998. "Does It Matter Who Answers the Race Question? Racial Classification and Income Inequality in Brazil." *Demography* 35(4): 465–74.

Telles, Edward E., and Tianna Paschel. 2014. "Who Is Black, White, or Mixed Race? How Skin Color, Status, and Nation Shape Racial Classification in Latin America." *American Journal of Sociology* 120(3): 864–907.

Telles, Edward E., and PERLA team, eds. 2014. *Pigmentocracies: Ethnicity, Race, and Color in Latin America*. Chapel Hill, NC: University of North Carolina Press.

Terry, Brandon M. 2015. "After Ferguson." *The Point* 10. Retrieved February 25, 2016 (http://thepointmag.com/2015/politics/after-ferguson).

Tesler, Michael, and David O. Sears. 2010. *Obama's Race: The 2008 Election and the Dream of a Post-racial America*. Chicago: University of Chicago Press.

Thelen, Kathleen, and James Mahoney. 2015. "Comparative-Historical Analysis in Contemporary Political Science." Pp. 3–38 in *Advances in Comparative-Historical Analysis*, edited by J. Mahoney and K. Thelen. New York: Cambridge University Press.

Thoits, Peggy A. 2011. "Resisting the Stigma of Mental Illness." *Social Psychology Quarterly* 74(1): 6–28.

Tilcsik, András, Michel Anteby, and Carly R. Knight. 2015. "Concealable Stigma and Occupational Segregation: Towards a Theory of Gay and Lesbian Occupations." *Administrative Science Quarterly* 60(3): 446–81.

Tilly, Charles. 1995. *Popular Contention in Great Britain, 1758–1834*. Cambridge, MA: Harvard University Press.

Tissot, Sylvie. 2015. *Good Neighbors: Gentrifying Diversity in Boston's South End*. Brooklyn, NY: Verso.

Todd, Jennifer. 2005. "Social Transformation, Collective Categories and Identity Change." *Theory and Society* 34(4): 429–63.

Tönnies, Ferdinand. 1887. *Gemeinschaft und Gesellschaft: Abhandlung des Communismus und des Socialismus als empirischer Culturformen*. Leipzig: Fues.

Truman, Jennifer L., and Michael Planty. 2012. *Criminal Victimization, 2011*. Washington, DC: U.S. Department of Justice: Bureau of Statistics. Retrieved August 8, 2013 (http://www.bjs .gov/index.cfm?ty=pbdetail&iid=4494).

Twine, France Winddance. 1998. *Racism in a Racial Democracy: The Maintenance of White Supremacy in Brazil*. New Brunswick, NJ: Rutgers University Press.

Tyson, Karolyn. 2011. *Integration Interrupted: Tracking, Black Students, and Acting White after Brown*. New York: Oxford University Press.

UNDP (United Nations Development Program). 2005. *Relatório de Desenvolvimento Humano Brasil 2005—Racismo, Pobreza E Violência*. Brasília: UNDP.

US Bureau of Labor Statistics. 2014. "Table A-2. Employment Status of the Civilian Population by Race, Sex, and Age." Retrieved July 31, 2014 (http://www.bls.gov/news.release/empsit .t02.htm).

———. 2015. "Median Weekly Earnings by Educational Attainment in 2014." *The Economics Daily*. Retrieved February 23, 2016 (http://www.bls.gov/opub/ted/2015/median-weekly -earnings-by-education-gender-race-and-ethnicity-in-2014.htm).

US Bureau of the Census. 2012. *US Census 2012*. Washington, DC. Retrieved December 4, 2015 (https://www.census.gov/library/publications/2011/compendia/statab/131ed/education.html).

———. 2010. "Metropolitan Statistical Areas with More Than 750,000 Persons in 2010— Population by Race and Hispanic or Latino Origin: 2010 [As of April 1]." In *ProQuest Statistical Abstract of the U.S. 2014 Online Edition*. Retrieved August 7, 2014 (http://statabs .proquest.com.ezp-prod1.hul.harvard.edu/sa/abstract.html?table-no=24&acc-no=C7095 -1.1&year=2014&z=CD410443D7348998F5A3C87EB0803381EF575D7B).

US Department of Housing and Urban Development. 2013. *Housing Discrimination against Racial and Ethnic Minorities 2012: Executive Summary*. Retrieved July, 31, 2014 (http://www .huduser.org/portal/Publications/pdf/HUD-514_HDS2012_execsumm.pdf).

Vargas, Joao H. Costa. 2010. *Never Meant to Survive: Genocide and Utopias in Black Diaspora Communities*. Lanham, MD: Rowman & Littlefield.

Véran, Jean-François. 2010. "'Nação Mestiça': as políticas étnico-raciais vistas da periferia de Manaus." *Dilemas: Revista de Estudos de Conflito e Controle Social* 3(9): 21–60.

Verba, Sidney, and Gary Orren. 1985. *Equality in America: A View from the Top*. Cambridge, MA: Harvard University Press.

Vertovec, Steven. 2015. *Super-diversity*. London: Routledge.

Vilela, Elaine Meire. 2011. "Desigualdade E Discriminação de Imigrantes Internacionais No Mercado de Trabalho Brasileiro." *Dados* 54(1): 89–128.

Waiselfisz, Julio Jacob. 2014. *Mapa Da Violência 2014: Os Jovens Do Brasil*. Rio de Janeiro: FLACSO. Retrieved December 3, 2015 (http://www.mapadaviolencia.org.br/pdf2014/Mapa 2014_JovensBrasil_Preliminar.pdf).

Walsh, Sophie D., and Rivka Tuval-Mashiach. 2012. "Ethiopian Emerging Adult Immigrants in Israel Coping with Discrimination and Racism." *Youth & Society* 44(1): 49–75.

Walzer, Michael. 1983. *Spheres of Justice: A Defense of Pluralism and Equality*. New York: Basic Books.

———. 1997. *On Toleration*. New Haven, CT: Yale University Press.

Warikoo, Natasha, and Janine de Novais. 2014. "Diversity and Colorblindness: Race Frames and Their Consequences for White Undergraduates at Elite US Universities." *Ethnic and Racial Studies* 38(6): 860–976.

Warren, Mark. 2010. *Fire in the Heart: How White Activists Embrace Racial Justice*. New York: Oxford University Press.

Waterhouse, Benjamin C. 2013. *Lobbying America: The Politics of Business from Nixon to NAFTA*. Princeton, NJ: Princeton University Press.

Waters, Mary C. 2000. "Immigration, Intermarriage, and the Challenges of Measuring Racial/Ethnic Identities." *American Journal of Public Health* 90(11): 1735–37.

Weber, Max. 1905. *The Protestant Ethic and the Spirit of Capitalism*. London: Routledge.

Weil, Shalva. 1997. "Religion, Blood and the Equality of Rights: The Case of Ethiopian Jews in Israel." *International Journal on Minority and Group Rights* 4: 412–97.

Welburn, Jessica S., and Cassi L. Pittman. 2012. "Stop 'Blaming the Man': Perceptions of Inequality and Opportunities for Success in the Obama Era among Middle-Class African Americans." *Ethnic and Racial Studies* 35(3): 523–40.

Western, Bruce, and Becky Pettit. 2010. "Incarceration & Social Inequality." *Daedalus* 139(3): 8–19.

Westreich, Elimelech. 2012. "The Official Rabbinical Court of Jerusalem in the 19th Century: Its Status among Jewish Communities and the Social and Cultural Background of the Judges." *Jewish Law Annual* 19: 235–60.

Williams, David R., Harold W. Neighbors, and James S. Jackson. 2003. "Racial/Ethnic Discrimination and Health: Findings from Community Studies." *American Journal of Public Health* 93(2): 200–208.

Williams, David R., and Michelle Sternthal, 2007. "Spirituality, Religion and Health: Evidence and Research Directions." *Medical Journal of Australia* 186(10): S47–50.

———. 2010. "Understanding Racial-Ethnic Disparities in Health: Sociological Contributions." *Journal of Health and Social Behavior* 51(Suppl): S15–27.

Williams, Rhys H. 2004. "The Cultural Contexts of Collective Action: Constraints, Opportunities, and the Symbolic Life of Social Movements." Pp. 91–115 in *The Blackwell Companion to Social Movements*, edited by D. A. Snow, S. A. Soule, and H. Kriesi. Malden, MA: Blackwell.

Willis, Paul E. 1977. *Learning to Labor: How Working Class Kids Get Working Class Jobs*. New York: Columbia University Press.

Wilson, William J. 1987. *The Truly Disadvantaged: The Inner City, the Underclass, and Public Policy*. Chicago: University of Chicago Press.

———. 1999. *The Bridge over the Racial Divide: Rising Inequality and Coalition Politics*. Berkeley: University of California Press.

———. 2012. *The Declining Significance of Race: Blacks and Changing American Institutions*. Third edition. Chicago: University of Chicago Press.

Wilson, William J., and Richard P. Taub. 2007. *There Goes the Neighborhood: Racial, Ethnic, and Class Tensions in Four Chicago Neighborhoods and Their Meaning for America*. Reprint edition. New York: Vintage.

Wimmer, Andreas. 2008. "The Making and Unmaking of Ethnic Boundaries: A Multilevel Process Theory." *American Journal of Sociology* 113(4): 970–1022.

———. 2013. *Ethnic Boundary Making: Institutions, Power, Networks*. New York: Oxford University Press.

Wimmer, Andreas, and Nina Glick Schiller. 2002. "Methodological Nationalism and Beyond: Nation-State Building, Migration and the Social Sciences." *Global Networks* 2(4): 301–34.

Winant, Howard. 2001. *The World Is a Ghetto: Race and Democracy since World War II*. New York: Basic Books.

Wingfield, Adia Harvey. 2010. "Are Some Emotions Marked 'Whites Only?' Racialized Feeling Rules in Professional Workplaces." *Social Problems* 57(2): 251–68.

Witte, Nils. 2015. "Can Turks Be Germans? Symbolic Boundary Perception of Turkish Residents in Germany." Pp. 105–118 in *Politics and Law in Turkish Migration*, edited by I. Sirkeci, D. Elcin, and G. Seker. London: Transnational Press.

Wolfsfeld, Gad. 1988. *The Politics of Provocation: Participation and Protest in Israel*. Albany: State University of New York Press.

World Bank. 2012. "Data." Retrieved August 6, 2014 (http://data.worldbank.org/indicator/SI .POV.GINI).

Yadgar, Yaacov. 2011. "A Post-Secular Look at Tradition: Toward a Definition of 'Traditionism.'" *Telos* 156: 77–98.

Yahia-Younis, Taghreed. 2010. "Politics of Loyalty: Women's Voting Patterns in Municipal Elections." Pp. 133–52 in *Displaced at Home: Ethnicity and Gender among Palestinians in Israel*, edited by R. A. Kanaaneh and I. Nusair. Albany: State University of New York Press.

Yiftachel, Oren. 1997. "Israeli Society and Jewish-Palestinian Reconciliation: 'Ethnocracy' and Its Territorial Contradictions." *Middle East Journal* 51(4): 505–19.

———. 2006. *Ethnocracy: Land and Identity Politics in Israel/Palestine*. Philadelphia: University of Pennsylvania Press.

Young, Alford A. 2004. *The Minds of Marginalized Black Men: Making Sense of Mobility, Opportunity, and Future Life Chances*. Princeton, NJ: Princeton University Press.

Young, Cristobal, Charles Varner, and Douglas S. Massey. 2008. *Trends in New Jersey Migration: Housing, Employment, and Taxation*. Princeton, NJ: Policy Research Institute for the Region, Woodrow Wilson School of Public and International Affairs, Princeton University.

Yuval-Davis, Nira, and Floya Anthias, eds. 1989. *Women-Nation-Gender*. London: Macmillan.

Zawdu Gebyanesh, Adane. 2011. "A View from Below: De-stigmatization Strategies among Ethiopian-Israeli." Tel Aviv University, Tel Aviv.

Zerubavel, Eviatar. 1991. *The Fine Line: Making Distinctions in Everyday Life*. New York: Free Press.

Ziv, Avner. 2010. "The Social Function of Humor in Interpersonal Relationships." *Society* 47(1): 11–18.

Zolberg, Aristide R., and Long Litt Woon. 1999. "Why Islam Is Like Spanish: Cultural Incorporation in Europe and the United States." *Politics & Society* 27(1): 5–38.

INDEX

Page numbers in *italics* refer to tables.